Sexuality and Authority in the Catholic Church

Sexuality and Authority in the Catholic Church

Monica Migliorino Miller

Scranton: University of Scranton Press
London and Toronto: Associated University Presses

Associated University Presses
440 Forsgate Drive
Cranbury, NJ 08512

Associated University Presses
25 Sicilian Avenue
London WC1A 2QH, England

**University of Scranton Press
Chicago Distribution Center
11030 S. Langley
Chicago IL 60628**

The paper used in this publication meets the requirements of the American National Standard for Permanence of Paper for Printed Library Materials Z39.48–1984.

Library of Congress Cataloging-in-Publication Data

Miller, Monica Migliorino, 1953–
      Sexuality and Authority in the Catholic Church / Monica Migliorino Miller.
          p.   cm.
      Includes bibliographical references and index.
      ISBN 0-940866-24-2 (alk. paper)
      1. Women in the Catholic Church.   2. Catholic Church--Doctrines.
3. Church--Authority.   4. Feminist theology--Controversial literature.
5. Patriarchy--Religious aspects--Catholic Church.
      I. Title
BX2347.8.W6M555   1995
282'.082--dc20   92-63037
                                                                          CIP

Printed in the United States of America

To my mother and my father

Contents

Acknowledgments   ix

Introduction   xi

1. Feminine Authority and the Covenantal Order of Salvation   3
    A Critique of Feminist Theology   3
    Women and the Fathers of the Church   28
    The Meaning of Authority   44

2. The Authority of Christ   48
    Christ—Head of the Church   48
    Christ—The New Adam   60
    The Meaning of Headship in 1 Cor. 11   63
    The Marital Order of Authority   73

3. The Meaning of Male Ecclesial Authority   76
    Christ the Good Shepherd   76
    The Gender of God   83
    The Authority of the Apostles   88
    The Fatherhood of Bishops and Priests   101
    The Male Person as Symbol of God   106
    Christ and the Saving of Humanity   113

4. The Authority of Mary   115
    Mary's "Fiat"—Source of the Incarnation   115
    Mary's Word: The New Genesis   119
    The Authority of Mary in the Mission of Christ   120
    The New Eve—Covenant Partner of Christ   134

5. The Feminine Authority of the Church   137
    Baptism and a Woman's Life-giving Authority   137
    The Biblical Testimony   147
    The Church Feeds Her Children   151
    Mother and Teacher   157
    The Feminine Side of Worship   159
    The Church—Mother of Priests   163
    The Divinization of Woman   165
    The Feminine Response to the Covenant   168

6. The Authority of Women   170
    Woman—Center of the World's Moral Order   170
    The Church and Women—Source of Human Unity   182
    The Woman as Teacher   189
    The Mediatorial Authority of Women   192

7. Women, the Covenant Partners of Christ   196
    Women of the Old Testament   196
    Early Christian Women   200
    St. Catherine: The Pope's Guide   207
    St. Margaret Clitherow   208
    The Authority of Consecrated Virgins   212
    Modern Examples of Women's Ecclesial Authority   215
    Some Final Words   220

Notes   223
Bibliography   275
Index   283

Acknowledgments

This book would not have been possible without the help of many friends to whom I am indebted. I would first like to thank Fr. Donald Keefe, S.J. for the enormous influence he has had upon the development of my theological thought. I have had the privilege of learning from a great and theologically creative thinker. He has pushed out the boundaries of my theological development, the impact of which will last me a lifetime. Moreover, Fr. Keefe has been a good and constant friend, a source of wonderful support to me.

I also would like to thank Fr. Joseph Murphy, S.J.—again from whose theological insight I have greatly benefited.

I am grateful to Dr. Wanda Zemler-Cizewski of the Marquette University Theology Dept. Her constant prompting and guidance was invaluable to me in my research of the Fathers of the Church and in tracking down Latin references for the footnotes. She deserves much credit in the scholarly quality of this book.

I also thank Frs. Earl Muller, S.J. and William Kurz, S.J. for their helpful comments and suggestions in the preparation of this manuscript. Their insights helped me to sharpen and clarify certain theological points that are important for this book's thesis.

I cannot thank enough my good friend Terry Orlowski who spent countless hours helping me with the computer work necessary for the writing of this book. I could not have begun nor finished this work without him. I thank him for his patience, reliability and advanced computer skill. I am also indebted to the staff consultants at the Marquette University Computer Services, especially Robert Ferguson who was of great help to me.

Finally, thank you Edmund—my dear husband—for your endless love, support, and encouragement.

Monica Migliorino Miller

Introduction

I told a nun whom I had met on a retreat that I wanted to write a book on the authority of women in the Catholic Church. She responded, "Well, that'll be a short book!"

Her statement reflects a definite sentiment of many people both in and outside the Church, especially among feminists. Because women cannot be priests in the Catholic Church, it is, therefore, commonly concluded that women simply do not have any authority. Many protest this situation while others even believe that by God's own design women ought not hold positions of authority anyway.

Most of the conflict surrounding the status and power of women in the Church is based on a false idea of authority. First of all, authority is nearly always associated with the holding of visible public office. Second, authority has become synonymous with the possession of power over others. If this is authority, then it is largely true that women have been and are deprived of the exercise of authority.

But authority ultimately has little to do with such things. In fact, frequently the holding of visible office and power over others amounts to the exact opposite of authority, its abuse and deformation. Recently a Milwaukee parish priest offered an excellent definition of authority that could well serve as a working definition for this book. He stated: "Originally authority merely implied those rights which the Author exercised in order to correctly maintain the created work."

This is a very refreshing approach to the meaning of authority. Authority is connected to the giving of life and has to do with the exercise of responsibility for life. This book intends to penetrate the true meaning of authority so that the authority of women in the Church may be fully understood and appreciated. Authority in the Catholic Church is not a juridicism. It is sacramental, liturgical, and moral before it is anything thing else.

The feminist challenge to hierarchical priestly authority requires a response that is insightful and creative. The feminist challenge to the Christian faith is a real one. Feminist theology in many ways represents a rival approach to the Church's sacraments and doctrine. This challenge has placed the Catholic Church in a state of crisis on the position of women. This crisis can only be resolved through a new appreciation for the essence of authority.

Authority is not simply a power possessed by a leader by virtue of his being the strong one within a group who then uses his strength to organize the group around his vision. Someone who has power can declare himself outside the group in a dominant position toward the group in a world where there is no inherent relation between the leader and the group. Order is achieved by outside force because there is no inherent relation among any members of the group. Indeed, if authority is the wielding of power, this presupposes that the group has no meaning or purpose outside of the leader's will. This is the Nietzcheian world where no ontological truth or harmony exists. But this is not the world of God the Father. God did not create a world where authority is arbitrary and a matter of mere quantifiable strength. The word "authority" comes from the Latin "auctor" which means the author, originator, source, maker of, or creator of something.

The creative authority of Christ exists within a covenant—namely that Christ is in a personal unity with what He has created. This means that authority is not monist, single, and atomized. Authentic authority exists within a covenant of love and is exercised from within this covenant. Authority in the Christian faith exists within the one flesh of the New Adam and the New Eve. What needs to be understood is how men and women are symbols of this covenant and how the covenantal authority of man and woman is exercised according to the glory of sexual differentiation. In short, how are men and women responsible for the order of redemption? More specifically, what have women been entrusted with that builds up the faith of the Church according to the meaning of their own sexuality?

This book is a theology of ecclesial authority. We begin with a full discussion of feminist theology as it is articulated by its major advocates, notably Rosemary Radford Ruether, Elizabeth Schüssler Fiorenza, and Mary Daly. Attention is also paid to lessor known authors whose contributions to feminist theology are nonetheless significant, i.e., Ida Raming and Naomi Goldenberg. Feminist theology is based in an egalitarian philosophy regarding the dignity of the person that considers sexual differentiation as purely functional without sacramental or liturgical significance. Feminist theology has detrimental effects upon the Catholic priesthood and Catholic Eucharistic worship. Insofar as feminist theology is rooted in a pessimism about the revelation of God and history, it is ultimately destructive of the Good Creation that is intrinsically bound to the order of redemption where man and woman speak the truth of God's unity with the world.

Feminist theology believes that the hierarchical structure of Catholicism and its sacramental system are bastions of all-male power that inherently discriminate against women. The theological task before the Church must demonstrate the covenantal dimension of authority and how women, without the status of ordained office, possess a true authority that is effective of salvation.

Feminine ecclesial authority is already articulated in what some might consider a most unlikely place, namely, the Fathers of the Church. These early Church thinkers can easily be accused of a negative and even misogynist view of women. But a careful examination of their works reveals that they frequently teach that the ecclesial role of women is constitutive of salvation in Christ. In many ways women are the true spiritual leaders in relation to men. Covenantal feminine authority is expressed, for example, by St. Irenaeus in his theology of the New Eve, by the important role given to consecrated virgins, by the eschatological necessity of the risen female body, by the moral virtue and spiritual maturity of women, etc., etc. The fact that female authority is recognized by the Fathers shows that this authority is intrinsic to Catholicism from the beginning. This book's dependence on the Fathers demonstrates that covenantal authority and the meaning of feminine authority are anchored in the very fabric of Christian tradition. Authority in the Catholic Church is covenantal; redemption is the result of a unity between Christ and the Church. Revelation itself discloses that male and female sexuality are the prime symbols of this covenant of redemption. The Church Fathers teach that the Church is necessary for salvation, and the Church is consistently spoken of by them as a woman—an exalted bride and mother. This bride and mother has a responsibility for redemption in which feminine symbolism, far from being disparaged by the Fathers, is essential to salvation in Christ.

In addition to Scripture and systematic theology, this book relies on the secular sciences such as anthropology and psychology in order to provide a comprehensive picture of male and female authority. Moreover, the theological point of this book is supported by several authors from different periods in Church history. The varied sources unlock the religious significance of male and female symbolism as this symbolism is the expression of the covenant of salvation.

Feminine authority, of course, cannot be examined in isolation. Therefore it is necessary to spend time looking at the meaning of male authority. Christ is head of the Church, but this does not mean that He is head as a dominant Lord. Christ is head because He is the arché, the *origin* of the Church's life and existence. Christ's headship, and thus His authority, is inseparable from His sacrifice on the Cross. From the Cross Christ is head to the Church as the New Adam to the New Eve. This truth about Christ and the Church is made manifest in the Eucharist and forms the basis for the Catholic priesthood. Priestly authority is bound to male sexuality because of the meaning of Christ's headship as source of the Church.

Furthermore, the Catholic priesthood reveals a truth about the fatherhood of God in the way that God is a life-giver. The fatherhood of God is not a mere metaphor. Fatherhood expresses a truth about the way God imparts life. Masculine sexuality sacramentally speaks a truth about the Trinity in its covenantal relation to the created world. Male gender is the proper liturgical–sacramental sign of God's life-giving authority.

Feminine ecclesial authority begins with Mary the Mother of God. By her *"fiat"* she is God's covenantal partner in the Order of Redemption. Mary is the source of Christ's incarnational life in the world. Thus her *"fiat"* makes her an *origin* of life that is intrinsically constitutive of the New Creation. Furthermore, Mary has authority in the mission of her Son. Yes, the Incarnation is dependent upon Mary's maternity, but this woman is also instrumental in the accomplishment of Christ's Passion. Finally, it is Mary as a woman who constitutes in salvation history the response of mankind to God's plan of salvation. Mary is the focus of a *theology of response* that demonstrates how women function as the co-cause of redemption.

Within the covenant of salvation, which is the one flesh unity of the Head and the Body, women are the life-giving center to which male authority is ordered. The life-giving powers of women are the center of the world's moral order. In relation to this the man knows his identity and his purpose.

Throughout Christianity the Church has been referred to as a Mother. As fatherhood is not simply a metaphor for God neither is motherhood simply a metaphor for the Church. Motherhood is inherent in the nature of the Church. Thus women are the Church's proper symbol. The secular sciences of sociology, psychology, and anthropology corroborate how this is so. We are concerned about the historical significance of the female person who, while certainly able to make many great contributions to society and culture, cannot be properly understood apart from her life-giving powers. By these powers the covenant of salvation is accomplished and achieves its historical expression in union with masculine authority.

While Mary is the paradigm of feminine authority, it is not enough to study Mary as if she were the only true expression of the Church. If feminine authority is real, it must be concrete in the lives of Christian women generally. If authority is connected to the ability to give life and the exercise of responsibility for life, then Christians will have a new place to begin this appreciation. The theology of authority articulated in this book may hope to have a deep impact on understanding the nature of the Church whose essence exists in her sacramental and liturgical life. Authority exists within a covenantal unity of persons. It exists for the sake of building this bond—the paradigm of which is the authority located in the one flesh unity of Christ and the Church. It is here that the differentiated authority of men and women is disclosed, made theologically explicit, and is appreciated as the authority upon which the order of redemption itself rests.

Within the last twenty years a number of theologians who support the Church's teaching on the all-male priesthood have written on the role of women in the Church, namely, Henri De Lubac, Louis Bouyer, E. L. Mascall, Han Urs Von Balthasar, Manfred Hauke, and Donald Keefe, S.J. Pope John Paul II's *Mulieris Dignitatem* is a significant contribution on the topic. Many of these writers were prompted to make an explicit response to the feminist challenge facing the Church. Yet there exists no systematic, comprehensive attempt to explain the meaning of ecclesial authority itself by which the authority of women can be understood in the light of faith. This book is at least a beginning in that direction. Cardinal Joseph Bernadin of Chicago recently stated the need for such a theology and Archbishop Weakland of Milwaukee stated, after the American bishops failed to approve a pastoral letter on women in November 1992, that the debate over women's role in the Church and society is "just starting."

Not only is it "just starting," but its importance and complexity seems to assure that the present controversy on the place of women in the Church is not soon to be resolved. The history of the Church has shown that whenever she has been challenged, the Christian faith has emerged enriched and enlivened—the Church achieves a more profound self-understanding. The author hopes this book will serve as at least a small step in that direction.

Sexuality and Authority
in the Catholic Church

1

Feminine Authority and the Covenantal Order of Salvation

I. A Critique of Feminist Theology

THE CRISIS OF ECCLESIAL AUTHORITY

"Woman ... is called upon to embody in her highest and purest development the essence of the Church—to be its symbol."[1]

The above statement, made by the great German philosopher and Catholic martyr Edith Stein,[2] sums up the essence of feminine ecclesial authority. Christian women possess authority in the Catholic Church, an authority that exemplifies the motherhood of the Church. This authority is other than that exercised by the Catholic priesthood. However, feminine ecclesial authority is complementary to the priesthood and is authority without which the sacramental life of the Church and redemption itself could not exist.

The Christian faith today faces a crisis brought on by a feminist challenge to the traditional role of women in society and the Church. This crisis is rooted in the larger crisis over the meaning of male and female sexuality in general. In the Catholic Church the eye of the storm is the relation between women and the exercise of ecclesial authority. Contemporary critics of the Church, particularly feminist theologians, believe the hierarchical structure of all-male priestly authority is a system inherently unjust and sinful in its exclusion of women from positions of authority. This attack on hierarchical priestly authority is not simply confined to a battle among theologians insulated within the confines of academia. Fundamentally the current crisis of authority concerning the position of women in the Church has to do with how Christians understand the order of redemption itself. The crisis of women and authority affects the very identity of the Christian people. This is because the issue of women and authority, related as it is to the meaning of the Catholic priesthood, strikes at the very heart of the structure of the Catholic Church and her worship. It is a crisis that troubles the faith life of the Church, particularly in the areas of morality and the sacraments.

Essentially the crisis arises out of a false perception of the meaning of authority itself. The secular world views authority as a quantifiable force, exercised visibly and publicly by persons who hold a special position or office. Those who do not possess public office are thought not to possess authority. Such persons are simply subjects ruled over by those who do possess public power. Feminist theologians believe that women in relation to the hierarchical priesthood are in a position of subjection because they are not permitted to share in the priestly authority of the Church. The notion that authority is equated with visible office is well articulated by Elizabeth Schüssler Fiorenza:

> Although the Church is called "our mother" and referred to with the pronoun "she," it is personified and governed by fathers and brothers only. Therefore, whenever we speak of the Church we see before our eyes the pope in Rome, bishops or pastors, cardinals and monsignors, deacons and altar boys, all of whom are men. Eucharistic concelebrations, televised bishops' conferences, or the laying on of hands in the ordination rite are manifestations of the Church as an "old boys club." No wonder that many Christians believe that God is a male patriarch and that the male sex of Jesus Christ is salvific.
>
> Women *as Church* are invisible neither by accident nor by our own default but by patriarchal law that excludes us from Church office on the basis of sex.[3]

Fiorenza's complaint is based on the presupposition that feminine visability in the Church is utterly dependent upon holding hierarchical office. As a leading spokesperson for women's liberation in the Church, Fiorenza identifies authority with office. The most common mistake made, not only by feminist theologians but by men and women everywhere, is that ecclesial office exhausts the essence of authority in the Catholic faith. It needs to be appreciated that the exercise of priestly office by males is only one side (a necessary side) of ecclesial authority. The "other side" of ecclesial authority is exercised by women as they symbolize the Church. Their authority is not dependent on formal office but is nonetheless real authority that exists, not in competition with, but in relation to the priestly office.

Because authority is equated with *office*, the denial of women to office is perceived by feminist theologians as a heinous injustice to women—an injustice utterly opposed to the gospel message of Jesus who preached the equal dignity of all persons. This injustice to women is believed to be inherent in the nature of the hierarchical Church itself because hierarchical structures of authority are the fruit of *patriarchy*. Fiorenza defines patriarchy as "a societal system in which all men have power over all women."[4] She explains, however, that this is to understand patriarchy in a narrow sense. Fundamentally patriarchy is an *ethic of power* that Fiorenza traces back to the Aristotelian political philosophy of domination and subordination which encompasses all sorts of injustices—racism, classism, as well as sexism. Domination and subordination are not the result of mere social convention but are rooted in "nature." Aristotle, "therefore, insisted that the discussion of political ethics and household management begin with marriage which he defined as 'the union of natural ruler and natural subject.'"⁵

Patriarchy is *any system of power* based on an intrinsic distinction between persons which results in those who rule and those who are subordinate to that rule. The patriarchal structure of the Church, which denies women leadership roles and authority, is the result of *androcentrism*, a male-centered view of the world based on the idea that masculinity defines what it means to be fully human. According to feminist theology, the all-male priesthood and Catholic hierarchy uses androcentrism to shore up its power structure which keeps women in a state of servility and subjection.⁶

An examination of the Fathers of the Church discloses that Catholic theology by association with Greek philosophy, especially that of Plato and Aristotle, has been tainted by androcentrism. However, the sacramental and moral life of the Catholic Church is not the result of Greek philosophy. It is based on the covenantal dignity of men and women—a dignity in Christ upon which creation itself rests—a dignity that not even the heavy influence of Platonism and Aristotelianism was able to utterly suppress in the writings of the Fathers.

According to Fiorenza the Church's oppressive power structure, rooted in androcentrism, must be reformed. In her quest to recover women's history suppressed by the patriarchal church, she describes exactly how the reform will occur:

> The debate between feminist "engaged" and androcentric academic "neutral" scholarship indicates a shift in interpretative paradigms. Whereas traditional academic scholarship has identified humanness with maleness and understood women only as a peripheral category in the "human" interpretation of reality, the new field of women's studies not only attempts to make "women's" agency a key interpretative category but also seeks to transform androcentric scholarship and knowledge into truly human scholarship and knowledge, that is, inclusive of *all* people, men and women, upper and lower classes, aristocracy and "common people," different cultures and races, the powerful and the weak.
>
> The shift from an androcentric to a feminist interpretation of the world implies a revolutionary shift in scientific paradigm, a shift with far-reaching ramifications not only for the interpretation of the world but also for its change. Since paradigms determine how scholars see the world and how they conceive of theoretical problems, a shift from an androcentric to a feminist paradigm implies a transformation of the scientific imagination. It demands an intellec-

tual conversion that cannot be logically deduced but is rooted in a change of patriarchal relationships.[7]

Fiorenza proposes that the Christian faith has been dominated by a male-centered interpretation of history—an interpretation that has minimized or suppressed the contributions women have made to the formation of the Church in its earliest centuries.[8] The feminist reform of the Church demands a shift "from an androcentric to a feminist interpretation of the world." However, this paradigm shift is not a reform of the Church at all but amounts to a manipulation of the faith. This manipulation is necessary in order to advance a particular sectarian ideology or philosophy whether this "interpretation of the world" is androcentric or feminist. The Christian faith, and more specifically the issue of women and authority in the Church, cannot be understood correctly by applying a sufficiently scientific interpretative model to its doctrines or its history. Scientific paradigms, whether androcentric or feminist, carry within them principles that suppress and misinterpret the faith because these paradigms stand outside the Revelation in judgment of it and will misread or misuse the Revelation to serve their own ends.[9]

Feminist theology teaches that by making "women's agency a key interpretative category," androcentrism will be overcome by a "truly human scholarship . . . inclusive of all people" which cuts across sex, class, and culture. In other words, feminist theology with its feminist interpretative paradigms (as opposed to androcentrism and patriarchy) is believed by its proponents to be a theology of liberation whose principles will usher in the Christian egalitarian community which is the fulfillment of Jesus' mission.

The shift from androcentrism to feminism that Fiorenza proposes simply will not provide an authentic understanding of the relation between sexual gender and authority in the Catholic Church. This is because *neither* paradigm confronts the Christian mystery of faith as it actually exists. Redemption is neither androcentric or feminist; it is *covenantal*. Both androcentrism and feminism fail to explain the equal dignity of men and women because ultimately, as we shall see in the following pages, these systems deny the goodness of God's created order.

The order of redemption is neither male-centered nor female-centered. The order of redemption is rooted in the covenantal union of Christ and His Church. Revelation discloses this covenantal union to be maritally structured. The world is saved by the one-flesh union of Christ and His Church. This union is at once the primordial creation of the first man and woman and its fulfillment. The marital structure of the covenant is the salvation of Christ mediated in the world. Salvation is realized, actualized by its own proper symbol: the nuptial union of Christ and His bride. Before all else—the Church is the Bride of the Lord. As bride she is the mystical Body of Christ. As bride she is the People of God.[10]

THE CRISIS OF SYMBOLS

The crisis concerning women and ecclesial authority is a crisis over symbols. As the Christian faith is dependent upon symbols for the effective mediation of Christ's redemption (whether these symbols be words or visible signs) any ambiguity or doubt concerning the symbols of the faith ushers in a crisis of faith itself. The Church is experiencing today not mere ambiguity or doubt about its symbols but an all-out attack upon their validity. The one symbol most attacked by feminists, because to them it is the source of the greatest injustice, is the all-male Catholic priesthood.

Rosemary Radford Ruether explains the feminist challenge to the Church's "patriarchal" system of authority as a conflict between experience and symbol. She defends feminist theology against the charge that feminist theology makes women's experience of oppression the sole criterion of truth by arguing that all theological reflection is ultimately rooted in human experience. Even "Scripture and tradition are themselves codified collective human experience."[11] For Ruether, experience of the divine, of oneself, of the community and the world produces symbols. A symbol ultimately is never *received*. A received symbol cannot dictate experience or the interpretation of it although systems of authority try to make received symbols do precisely this. "If a symbol does not speak authentically to experience, it becomes dead or must be altered to provide a new meaning."[12]

In feminist theology a symbol is a relative sign. Symbols only serve to interpret revelatory experience, and they are most often simply borrowed from the culture that surrounds the people who are subjects of this experience.[13] There is nothing absolute or lasting about any religious symbol. As experience changes and grows, symbols may lose their authenticity because they fail to communicate the change or because they were never valid to begin with but merely imposed by "systems of authority." "Exclusive language," that is, words that speak of human beings in terms of the primacy of the masculine would be an example of invalid symbols. The use of the words "man," "mankind," "men," "he," and "him," etc., when one means to include all persons male or female, are, according to feminist philosophy, invalid or failed symbols because they result from a patriarchal view of the world contrary to the feminist experience of liberation.

In order for women to have their dignity, equality, and power, recognized religious symbols must be changed. This change of symbols to achieve women's liberation is very clearly illustrated by the feminist attraction to "Goddess religion." Mary Jo Weaver in her book *New Catholic Women:*

A Contemporary Challenge to Traditional Religious Authority observes
that the use of the word "Goddess" (instead of "God") is "after all, the
conscious re-creation of a religious symbol."[14] Such word changes are
necessary to foster new attitudes and feelings in order to achieve feminist
social and political goals. Weaver points out that while Ruether is hesitant
to endorse "Goddess" religion, she nevertheless creates a new religious
symbol in her book *Sexism and God-Talk: Toward a Feminist Theology* by
introducing the word "God/ess." This new symbol sounds like "Goddess"
and is invented by Ruether to combine "the masculine and feminine forms
of divinity while still affirming the divine unity."[15]

Naomi Goldenberg also recognizes that the feminist quest for equality
and power is achieved by altering or even destroying religious symbols.

> When feminists succeed in changing the positions of women in Christianity
> and Judaism, they will shake these religions to their roots. The nature of religion
> lies in the nature of the symbols and images it exalts in ritual and doctrine. It is
> the psychic picture of Christ and Yahweh that inspires the loves, the hates and
> behavior patterns of Christians and Jews. The psychology of the Jewish and
> Christian religions depends on the masculine image that these religions have of
> their God. Feminists change the major psychological impact of Judaism and
> Christianity when they recognize women as religious leaders and as images of
> divinity.[16]

This alteration of symbol is not simply a matter of changing certain religious words. Feminist theology is a comprehensive reform of the very
vehicles of Revelation; by it, for example, the Holy Scriptures are given a
new interpretation. The New Testament—that is, the twenty-seven books
that make up the *canon*—is a *symbol* by which the "revelatory experience"
is communicated and interpreted. However, Scripture itself, according to
feminist theology, is the result of a "system of authority" or power. Early
Christian leaders sought to codify the "revelatory experience" by suppress-
ing writings that came from what they regarded as "deviant communities."[17]
Scripture is the result of "historical winners." It is not necessarily inerrant
nor is it regarded by most feminist theologians as the divinely inspired
Word of God.[18] Fiorenza interprets Scripture according to a *hermeneutics of
· suspicion*[19] whereby feminist principles judge what is authentic in the Bible
and what is not. According to the feminist experience of oppression and
liberation, whole parts of Scripture are "dead or must be altered to provide
a new meaning." The New Testament canon was formulated according to
a patriarchal mindset that sought to suppress the leadership and authority
of Christian women.

While the androcentric transmission and redaction of early Christian traditions can be attributed partially to an early Christian cultural-political apologetics, the canonization of early Christian writings took place at a time when different parts of the church were engaged in a bitter struggle for or against women's leadership. The struggle was engendered by the gradual patriarchialization of early churches. The textual and historical marginalization of women is also a by-product of the "patristic" selection and canonization process of Scripture. Therefore, feminist studies in religion must question the patristic interpretive model that identifies heresy with women's leadership and orthodoxy with patriarchal church structures.[20]

Feminist experience of the divine and the world gives rise to a *canon within the canon* approach to biblical interpretation. Buried beneath the androcentric texts are the feminist texts based in a prophetic tradition of liberation that represents the original "revelatory experience" of Jesus. These feminist texts must be uncovered and then used to judge and condemn the patriarchy of Scripture.

. . . the prophetic liberating traditions can be appropriated by feminism only as normative principles of Biblical faith which, in turn, criticize and reject patriarchal ideology. Patriarchal ideology thus loses its normative character. It is to be denounced, not cleaned up or explained away. . . .

Feminist theology that draws on Biblical principles is possible only if the prophetic principles, more fully understood, imply a rejection of every elevation of one social group against others as image and agent of God to justify domination and subjection. Patriarchy itself must fall under the Biblical denunciations of idolatry and blasphemy, the idolizing of the male representative of divinity. It is idolatrous to make males more "like God" than females. It is blasphemous to use the image and name of the Holy to justify patriarchal domination and law. Feminist readings of the Bible can discern a norm within Biblical faith by which the Biblical texts themselves can be criticized. *To the extent to which Biblical texts reflect this normative principle, they are regarded as authoritative. On this basis many aspects of the Bible are to be frankly set aside and rejected.* (Emphasis added.)[21]

Only those symbols that communicate and interpret the feminist experience are valid. Like various Scripture texts, symbols that sustain the Feminist patriarchal system of power in its domination and subordination "must be set aside and rejected."

For a person or a privileged caste of persons to identify themselves as special mediators of the divine presence militates against the egalitarian community feminist theology believes Jesus to have initiated. Anyone or anything that claims to represent God to the people is idolatry.

In the patriarchal ethic of power men have been associated with mediating divinity to the world. The male Catholic priest as symbol of Christ is the one symbol feminists most associate with the subjection and oppression of women. Because the Catholic priesthood is intrinsically bound to the celebration of the Eucharist, it is against these two symbols in the Church—whereby the Church lives and understands herself—that feminist theology launches its most severe attack. The first principle of feminist theology demolishes any validity in these symbols. The all-male priesthood (indeed any clerical system because it assigns power to a special caste), from a feminist perspective, denies woman their full humanity insofar as the priesthood means women cannot image the divine equally with men. This means that the entire means of salvation in the Catholic Church through her sacramental worship is not, in Ruether's words, the "work of an authentic redeemer."[22] The Church, most particularly in the priesthood and Eucharistic sacrifice (the very symbol the Catholic Church teaches is the source of her unity), has betrayed her Lord. These things are not the will of Christ. They do not flow from Christ's mission but exist contrary to His mission of ushering in the egalitarian community of justice in which systems of domination and subordination are abolished.

Feminist theology ranges from Fiorenza and Ruether, who attempt to accommodate Scripture and Christian tradition to the feminist view, to the work of Mary Daly who has long since abandoned Christianity and its symbols as inherently sexist.[23] However, for all of these thinkers femininism is a view of the world in which justice for women is gained by eliminating the significance of the sexual difference. For them, sexual difference is the cause of systems of submission and dependence. Feminism must dissolve the male priesthood and the sacrifice of Christ in the Eucharist because these are symbols in which all-male power is sustained and perpetuated.

Feminism and Christ

The feminist challenge to these sacramental symbols of faith starts with a crisis of faith regarding the symbol of Jesus Himself as He appears as Savior in the form of a masculine person.

> In traditional Christian theology, Christ is the model for this redeemed humanity that we have lost through sin and recovered through redemption. But Christ as a symbol is problematic for feminist theology. The Christological symbols have been used to enforce male dominance, and even if we go back beyond masculinist Christology to the praxis of the historical Jesus of the synoptic Gospels, it is questionable whether there is a single model of redeemed humanity fully revealed in the past. This does not mean that feminist theol-

ogy may not be able to affirm the person of Jesus of Nazarath as a positive model of redemptive humanity. But this model must be seen as partial and fragmentary, disclosing from the perspective of one person, circumscribed in time, culture, gender, something of the fulness we seek. We need other clues and models as well, models drawn from women's experience, from many times and cultures.[24]

Ruether has stated the fundamental challenge of feminist theology to the Catholic faith. Feminist theology is struggling to find a symbol of redeemed humanity. Not even Jesus seems to sum it up. Jesus as a model of redeemed humanity is "partial and fragmentary." He is only one person whose effectiveness as a symbol is burdened by His gender, culture, and history. The feminist crisis is over the issue of whether Jesus the *man* can serve as a model of redemptive personhood for women.[25] The answer *in a sense* is rightly "No." Christ alone does not sum up what it is to be redeemed although He alone is the source of redemption. Feminists try to find other models but because history and corporeality relativize and degrade any model, feminists are forced to live in a fragmented world where the "fulness of redeemed humanity is only partially disclosed."[26] In feminism models of redemption will forever be somewhat arbitrary—never absolute—kept in service only for a time until growth in the "revelatory experience" renders the sign obsolete.

The feminist "despair" of finding full symbols of redemption is rooted in a sensitivity exacerbated by a false perception of the Catholic faith, which would hold that Christ *alone* is the sign of redemption. This is a Christo-monism that inevitably leads to a despair of historically mediated redemption. The great flaw in feminist theology is that it abandons the faith to seek liberation elsewhere. It fails to understand that redemption is not summed up by the male Christ alone who must then assimilate all creation—and women—to Himself in the manner of a gnostic anthropos. Redemption is not mediated by Christ alone *as symbol* but by *Christ and the Church*. Redemption is only mediated by the covenant Christ established with the Church. The Church gives a response to the mission of the Son that is authentically hers—thus she is a model of redemption in union with her Lord and has responsibility for the covenant that is equal in human and mediatorial freedom, and thus in dignity, to His. Christ as model and source of redemption is so only as in union with the Church. As we shall soon see, the feminist quest for faith-symbols other than the "Whole Christ" results in another monism accomplished by a flight from history. The new egalitarian Christian community becomes the sign of redemption to which Christ as source of salvation to this community is no longer central or important.

THE FEMINIST DENIAL OF GENDER

The first symbols to be discarded in the feminist quest for liberation, power, and equality are male and female gender. Because gender is a source of isolation and domination, the male gender of Christ has no salvific value. Ruether states:

> Theologically speaking. . . the maleness of Jesus has no ultimate significance. It has social symbolic significance in the framework of societies of patriarchal privilege. In this sense Jesus as the Christ, the representative of liberated humanity and the liberating Word of God, manifests the *kenosis of patriarchy*, the announcement of the new humanity through a lifestyle that discards hierarchical caste and privilege and speaks on behalf of the lowly. In a similar way, the femaleness of the social and religiously outcast who respond to him has social symbolic significance as a witness against the same idolatrous system of patriarchal privilege.[27]

The male body of Jesus is not important. Salvation is not through His body. Christ's maleness is important only to express in the face of patriarchy that it is not important. Christ's male body has no redemptive sacramental value. The only thing of ultimate importance is His preached message, His vision of the world that discards "hierarchical caste privilege." It is not really significant whether one is male or female. A person exemplifies redemption to the extent that he or she has appropriated it, and one's gender is not meaningful or necessary for this appropriation.

Because Christ's masculinity has no intrinsic redemptive meaning, the door is open to a priesthood that admits both men and women. Justice itself precludes the exclusion of women. To image "redeemed humanity" does not depend on any ontological sign of grace. To be *a sign* one must simply take on Jesus' vision of the egalitarian community. Some feminist theologians who still believe in some form of clerical leadership, but believe this leadership should be open to women, locate the sign value of this leadership in the leader's power of personal devotion, in the ability to nourish the Church. A person could only assume office when they have achieved an inner transformation, an attachment to Christ, which lies beyond gender, becoming transparent for Him. Sexual gender is not relevant to this sign as the priest does not stand sacramentally *in persona Christi*.[28]

In this feminist reform of Church office the priesthood does not depend on sexuality for its effectiveness as a sign; nevertheless, feminist theology makes an attempt to render female sexuality meaningful within the economy of salvation. Ruether argues that according to Scripture women are the "oppressed of the oppressed." They are at the bottom of the social hierarchy in biblical times and hence are in a special way the last who shall be first in the kingdom of God.[29]

In this scheme Mary, the mother of Jesus, is elevated to symbolize the Church. Mary as symbol of the Church is expressed in the Magnificat of St. Luke's Gospel. Mary's words are interpreted according to a political scale of values: "she represents the oppressed community that is to be lifted up and filled with good things in the messianic revolution."[30]

Because women represent the poorest of the poor, they serve as preeminent models of faith as their liberation is the most pronounced instance of the redemption of Christ, who came to rid the world of all systems that foster domination and dependency. In feminist theology women as victims of oppression, now redeemed, stand in for all oppressed peoples in need of God's favor.[31]

Women especially represent the Church by calling others out of bondage into freedom. The despised woman as poorest of the poor has symbolic priority in the Church.[32]

It is extremely important to understand *how* woman is a symbol in feminist theology. Woman is a sign of redemption because she has been oppressed. This condition of oppression is the source of her symbolic power. The oppression of women is the effect of androcentrism upon history. It is important to notice, therefore, that oppression of women is not something intrinsic to them as *women*. This oppression, can be, should be, and possibly will be eliminated. Apart from the reality of this oppression women would have no symbolic value.

This is where feminist theology fails to serve the real equality and dignity of women. It is not women but the condition of oppression alone which has value—a condition that is not a fact concerning the *nature* of women. To say women are symbols of redemption or even symbols of the Church does not explain what it is about the female sex *as female* that is good, valuable, and worthy of being cherished. Feminine goodness is not rooted in the feminine person.[33] Women as such have no symbolic value. In the end, existence as a female is meaningless. Women only gain symbolic meaning from the extrinsic condition of oppression. In feminist theology the conditions of oppression/liberation have meaning. The female body, that is, the concrete expression of women's existence, has no real theological value as a sign of the Church as Christ's male body is emptied of its salvific value. Ultimately, Ruether has failed women. Theoretically a woman's symbolic priority could be swept away, supplanted by some other group that more adequately expresses oppression/liberation. According to Ruether's theology, Jews, blacks, battered children easily could serve as symbols of redeemed humanity as their oppression has been very great.[34]

The Elimination of Christ's Sacrifice

Feminist theology would achieve equality and leadership for women by eliminating the sacrifice of Christ as the single source of the world's salvation. Fiorenza argues that Christ's death as a sacrifice for sin is a later cultic development within the early Church:

> While the earliest Jesus traditions eschew any understanding of the ministry and death of Jesus in cultic terms as atonement for sins, it was precisely this interpretation which soon took root in some segments of the early Christian movement. Yet such an interpretation of Jesus' death as atonement for sins is much later than is generally assumed in New Testament scholarship. The notion of atoning sacrifice does not express the Jesus movement's understanding and experience of God but is a later interpretation of the violent death of Jesus in cultic terms. The God of Jesus is not a God who demands atonement and whose wrath needs to be placated by human sacrifice or ritual. . . . Although such an interpretation of the death of Jesus is soon found in early Christian theology, *the death of Jesus was not a sacrifice* and was not demanded by God but brought about by the Romans. (Emphasis added.)[35]

Christ's death is theologically significant only in the sense that He is killed as a result of His message in the same way that other prophets like John the Baptist were violently put to death. But in no sense is Jesus' death salvific. His death is not the will of the Father, nor is it the means whereby sin is atoned for and man reconciled to God by the grace won by Christ.[36]

Feminist theology must reject the sacrifice of Christ because the sacrifice of the God/man is antithetical to the principles of the egalitarian community. The notion of sacrifice is part of the patriarchal system of power and domination. The sacrifice of Christ is essentially what constitutes Him a priest, with power no human individual can be said to possess or exercise. Marie Zimmerman in her article "Neither Clergy nor Laity: Women in the Church" argues that if women are equal with men the priesthood must be disassociated from power.

> It is to proclaim the end of the priesthood of the temple in favor of the Christian priesthood. In this way we leave power all its position, a firmly human position which no function can any longer assume in the name of God. The God of Jesus is neither the god eager for sacrifices for whom his own son would be the only satisfactory victim, nor the god of the renewal of this expiatory sacrifice, be it merely an efficacious symbolic action. He is the God who saves man's longing in order to allow him to realize this longing in a work of life. Hence priesthood cannot and must not dig itself in behind an efficacious

symbolism in order to defend the prerogatives of the masculine institution of *potestas sacra*.[37]

Christ's sacrifice and the renewal of it (the Eucharist) are unnecessary for salvation. Consequently, if the renewal of the sacrifice is unnecessary, so is the Catholic priesthood as a sacrificing priesthood.

The sacrifice of Christ on the Cross as source of salvation is rejected in feminist theology because such sacrifice is a threat to the feminist view of equality. If Christ's *person and personal work* is salvific, this means that some *one* possesses a "power," a "quality" that stands outside of the world and Church, over and against the world and Church upon which people are made absolutely dependent. For the feminist, Christ is not Lord and those who represent Him are not "lords" in this sense. The ministerial priesthood claims (as it stands *in persona Christi*) to be the restorer of things. This restoration depends upon distinction and separation of the sexes.[38] The Catholic priesthood perpetuates the *otherness* of God and Christ and this type of distinction between the sacred and profane gives rise to hierarchical systems of domination and dependency— if not oppression. In order for equality to be real, Christ must not possess anything that the Christian community does not possess.

Ruether explains that the Christian community continues Christ's identity.[39] This idea is, of course, quite consistent with Catholic teaching. The Church does "continue Christ's identity." Christians have "put on Christ" through baptism. In the sacraments of her worship Christ shares His redemption with the faithful. However, feminist theology hesitates to make any real distinction between Christ and the Church because distinctions are the seeds of inequality. In the feminist notion of the Eucharist there is very little emphasis on Christ as an object of worship. In short, Christianity is no longer the worship of a "person."[40] The community is not turned toward Him as the source of its salvation and praise. Gone, too, are any effective symbols (i.e., the sacrificing priesthood and consecrated species) that are causative of the Church's worship.

The feminist challenge seeks to reform the Catholic Church by dissolving its hierarchical clerical structure to make way for the egalitarian community in keeping with what is affirmed by them to be Jesus' original vision of redemption. In such a community all Christians are empowered by the Spirit and no one individual or special caste in the Church has exclusive claim to represent to the community the presence and power of God.

The liberation of the Church from clericalism also means reclaiming the sacraments as expressions of the redemptive life of the Church that the people are

feminist

empowered to administer collectively. The community may designate various people at different times to develop and lead liturgical expressions, but *this does not mean these persons own or possess a sacramental power that the community does not have.* Rather, it means these persons represent and gather into a collective experience the sacramental life processes of the people. . . . Reappropriation of the sacraments means that not only the exercise but also the interpretation of the sacraments *arises from the community's collective experience of its life in grace. The baptism of each individual involves all members of the community, who midwife each other's rebirth from alienated to authentic life. Penance means forgiving one another. It is not the disciplinary tool of any elite. Eucharist is not an objectified piece of bread or cup of wine that is magically transformed into the body and blood of Christ.* Rather it is the people, the ecclesia, who are being transformed into the body of the new humanity, infused with the blood of new life. The symbols stand in the midst of and represent that communal reality. (Emphasis added.)[41]

not even Christ

Prescinding from her caricature of the Catholic Eucharist, Ruether's statement demonstrates that in the feminist understanding of equality the *community is all.* Nothing—no person, no symbol stands over/against the community. Persons who lead liturgical celebrations "do not own or possess a sacramental power that the community does not have." What is represented in the new eucharist is not Christ to the people but the "community's collective experience." The Eucharist is no longer worship of Christ, the Lord and Savior, in which He is objectively present as source of that worship. The Eucharist represents the *Church.* But this Church is not Christ's Body either (a body in complement to and in relation to its head). Rather, the Eucharist represents the "new humanity."

Feminist

Feminist theology, when taken to its logical conclusions, does not advocate the ordination of women to the Catholic priesthood. It seeks to dissolve the priesthood. The majority of feminist writers, however, continue to advocate the ordination of women within some concept of Holy Orders.[42] However, in order for women to be priests the meaning of the priest as *sign* must be altered.

The horror of *distinction* (as it is seen to be the cause of the oppression of women and all other injustices) permeates every aspect of feminist theology. The quest for unity, dignity and equality among all human beings and most especially between men and women is an ancient quest. Feminist theologians are by no means alone in their desire for unity and equality at the expense of the goodness of the created order. Feminist theology departs radically from the Catholic faith regarding the relation between history and the validity of the sacramental priesthood. The Catholic Church teaches that her sacraments and doctrinal teaching flow from the covenant instituted by the one sacrifice of Christ Himself. The sacraments and doctrinal tradition are essential to the Church's historical mediation of the one sacrifice. Any development of sacramental worship and of dogma occurred *in history* under the inspiration of the Holy Spirit. Most importantly, the Eucharist as a sacrifice was instituted by Christ as part of His historical mission. This truth was affirmed at Vatican II when it taught that the Eucharist was instituted by Christ Himself on the night He was betrayed in order to perpetuate the sacrifice of the Cross "throughout the ages."[43] The efficacy of the Eucharist is not diminished or rendered beyond our grasp by history as if time and concrete circumstances stood as a barrier between us and the original truth of this symbol.

THE FEMINIST VIEW OF THE CHURCH

In contrast to this, feminist theology regards historical circumstances as the enemy of Christ's original pristine message. Christ's mission was to usher in the egalitarian community.[44] In the feminist perspective Christianity was corrupted early, when the Christian community moved from charismatic leadership—not based on sexual role differentiation—to office. This move is from equality to patriarchy, and it came about when the charismatic millenarist Church had to deal with the delay of Christ's return and accommodated to continued historical existence in the world.[45] But this transition from charism to office was neither historically necessary nor theologically correct.[46]

The original mission of Christ is uncovered by Fiorenza by the hermeneutics of suspicion which makes Christ's compassion for the poor and the outcast and his antiauthoritarian statements (i.e., "call no one your father") paradigms for understanding what the Kingdom of God and salvation are all about. Gal. 3:27–28 expresses the essence of Jesus' mission. This is not an eschatological/millenarist ideal but the reality of the Christian community.[47] Fiorenza states that Christianity's new vision of humanity was a threat to Graeco-Roman patriarchal order.

> I have argued that the pagan perception of Christians interfering with the patriarchal order of the house was not unfounded. Insofar as Christians accepted slaves and women from pagan households as converts and members, they clearly broke the ancestral laws. Their self-understanding as the new eschatological community, the new creation, the new humanity, in which the social/political statification of religion, class, slavery, and patriarchal marriage are abolished, and all are equal in Christ, was an alternative vision that clearly undermined the Graeco-Roman patriarchal order. The Christian message was so attractive and convincing for women and slaves, precisely because it promised them liberation

from the patriarchal order and gave them a new freedom in the community of equals.[48]

This inclusive (versus exclusive) egalitarian vision is later replaced by hierarchy and office. Fiorenza places the beginnings of this transition in the early Church's need to accommodate itself to the ethics and behavioral customs of the time. The Church needed to tone down and domesticate its eschatological egalitarian enthusiasm which made the Christian community stand out from its surrounding culture. By doing this the Church would be accepted by its time and thus ensure its survival in its postmillenarist phase.

Graeco-Roman culture is based on hierarchical relationships with power located in a dominant male authority figure. Fiorenza states that the household codes found in the Pauline and Petrine epistles are based on Graeco-Roman patriarchal order. These codes become the norm of Christian ethical behavior as a means of demonstrating, contrary to the accusations of pagan critics, that the Church is not a threat to traditional familial patriarchal authority.[49]

Contrary to the *paterfamilias*, early Church authority is characterized by role interchangeability.[50] According to Fiorenza, in the early Church all Christians, based upon their baptism, had "equal access to authority, leadership and power." Fiorenza is in complete agreement with Ruether that no one possesses a sacramental power that the community as a whole does not possess.[51] The only difference between the authority of the apostles and anyone else exercising leadership is that the apostles' authority was translocal and derived "its legitimacy from the direct revelation and authority of the resurrected Lord." The authority of bishops and heads of house churches was limited to a local community.[52]

A change occurred, however, in the early life of the Church from an egalitarian view of authority to the present patriarchal/hierarchical model. Fiorenza believes this shift, which occurred in the second century, was from charasmatic leadership to an institutional centralization of power. Now the local leaders absorb all ecclesial power—that of prophet, apostle, and the power of the community to make decisions. At first, leadership was accessible to all the baptized, but gradually, over time, it became a patriarchal leadership restricted to male "heads of households."[53]

Fiorenza believes this shift is articulated in the Pastoral epistles in which the bishop/overseer is understood in terms of a *paterfamilias*. Ecclesial structure and authority is the authority of the familial household codes writ large in which subordinate members of the household must subject themselves to the head.[54]

Ruether also characterizes the early Church as a millenarist, egalitarian, spirit-filled community. A conflict soon develops between the "original; charismatic order" and a developing institutional order. Ruether portrays the conflict as a struggle for power with the institutional office of the bishop winning. The leaders in the charismatic order, inspired by the spirit, take it upon themselves to speak in the name of Christ. The institutional ministry "felt the need" to cut off this type of prophesying, characteristic of a Church in its infancy and marked by an enthusiasm for the return of the Messiah.[55] As the Church loses its eschatological fervor, it becomes institutionalized.[56]

> Those who continue to speak in the name of Christ become heretics (Montanists). Revelation is said to be closed and located in the past in a historical Christ and a past apostolic community. The ongoing power of the Spirit sent by Christ to the community is no longer to "blow where it will" but is institutionalized in the authority of bishops. They received the original "deposit of faith" from the apostles and they pass it down unaltered in their official teaching traditions. Both the interpretation of the words of Christ and the power of reconciliation with God is to be wrested from the hands of the charismatics, prophets, and martyrs and placed in the hands of the episcopacy, which takes over the claims of apostolic authority.[57]

The final phase of the Church's fall into "patriarchalization" occurs in the fourth century when the Church is established by an edict of Constantine as the imperial religion of the empire. Messianic kingship theology takes over because the dominant symbol of glory and power in the Graeco-Roman world is the emperor.

> All is integrated into one vast hierarchy of being. Just as the *Logos* of God governs the cosmos, so the Christian Roman Emperor, together with the Christian Church, governs the political universe; masters govern slaves and men govern women. Women, slaves and barbarians (as well as religious minorities, Jews, pagans, and heretics) are the *a-logoi,* the "mindless" ones, who are to be governed and defined by the representatives of the divine *Logos*. Christ has become the Pantocrator (All-Ruler) of a new world order. Christology becomes the apex of a system of control over all those who in one way or another are "other" than the new Christian order.[58]

According to feminist theology the story of the Church is one of a pure original community, which, almost from its very conception, fell gradually more and more into a corrupt view of authority and power as it was tainted by the unjust patriarchal culture around it. The sacramental system, male priests, and the authority of bishops are the result of historical corruption. Ruether believes that the remedy for this corruption is to go back to the beginning and uncover the true vision of Christ. This return involves doing an end run around the institutionalized authorities and historical tradition. But even Ruether concedes that there really is no way to get back to the uncorrupted start of things. Going back, therefore, becomes a way to impose a radical new interpretation upon the faith—this time an interpretation that is, of course, feminist.[59]

This feminist *return* to the original moment when the Christian faith was pure falls just short of a total despair of history in the sense that Ruether believes the moment is at least "discoverable" beneath the layers of historical corruption and that this corruption of history does not stand in the way of a reform of the Church. Nevertheless, we are confronted here with a position quite contrary to the Church's self-understanding in relation to history and God's providence. The Church is not the result of "collective experience." The Church has *received* her being from Christ. She has received her symbols, i.e., the priesthood, the Eucharist, and her motherhood. Ruether makes a caricature of these symbols when she accuses "systems of authority" of making received symbols dictate what can be experienced as well as the interpretation of that which is experienced.[60] The symbols of the faith make present the covenant between Christ and the Church. Far from being the result of history's corruption, they are the very symbols by which fallen history is yet given its meaning and direction. The Church's celebration of the covenant by way of these symbols, rooted in the order of creation and redemption, cannot be dictated. The covenant of Christ and His Church and its tangible expression is either a free event, or it is not a covenant at all.

As we noted previously, one of the most basic principles of feminist theology is a horror of any sort of inherent distinction on the level of being that gives rise to role differentiation forming systems of domination and oppression. As long as the Church excludes women from office and positions of leadership, it is held to be a corrupt institution whose whole tradition has been shaped by androcentrism and not by the Holy Spirit.

For women to achieve equality in the Church, the Church's doctrinal history on this view must be rewritten to recover the traditions of early Christian sects that advocated the equality of women but which were condemned as heretical by the orthodox Church. The feminist rehabilitation of these sects calls into question the Church's entire doctrinal history.

There is a problem of historical and theological perspective that must be kept in mind from the beginning. We know from a variety of ancient sources that many Christian communities of the first four centuries allowed extended leadership roles to women, including the ordained ministry in many cases.

feminist

These groups for the most part represented strains of early Christianity which did not become contributors to the formation of the Christian tradition which we have inherited.

Feminist

Rather, they were considered "heretical" by the "orthodox" tradition which eventually became the only legitimate Christianity; they are known to us as Gnostics, Montanists, Marcionites, and others. Whatever the theological factors involved, it is important to understand that what has survived is basically one theological tradition, the "orthodox" one, represented by writers known to us as the Church Fathers, whose bias against "heretical" Christianity is obvious.[61]

The Catholic tradition that excludes women from formal leadership positions is therefore invalid. The Church's rejection of these heretical sects is not the result of a history under the influence of the Holy Spirit protecting the Church against false teachings. For example, Montanism ought now be used as a corrective force on the corrupt "orthodox" position which is simply the result of a struggle for power in which one view of the Church as hierarchical and sacramental became the "historical winner."[62]

It is true that the Fathers of the Church held clearly misogynist views under the influence of Platonic and Aristotelian philosophy. Nevertheless, when the Church battled against and rejected gnostic sects, she was being true to her self-identity as a community founded by the historical Christ in covenantal/Eucharistic worship. When the Fathers reject certain sects and their teachings, sects that may have allowed women prominent leadership roles, this is the result of a will to be true to the historically received teaching of the Apostles. The Fathers' rejection of these sects is primarily the rejection of underlying philosophical principles and teachings upon which these sects were based, principles and teachings that threatened the moral, liturgical, and sacramental life of the Church. What the Fathers' protected in their rejection of gnostic sects was not their "male supremacy and power" but the worship of the Church. Conflicts between the orthodox Church and certain sects rarely, if ever, centered on the power and authority of males versus females. An example of this is in the Fathers' opposition to Montanism. While the Montanist sect gave certain followers of Montanus special status, i.e., Priscilla and Maximilla were considered prophetesses, the sect was condemned on other grounds. St. Jerome criticizes it for its extreme and false asceticism, its emphasis on members being inspired by the Holy Spirit while rejecting the Church's apostolic tradition and hierarchical/institutional authority. In short, Montanism's pneumatic extremism was a threat to Catholic sacramental worship.

THE GNOSTIC PRINCIPLES OF FEMINISM

Ancient Babylonian cosmology portrayed the creation of the universe—the separation of the sky from earth—as a violent conflict.

> In Babylonian cosmology, from which that of *Genesis* is derived, Marduk cut in two pieces the monstrous Tihamat, and 'one half of her he set in place, he spread out as heaven.' The primitive Egyptians, likewise, described *Shu* as separating the sky (*Nut*) from the earth (*Seb*). In the Taoism of China, an original 'Chaos' splits of its own accord into the two opposed moieties called *Yang* and *Yin*, the regions of light and darkness associated with heaven and earth.[63]

This cosmology from culture to culture has a universal representation.

> ... the world began as an undifferentiated mass, without internal boundaries or limits—an apeiron $\alpha\pi\epsilon\iota\rho o\nu$. This mass separated into two parts, which were opposed or 'contrary'—male and female. Finally, the male and the female were united by Eros, the contraries were combined, and gave birth to individual existence—to Gods [*sic*] or to things.[64]

Earth and heaven in Greek cosmology are essentially male and female principles. In Plato and Aristotle, for example, the male and female principles are associated with the two great contraries—Form and Matter.[65]

In Orphism, dating some two centuries before Plato, the universe is structured according to a cosmic dualism in contrasts that are in constant tension and irreconcilable—notably that between good and evil. This cosmic tension reflects that inner sense of the double man and the war in our members that is called the "sense of sin."[66] This tension throws man into a crisis as he experiences his own self-conscious individuality which is to feel a profoundly terrifying isolation from God and the common life and common consciousness. The conflict is experienced as one between body and soul.

> To the 'body' are assigned those senses and lusts whose insurrection destroys the inward harmony. 'Soul' still covers the field of the common consciousness, or 'conscience'; but it has shrunk from being the pervasive soul of the whole group to being one among an aggregate of individual selves, weakened by their novel isolation, and always longing for the old undivided communion.[67]

The Orphics, in contrast to Dionysiac religion which sought immediate reunion with God through orgiastic ecstasy, turned to the Way of Righteousness: "a long and painful round of ritual forms."[68] The Pythagoreans, who inherited the Orphic tradition, taught that salvation could only be achieved through a series of purgations leading in the end to the soul's reunification with God.[69]

In Plato's *Phaedo* the soul is likened to the eternal true "natures' or Ideas. Salvation is release of the soul from the corruption of the body. F. M. Cornford explains:

> The immortal thinking soul, which alone knows reality, is sharply distinguished from the body, with which are associated the lower faculties of sense, emotion, and desire. Death is the complete release of the soul from the infection and impurity of that lower nature; philosophy is the rehearsal of death, in which the soul retires by herself, shaking off, so far as she can, the senses and lusts of the body, to commune with those invisible and passionless existences, Justice, Beauty, Goodness, and the rest. . . . The world of the body is a prison, or a tomb; that other world of the soul and of Ideas is the realm of true life and reality, in which all worth resides.[70]

In the *Timaeus* the male is the symbol for the pure Forms or Ideas, for what is spiritual and unchangeable, while the female is symbolic of matter, of what holds the soul back from union with the One.

Philo (born 13 B.C.) was the greatest Jewish philosopher of the Alexandrian school during the Graeco-Roman period, who, under the dominant influence of Plato, associates the material world with becoming and change. "These phenomena, which are closely associated with the reproductive process, belong to the world of sense perception, not to the world of ideas and the invisible mind."[71] In Philo's thought, peace, harmony, and unity between God and man and the world are achieved through the dissolving of particularity. Nothing in God is divided. God is "himself the sole standard for the monad."[72] For man to be at peace nothing in him must be divided; his only reality is his similarity to God.

In Philo's exegesis of Genesis there are actually two men created by God. The first man is that of Gen. 1:27 who is "what one might call an idea. or a genus, or a seal, an object of thought, incorporeal, neither male or female, by nature incorruptible."[73] The second man is that of Gen. 2:7. This is the man of flesh and sense who is male or female.[74] The first man is nonsexual, or asexual, only potentially male or female but not actually.[75] The rational soul can rule over the undivided "body" of the first "man." Sense perception and body do not fight the rational soul but are subservient to it.[76] From the very beginning however, the man of Gen. 2:7 is susceptible to a fall as nothing is constant in any created thing. The fall occurs with the appearance of woman.[77] On the creation of Adam Philo writes:

For so long as he was one, he was like the world and God in his singleness and received in his soul the impressions made by the nature of each, not all of these but as many as one of mortal composition can find room for. But when woman too was formed, beholding a figure like his own and a kindred form, he was gladdened by the sight, and approached and greeted her. She, seeing no living thing more like herself than he, is filled with happiness and modestly returns his greeting. Love supervenes, brings together and fits into one the divided halves, as it were, of a single living creature, and sets up in each of them a desire for fellowship with the other with a view to the production of their like. And this desire begat likewise bodily pleasure, which is the beginning of wrongs and violation of law, and for the sake of which they bring on themselves the life of mortality and wretchedness in lieu of that of immortality and bliss.[78]

The following comment on the thought of Philo is helpful:

The first man originally existed in a state of unity or oneness, and so long as he remained in this state, he was like both God and the world in his singleness (μονωσις). But this original state of oneness or singleness was interrupted by the appearance of woman who became for the first man the ἀρχὴ τῆς ὑπαίτιου ζωῆς .[79]

In Philo's system of thought woman is the repository of irrational sense perception—that lower part of the human soul which is tied to the physical temporal world. In Philo's thought the male represents "mind" and woman "sense."[80] As long as mind dominates sense all is well. But the male allowed woman (sense) to pull him into pleasure and thus distract him from the higher things of God and the spiritual world.

Pleasure is not able to deceive the mind (the male) directly, but can only do so through sense (the female).[81] She is the symbol of all that would keep man from experiencing oneness in himself and with the divine and unchanging. Salvation, therefore, is a flight from woman and everything associated with the feminine.[82]

Feminist theology as it is articulated by its major thinkers is fundamentally a retrogression—a retreat back either to ancient cosmology or to Platonic and Gnostic views of salvation. Mary Daly provides the most unabashed articulation of this tendency in her books *Beyond God the Father* and *Gyn/Ecology*. For this she is mildly criticized by Ruether in her book *Sexism and God-Talk*. However, while Ruether repudiates Daly for her fall back into Gnostic salvation, Ruether herself, because she must reject the goodness of differentiation, ends up producing a soteriology that is equally an attack on the good of creation. In the thought of Mary Daly, not only is Christianity irretrievably sexist, but the entire world is steeped in the corruption of male influence.[83] According to Daly, men have been responsible for all the evils of the world.[84] The greatest evil men perpetrate is their quest to dominate and eliminate all that is feminine from the world.

> For men in the past—and most are living in the past rather than now—life has meant feeding on the bodies and minds of women, sapping energy at the expense of female deaths. Like Dracula, the he-male has lived on woman's blood. Perhaps this is one reason why patriarchal lore has expressed such a horror of female blood. The priests of patriarchy have eaten the body and have drunk the blood of the Sacrificial Victim in their Mass, but they have not wished to know *who* has really been the Victim whose blood supported this parasitic life.[85]

The patriarchal forces of the male world sap and suck out the life energies of women. In Daly's philosophy, salvation for women from this oppression mirrors that of Philo. Salvation for Daly is to escape the world—to get out of this evil realm of the "land of the Fathers."

> Breaking through the Male Maze is both exorcism and ecstasy. It is spinning through and beyond the fathers' foreground which is the arena of games. This spinning involves encountering the demons who block the various thresholds as we move through gateway after gateway into the deepest chambers of our homeland, which is the Background of our Selves.[86]

This escape is accomplished by women turning in upon themselves wherein she "dis-covers" her "Be-ing."[87] It is within the Self alone, isolated and apart from the world and from men that salvation is achieved. The woman possesses herself and creates herself and in so doing creates the "Otherworld."[88]

Ruether describes this notion of salvation as "primarily spiritual," and while (along with goddess religion) it may be attractive in many ways, it is nevertheless "delusive."[89] Ruether criticizes separatist views of salvation because a woman's affirmation of her own humanity demands a like affirmation of the humanity of men.[90]

If Daly's soteriology reinvents Philo, Ruether's soteriology, while different from Daly's, is likewise utterly incompatible with the Christian insistence on the good of the body, the individual self and creation. Since for Ruether as well as for Daly, injustice is rooted in differentiation, there can be no "dualism" or split between spirit and matter. Even God, according to Ruether, is not simply a spiritual being. The "God/ess" is both spirit and matter.

The God/ess who is primal Matrix, the ground of being-new being, is neither stifling immanence nor rootless transcendence. Spirit and matter are not dichotomized but are the *inside and the outside of the same thing*. When we proceed to the inward depths of consciousness or probe beneath the surface of visible things to the electromagnetic field that is the ground of atomic and molecular structure, the visible disappears. Matter itself dissolves into energy. Energy, organized in patterns and relationships, is the basis for what we experience as visible things. It becomes impossible anymore to dichotomize material and spiritual energy.[91]

Stated simply, spirit and consciousness are only a different form of matter. There is no transcendent God who can be named as Other than the world. All reality—spirit, matter, God—is the same entity. Therefore, not only can it be said that men and women do not differ from each other in any significant way, but gone is any significant difference between God and creation. Ruether strives to achieve unity in a world seemingly torn and atomized and thus filled with injustice. Salvation, however, is not for her a process (as it is for Philo and Daly) of getting out of the world. Ruether, instead, goes to the opposite extreme. In *Sexism and God-Talk* she asks whether immortality serves feminism. Because Ruether regards differentiation as the enemy of unity, her theology inevitably preaches the annihilation of the individual: to be rid of the *self*. This is salvation.

She explains that with death, personal reality comes to an end.

Consciousness ceases and the organism itself gradually disintegrates. This consciousness is the interiority of that life process that holds the organism together. There is no reason to think of the two as separable, in the sense that one can exist without the other.

What then has happened to "me"? In effect, our existence ceases as individuated ego/organism and *dissolves back into the cosmic matrix of matter/energy, from which new centers of the individuation arise. It is this matrix, rather than our individuated centers of being, that is "everlasting," that subsists underneath the coming to be and passing away of individuated beings and even planetary worlds.* Acceptance of death, then, is the acceptance of the finitude of our individuated centers of being, but also our identification with the larger matrix as our total self that contains us all. (Emphasis added.)[92]

Feminist theology "solves" the ancient problem of the One and the Many by wiping out "the Many." Salvation is annihilation. Justice and harmony is achieved by a collapse of the many into the depersonalized One. While a Christian lives, this One is the Christian community and when we die it is the earth that swallows up everything. Ruether attempts to soften this picture by stating that the individuated self is not lost, but changed. We become food for new beings to arise from our bones.[93] Ruether's doctrine is the rediscovery of the primitive notion of reincarnation, predating the Orphic discovery of the self, which longs for "the old undivided communion."[94] Feminist philosophy is the rehearsal of death. The individuated self is lost. When the human being is reduced to food for other selves, this assumes that the individual *person* is ultimately insignificant.

The old cycle of reincarnation is described by Cornford:

> That primitive belief belonged to earth not to heaven: it taught the revolution of all life or soul in man and nature, passing in an endless round from the underworld into the light of day, and back again. There was no hope or possibility of any release; indeed, such an idea would have no meaning, since the individual soul did not persist after death, but was reabsorbed in the one life of all things. No part or fragment of this life had any separate persistence. It had not come from the aether, and could not fly off thither; it came from earth and returned to earth again.[95]

Not only does feminist theology revert back to prephilosophical primitive cosmologies, but it shares many elements of Platonic salvation as articulated by Philo. Daly may be the most radical among feminist theologians but in a real sense hers is the quintessential statement of where feminist theology leads. It does not matter that her idea of salvation for women is a spiritual salvation of the Mind while Ruether's seems to emphasize the eternal life and goodness of the earth. Both views deny the goodness of human sexuality. The individual self insofar as it is a sexual, concrete, physical entity is not important and in the end is destroyed. Ruether tries to escape Daly's completely spiritualized salvation but only succeeds in providing a clever camouflage for what is still fundamentally a pessimistic and un-Christian view of human beings and their relation to God and the world. For Plato, salvation meant escaping the body (that is, the individual self) so that the soul could be joined to the One. Ruether's idea of salvation differs from this only in the sense that instead of escaping matter—the self is dissipated in matter understood as the One. The goodness of the created order is founded on the primordial covenant in which God the Creator names something *else*, something *other* than Himself as *good*. This *something other* is His creation constructed according to the beauty of covenantal differentiation. The primary symbols of this covenant are the male and female person. Salvation does not annihilate the self, thus it does not annihilate sexual difference, but according to the faith of the Church, the order of redemption rests upon the bodily *symbols* of man and woman. The manner in which these symbols function redemptively in the order of grace is the basis for male and female authority in the Catholic Church.

II. Women and the Fathers of the Church

THE INFLUENCE OF PLATONISM

The role of women in the Church—more specifically, the exercise of feminine ecclesial authority—exists in the covenantal structure of salvation in which male and female sexuality serve as the prime symbols of the unity between Christ and His people. This covenantal structure of salvation is taught even by the Fathers of the Church—a place one would not expect to find such teaching. The Catholic view of the equality of the sexes is evident in the Fathers' writings when they speak with an authentic Christian sacramental vision of the world that is not as heavily tainted by Neoplatonism. The Fathers, deeply influenced by the cosmological worldview of their time, look upon the female as the inferior sex by nature. The writings of the Fathers are full of a condescending and even hostile view of women. The Fathers, guided by Platonic principles, associate the female body with sense and matter.[96] Women are intellectually and morally inferior to men because of the limitations of their physical sex.[97] Because a woman's body links her to what is passing and temporal, it was thought more likely a priori that women personified in Eve would be the cause of Original Sin.[98] Some of the Fathers express the idea that women collectively bear the guilt of Eve for the fall.[99] Women are not permitted to teach in the assembly because they are morally the weaker vessel and subject to the authority of men who are regarded as the superior sex.[100] In many instances the Church Fathers, under the influence of Platonism, associate spiritual unity and perfection with what is male. A woman's existence is justified by her functional capacity as a helpmate to the man in procreation. According to a passage from St. Augustine, procreation is a woman's sole reason for existence; another man would have been a better companion for Adam in everything else.[101] Cosmological harmony and unity is achieved by associating what is fully human and complete with what is masculine. In the words of St. Clement of Alexandria, a woman is an imperfect man.

> This, then, the mark of the man, the beard, by which he is seen to be man, is older than Eve, and is the token of the superior nature. In this God deemed it right that he should excel, and disperse hair over man's whole body. Whatever smoothness and softness was in him He abstracted from his side when He formed the woman Eve, physically receptive, his partner in parentage, his help

in household management, while he (for he had parted with all smoothness) remained a man, and shows himself man. And to him has been assigned action, as to her suffering; for what is shaggy is drier and warmer than what is smooth. Wherefore males have both more hair and more heat than females, animals that are entire than the emasculated, perfect than imperfect.[102]

A woman is an emasculated male. This tendency in the Fathers to denigrate women, to look upon them as creatures who are inherently inferior and unequal to men is the result of the Platonic search for unity. Unity in the Middle and Neoplatonism of the Fathers is not trinitarian but radically monist. When the Fathers succumb to this non-Christian point of view, female existence can only be defined and justified according to male priority—a priority that must overwhelm and exhaust what is different from itself, namely, the female member of the species. The subjection of what is perceived to be less perfectly human to what is more perfectly human (i.e.,: to what is physically stronger, more rational, and more spiritual) is the means of achieving order and unity in creation. St. Augustine's teaching that only when women are joined to males do they bear the image of God is a prominent example of the Platonic tendency to find in a single entity the source and meaning of spiritual unity and perfection. Concerning the manner by which women are in God's image, St. Augustine states:

> . . . according to that which I have said already, when I was treating of the nature of the human mind, that the woman together with her own husband is the image of God, so that the whole substance may be one image; but when she is referred separately to her quality of help-meet, which regards the woman herself alone, then she is not in the image of God; but as regards the man alone, he is the image of God as fully and completely as when the woman too is joined with him in one.[103]

In this passage from *On the Trinity* St. Augustine attempts to reconcile 1 Cor. 11:7–8, where St. Paul states that man is in God's image while women reflect man's glory, with the teaching in Gen. 1:27, which teaches that both males and females are made in God's image. Augustine's reconciliation of the texts is done according to Platonist teaching on the relation between the male and female body to the soul.[104]

The image of God is shared by men and women equally according to the rational part of the mind, more specifically when the human mind is turned toward eternal truth. Because the female body serves to help men as a "helpmeet" in temporal and corporeal affairs, the woman, insofar as her mind is turned toward these affairs because of her body, is not in the image of God. As Augustine states:

... when as a whole [the mind] contemplates the truth it is the image of God; and in the case when anything is divided from it, and diverted in purpose to the dealing with temporal things; nevertheless on that side on which it beholds and consults truth, here also it is the image of God, but on that side whereby it is directed to the dealing with the lower things, it is not the image of God.[105]

Man is made according to the image of God "where there is no sex, that is, in the spirit of his mind."[106] However, the male and female body are symbols for the higher and lower parts of the soul. Because the female body stands for that part of the soul turned from God to temporal things in her role as a "helpmeet" for man—women as women are not in God's image.

Because she differs from the man in bodily sex, it was possible rightly to figure under her bodily covering that part of the reason which is diverted to the government of temporal things; so that the image of God may not remain, except on that side of the mind of man on which it cleaves to the beholding or the consulting of the eternal reasons of things; and this; it is clear, not men only, but also women have.

A common nature, therefore, is recognized in their minds, but in their bodies a division of that one mind itself is figured.[107]

Because a man's bodily function in the world is more consistent with the purpose of the rational mind, he alone *as man* exemplifies the image of God in the world. Only when the woman is assumed by (is made one with) the man does she participate substantially in the image of God.

Based upon Platonic principles two ideas are linked in the thought of Augustine. First, that only the mind and not the body, whether male or female, participates in the image of God.[108] Second, nonetheless the male body stands for the spiritual part of man which is closest to God while the female body stands for what is in opposition to God and thus needs to be under subjection.

Do women not have this renewal of their mind where the image of God is? Who said that? But they do not signify it by the sex of their body, for which reason they are bidden to veil themselves. Truly, in so far as they are women, they show that part which can be called concupiscible, which, when the woman lives according to God's law and order, is dominated by the mind subject to its God. What, therefore, in one person are mind and concupiscence (for the one rules, the other is ruled; the one dominates, the other is subdued), that in two human beings, man and woman, is represented according to the sex of the body.[109]

There are other passages in St. Augustine where the significance of the female body and feminine existence is given a far more positive treatment—a treatment that in the light of faith discards Platonic dualisms when dealing with the role of the Virgin Mary and the Church in the redemption of Christ. Indeed, a close and careful reading of the Fathers reveals that their philosophical and theological treatment of women is full of healthy conflict and inconsistencies. The Fathers are embedded in a pagan philosophical worldview whose degrading view of women is, however, coming up against the faith of the Church which teaches according to its sacramental and moral life that men and women share an equal dignity and are partners in redemption. One may go so far as to say that in the writings of the Fathers on women it is not Greek philosophy that is obscuring Christian revelation, but rather it is the revolutionary teaching of the Church that is, albeit slowly and painfully, displacing the dominant philosophical view that women are inferior to men. When the Fathers base their writings upon the Revelation of Christ, a view of women begins to emerge that recognizes that concrete feminine existence is essential to the fulfillment of the world's redemption in Christ. In this role woman is in relation to man, as *sign* of the marital covenant between Christ and His Church. The Fathers' teachings on women show that women bear authority for the building up of the Christian faith. The redemption of Christ is dependent upon women—a dependency that is rooted in the created goodness of women as such.

St. Augustine

Against those who in his day denied the importance and goodness of the human body and thus disparaged the Christian faith that God has taken on flesh through a woman, St. Augustine taught vigorously that the Incarnation honored both the male and the female sex.

> Those likewise are to be detested who deny that our Lord Jesus Christ had Mary as his mother on earth. That dispensation did honor to both sexes male and female, and showed that both had a part in God's care; not only that which he assumed, but that also through which he assumed it, being a man born of a woman.[110]

In this passage from *Faith and the Creed*, the male and female sex are equal. The fact that Christ became male does not render the male sex superior to the female. The Incarnation expresses God's acknowledgment of both sexes. Christ's male sex is relative to the Church. The mission of the Son terminates not in Christ but in the New Covenant. As regards the role of women in redemption, the human Christ is dependent upon the woman. Augustine states that Christ certainly had no mother as far as his divine nature is concerned. But the crucifixion—the act by which the world is saved—was rendered through Christ the man, born of Mary and that is why in *the hour* of His Passion He recognizes her.[111]

The respect Augustine shows to the Mother of Christ as regards the work of redemption in the passage just quoted is remarkable. St. Augustine bases his respect for Mary on Christ's own respect for her in His salvific work. Christ recognizes Mary *as His Mother*. Far from disowning her, Christ recognizes her as necessary to His redemptive act on the Cross.[112] St. Augustine then goes on to admonish believers not to be repelled by the Faith because the Son of God was born from a woman.

> Nor should our faith be lessened by any reference to "a woman's internal organs," as if it might appear that we must reject any such generation of our Lord, because sordid people think that sordid. "The foolishness of God is wiser than men" (1 Cor. 1:25); and "to the pure all things are pure" (Tit.1:15) as the apostle truly says.[113]

The contrast of the above passage with the prevailing Neoplatonism of the time cannot be overemphasized. Origen, for example, whose platonic Christian thought had great influence upon the later Fathers, associated women and femininity not only with what is corporeal and thus supposedly contrary to the spirit, but also with sin itself.[114] For this reason he declared that God did not condescend to look on what is feminine and bodily.[115] Furthermore, as far as redemption is concerned, male and female embodied existence is meaningless to God. The male and the female stand for the quality of the soul only. However, St. Augustine, in *Faith and the Creed*, taught that, far from salvation having nothing to do with human sexuality, the male and female persons are part of the economy of salvation according to the Incarnation. Most startling, in contrast to the extreme Platonism of Origen, is Augustine's statement that the Incarnation took place through a "woman's internal organs" and that such contact in no way sullied divinity. Rooted in Christian teaching, Augustine concludes that indeed God *does look* upon what is womanly and corporeal. It is a look that is favorable—a look that causes the feminine to be caught up in the work of redemption. The passage from Augustine is dominated by a theology of the body and the Incarnation. Origen's denigration of women, based in his Platonic thought, is therefore undone by the Bishop of Hippo.

St. Jerome, although a student of Origen, also teaches that the female body participates in an essential way in the order of redemption—in a way that is equal in importance and dignity to the male existence Christ took on. In Jerome's *Letter 22 to Eustochium* again, similar to Augustine, we find salvation dependent on the female person as the pure body of Christ came from the pure Virgin.

> "There shall come forth a rod out of the stem of Jesse, and a flower shall grow out of his roots." The rod is the mother of the Lord—simple, pure, unsullied; drawing no germ of life from without but fruitful in singleness like God Himself. The flower of the rod is Christ, who says of Himself: "I am the rose of Sharon and the lily of the valleys." In another place He is foretold to be "a stone cut out of the mountain without hands," a figure by which the prophet signifies that He is to be born a virgin of a virgin. For the hands are here a figure of wedlock as in the passage: "His left hand is under my head and his right hand doth embrace me."[116]

It should be acknowledged that in this section of the letter St. Jerome compares virginity to marriage in which virginity as a vocation is exalted. However, regarding St. Jerome's attitude toward women, it is important to note that there is an equivalence between Christ and His mother and that the passage implies a dependency of Christ upon the human Mary. In addition, it is not Christ alone who exemplifies virginity. Christ and His mother share equally the dignity of this state as Jerome writes: "For me virginity is consecrated in the persons of Mary and Christ."[117] Finally, St. Jerome does not at all hesitate to say that Mary in her fruitful virginity is "like God (Christ) Himself." It can be argued that what is important for Jerome is the virginity common to the Savior and to Mary. Nevertheless, it is important that Jerome at the same time recognizes that Mary's virginity does not deny her womanhood. Mary is not like Christ because virginity causes her to become male or a spirit. While Mary is a virgin she is still a woman—"the mother of the Lord."

St. Augustine's theology presents the Church as the New Eve. This teaching, while it does not directly bear upon the role of individual Christian women, nevertheless explicitly recognizes that femininity is part of the order of salvation and thus serves as a very valuable foundation for building a theology of the role of women in the Church. In Augustine's exegesis on Psalm 127 we see that salvation is centered on a pair: Christ and His Church. This is a nuptial pair as Christ and His Church are prefigured in the first couple.

> But where did He sleep? On the Cross. When He slept on the Cross, He bore a sign, yea, He fulfilled what had been signified in Adam: for when Adam was

asleep, a rib was drawn from him, and Eve was created; so also while the Lord slept on the Cross, His side was transfixed with a spear, and the sacraments flowed forth, whence the Church was born. For the Church the Lord's Bride was created from His side, as Eve was created from the side of Adam. But as she was made from his side no otherwise than while sleeping, so the Church was created from His side no otherwise than while dying.[118]

As salvation is centered on a pair, Christ is not effecting salvation alone. Salvation is effected by Christ *through the Church* who is His bride and who as His bride exemplifies all that is feminine. It can be said that in St. Augustine's theology there is a sense in which the feminine Church is a co-cause of salvation. It is she who gives birth to Christ's children.

There is a certain woman, in whom what was said unto Eve, "in sorrow shalt thou bring forth children," is shown after a spiritual manner. The Church bears children, the Bride of Christ; and if she bears them, she travails of them. In figure of her, Eve was called also "the Mother of all living." . . . The Church groans for them, the Church travaileth of them; but in that resurrection of the dead, the offspring of the Church shall appear, pain and groaning shall pass away.[119]

The Church is a woman. Again, St. Augustine, far from denying women or disparaging what is feminine in order for salvation to be effected, indeed states that the salvation of Christ is accomplished through the feminine, and his thought at least implies that, according to a nuptial order, an equal dignity exists between the male Christ and the female Church. This is, of course, the "whole Christ," the *Christus totus*, Head and Body, *sponsus and sponsa*.

St. Irenaeus, as no other Church Father, provides a well-developed theology of Mary as the New Eve. Similar to Augustine, his teaching on the role of Mary is articulated in defense of the good of the human body and the Incarnation.[120] In his work *Against Heresies* Irenaeus very explicitly teaches that by a woman salvation is accomplished. The bodily presence of Christ is dependent on the body of Mary.[121] He is the New Adam only through the obedience of the New Eve.

For inasmuch as He had a pre-existence as a saving Being, it was necessary that what might be saved should also be called into existence, in order that the being who saves should not exist in vain.

In accordance with this design, Mary the Virgin is found obedient, saying, "Behold the handmaid of the Lord; be it unto me according to thy word."[122]

The obedience of Mary is not simply passively functional in relation to the Incarnation. Rather, Mary's "yes" is *causative* of salvation as Eve's disobedience was the source of man's damnation.

> But Eve was disobedient; for she did not obey when as yet a virgin. And even as she, having indeed a husband, Adam, but being nevertheless as yet a virgin. . . was made the cause of death, both to herself and to the entire human race; so also did Mary, having a man betrothed [to her], and being nevertheless a virgin, by yielding obedience, *became the cause of salvation*, both to herself, and the whole human race. (Emphasis added.)[123]

Far from overlooking or rejecting what is feminine, on the supposition that the feminine would be incapable of being a vehicle of grace, what is feminine is placed at the center of salvation according to God's design for the Incarnation. Mary's "yes" is not a consent simply to bear God's Son. Her "yes" to bear the Son of God is causative of redemption. Mary's consent to be the Mother of God undoes the bonds of death forged by Eve's disobedience. The order of salvation is bound up with Mary's "yes." Through a woman grace bursts forth into the world and in this way Mary is a co-redemptrix with Christ.[124] This theme is also found in Justin Martyr's *Dialogue with Trypho* where we again see Christ in the Incarnation dependent on Mary.[125]

Prudence Allen in her thorough study of Western philosophy's teachings on women states that it is with the dawn of Christian philosophy that a view of women emerges which recognizes that women and men are equal in rights and dignity in contrast to Stoicism and Neoplatonism.[126] Ancient pagan philosophy taught theories of either sex polarity or sex unity. The former theory teaches that men and women are so radically different, with men occupying a superior position, that there can be no real unity between them. The latter theory states that sexual unity is possible by ignoring sexual difference and treating the male and female body as irrelevant to the person who is identified with the soul alone. According to Allen the Christian teaching on the resurrection of the body was the basis for a new understanding that women are equal to men. The Christian faith believes that the human body has not only a temporal dimension but an eternal one, and, moreover, the bodies of men and women are eternally differentiated. The body and not only the soul constitutes human identity. Salvation in Christ means having one's body saved. It means having one's sexuality, male or female, called forever good. The eternal differentiation of male and female "had serious consequences for philosophy" Allen notes. Greek and Roman philosophy, with its ideas of sex unity and sex polarity, formed the basis of Christian thought but now, thanks to the Christian revelation, a new idea on the relation of the sexes was emerging. The conflict among these ideas produced a tremendous tension that was never satisfactorily resolved by the Fathers. However, Allen believes St. Augustine is the "meeting point of the different traditions. His inconsistency. . . marks a step forward in the history of the concept of woman in relation to man."[127]

Not only does the Christian teaching on the equality of women flow from the Church's teaching on the resurrection, but according to St. Augustine the resurrection of women is necessary for the fulfillment of salvation in Christ. The following passage from *The City of God* is of extreme importance regarding the relationship between human sexuality and redemption.

> For my part, they seem to be wiser who make no doubt that both sexes shall rise. . . . And the sex of woman is not a vice, but nature. It shall then indeed be superior to carnal intercourse and childbearing; nevertheless the female members shall remain adapted not to the old uses, but to a new beauty, which, so far from provoking lust, now extinct, shall excite praise to the wisdom and clemency of God, who made both what was not and delivered from corruption what he made. For at the beginning of the human race the woman was made of a rib from the side of the man while he slept; for it seemed fit that even then Christ and His Church should be foreshadowed in this event. For that sleep of the man was the death of Christ, whose side, as He hung lifeless upon the cross, was pierced with a spear, and there flowed from it blood and water, and these we know to be the sacraments by which the Church is "built up." For Scripture used this very word, not saying "He formed" or "framed," but "built her up into a woman"; whence also the apostle speaks of the *edification* of the body of Christ, which is the Church. The woman, therefore, is a creature of God even as the man; but by her creation from man unity is commended; and the manner of her creation prefigured, as has been said, Christ and the Church. He then, who created both sexes will restore both.[128]

True to Augustine's Neoplatonism, childbearing and carnal intercourse are held in low regard in this passage. They are mere functional capacities that have no religious symbolic value. Nevertheless, he accounts for the resurrection of both men and women precisely on the grounds that the male and female body are *signs* of the redemptive order from the very beginning of creation.[129] As God "built up" Eve from the rib of Adam, Christ builds up His Church. St. Augustine quotes Eph. 4:12 in which the "building up" of the Church is called the *edification* of the body of Christ. A woman's body stands for the body of Christ. Christ has built this body, and the unity between Himself and the Church is a marital one prefigured by the marriage between Adam and Eve. Augustine's theology of the resurrection of the body rests on the sexually symbolic meaning of the body, a meaning already given in Adam and Eve which is finally and ultimately fulfilled when the body is raised from the dead. In the thought of Augustine the significance of gender is not erased in the eschaton. From the very beginning of creation the male and female persons were imbued with religious and spiritual meaning. Redemption means that both sexes, imbued with this meaning and because of this meaning, shall be raised up.

The significance of St. Augustine's teaching for women and their place in the Church resides precisely in the fact that, as the above passage itself testifies, there is equality between men and women, and women themselves contribute to and are a necessary part of what it means for the world to be saved.

The significance of the female person for salvation can also be seen in the Fathers' discussion of the role of consecrated virgins. St. Jerome acknowledged that women were more favored with this vocation than men. He states: "Death came through Eve, but life has come through Mary. And thus the gift of virginity has been bestowed most richly upon women, seeing that it had its beginning from a woman."[130] In the thought of the early Church Fathers feminine virginity was a unique charism with a special significance that male virginity did not have. The female virgin was an ecclesiological symbol rendering present a spiritual reality. St. Jerome states "assuredly no gold or silver vessel was ever so dear to God as is the temple of a virgin's body. The shadow went before, but now the reality is come."[131] The reality that a consecrated virgin's body makes present is the marital/covenantal redemption of Christ. Throughout *Letter 22* the virgin is spoken of as Christ's bride. In this letter virgins are like Mary, the Mother of God. Indeed, one might say that a consecrated virgin is *another Mary*. St. Jerome writes "Now you too, may be the Lord's mother." Virgins give birth to the spirit of Christ's salvation which they "have wrought upon the earth."[132] This last statement is especially significant regarding the great dignity of women's purpose and place in the Church. The female virgin, precisely because of the nuptial meaning of her body, causes the salvation of Christ to be present on earth. The presence of Christ's salvation is "wrought" by these women. It is their work. It should be noted that St. Jerome defends the good of the female body against heretics such as the Manichees who allege that the devil is the author of the body.[133] St. Augustine, in his treatise *Holy Virginity*, also teaches that the consecrated virgin is a fleshly sign of what the Church is in faith.

> Since, therefore, the whole Church is espoused as a virgin to one man, Christ, as the Apostle says, how great honor her members deserve who preserve in their very flesh this which the whole Church, imitating the Mother of her Spouse and Lord, preserves in the faith. The Church too, is both mother and virgin. For, about whose integrity we are solicitous if she is not a virgin? Or of whose progeny do we speak if she is not a mother?
>
> Mary bore the Head of this body in the flesh; the Church bears the members of that Head in the spirit. In neither does virginity impede fecundity; and in neither does fecundity destroy virginity.
>
> Therefore, since the whole Church is holy, both in body and in spirit, yet is not exclusively a virgin in body, but only in spirit, how much more holy is she in those members where she is a virgin both in body and in spirit.[134]

Augustine has effectively linked the espousal of the Church, Mary, and the meaning of consecrated virginity. Consecrated virgins *preserve in their very flesh* the espousal of the Church to Christ. In this way it is women—indeed, the female body—which is a sign of redemption. And of course there is no way in which the male body would be just as well suited to this sacramental purpose.

In the thought of St. Ambrose we find again a comparison between consecrated virginity and the Church. Not only are female virgins a sign of the Church's virginity, but they also exemplify in their vocation the Church's *motherhood*.

> "So the holy Church, ignorant of wedlock, but fertile in bearing, is in chastity a virgin, yet a mother in offspring. She, a virgin, bears us her children, not by a human father, but by the Spirit."[135]

Feminist authors, for example, Mary Daly, complain that the Fathers' praise for female virginity was rooted in the idea that women could only become truly holy by shedding their female sex equated with the child-bearing function. Virginity allowed women to escape the "curse of Eve." Having escaped this curse, virginity rendered women manly, and manliness, as opposed to what was feminine, was associated with sanctity. For example, St. Jerome stated:

> As long as woman is for birth and children, she is different from man as body is from soul. But when she wishes to serve Christ more than the world, then she will cease to be a woman and will be called man (*vir*).[136]

There can be no question that Middle- or Neoplatonic principles are at work behind such a statement and similar statements made by other Church

Fathers.[137] Since there was a tendency in the Fathers such as St. Augustine to identify women solely with their power to procreate, consecrated virginity, by which this function was abandoned, caused women to become like men. Furthermore, in Neoplatonic and Middle-platonic thought, masculinity and femininity were spiritual categories associated with holiness and sin, good and evil, body and soul. We saw above how Origen held to such a view. Nevertheless, it cannot be said that this equation of female virginity with manliness represents in any way the thought of the Church Fathers concerning the religious meaning of the female body and the role of women in the Church. Women were not to become men. Even St. Jerome in his letter to Eustochium sharply criticized women who desexed themselves in this fashion: "Others change their garb and assume the mein of men, being ashamed of what they were born to be—women. They cut off their hair and are not ashamed to look like eunuchs."[138]

Concerning the ambivalence and contradictions one encounters in the Fathers' view of women, one female author insightfully observed:

> Despite the initial confusions in their language and the distortions developed in the minds of the vulgar, it was certainly not the object of the fathers to turn women into men through the virginal life. Rather they were seeking to express the absolute equality which the two sexes enjoyed outside the limitations of marriage.[139]

This is an important insight. The Fathers do not want to turn women into men. They are steeped in a culture dominated by Platonic ideas of equality and unity. The Platonic idea of unity is monist. The male is the paradigm of what is unified, perfect and single. Thus, within the Platonic mode manliness is the only way the Fathers know how to express equality between the sexes, and they are not consistent in their thought. As we saw in the discussion of virginity, the importance of the female body *as female* is recognized and praised by the Fathers.

WOMEN AND MARRIAGE ACCORDING TO THE FATHERS

In addition to affirming the significance of the female body, the Fathers testify in their writings to women's equality and authority in the Church's moral and sacramental life. Women were deemed equal in marital consent and in marital rights and were looked upon as exemplary in their love for Christ.

Regarding marriage, the Fathers, impelled by the revelation of Christ, taught that a woman should be free to choose her spiritual vocation. A

young woman could not be compelled by her family or even by her father
to marry if it were against her will. This assertion of the right of a woman
to defy her family regarding marriage flew in the face of the prevailing
custom and attitude of the time.[140] Clement of Alexandria, giving advice
about marriage in *The Stromata*, teaches that a man could not force a woman
to marry him or to love him.[141] St. Ambrose in his work *Concerning Virgins*
supports the Roman law allowing women to choose their own husbands
and the freedom of a woman to choose perpetual virginity.[142] He also
severely criticizes the dowry system as treating women as merchandise to
be sold for a price. "Slaves are sold under more tolerable conditions" and
possess more dignity, as they can often choose their own masters but if
a "maiden chooses it is an offense, if not it is an insult."[143] Women who
desire consecrated virginity in order to be wedded to Christ ought to defy
their angry parents and not be concerned about losing the security of the
household or their father's inheritance. To fulfill the call of Christ they are
to renounce all these things: "Conquer your affection first, O maiden. If
you conquer your home, you conquer the world."[144]

St. Jerome teaches in his letter to Eustochium that consecrated virginity
by God's own design is to be freely given, and, therefore, mothers should
not hold daughters back from this choice. Indeed, the daughter's vow
raises the mother's own status as she becomes "now the mother-in-law of
God."[145]

According to Augustine this freedom of the woman to choose her vocation has its preeminent model in Mary. Her virginal consecration was not
due to a precept or compulsion but by a "love of her own choice."[146]

> Thus, Christ, in being born of a virgin who, before she knew who was to
> be born of her, had resolved to remain a virgin, chose rather to approve holy
> virginity than to impose it. So, even in that woman in whom He took upon
> Himself the nature of a slave, He desired virginity to be free.[147]

This idea of personal freedom and consent marks a new anthropology
founded on the Christian teaching concerning the nature of marriage. Personal will, whether of the man or of the woman, is to be respected. Marriage
is a free giving of the self. Consecrated virginity is a type of marriage, and
so, too, the woman cannot be forced into it.

Christian teaching on marriage as a sign of the New Covenant required
personal freedom. A woman's free consent was as necessary to the validity
of the bond as the man's. Her consent, equally with his, entered into the
causality of the sacramental sign. Free consent to marry is inextricably

bound to conjugal rights, that is, the authority spouses have over one another's body. Husbands do not possess more conjugal or sacramental rights
than the wives. The marriage bond is one of equality, rooted in the mutual
authority spouses possess over one another's body. Because of this mutual
authority, the ban on divorce is equally binding on both husband and wife
as St. Augustine explains.

> In this law of marriage, therefore, if the rule as to both husband and wife is so
> similar that the same Apostle has not only mentioned it with regard to the wife,
> but has not even remained silent about it with regard to the husband (for, with
> reference to her, he says: 'Not the wife, but the husband, has authority over her
> body'; and with reference to him, he says: 'The husband likewise has not, but
> the wife has authority over his body')—therefore, if the rule is the same, we
> must understand that a wife is not allowed to put away her husband except for
> the same reason for which a husband is allowed to put away his wife, that is,
> fornication.[148]

St. Augustine recognizes that this mutual authority that the spouses have
over each other's body is the foundation of marital equality. No question
exists but that the wife is "unequal" and subordinate in all else regarding
the marriage but regarding the essence of marriage spouses are equal.[149]
For example, St. Augustine teaches, based on 1 Cor. 7:4, that a husband
could not make a vow of perpetual continence without the *consent* of his
wife.[150] In addition, contrary to the surrounding culture, Christian marriage
demanded total fidelity of husbands as well as wives. St. Augustine in his
sermon *To the Married* is adamant that wives must not tolerate infidelity
in their spouses.[151] Perhaps there is no clearer statement in the Fathers
regarding the authority a woman has over the moral life of her husband.
Augustine tells Christian husbands: "I commend you to the guardianship
of your wives." And to the wives he states:

> Do not allow your husbands to fornicate! Hurl the Church herself against
> them! Obstruct them, not through the law courts, not through the proconsul. . .
> not even through the Emperor, but through Christ. . . . *The wife has not authority*
> *over her body, but the husband.* Why do men exalt? Listen to what follows.
> *The husband likewise has not authority over his body, but the wife.* . . . Despise
> all things for love of your husband. But seek that he be chaste and call him to
> account if his chastity be amiss. . . . Who would tolerate an adulterous wife?
> Is the woman enjoined to tolerate an adulterous husband? . . .
> Those of you who are chaste women, however, do not imitate your wanton

husbands. May this be far from you. May they either live with you or perish alone. A woman owes her modesty not to a wanton husband but to God and to Christ.[152]

The above passage is a very good illustration of early Christian teaching that links equality and authority. Augustine's sermon contains much that would offend the modern sense of marital equality, nevertheless, the Fathers of the Church understand that sexual equality forbade a double standard of morality. There are many instances in the writings of the Fathers in which such a notion is condemned. St. Caesarius of Arles is notable for the connection he draws between the moral equality of men and women and their equal participation in the sacramental life of the Church.

> How is it that some men are so insolent that they say cruel vice is lawful for men but not for women? They do not reflect that men and women have been redeemed equally by Christ's Blood, have been cleansed by the very same baptism, approach the Lord's altar to receive His Body and Blood together, and that with God there is no distinction of male and female. 'God is not a respecter of persons.' Therefore, what is unlawful for women similarly never was and never can be lawful for men.[153]
>
> Now, in the Catholic faith, whatever is not lawful for women is equally unlawful for men. Man and woman were redeemed together for one price, the precious blood of Christ; they are called to one faith, and are assembled in one body of the Church.[154]

Women had a right to demand moral righteousness in their husbands and despite the Fathers' constant teaching, on the one hand, that women are naturally weaker in virtue,[155] on the other hand the Fathers' acknowledge that women are most often the ones practicing virtue and are to lead their husbands to do the same.

St. John Chrysostom taught in one of his homilies that women were to instruct, advise, and admonish their husbands in the moral life. The following passage clearly illustrates the authority of Christian wives.

> Indeed, nothing—nothing, I repeat—is more potent than a good and prudent woman in *molding* a man and *shaping his soul* in whatever way she desires. For he will not bear with friends, or teachers, or magistrates in the same way as with his wife, when she *admonishes* and *advises* him. Her admonition carries with it a kind of pleasure, because of his very great love of the one who is admonishing him. . . . She is devoted to him in all things and is closely bound to him as the body is fastened to the head. . . .

Therefore, I beseech women to carry this out in practice and to give their husbands only the proper advice. For, just as a woman has great power for good, so also she has it for evil. A woman destroyed Absalom; a woman destroyed Amnon; a woman would have destroyed Job; a woman saved Nabal from being murdered; a woman saved an entire nation.

Furthermore, Deborah and Judith and innumerable other women directed the success of men who were generals. And that is why Paul said: 'For how dost thou know, O wife, whether thou wilt save thy husband?' In his day too we see Persis and Mary and Priscilla sharing in the Apostles' difficult trials. You also ought to imitate these women, and *mold the character* of your husbands, not only by your words but also by your example. . . .

But when you provide him with instruction, not only by your words but also by your example then he will both show approval of you and be the more effectively convinced. (Emphasis added.)[156]

A woman has power for great good or evil. We are very far here from any intimation that women are morally weak and thus prone to evil. The power of women is seen here to direct the destiny of men. Men who are in positions of authority are directed by women to success or failure. Indeed, a wife even has the power to save her husband from damnation. Chrysostom does not hesitate to say that wives *instruct* their husbands, teach them, mold them, shape them, and admonish them. Wives are not alone in the position of being instructed. Rather, husbands, too, are to be instructed. They should listen to their wives because wives possess moral authority.

Most importantly, the authority of wives [and husbands] is rooted in the covenant of marriage itself. The meaning and essence of marriage is the basis for the proper exercise of authority and obedience. The authority of the wife (in this case) is moral and sacramental, and therefore put to the service of her spouse's salvation. It is a moral authority based on a bond of love as the body is bound closely to the head.

St. Chrysostom, in his homily on the *First Letter of Timothy*, denies women have authority over men when arguing why they should keep silent in the assembly. He states men are superior to women, and St. Paul wishes them to be preeminent in everything. Yet it is interesting to note that in the same homily Chrysostom teaches that women originally did have authority to teach men, but Eve abused it in leading Adam to sin and he acknowledges that Eve was Adam's equal. "For the woman taught the man once, and made him guilty of disobedience, and wrought our ruin. Therefore because she made a bad use of her power over the man, or rather her equality with him, God made her subject to her husband."[157]

Chrysostom is looking for a reason to support the ban on women speaking in the assembly, but as we have seen above, he does believe women have marital authority over their spouses and that this authority should be exercised.

St. Paulinus of Nola's teaching is very similar to Chrysostom's. He has a further insight that the wife's moral leadership is a sign of God's marriage with the Church.

> . . . your wife, who does not lead her husband to effeminacy or greed, but brings you back to self discipline and courage to become the bones of her husband, is worthy of admiration because of her great emulation of God's marriage with the Church.[158]

The phrase "to become the bones of her husband" is very significant. In *Gen.* 2:24 Adam declares that Eve "is bone of my bones and flesh of my flesh." Paulinus is using the verse to refer to what a good wife does for her husband. She in fact *builds him up* as husband in building up his moral life. The passage might also be read that the wife *is the bones* of her husband causing him to stand morally upright as a man.

Finally, it should not be overlooked that the Fathers constantly praise women for their supremacy in the practice of Christian virtue. Despite the Fathers' frequent statements degrading the nature of women, when all is said and done, female sexuality is no bar to holiness and in some cases is an aid to holiness; as St. Jerome noted, virginity is more richly bestowed on women. St. Augustine in his treatise *On Virginity* taught that Thecla and Chrispina were models of discipleship. *Matt.* 20:22, addressed to male disciples, connected discipleship with the ability to drink from the cup of Christ's Passion, yet women are seen by Augustine to have equal strength to drink from this cup as well.[159] St. Cyprian taught that women martyrs were stronger than their male torturers.[160] St. Ambrose praises a female martyr for having kept her chastity from abuse by men.[161] Eusebius records the martyrdom of Blandina who, before her own death, gives encouragement to the men who are to follow her.[162] In the writings of the Fathers, Mary Magdelene is regarded as the preeminent model of penitence for both *men and women.*[163]

III. The Meaning of Authority

The writings of the Church Fathers contain the principles upon which authority in the Catholic Church is built and upon which, more specifically, an understanding of feminine ecclesial authority can be obtained. Authority is not to be identified with mere rulership or official positions of power.

Even in the theology of the Fathers feminine authority emerges whenever authority is treated covenantally.

The source, meaning, and function of feminine ecclesial authority is discovered first from within the essence, or as one might call it, the structure of the Catholic faith itself. The feminist grievance against the Church is that only ordained males hold authority and power. While feminists may seek the dissolution of the Catholic doctrine of Eucharistic worship, it is precisely in this worship and by the lived meaning of this worship that any authority, whether male or female, exists in the Church.

The truth of Christianity is embedded in the Church's worship—a worship centered on the Lord present in history. Eucharistic worship, as the integration of the Old Covenant, the New Covenant, and the Kingdom of God, is the ground of history as it is the locus of the covenant whereby in history the world knows and has access to its salvation. Feminist theology challenges the validity of the Eucharistic symbol. If this symbol is erased, all of Christian history is erased. This the feminists desire because the male priesthood and the sacrifice of Christ militate against their "experience" of equality and liberation which they would raise up as the paradigm to judge the teachings of the Catholic faith. However, the Catholic faith rooted in the marital structure of Eucharistic worship presupposes the sexual equality and authority (thus the full humanity) of women and is a worship that could not exist without that authority.

By examining the teachings of the Fathers on women, the meaning of male and female authority begins to emerge. It is a meaning that perhaps would not become evident if we were simply to examine authority as it is exercised by the pope and bishops. The function of hierarchical authority can only be fully understood from within the Church's worship, that is, where male and female authority is exercised in the sacramental life of the Church. The authority of the Church, which is not other than its covenantal freedom, is not exhausted by bishops and priests—in other words—by those (men) who through Holy Orders stand in the place of Christ. The Church and hierarchical authority in the Church exist within the free historical order of the New Covenant. The New Covenant is the marital union between Christ and the Church. This New Covenant is the order of redemption that fulfills the order of creation. The meaning of ecclesial authority is therefore *marital*. This is because the New Covenant between Christ and the Church *is a marriage* and the ground of all marriage. Therefore, ecclesial authority is marital and functions nuptially.

Salvation history is the history of God's covenant with His people. This covenant is a restoration of the primordial order of the good creation in which the one-flesh union of the first man and woman serves as the primordially effective symbol of God's own love for the world. Because

salvation is mediated to the world by the maritally structured covenant between Christ and the Church, the current crisis of faith regarding women
and authority can only find its resolution by understanding how men and
women participate in the order of redemption.[164] Contrary to the feminist
position, human sexuality is essential to the order of redemption. The unity
of marriage is the primordial symbol by which the love of God is disclosed
in the world.

The nuptial structure of redemption wrought by Christ then determines
what authority is within the Catholic Church. Authority (for example, as
held by the pope and bishops) is fundamentally *service*. In other words,
authority, rooted in the marital structure of the New Covenant, is *responsibility for the faith*. We are concerned about understanding this responsibility. If the model of redemption is marital, then male and female sexuality
according to the very order of creation are the *symbols* of the covenant.
The covenant is dependent on these symbols and would have no concrete
expression without them. Therefore, one can say that male and female sexuality are imbued from the very beginning with salvific meaning: they are
sacramental signs. Since the New Covenant exists in the world according to
a marital structure, *responsibility for the faith* (authority) is differentiated
according to the sexual symbols of this covenant. The responsibility of
men in ecclesial office exists over and against the feminine Church whose
femininity is expressed in the concrete lives of Christian women. To the
extent that this differentiated responsibility becomes blurred, Christianity
itself, as rooted in the meaning of sexuality, ceases to be effectively expressed in the world. To undo the meaning of sexual symbols is to undo
the Christian faith.

Authority is not sheer power that could be used for either good or evil.
Authority as it resides in the Trinity and in the person of Christ is that which
is an effective cause of life and redemption. According to the meaning of
the marital covenant, men and women in their covenantal equality are not in
the same identical fashion effective causes of life and redemption. Redemption is rendered present and effective in the free, i.e., morally responsible,
relation between these symbols. Authority is covenantal, meaning that
male responsibility for the faith is effective in relation to and in complete
dependence upon feminine responsibility for the faith. The relation of male
and female responsibility is *causative* of salvation. Authority is exercised
according to a *one flesh union* (the head and the body) in which the *symbols*
effecting this union are not dissolved or confused, but fulfilled.

The teaching of the Fathers on women illustrate the covenantal authority
of the Church—authority that is power to effect salvation as mediated
according to the meaning of male and female sexuality. The "yes" of
Mary is causative of the Incarnate Christ, the motherhood of the Church is

causative of Christ's children, the position of a wife in Christian marriage builds up the salvation of her husband, etc., etc.

Catholic consciousness has always been centered on the authority of the Apostles and derivatively on the authority of bishops and priests. But with respect to feminist theology, the present crisis over the place of women in the Church is the fruit of a false perception regarding the essence of hierarchical authority and in general of how authority functions in the Catholic community. Ecclesial authority is covenantal—bound up with the very order of redemption itself. Authority as responsibility for the faith has its preeminent source, derives its ultimate meaning and has its ultimate expression within Catholic worship, namely, the celebration of the Eucharist. Here the one flesh union of Christ and the Church is celebrated, and the New Covenant made present in the world.

2

The Authority of Christ

I. Christ—Head of the Church

THE MALE PRIEST AND THE COVENANTAL ORDER OF AUTHORITY

Men and women, according to the inherent truth, goodness, and dignity of their sexuality, are symbols taken up into the order of redemption in which the unity between Christ and His Church is sacramentally effected and revealed.

Because the order of redemption is marital, women possess, according to the meaning of their own sexuality, an authority in relation to the ministerial priesthood that is integral to the world's salvation in Christ. The authority of women exists in relation to, as complement of, and over/against the masculine authority of clerical office, i.e., of the Catholic priesthood. Feminine authority is equal to but qualitatively differentiated from the ministerial priesthood.

As a result, authority within Catholicism is not quantitative power exercised as force to accomplish certain ends. Authority is not simply the exercise of leadership wherein the leader, due to some preeminence of personal talent and personality, directs the course of a person or group of persons subordinate to him. The authority by which redemption is effected in the Catholic Church is the love of God in Christ appropriated liturgically by men and women in their imaging of God as *source* and *cause* of life. In short, authority in the Church is the power to effect supernatural life; more specifically, the power to appropriate and make effective the covenantal redemption of Christ in the world.

Feminine authority exists as women exemplify the Church as mother. The authority of woman as *Mater Ecclesia* is so prerational, so close to us, and perhaps most importantly by its own nature, unenshrined by sacramental office, that it easily goes unnoticed and is misunderstood. Ecclesial authority is not synonymous with, nor solely identified with, male clerical office, though this office of the priesthood is utterly indispensable to the life of the Church.

The authority of the Church exists according to the order of redemption which, as covenantal, is marital. The meaning of such authority is expressed by St. Paul when he states: "In the Lord, woman is not independent of man nor man independent of woman. In the same way that woman was made from man, so man is born of woman; and all is of God" (1 Cor. 11:11–12). The meaning of the Catholic priesthood exists within the marital order of redemption as the priest is *arché* (source) of Christ's salvific presence and grace to the Church. The meaning of this *arché* (as differentiated from the the woman as source) is inherently masculine. The male person is its appropriate sign if the covenant is to be effected and real in the world. If we are to understand feminine authority, it is necessary to understand how salvation is maritally ordered and what is the place of the priesthood within this marital order.

The marital order of redemption is the "one flesh" of Christ the *Head* and His *Body* the Church. The marital order of the New Covenant is effected in history as the presence of the risen Christ and the risen bride in the *one flesh* of the Eucharist. If the New Covenant is marital, the worship of this covenant is constituted by masculine and feminine symbols and not apart from these symbols. The meaning of male and female sexuality is the fundamental expression in the Church's worship of what it means for Christ to be united with His people and what it means for this people to be in relation to the source of their redemption. Here in the Eucharist, Christ the head and the Church, His body, are one.

The authority of Christ as head means that He is the *arché* of the New People of God. Christ is the cause of the Church. The Church having received her being in turn makes it possible for Christ's redemption to be accomplished in the world. The authority of Christ as head continues sacramentally in the bishops and in priests for the purpose of effecting true worship through the Church, in a "one flesh" or nuptial and free unity with the Church. True worship is the ground of the covenant existing in and made present and available to the world in the Eucharistic sacrifice. The Catholic priesthood is the sacramental *arché in persona Christi* of this sacrifice.

The 1976 Vatican document entitled *Declaration on the Admission of Women to the Ministerial Priesthood* (*Inter Insigniores*) teaches that the masculinity of Christ "cannot be disassociated from the economy of salvation."[1] The document goes on to state that the masculinity of the Redeemer is according to the "mystery of the Covenant" which is maritally ordered.

> For the salvation offered by God to men and women, the union with him to which they are called—in short, the Covenant—took on, from the Old Testament prophets onwards the privileged form of a nuptial mystery: for God the Chosen People is seen as his ardently loved spouse. . . . . When the "fullness of time" (Gal. 4:4) comes, the Word, the Son of God, takes on flesh in order to establish and seal the new and eternal Covenant in his blood, which will be shed for many so that sins may be forgiven. His death will gather together again the scattered children of God; from his pierced side will be born the Church, as Eve was born from Adam's side. At that time there is fully and eternally accomplished the nuptial mystery proclaimed and hymned in the Old Testament: Christ is the Bridegroom; the Church is his Bride, whom he loves because he has gained her by his blood and made her glorious, holy and without blemish, and henceforth he is inseparable from her.[2]

The above passage states several principles of ecclesial authority. First, Christ is *arché* of the New Covenant as He is the one who unifies what is scattered and is the source of the Church's being (from his pierced side will be born the Church). Second, *Inter Insigniores* teaches that the ordained priest does not exemplify, personify, or symbolically represent the Church as the Body of Christ. The priest represents sacramentally the headship of Christ to the Church. The document states that the priest represents the Church only because he first stands in the place "of Christ himself, who is the Head and Shepherd of the Church."[3] It is important for us to keep clearly in mind, in order to safeguard the meaning of feminine authority, that the priesthood does not take the place of the Church as Body of Christ in the Eucharistic worship. The priest takes the place of Christ and represents the Church only within the one flesh union that the headship of Christ constitutes. *Inter Insigniores* teaches that for the priest to stand *in persona Christi* he must stand in the place of Christ as Head and Shepherd: "It is in this quality that the priest presides over the Christian assembly and celebrates the Eucharistic sacrifice 'in which the whole Church offers and is herself wholly offered.'"[4]

The authority of the priest consists in his sacramental representation of Christ as Head and Shepherd to the Church. It is therefore essential for an understanding of masculine authority to uncover what it means for Christ to be Head and Shepherd of the Church.

THE MEANING OF CHRIST'S HEADSHIP IN THE PAULINE EPISTLES

The Pauline tradition teaches, particularly in the epistles to the Colossians and Ephesians, that Jesus Christ's relation to and unity with the Church is that of head to body. These letters reveal the meaning of Christ's authority to the Church. Christ's authority is constituted by the sacrifice of His life upon the Cross which brings into being the New Creation, His body, the Church. Christ in His sacrifice is the font of life establishing the New Covenant in which the covenant partner in redemption, the Church, is intimately united with Him according to the unity of "one flesh" but which remains always differentiated from Christ and is the complement to Him in His salvific work.

The Letter to the Ephesians 1:22[5] states: "He has put all things under Christ's feet and has made him, thus exalted, head of the Church, which is his body: the fullness of him who fills the universe in all its parts."

Perhaps nowhere else in the New Testament is the relation of Christ the head to His body the Church given a more clear, full, and sophisticated exposition than in the Letter to the Ephesians. Here this Pauline theme comes to full expression as the head/body relation becomes the means by which the mystery of God's plan for redemption is accomplished. In Ephesians the nature of the Church is understood only in connection with Christ as He is her head and Savior. At the same time, however, the person of Christ cannot be comprehended except in relation to His body. In all of Pauline thought, the head/body relation exists according to a marital order. This marital order of salvation is the foundation upon which ecclesial authority rests.

St. Paul's Letter to the Ephesians describes the meaning of redemption in terms of bringing all things under Christ's headship.[6]

> It is in Christ and through his blood that we have been redeemed and our sins forgiven, so immeasurably generous is God's favor to us. God has given us the wisdom to understand fully the mystery, the plan he was pleased to decree in Christ, to be carried out in the fullness of time: namely, to bring all things in the heavens and on the earth into one under Christ's headship. (Eph. 1:7–10)

The mystery (μυστήριον) of God is indissociable from the plan (θελή-ματος) of salvation, this plan of salvation that is accomplished by what it means for all things (πάντα) to be under Christ's headship (ἀνακεφαλ-αιώσασθαι).

The mystery of salvation mentioned in Eph. 1:10 concerning Christ's headship receives a more full and precise definition in vs. 19b–23.

> It is like the strength he showed in raising Christ from the dead and seating him at his right hand in heaven, high above every principality, power, virtue, and domination, and every name that can be given in this age or in the age to come.

He has put all things under Christ's feet and has made him, thus exalted, head of the church, which is his body: the fullness of him who fills the universe in all its parts (τὸ πλήρωμα τοῦ τὰ πάντα ἐν πᾶσιν πληρουμένου).

Because Eph. 1:19b–23 is a fuller exposition of the mystery first mentioned in 1:9–10 we see that the relation of Christ (head) to His body (the Church) is constitutive of this mystery whose meaning progressively unfolds in the letter. The relation of Christ and the Church in 1:23 emerges later in the letter's climax as a marital unity of "all things . . . . under Christ's headship."[7]

The meaning of Christ's authority in relation to the Church is set out in Eph. 1:19b–23. Christ's authority over the Church is significantly different in kind from the type of dominion He possesses over "principalities, powers, virtue, and domination" (ἀρχῆς, ἐξουσίας, δυνάμεως, κυριότητος). Christ subjects all rule and authority to His rule. He sits *over—high above* all rule and authority and power and domination, and "above every name that is named" (1:21). The Father has put all things under Christ's feet (1:22). We have the idea here that the powers are subjected—put down by force. Christ's relation to the Church is significantly different. His relation to the Church is not domination. He is not depicted as spatially above her as He is over the powers. The language of being "above" or "over" depicts a separation between Christ and that which He is over. Instead the Church is one with Christ—she "is his body" (1:23a).[8]

> . . . . we must ask what we mean by the headship of Christ to the Church. Some commentators take it to imply 'sovereignty': Christ rules over the Church; he is Head in the sense of 'overlord'. But if this is the full meaning of 'Head' in this connection, then v.22b adds nothing to v.22a, 'he put all things in subjection under his feet.' The relationship of Christ to the Church is, consequently, the same as his relationship to the remainder of creation. To interpret 'Head' we must go forward in the verse and not backward; it must be explained in relation to 'Body.' A 'head' may certainly be said to rule its 'body'; the conception of 'sovereignty' alone, however, seems to imply that the ruling power is separated from what it rules; head and body are not separate but form a unity. Thus Christ and the Church are organically related and are a unity.[9]

Second, the words κεφαλὴν ὑπὲρ in the passage κεφαλὴν ὑπὲρ πάντα τῇ εκκλησία "made him the head over all things to the church" (1:22), also reveal the meaning of Christ's authority as head. Christ's headship is over all things *to* the Church. Sometimes τῇ is translated not *to* the Church but *for* the Church. Christ is head over all things, but there appears to be a differentiation between *all things* and *the Church*. Christ's headship to the

Church is much different than the headship He exercises over all things. Why did not the author of Ephesians simply say Christ is head over all things *including* the Church instead of *to* or *for* the Church?

Verse 1:22 calls Christ "exalted" precisely because He has bound all the powers. This verse gives the distinct impression that Christ is not simply head of the Church—He is her head in His glory and triumph— as if to say Christ can only be her head because He has subjected all other powers *for* her. The Church as Christ's bride has an exalted head, and she is in a privileged position in relation to Him. Concerning the use of the word *head* (κεφαλή) in Ephesians, Stephen F. Miletic explains that the term expresses a basic idea about Christ—namely, His absolute lordship. Verse 1: 22–23 links Christ not only to the Church but also to the cosmological powers. He is "head over all things for the Church" (v. 22). The term κεφαλή connects Christ to both the Church and the cosmos without making any distinctions between the two relations. This suggests that there are at least two meanings for the term.[10]

Christ is not merely "head" as an overlord. Colossians and Ephesians teach that Christ is head as *source*. "Christ relates to the Church as its 'source' of life (4:15–16) as well as its groom (5:31–32). He does not relate to cosmological forces in this fashion."[11] S. Bedale has shown that headship functions according to two meanings in St. Paul: "Head (κεφαλή) does not only mean 'overlord' but according to its use in the Old Testament the word also means 'first' or 'beginning' (ἀρχή)."[12]

> It seems a fair inference that St. Paul, when using κεφαλή in any but its literal sense, would have in mind the enlarged and metaphorical uses of the term "head' familiar to him from the Old Testament: and these, as we have seen, include the meaning of the "beginning" of something. Consequently, in St. Paul's usage, κεφαλή is very approximate in meaning to ἀρχή [beginning].
>
> If this virtual equation of κεφαλή with ἀρχή be conceded a new and illuminating interpretation of several Pauline passages becomes possible.
>
> In Col. 1:18 κεφαλή in the sense of "ruler" of the Church would be an irrelevant intrusion into the context, which is otherwise wholly concerned with Christ as ἀρχή, the "beginning" and "principle" alike in Creation and Redemption.[13]

Furthermore, the use of the verb ἔδωκεν (gave) in the Ephesians verse "and him gave to be head over all things to the church" (καὶ αὐτὸν ἔδωκενκεφαλὴν ὑπὲρ παντα τῇ ἐκκλησια) expresses the gift character of Christ's authority. Miletic points out that in the Greek version of the Scriptures the verb δίδωμι expresses, especially in Genesis, the covenantal action of God.[14] The verb "emphasizes the donative character of Christ's headship for the church."[15] The gift character of Christ's headship carries great significance for the meaning of authority. If the gift character of Christ's authority is to be taken seriously, then this authority must be *received* freely by the Church. This giving and its reception is consonant with the marital order of the Christ/Church relation expounded fully in Ephesians 5.

Headship, denoting the authoritative position of Christ to the Church, as "source" represents an innovation upon the meaning of authority. The head/body imagery was commonplace in antiquity as an expression of an authoritarian social and political solidarity. In antiquity authority means domination. Authority as "source" of life is a notion foreign to classical, postclassical, or Hellenistic Jewish thought.[16]

Headship and *source* are explicitly identified in Eph. 2:20–22 and 4:15–16 as well as Col. 2:19. Eph. 2:20–22, referring to the Jews and Gentiles who make up the Church, states:

> You form a building which rises on the foundation of the apostles and prophets, with Jesus Christ himself as the capstone. Through him the whole structure is fitted together and takes shape (grows—αυξει) as a holy temple in the Lord; in him you are being built into this temple, to become a dwelling place for God in the Spirit.

The building is not its own cause. First of all it "rises on the foundation of apostles and prophets." Jesus alone is the central stone of the structure (cornerstone—ἀκρογωνιαίου). He is the source of the structure's unity and order. It is *through Him* (ἐν ᾧ) that the whole structure is fitted together. It is *in the Lord* (ἐν Κυρίῳ) that the building grows into a holy temple. The builder of the edifice described in Eph. 2 is God (in Christ).[17] In Ephesians the building is also the body made of Jew and Gentile referred to earlier in 2:16 and later in the letter the body is explicitly in a marital relation to Christ. The reference to Gen. 2:24 in Eph. 5:31 teaches that the primordial *one flesh* union of Adam and Eve foreshadows the marital union of the New Adam and the New Eve. The Church has her source in Christ the head. In 2:20–22 a form of the infinitive "to build" is used twice in relation to the Church, the holy temple. She "having been built" (συναρμολογουμένη) and "are being built together" (συνοικοδομεῖσθε) reminds us of Gen. 2:22 in which God, after casting Adam into a deep sleep, "built up into a woman the rib that he had taken from the man" (Καὶ ᾠκοδόμησεν ὁ Θεὸς τὴν πλευρὰν ἣν ἔλαβεν ἀπὸ τοῦ' Αδαμεὶς γυναῖκα καὶ ἤγαγεν αὐτὴν πρὸς τὸν Αδάμ). The Greek word in the Septuagint version of Genesis, οἰκοδομεῖν ("to build"), has the same root used by Saint Paul in Eph. 2:20–22 when he speaks of the Church which, we have already noted, is the New Eve to the New Adam.

Christ is *head* because He is the source of the structure's being. The holy temple rests upon Him and is fitted together "in him." Furthermore, Christ is not separate from the structure. J. Armitage Robinson points out: "He is part of the Body which He brings into being, for He is its Head: He is part of the house which He founds, for He is its Cornerstone."[18]

Joseph Huby states that the Greek term "cornerstone" or "keystone" can mean that Christ is the fundamental stone of the building that unites two walls "comme le Christ unit les deux groupes, paien et juif."[19] This interpretation is consistent with Eph. 2:14–16 which speaks of Christ reconciling the pagans and the Jews, "creating one new man out of the two" and reconciling "both of them" in "one body." Huby, however, prefers the interpretation of J. Jeremias who argues that Christ is the cornerstone in the sense of being the stone that crowns the structure.[20] According to Jeremias "cornerstone" does not indicate a stone at the structure's foundation "but the stone used to top an arch" in the sense of a "keystone." The word *akrogōniaios* (ἀκρογωνιαῖος) etymologically means "the one on the high corner."[21] Marcus Barth, in support of Jeremias's exegesis, notes that early Fathers of the Church called Christ the "the cornerstone at the head which supports all."[22]

> Further alternatives would identify the "stone" in question not just with one specific stone but with an outstanding high corner or pinnacle of the temple, or with the rock and altar in the Jerusalem temple which was considered the groundstone or navel of the earth. Consequently Eph. 2:20 would describe Christ either as a most conspicuous and impressive feature of the temple, or at the ground and turning point of the new creation. . . .
>
> But among the competing interpretations of the chief stone mentioned in Ephesians 2:20, J. Jeremias' suggestion has the strongest support from the rest of Ephesians. In this letter Christ is called the "head of the body" (1:22 etc.). The body "grows to the head" (4:15). . . . The growth "from the head" mentioned in 4:16 hardly means a growth higher and higher up and away from Christ, the foundation stone![23]

Whether cornerstone means a rock forming the chief part of the foundation or the centerstone of the structure, the important theological point to be made from Eph. 2:20–22 is that Christ as the cornerstone is the source of the Church's being and unity.[24]

In 2:20–21 Christ the ἀκρογωνιαίου is the source from which the Church is "fitted together" and "grows." Eph. 4:15–16 also teaches that the head is the source of the body's growth and unity.

> . . . . let us profess the truth in love and grow to the full maturity of Christ the head. Through him the whole body grows, and with the proper functioning of

the members joined firmly together by each supporting ligament, builds itself up in love.

A parallel passage in St. Paul's Letter to the Colossians 2:19 states:

. . . . he should be in close touch with the head. The whole body, mutually supported and upheld by joints and sinews, *achieves a growth from this source* which comes from God.

These passages show clearly that Christ is not the head only because of a preeminence in rank over the Church but because as head He is the Church's vivifying principle.[25] Bedale points out:

In Col. 2:19 and Eph. 4:15, where the body is said to derive its growth and development from the 'head' . . . . it is very difficult to make any sense at all so long as κεφαλή is regarded as 'over-lord'. But when it is realized that Christ is in relation to the Church, it is possible to see how Christians can be said to 'grow up into him' . . . . as the archetypal image of the Second Adam is progressively realized in them.[26]

Finally, Christ is the head of the Church specifically and most importantly through His sacrifice. Eph. 3:13–16 presents one of the most explicit teachings regarding the sacrifice of Christ as the cause of the Church.

But now in Christ Jesus you who were once far off have been brought near through the blood of Christ. It is he who is our peace, and who made the two of us one by breaking down the barrier of hostility that kept us apart. In his own flesh he abolished the law with its commands and precepts, to create in himself one new man from us who had been two and to make peace, reconciling both of us to God in one body through his cross, which put that enmity to death.

Eph. 1:22–23 declared that Christ is the head of the Church which is His body. Now we are told that this body, the Church, is composed of reconciled Jews and Gentiles. Christ (who is the head of this body) is the cause of the New Creation, the one new man (ἕνα καινὸν ἄνθρωπον) specifically through His death on the Cross. Christ's sacrifice is the cause, source, origin of the body that is understood in Eph. 5 as the bride of Christ. Headship is linked with sacrifice, a sacrifice causative of the New Creation.

The Gentiles have been "brought near" to the covenant "through the blood of Christ." The barrier or wall identified in Eph.2:15 as the law that kept Jew and Gentile in hostile alienation has been abolished through Christ's own flesh. Verse 16 states that the body (of Jew and Gentile) is effected "through his cross." The sacrificial headship of Christ as cause of the Church is taught in Eph. 5:23–27. In v. 23 Christ is head in terms of His being the savior of the body (Χριστὸς κεφαλὴ. . . .σωτήρ τοῦ σώματος). And of course this Christ/Church, head/body relation in Ephesians 5 exists according to the "one flesh" of the primordial couple. Christ is head of the body through His sacrifice on the Cross. The Old Testament people realized that covenants were ratified by blood. In this light the death of Christ is seen to be a necessary part of His work. He Himself describes His death on the night before He died as a blood sacrifice that would effect the New Covenant. The blood of Christ is the fulfillment of all the Old Covenant blood-shedding bringing forth the New Covenant whereby Jew and Gentile have access to the one true God.[27]

THE EVIDENCE FROM ROMANS AND 1 CORINTHIANS

The authority of Christ as head of the Church is authority because Christ is a source of life. This is the essence of His authority and thus of all authority. He can be head, and be respected as head not because Christ dominates the Church, not because His lordship is in any way quantified power, but because the Church is given life by Him. This sense of Christ's authority—authority as *source*—defines and is the principle of the kind of authority exercised by priests in His name. Appreciation of authority on this level reshapes how priestly authority is understood in relation to the Church.

The meaning of Christ's authority as head is revealed in Rom. 12:5 and I Cor. 12:12, 27. These passages explain how even though the Church is comprised of many members, this diversity is not opposed to ecclesial unity, and how the headship of Christ relates to this unity and is the cause of this unity. Rom. 12:5 states:

> Just as each of us has one body with many members, not all the members have the same function, so we too, though many, are one body in Christ and individually members of one another.

The phrase ἐν Χριστῷ (in Christ) indicates the source of the body's unity. Ernst Käsemann argues that the phrase "one body in Christ" means "We, who are many, are one body, in so far as we are in Christ."[28] St. Paul, even prior to Ephesians, treats the relation between Christ and the Church as one of distinction and unity with Christ as the source of that unity. In 1 Cor. 12:12 the same theological issue is treated: "The body is one and has many members, but all the members, many though they are, are one body; and so it is with Christ."

After explaining in vs. 14–26 the necessity of all the members of the body, St. Paul concludes in v. 27: "You, then, are the body of Christ. Every one of you is a member if it."

The first thing to be gained from these Pauline passages on the body in reference to the Church is that unity is not at all a matter of dissolving differences. Unity is not monistic.[29] Nowhere in 1 Cor. 12:12–27 is Christ mentioned as a member of the body. Rather, individual Christians, formed into one body by the power of baptism (v. 13), are "the body of Christ" (v. 27). The entire sense of the passage gives rise to the interpretation that the one body formed by diverse members is in relation to Christ. The Church is the body of Christ in the sense that she belongs to Him, is dependent upon Him, and derives her life from Him. Joseph Huby points out that for St. Paul Christ is always the personal Christ.[30] The phrase "and so it is with Christ" (v. 12) is not to be taken as the Church existing in the manner of being Christ, but according to His activity as the principle source of the body's unity.[31] After explaining the unity of the members of the body (vs. 15–25), St. Paul finally declares the essential reality of the Church: "You then are the body of Christ" (v. 27), which is to say a body, dependent on Him, a body that He has organized and to which He communicates His own life.[32] We can see, therefore, that even in the earlier Pauline epistles, Christ's relation to the Church is *source* to the body, a relation that is consistent with the later Pauline theology of Christ the Head presented in Ephesians and Colossians.

WOMAN—THE BODY OF HER HUSBAND

The Church as the body of Christ can be traced back to Hebrew theology of the husband/wife relation taught in the book of Genesis.[33] The key to Pauline thought on the Church as the "body of Christ" is the Adam/Eve marital unity. Some scholars[34] interpret the expression σῶμα Χριστοῦ in an explicative sense: the Church is actually Christ himself. The term, however, can be understood in the possessive genitive. In this sense Christ is the author or origin of the Church. The Church is His body because it is issued from His side, it resembles him, or because the organism that makes it up belongs to the Lord.[35] St. Paul, who was certainly well versed in the rabbinical school, was familiar with the Hebrew understanding that a man knew himself in two bodies, his own and his wife's.[36] The Christ/Church relation is founded upon the Adam/Eve marital unity.

Adam's spouse is called a helpmate, a person like him, literally his "face-to-face" (*kenegdo*: Gen. 2:18, 20). She is given the name *isshah* because she is taken from a man, *ish* (Gen. 2:23). For Adam, she is like the reflection of himself in whom he recognizes himself. Hence his exclamation: "This at last is bone from my bones, and flesh from my flesh," body from my body.... Eve is shown to be Adam's body (since she issued from it) in order that she might form with him the highest conceivable unity; she is as close to man as his own body. For this reason man will cling to his wife . . . and they will become one flesh (2:24) or as Paul will say, one body (1 Cor. 6:16).[37]

Gen. 2:24 serves as the basis of unity in Christ as expressed in Eph. 5. St. Paul teaches in 1 Cor. 6:15–17 that even the union of the Christian disciple to Christ is according to the marital order of the first couple.

Do you not see that your bodies are members of Christ? Would you have me take Christ's members and make them the members of a prostitute? God forbid! Can you not see that the man who joins himself to a prostitute becomes one body with her? Scripture says, "The two shall become one flesh." But whoever is joined to the Lord becomes one spirit with him.

The terms "being joined" (κολλώμενος) to a harlot denotes physical conjugal union and is precisely the same word used by Paul to describe the Christian's union with Christ (κολλώμενος). Gen. 2:24 quoted in 1 Cor. 6:16 illustrates that the meaning of being *joined* is to take *two* and make them *one*. The Christian is in relation to Christ nuptially as body to head.

Later in the very same epistle St. Paul will speak of the members' union with Christ (12:12, 27). Pierre Benoit points out that the theme of the body of Christ in 1 Cor. 12:12ff was already present in the Apostle's mind when he stated earlier, "Do you not see that your bodies are members of Christ?" and this according to a conjugal unity.[38] Because St. Paul uses this expression in a conjugal sense, the body of Christ must also be understood in this way. In St. Paul's theology of the body he teaches "Now you are the body of Christ, and individually members of it" (12:27). This theology of the body of Christ reaches its nuptial climax in Eph. 5:30. The parallel, Paulus Andriessen notes, is "clear enough to remove any doubt."[39]

The Hebrew religious thought of Genesis regarding the marital unity of Adam and Eve provides a sound explanation for the fact that in the Christian dispensation the Church is both body and bride of Christ.[40] Whether we are looking at earlier or later Pauline epistles, it is clear that Christ stands over

against the Church as her source and that the meaning of Christ's headship
is according to the marital order of the New Adam to the New Eve as the
wife is "body" of her husband.

II. Christ—The New Adam

In Ephesians Christ is "head" because He is the source of the body through
His sacrifice, and the relation between head and body exists according to
a marital "one flesh" unity (Eph. 5:21). In Rom. 5:12–21 Christ is "head"
or source of the New Creation because He is the New Adam.[41]

> Therefore, just as through one man sin entered the world and with sin death,
> death thus coming to all men inasmuch as all sinned—before the law there was
> sin in the world, even though sin is not imputed when there is no law—I say,
> from Adam to Moses death reigned, even over those who had not sinned by
> breaking a precept as did Adam, that type of the man to come.
> But the gift is not like the offense. For if by the offense of one man all died,
> much more did the grace of God and the gracious gift of the one man, Jesus
> Christ, abound for all. . . .
> To sum up, then: just as a single offense brought condemnation to all men,
> a single righteous act brought all men aquittal and life. Just as through one
> man's disobedience all became sinners, so through one man's obedience all
> shall become just.

Adam and Christ are the origins of two races of men. The first Adam is
the source of the mankind of sin and death; the Second Adam is the source
of the mankind of the righteousness and life. Robin Scroggs explains that
both Adam and Christ are a *Stammvater*, "the original ancestor, of his
particular humanity":

> For Paul the church is now the chosen people of God (Rom. 9:25) and may
> once even be labeled the "Israel of God' [Gal. 6:16]. Of this chosen people it
> is Christ who is the first born of many brethren and the first fruits. Thus Paul
> may imply that Christ is the first patriarch of the new creation in his status as
> exalted, resurrected man. The antitheses in Rom. 5:15–21 suggest a contrast
> between the two heads. Adam mediates death to his brethren, while Christ,
> life. The one acted in disobedience; the other, in obedience. Stemming from
> these two acts are two radically different results affecting the offspring of the
> two founders. . . .
> . . . . a reasonably close parallelism exists between Jewish logia about Adam
> as first patriarch and the statements about Christ by Paul. Just as Adam, for

Judaism, exhibited in his original existence God's intent for Israel, so Christ is the reality of God's design for man and is the first patriarch of the new creation.[42]

Rom. 5:14 states that Adam was "the 'type' (τύπος) of the man to come." We have seen that Adam is a type of Christ in that like Christ he is the beginning of a people.[43] Furthermore, Adam is the image of the humanity God intended in creation, a humanity that is restored in the image of Christ in the New Creation.[44] Adam has an eschatological significance. The true meaning of the first Adam is definitively revealed in the Second.[45] A correlation exists between creation and redemption. Regarding the meaning of Rom. 5:14 Karl Barth states that both Adam and Christ are alike as both are one source for "the many." But if the correlation between creation and redemption is a true one, Adam is not simply a type of Christ because his action (in his case sin) determined the destiny of all men. Adam is the cause of sin for all because he stands at the beginning, as the primordial source of man. Christ is head because He definitively and gloriously fulfills the role and place of Adam as the New Beginning: the source of the "one new man" (Eph. 2:15) which is the Church.[46]

"One man because of his offense brought death," the one man's "single righteous act brought all men acquittal and life" (v. 18). Adam's single offense, an act of disobedience, is juxtaposed to Christ's single righteous act of obedience (vs. 18–19). This righteous act of obedience is Christ's sacrifice on the Cross. Thus the headship of the New Adam as cause of life for all men is indissociable from the laying down of His life (Rom. 5:6–7). Rom. 5:1–11 speaks several times of the death of Christ in relation to rendering men righteous before God (v. 6, 7, 8, 9, 10). Verse 9 states: "We have been justified by his blood." The word δικαιωθέντες "having been justified" in relation to Christ's blood has the same root as δίκαιοι "justified" used in v. 19 regarding the effect of Christ's obedience. Condemnation was brought by a single offense of Adam, an act of disobedience. Christ's "single righteous act" is parallel to this, and since St. Paul already spoke of Christ's Passion as the cause of righteousness in the section just previous to vs. 12–21, certainly we are right to conclude that the Second Adam's obedience referred to in v. 19 is the sacrifice of Christ's life on the Cross.[47] Many scholars believe that Philippians 2:5–11 is a contrast between Adam and Christ in which Christ's obedience is linked to His death "on a cross" (v.8).[48]

Christ's headship exists in that he is the New Adam who has given up His life for the New Eve which in turn is "the body of Christ." The marital meaning of Christ's authority is brought out even more strongly by the fact that Eph. 1:19–23, which is parallel to 5:22–32, has for its background 1 Cor. 15:21–28. Here Christ is the New Adam who by His resurrection is the source of life (v. 22). As the Last Adam all things have been made subject to Him. The status and position of the Last Adam in 1 Cor. 15:21–28 is described exactly in terms of the headship of Christ over "every principality, power, virtue, and domination" which is stated in Eph. 1:19–23 in which this headship exists "for the Church." Stephen F. Miletic has provided a detailed exegesis of both passages to show the striking similarity between them and concludes:

> Clearly the structure and content of 1 Cor. 15:20–28 has been adopted and adapted at Eph. 1:19–23. This alone suggests that the image of Christ as the New Adam may be lurking in the shadows of Eph. 1:19–23. When we recall that the term is associated with Genesis twice in the Pauline corpus prior to Ephesians (i.e. 1 Cor. 11:2–16 and Col. 1: 15–20) and that at Eph. 1:19–23 the author clearly develops the structure and content of a text which contains a clear example of Christ/Adam typology (i.e. 1 Cor. 15:20–28), the possibility that Eph. 1:19–23 expresses Pauline theological reflections about the New Adam is greatly enhanced.[49]

Christ's headship as *source* is also explicitly taught by St. Paul in Col. 1: 15–20.

> He is the image of the invisible God, the first-born of all creatures. In him everything in heaven and on earth was created, things visible and invisible, whether thrones or dominations, principalities or powers; all were created through him and for him. He is before all else that is. In him everything continues in being. It is he who is head of the body, the church; he who is the beginning, the first-born of the dead, so that primacy may be his in everything. It pleased God to make absolute fullness reside in him and, by means of him, to reconcile everything in his person, both on earth and in the heavens, making peace through the blood of his cross.

Christ is the *source* and the *beginning* of all that exists and "In him everything continues in being." V. 18 links together Christ's headship to the Church with His being "the beginning, the first born of the dead." This is quite similar to 1 Cor. 15:22–23 which states that the resurrection of the New Adam is the "first fruits" of the New Creation. It is important to notice in Col. 1:20 that Christ's headship is effected through his sacrifice "making peace through the blood of his cross." Once again we have a Pauline passage in which Christ as source and beginning and His Passion are constitutive of His headship and thus constitutive of his authority. The Church is brought forth from this headship and exists in union with it.

III. The Meaning of Headship in 1 Cor. 11

THE AUTHORITY OF CHRIST AND MALES IN 1 COR. 11

1 Cor. 11:3–16 provides one of the clearest theological statements on the relationship between the headship of Christ and the masculine sex as the primordial symbol of this headship. The passage is frequently interpreted to mean that women are subordinate and inferior to men. Feminist theologians regard the passage as an example of Pauline misogynism.[50] The passage, however, concerns the marital and covenantal order of the man/woman relation and grounds this relation in (at least implicitly) the trinitarian ordering of the Father and the Son.[51] 1 Cor. 11:3–16 reads as follows:

> I want you to know that the head of every man is Christ; the head of a woman is her husband; and the head of Christ is the Father. Any man who prays or prophesies with his head covered brings shame upon his head. Similarly, any woman who prays or prophesies with her head uncovered brings shame upon her head. It is as if she had had her head shaved. Indeed, if a woman will not wear a veil, she ought to cut off her hair. If it is shameful for a woman to have her hair cut off or her head shaved, it is clear that she ought to wear a veil. A man, on the other hand, ought not to cover his head, because he is the image of God and the reflection of his glory. Woman, in turn, is the reflection of man's glory. Man was not made from woman but woman from man. Neither was man created for woman but woman for man. For this reason a woman ought to have a sign of authority on her head, because of the angels. Yet, in the Lord, woman is not independent of man nor man independent of woman. In the same way that woman was made from man, so man is born of woman; and all is from God. I will let you judge for yourselves. Is it proper for a woman to pray to God unveiled? Does not nature itself teach you that it is dishonorable for a man to wear his hair long, while the long hair of a woman is her glory? Her hair has been given her for a covering. If anyone wants to argue about this, remember that neither we nor the churches of God recognize any other usage.

We seek to discover the meaning of "headship" in the Pauline passage. First we must look to v. 3 where it states that Christ is the head of all males. The word ἀνδρὸς means "male" and not "mankind" which would of course include both men and women. St. Paul knew very well that Christ is the Lord of both men and women, but here the headship of Christ is only in relation to the masculine sex. This leads one to speculate that *head* (κεφαλή) in v. 3 has a meaning apart from Christ's lordship or at least is not strictly associated with it alone.[52] Verse 7 explains the relationship between males and God. Men are "the image of God and the reflection of his glory." Verses 8–9 go on to explain the headship of men to women (husbands to wives) which was also articulated in v. 3: "Man was not made from woman but woman from man. Neither was man created for woman but woman for man."

Scripture scholar C. K. Barrett explains in his commentary on 1 Cor. 11: 3–16 that *head* (κεφαλή) equals *origin* according to the Greek usage of the word. He argues that the sense of the word is strongly suggested in v. 8. Here St. Paul says that the man is the origin of woman's being. He does not say that man is her lord (κύριος). When St. Paul says that man is woman's origin, he is directly dependent on Gen. 2:18–23 where it teaches that woman is created by the removal of Adam's rib.[53]

According to the second Genesis account of the primordial creation, the man is the source of the woman. Furthermore, the man is in the image of God (v. 7) as well as his glory while the woman is the reflection of man's glory. How is it that the man is in the image of God but not the woman when St. Paul knew very well that Gen. 1:27 taught that both the male and the female are made in the image of God? 1 Cor. 11:3–16 teaches that there is a specific imaging between Christ and men. In other words, Christ is the head of males and husbands the heads of their wives because headship is something shared by Christ and men. They are both *origins* as also the Father is the head or source of the Son (v. 3). Barrett explains:

> *Man is the head of woman* in the sense that he is the origin, and thus the explanation of her being. That *God is the head of Christ* can be understood in a similar way. The Father is *fons divinitatis*; the Son is what he is in relation to the Father . . . . as the existence of Christ is given in the existence of God, and as the existence of woman is given in the existence of man, so the existence of man is given in the existence of Christ.[54]

There is a correlation between Christ and males. Col. 1:15 states of Christ that "He is the image of the invisible God." 1 Cor. 11:7 states that men are in the image of God. There is something about both Christ and men which images God, with Christ, of course, being the head of males. Christ's headship in relation to males is of the Archetype to the image. Men are not directly images of the Father. Only Christ is the image of the Father as the Father is the head of Christ. Men are images of God insofar as they have Christ as their head. Paulus Andriessen states:

> Christ is man's head (and therefore indirectly also the head of the woman: Ep. 5:22; Col. 3:28), not only because he is lord and Master, but first of all and especially because he is the origin, the Archetype, of which man is the

reflection; man is the image and the *glory* (v. 3) of the Lord. . . . For the same reason God is Christ's *head* (v. 3) although this reason is not given here but elsewhere (2 Cor. 4:4; Col. 1:15; Heb. 1:3).[55]

God (the Father) is Christ's head because Christ is His image. Christ is the head of men because men are Christ's image. Men have a representative, sacramental role. They are symbols of Christ: "in him everything continues in being" (Col. 1:17) and derivatively symbols of God from whom everything comes (1 Cor. 11:12). Men have Christ as their head which indicates that the meaning of being male and the meaning of masculine authority is derived from Christ and thus men exist as "the image of God and the reflection of his glory" in a way that women do not.[56] Husbands are the *heads* of their wives because as v. 8–9 explains man is the origin of the woman.

> That is to say, the male is κεφαλή in the sense of ἀρχή [beginning] relatively to the female; and in St. Paul's view, the female in consequence is 'subordinate' (cf.Eph. v.23). But this principle of subordination which he finds in human relationships rests upon the order of creation, and includes the 'sonship' of Christ himself. Thus, παντὸς ἀνδρὸς ἡ κεφαλὴ ὁ ριστός ἐστιν and κεφαλὴ τοῦ Χριστοῦ Θεός. That is to say, while the word κεφαλή (and ἀρχή also, for that matter) unquestionably carries with it the idea of 'authority', such authority in social relationships derives from a relative priority (causal rather than merely temporal) in the order of being.[57]

St. Thomas Aquinas provides an insight regarding how males bear the image of God insofar as they, like God, exist as source and beginning.

> . . . as regards a secondary point, God's image is found in man in a way in which it is not found in woman; for man is the beginning and end of woman, just as God is the beginning and end of all creation. Thus after saying that *the man is the image and glory of God, while the woman is the glory of man*, the Apostle goes on to show why he says it, and adds: *for the man is not from the woman, but the woman from the man; and the man was not created for the woman, but the woman for the man.* (Emphasis in original.)[58]

The male is like God in the sense of bearing a trace (*vestigium*) of God as creator, that is, as He is source of all things.

> It was right for woman to be formed from man in the original establishment of things, for reasons that do not apply to other animals. In the first place this was desirable in order to maintain a certain style and dignity for the first man,

by making him, *in virtue of his likeness to God, the original of his whole kind, just as God is the original of the whole universe.* (Emphasis added.) So Paul says that God *made the whole of mankind from one.*[59]

The quotation above is, of course, a reference to Adam who is the originator of his kind and because he is a source, Adam (and the masculine sex in general) is like God. Woman, however, is the reflection of man's glory (v. 7). She is the glory of the man because the man is her source. She is drawn from his side, she is a part of his being; man's indispensable complement. Woman is man's glory—not because she is his image or reflection—but precisely because she is different from him.[60] Taken from the man and yet being different from him she reveals who he is—she defines him.[61] The man is completed with the creation of the woman: "This one at last is bone of my bones and flesh of my flesh; this one shall be called 'woman' for out of 'her man' she has been taken" (Gen. 2:23).

Once again we see from I Cor. 11 that authority means to be a source. The passage cannot be used to argue the subordination of women. The authority of headship in the passage has to do with the ordering of relations. Even Christ has a head because the Father is His source.

THE AUTHORITY OF WOMEN IN 1 COR. 11

The issue of headcovering for the woman when she prays or prophesies has long been interpreted as a sign of female inferiority. But the passage, far from establishing their inequality, teaches how women exercise their own authority according to their feminine dignity. 1 Cor 11:3–16 has to do with marital ordering rooted in Gen. 2:21–23. The ordering has to do with who came first and who is from whom and thus is concerned about sexual differentiation.[62] St. Paul teaches that the woman is not to speak in the assembly with an unveiled head. Her covering sharply and publicly differentiates her from the man. Oneness in Christ taught in Gal 3:28 does not at all obliterate sexual difference in St. Paul's theology. The distinction is given in creation itself. Man disgraces himself if he wears a veil—but woman disgraces herself by not wearing one.[63]

Furthermore, the word ἐξουσίαν in v. 10 does not mean "submission" as it is translated in some editions of the New Testament. The word means "authority"; "For this reason a woman ought to have authority on her head (διὰ τοῦτο ὀφείλει ἡ γυνὴ ἐξουσίαν ἔχειν) because of the angels." Andre Feuillet points out that *exousia* (power) is not something exercised by someone over someone else. The word indicates power that someone possesses and exercises themselves.[64] In this case *exousia* is the woman's own authority and not what the man exercises over her. According to

William Ramsay the Oriental roots of the word give it this meaning. The veil is not a sign of the male's authority over the woman. The veil indicates the woman's own power, her own control. She exercises her authority as a willing acknowledgment of her relation to her husband.[65]

Earl Muller and C. K. Barrett have shown that the covering of the woman is a sign of her liturgical authority.[66] Through a very careful exegesis of "covering" in the Old Testament, Muller demonstrates that "covering" has a covenantal meaning. The one who is covered is in relation to Yahweh, Lord and Husband of His people. St. Paul states that the uncovered woman in the assembly brings shame on her head. In the Oriental world veiling was a sign of honor, not submission.[67] In the Old Testament shame is what is uncovered, and it is equated with having one's head shaved (Isa 3:24, Eph. Jer. 31, Ezra. 7:18).[68] Being uncovered is a sign of harlotry and idolatry. As Muller states: "The imagery is tied particularly to Yahweh's marriage to Israel or Jerusalem."[69] In the Book of Hosea, for example, God expresses His wrath against His covenanted people for their religious infidelity. This infidelity is explicitly spoken of in terms of harlotry. The nation of Israel is an unfaithful wife to her husband, Yahweh. The sign that God renounces his covenant, thus his relation to Israel as her husband is that He will "strip her naked, leaving her as on the day of her birth" (Hos. 2:5). All the covenantal benefits God gave to His bride, with which she covers herself, He will take away: "I will snatch away my wool and my flax with which she covers her nakedness. So now I will lay bare her shame before the eyes of her lovers, and no one can deliver her out of my hand" (2:11–12).

The Book of Ezekiel provides another striking example of the theological meaning of "covering." Chapter 16:6–8 states:

> Then I passed by and saw you weltering in your blood. I said to you: Live in your blood and grow like a plant in the field. You grew and were developed, you came to the age of puberty; your breasts were formed, your hair had grown, but you were still stark naked. Again I passed by you and saw that you were now old enough for love. So I spread the corner of my cloak over you to cover your nakedness; I swore an oath to you and entered into a covenant with you; and you became mine, says the Lord.

When Israel, the Bride of Yahweh, turns to foreign gods and thus commits harlotry, God declares: "I will gather together all your lovers whom you tried to please . . . . I will gather them against you from all sides and expose you naked for them to see" (16:37). To be covered has marital/covenantal meaning while being uncovered denotes being outside of the covenant or in violation of it. In 1 Cor. 11:3–16 a woman's hair is associated with covering. The veiling of her hair is a liturgical action as though such a covering affirmed or enhanced the significance of her hair. It is her glory and her covering (vs.15–16), and it differentiates her from men (v. 14). Muller explains that the woman's covering is a liturgical expression of the female's covenantal significance and thus of her authority. Her hair:

> *is a covering given by God. But the covering given by God is the covering of the covenant, the nuptial covering which establishes the context for any genuine worship of God.* Of course Woman has authority to pray and prophesy to her Husband, her Source. Her authority is on her head! (Emphasis in original.)[70]

WOMAN IS THE COMPLETION OF MAN

As we have seen, the headship of the male reflects Christ as source and thus archetype of the man. However, the headship of the man and the woman's own authority, which we discussed above, is ordered according to the meaning of human sexuality as it is maritally grounded. St. Paul goes "back to the beginning" of creation and discovers that authority is imbedded in the very structure of the male and female relation. Yes, man is the head because like Christ, he is a cause. The woman is from him and for him (vs. 8–9). Ultimately, however, the man and the woman are defined in relation to each other: "Yet, in the Lord, woman is not independent of man nor man independent of woman. In the same way that woman was made from man, so man is born of woman; and all is from God" (vv.11–12). This passage is a key to understanding male and female authority. Masculine headship, which stands on the side of Christ, is stated in v. 12. The woman being "of (ἐκ) the man" refers back to Gen. 2: 21–22, which relates that Eve was formed by the rib that had been taken from Adam. The woman "made from man" serves as the primordial prophecy, from the beginning, of the Church who receives her being from Christ. V. 12 is followed immediately by the equivalent of feminine authority: "man is born of woman." The word "born" used here in the New American Bible is in Greek διά— or "through." The passage indicates the dependency of men (males) upon women for life. The passage accounts for the differentiation—not simply between men and women, but the differentiation between male and female authority. Women are not "heads" as they do not stand sacramentally in the place of Christ to the world, yet women are a true source of life. They are a source of life that completes the true meaning of authority as it exists only within, and never apart from, the unity of the *one flesh*. Feminine authority exists in women as *source* of the man. In other words the essence of feminine authority resides in the woman as bride and mother. 1 Cor. 11:11–12 is the doctrine of Genesis: "It is not good for the man to be alone. I will make a suitable partner for him"(Gen. 2:18). 1 Cor. 11:11 teaches that man is not independent of woman, which leads us back to Gen. 2:23–24, where the First Adam exclaims:

> This one at last is bone of my bone and flesh of my flesh. This one shall be called 'woman' for out of 'her man' this one has been taken.
>
> That is why a man leaves his father and mother and clings to his wife, and the two shall become one flesh.

The above passage speaks of the differentiation and codependency of man and woman upon which the order of Christ and the Church, and thus the order of ecclesial authority, is based. The creation of the woman is the climax of creation. Eve, though derived from Adam, completes him. She is his body "bone of my bones, flesh of my flesh." Eve provides Adam with his masculine self-identification.[71] Furthermore, in relation to Adam she is a source: "The man called his wife Eve, because she became the mother of all the living" (Gen. 3:20).[72]

The differentiation and codependency of man and woman as the ground of ecclesial authority expressed in 1 Cor. 11:11–12 are paralleled in Ephesians. 1 Cor. 11:3 states that the "head of a woman is her husband." This is repeated in Eph. 5:23 in direct relation to the marital order of Christ's headship to the Church, "the husband is head of his wife just as Christ is head of his body the church." Furthermore, 1 Cor. 11:3–16 is based on the marital doctrine of Genesis as is much of the theology of the Christ/Church relation presented in Ephesians, most explicitly 1:22–23 and 5:22–32.[73]

The marital order of the man/woman relation in 1 Cor. 11:11–12, in which both are sources in their sexual differentiation and dependent upon one another, is taught even more fully in Ephesians. We have seen that Christ is head in the sense that He is the cause of the body, the Church. However, because the Christ/Church relation is inherently marital, the Church actually completes Christ and is His partner in the work of redemption. Eph. 1:22–23 states: "He has put all things under Christ's feet and made him thus exalted, head of the Church, which is his body: the fullness of him who fills the universe in all its parts." Some commentators take plērōma to mean that the Church is the fullness of Christ in the sense that she is a passive receptacle into which He has poured His benefits.[74] However, while affirming that all the graces of the Church flow from Christ, Pope Pius XII in the encyclical *Mystici Corporis* teaches:

> This communication of the Spirit of Christ is the channel through which all

the gifts, powers, and extraordinary graces found superabundantly in the Head as in their source flow into all the members of the Church, and are perfected daily in them according to the place they hold in the Mystical Body of Jesus Christ. *Thus the Church becomes, as it were, the filling out and the complement of the Redeemer, while Christ in a sense attains through the Church a fulness in all things.* Herein we find the reason why, according to the opinion of Augustine . . . .the mystical Head, which is Christ, and the Church, which here below as another Christ shows forth His person, constitute one new man, in whom heaven and earth are joined together in perpetuating the saving work of the Cross: Christ We mean, the Head and the Body, the whole Christ.[75] (Emphasis added.)

The word πληρουμένου (filling) at the end of Eph. 1:23 can be interpreted according to the active or passive sense. The word *"plērōma"* (πλήρωμα) preceding πληρουμένου is then rendered in the active sense that the Church is completing Christ and is the complement of the head.[76] Joseph Huby points out that this interpretation has great support from the Fathers of the Church, notably Origen, St. Jerome, and St. John Chrysostom and his school.[77]

Scripture scholar George S. Hitchcock explains how the Church is the fullness of Christ in Eph. 1:23:

> We note that it is parallel to the description of the Church as our Lord's Body; and since the body completes the head, the Church is then spoken of as our Lord's complement, that which fills Him, His Fullness. . . .
>
> To suppose that this implies any lack in our Lord, the Divine Word, is to miss the significance of the figure, which is used of our Lord in His particular office as the Christ, and in His particular relation to the Church as its Head. . . .
>
> We have already learned from the *Epistle to the Colossians* ii.9, that all the Fullness of the Godhead dwells in Christ bodily. . . . But even so, the Christ, as the Christ, is not complete. He must have a human nature, body and soul; and therefore, the Fulness of the Godhead must dwell in Him bodily. Still, for all that, the Christ is not yet complete. To the Godhead and the humanity must be added the Church . . . . the Church therefore, is His Fulness, His complement, that which fills and completes Him. . . .
>
> Of course, our Lord is perfect. But as we have seen, that is not the question here. Now we are dealing with His Mystical Body and His channels of grace to the Universe. We are getting a glimpse of the Sacramental Order in the Universe.[78]

The Church is the completion of Christ according to the meaning of His Incarnation and thus according to the order of redemption. The Church as the Body of Christ exists according to a marital relation. Christ stands as head, and He is source of the Church. But this is not the whole truth. The head and body together is the Christ—thus she is His *plērōma*. Without her Christ is not complete.[79]

We saw that even in the earlier Pauline epistles a distinction exists between Christ and the Church: Christ is not the body—the Church is the body. Eph. 1:23 conveys this sense of differentiation and complementarity between Christ the head and His body which is in evidence throughout the epistle.[80]

The relation of the Church relative to the head is free: that of the bride to her husband. The key to understanding how the Church is the *plērōma* of Christ is found in Eph. 5:29 where St. Paul teaches that the Church is Christ's flesh as the body of a wife is the flesh of her husband. Let us also note that headship is defined in terms of how the Divine Spouse and husbands care for their wives who are "their own bodies."

> Husbands love your wives as Christ loved the Church. He gave himself up for her to make her holy, purifying her in the bath of water by the power of the word, to present to himself a glorious church, holy and immaculate, without stain or wrinkle or anything of that sort. Husbands should love their wives as they do their own bodies. He who loves his wife loves himself. Observe that no one ever hates his own flesh; no, he nourishes it and takes care of it as Christ cares for the church—for we are members of his body. (Eph. 5:25–30)

The man is not independent of woman (1 Cor. 11:11). The first man, Adam, declared that the woman was "flesh of his flesh and bone of his bone." She alone is the answer to his solitude (Gen. 2:18). She is his suitable partner fulfilling what it means for him to be male and to be a head. The wife is the body of her husband (5:28–29), and the Church is the body of Christ—the body through which His headship and salvific activity is exercised. The Church is Christ's covenantal partner in the New Creation (Eph. 2:15–16). Eph. 3:10–11 teaches that "through the church, God's manifold wisdom is made known to the principalities and powers of heaven, in accord with his age old purpose, carried out in Christ Jesus our Lord." It is through the Church (in union with Christ) that God's wisdom is revealed. This wisdom is linked to the mystery of God, his secret plan (1:9–10, 3:3:4), which is nothing less than the establishment of the New Covenant "to bring all things in the heavens and on earth into one under Christ's headship" (1:10). The Church is Christ's active partner in redemption as the New Eve to the New Adam. The plan to unite all things in Christ begins with the New Adam/New Eve relation.[81] Furthermore, the Church, like her head, is to do battle with the cosmic forces of evil

(Eph. 6:10). Stephen Miletic explains:

> . . . the church is given a *cosmological* role in Ephesians.
>
> She has been raised up with Christ "in the heavenly places" (2.6) where she has been blessed with all spiritual blessings (1.3) . . . . like Christ in 1 Cor. 15: 20–28 and the Spirit (1 Cor. 2.8, 10, 12), the church plays a key role vis-a-vis God's plan of salvation. The church reveals that plan to the cosmological powers in the heavenly places (3:10) and does combat with the forces of the devil (6.12). That is, in Ephesians the church is an important agent effecting the unity of (literally) everything with Christ (1:10).[82]

Redemption is not accomplished by Christ alone. It is accomplished by Christ in union with His Church. This union is maritally ordered insofar as Christ is the source of the Church, the Church is His *plērōma*, both are dependent yet differentiated. Together they are the New Covenant which is no less than that of the "one flesh."

Because redemption is maritally ordered, masculinity and femininity are entirely bound up with its accomplishment and expression. Eph. 5:23–27 teaches that Christ's headship exists according to his sacrifice as bridegroom and thus Christ's authority defines what it means to be masculine. Pope John Paul II affirms this primary truth about Christ:

> Christ is the Bridegroom. This expresses the truth about the love of God, who "first loved us" (cf. 1 Jn. 4:19) and who, with the gift generated by this spousal love for man, has exceeded all human expectations: "He loved them to the end" (Jn. 13:1). The bridegroom—the Son consubstantial with the Father as God—became the son of Mary; he became the "son of man," true man, a male. The symbol of the bridegroom is masculine. This masculine symbol represents the human aspect of the divine love which God has for Israel, for the church and for all people. Meditating on what the Gospels say about Christ's attitude toward women, we can conclude that as a man, a son of Israel, he revealed the dignity of the "daughters of Abraham" (cf. Lk. 13:16), the dignity belonging to women from the very "beginning" on an equal footing with men. At the same time Christ emphasized the originality which distinguishes women from men, all the richness lavished upon women in the mystery of creation. Christ's attitude toward women serves as a model of what the Letter to the Ephesians expresses with the concept "bridegroom." Precisely because Christ's love is the love of a bridegroom, it is the model and pattern of all human love, men's love in particular. . . . Christ is the bridegroom because "he has given himself."[83]

IV. The Marital Order of Authority

How do we know that the masculine headship of Christ and the femininity of the Church, His body, are not merely arbitrary symbols, time bound and historically conditioned? How do we know that such sexual symbolism is not only one model of redemption, a merely extrinsic metaphor that can be replaced with another, or at least a model in which the roles can be blurred, can overlap or be exchanged? We know that redemption is maritally ordered and thus ecclesial authority because the relation of Christ and the Church fulfills the order of Creation. From the very beginning male and female sexuality was meant by God to be signs of Christ's union with His Church. Through such marital ordering God's love itself is expressed. The symbols are not arbitrary. *They are constitutive of the covenant as they are constitutive of creation.* To dismantle the marital order of Christ and the Church is to dismantle the Christian faith itself. Eph. 5:31–32 explicitly teaches that redemption, (namely the Christ/head, Church/body relation) is bound to the marital order of the "one flesh" founded "in the beginning."

'For this reason a man shall leave his father and mother, and shall cling to his wife, and the two shall become one flesh.'
This is a great mystery; I mean that it refers to Christ and the Church.

Because the order of redemption is rooted in the order of creation, to deny the sacramental value of male and female sexuality is also to deny the goodness of creation. As we saw in the previous chapter the feminist solution to ecclesial authority is to erase all differentiation, first between men and women, but also between God and matter and between human beings and the earth.[84] Peace and equality will only be achieved when everything is absorbed into the faceless, impersonal, monistic, platonic One. Such a view of authority is absolutely antithetical to the entire meaning of Creation coming from the hand of God who called something "good" that was not Himself (Gen. 1). The New Covenant between Christ and the Church exists maritally, and thus it is within the "one flesh" union of the New Adam and the New Eve that male and female authority is constituted. In his pastoral letter on the priesthood Emmett Cardinal Carter of Toronto stated:

As has been seen, this sacrifice is that of the Head of the Body, offered for the Body. The Head-Body relation is marital, covenantal. In this relation, the authority-structure of the Trinity is imaged: the subsistent relations of Father, Son and Spirit have their created analogue in the Head, the Body, the One Flesh of the New Covenant. As the persons who mutually constitute the Triune God are defined by their relatedness, as their authority is thereby qualified while remaining undiminished, wholly divine, so in the New Covenant the Head, the Body, and the One Flesh of their sacrificial union are constituted by their interrelation, and their mutual authority is qualitatively differentiated without subjection. The head gives Himself totally to the Bridal Church who gives herself totally in reply and both are under the authority, the irrevocability, of their union in One Flesh.[85]

The essence of Christ's authority resides in His existing as *source* of the Church through His sacrificial death on the Cross: "He gave Himself up for her" (Eph. 5:2, 25). Authority can, therefore, never be disassociated from "giving up oneself" to another. This truth serves as the foundation upon which to understand the meaning of "submission." Wives' submission to their husbands as taught by St. Paul (Eph. 5:22, Col. 3:18, 1 Tim. 2:11–12 and also in 1 Pet. 3:1) is considered by many believers today as merely an antiquated custom, inherently demeaning to women that serves no religious or redemptive function. Subordination, however, begins with Christ Himself and is essentially soteriological. Christ submitted Himself to the will of the Father in everything for the accomplishment of salvation, as many Scripture passages attest (Matt. 26:42, Mark. 14:36, Luke. 22:42, John. 5:19, 6:37–38, 7:16, 28, 8:28, 42, 12:49, 14:10, 24, 31, 15:15, 17:4). Furthermore, Christ, the bridegroom, submitted Himself to the Church by dying for her, and the Church, in turn, is to submit herself to Christ. This is a marital submission for the sake of the Covenant of the "one flesh" (Eph. 5: 31–32). The ordering between husbands and wives is its expression. Manfred Hauke explains that if a wife is to be subordinate to her husband it is *not* because he is her lord but because he is *like* the Lord. And since the husband appears in the image of Christ, the command that he "love his wife" (as the masculine paradigm of love is Christ's sacrificial death) contains an even stronger obligation (or at least an equal obligation) for self-surrender than the remark that gives offense to so many women that they are to be "subject" to their husbands.[86]

Miletic explains the soteriological role of feminine subordination in relation to the subordination of Christ. 1 Cor. 15:20–28 teaches that the subordination of the Son to the Father is to bring about the reconciliation of all things in God. In Ephesians this subordination is transferred to the Church.

> The relocation of Christ's subordination in the Christ/church relationship at 5.24a is understandable given the nature of that relationship. Christ's relationship to the church involves salvation. He saves the body (5.23c) by loving it and dying for it (5.25b–27), by initially creating it (2.15–16) and by maintaining its resurrected life and growth (4.15–16). All of these activities are salvific and contribute towards the unity between Christ and the church. Within such a con-

text, the subordination of the church to Christ (Eph. 5.24a), like that of Christ to God (1 Cor. 15.28b), must be understood as a critical element in the salvific plan of uniting all things to God (1 Cor. 15.28c) or to Christ (Eph. 1.10). In the context of Ephesians, the church's subordination to Christ represents an initial realization of Eph. 1.10. That is, the unification of all things in subordination to Christ. They are "one flesh" (Eph. 5.31) in this soteriological sense.[87]

Subordination, first of all, is mutual but differentiated.[88] Feminine subordination is at the service of the covenant; thus it is constitutive of redemption. For this reason, if we keep in mind the christological character of subordination, subordination because it is causative of redemption is part of what it means to exercise masculine or feminine authority.

Redemption is accomplished within the New Covenant between Christ and the Church which is ordered according to the "one flesh" of the first couple. Christ is the head in this covenant because He is the initiatory source of it as bridegroom to bride. The Church is the body of Christ, fulfilling Him, completing Him, and thus she is the covenantal partner in redemption. Male and female authority is the sacramental expression of this reality. Male and female authority is a matter of being *entrusted* with a responsibility for redemption according to the marital order of the covenant. The theological task is to understand more deeply and articulate this entrusting. Priestly authority has the task of imaging Christ who is the icon of the Father to the world, for the sake of an effective worship. Gertrud von le Fort has stated:

> The priesthood could not be confided to a woman, for thereby the very meaning of woman in the Church would have been annihilated. A part of the essential nature of the Church of which woman is the symbol would likewise have been annihilated.[89]

The masculine priesthood represents Christ as *source* of the Church. But this authority does not sum up the essence of ecclesial authority or the essence of the Church. We will see how the headship of Christ is sacramentally ordered to male sexuality. But what we must always keep in mind is that we are dealing with a covenant. Christ is a man, but He is only fully so through the womanly role of the Church. He needs her to be filled with His presence—like a womb full of life to bear Him and keep him in the world. He sees Himself reflected in her as she is sprung from His side as He died upon the Cross. The words of the First Adam are now the words of the Second. In the ancient and eschatological cry of covenantal love, Jesus in union with His Church utters: "This one at last is bone of my bones and flesh of my flesh."

3

The Meaning Of
Male Ecclesial Authority

I. Christ the Good Shepherd

PRIESTLY AUTHORITY AND MASCULINE SEXUALITY

The authority of Christ cannot be separated from His sacrificial offering—
the offering that creates the Church and keeps her in being. Essentially
authority has to do with offering and receiving in a freedom that is constitutive of covenantal unity between Christ and the world He redeemed. The
crucial question before us at this moment of the Church's history is how
male and female sexuality serve as the essential, as opposed to arbitrary
or time-conditioned, liturgical expression of salvation in Christ. At stake
is not merely how the Mass is celebrated; the issue before us is bound up
with a theological view of creation itself—its freedom, its beauty, and its
order. Male and female sexuality are not secular realities or mere biology.
The man and the woman speak a truth about the order of God's love for the
world. In this order *equality* does not mean *identity* in which difference
itself is associated with injustice. Rather the difference is the very means
by which the created order serves as the divinely ordained expression of
the order of redemptive grace.

> ... the movement for the ordination of women is in practice unanimous in
> accepting as a matter of course the postulate of equality as identity and identity
> as unqualified, therefore as finally quantitative and monadic. It is obvious that
> the covenantal equality, the baptismal equality, of men and women is entirely
> alien to this sociology, this anthropology, this "ecclesiology," for covenantal

76

equality demands a sacramental valuation of sexual differentiation as intrinsic and indispensable to Catholic worship, a valuation which is explicit in the Eucharist and in marriage, and which has obvious application to the sacrament of priestly orders; the priest acts *in persona Christi*, and only because he so acts does he represent also the congregation at worship; his authority is that of the Head, and it is a covenantal authority.[1]

The Church rests on the fact that Christ Himself historically established her worship. He Himself is the guarantee that the worship the Church offers to the Father is efficaciously pleasing to Him because what the Church offers in the Eucharist is the one sacrifice of Christ offered by His own authority.[2]

Priestly power is inherently connected to masculine sexuality. Priestly power has to do with engendering and maintaining the divine life of God in us. The priest has a delegation from God. His authority is not self-bestowed. Christ, who is the only true priest, has chosen certain men to be his instruments whereby Christ maintains His presence in the Church. To this end Christ passes on to priests what He received from His Father.[3]

The meaning of priestly authority is bound to male sexuality because of the relation between the headship of Christ and His engendering of the Church. This is the manner in which Christ exists as *source*. Furthermore this divine life transmitted via the priesthood is *received* by the Church. Her life is bestowed upon her from the outside. The Church is not her own cause. The male body is related to priestly action because the meaning of masculinity does not rest in itself but derives its meaning by being a transparency for what is transcendent as opposed to what is immanent. A priest's authority is not his own. He is a sacrament of the one true priest who is Christ. Ultimately a priest is not only a sign of Christ. As an effective sign the sacrament of Orders makes a truth about the fatherhood of God real in the world. The feminist restructuring of ecclesial authority, as we saw in chapter 1, must demolish the religious significance of fatherhood. God as the source of life has no way to speak Himself in the order of creation that signifies His unique power in relation to what He has made. In feminist theology, fatherhood, and thus God Himself, is not only remote; He is invisible.[4] The masculinity of the priesthood, however, speaks a truth about the authority of God, about how God relates to the world. Fundamentally, when the Church insists on the masculinity of the priesthood, she is preserving the order of God's love for the world which is inherently marital.

By entrusting His authority to males Christ preserves a truth about His love in relation to His creation. His sacrifice is uniquely His own offered *for the Church*. The particularity of His sacrifice has its historical and eternal expression in the marital order of the New Covenant. In marriage nothing can substitute for the unique gift a husband makes to his wife and the wife to her husband. The gift of self is embodied in a personal word of the man as man and the woman as woman out of which the unity of their "one flesh" is formed. The male priesthood speaks of the uniqueness of Christ's gift of self—a complete personal self-donation that is the source of a unique covenantal response. A bisexual priesthood would render Christ's sacrifice unintelligible. The economy of Christian worship would be dissolved and thus the Christian revelation. The feminist quest for a female priesthood is rooted in the mistaken notion that all words are basically the same, that symbols as such are meaningless, that Revelation has no language except what is contrived by an historical relativism. Feminist thinkers tend to view the male body and the female body as virtually irrelevant. What counts for them is the *person* and what the person is able "to do" despite their sexual gender. One's sex should not matter when considering whether someone is "qualified for the job." However, when "the job" is to image the marital/covenantal structure of God's love and authority in the world, the bodily reality of masculinity and femininity cannot be dispensed with. The human body as male or female—indeed, the entire person—as male or female serves as a communicator of God's covenantal love.

CHRIST AND THE REVELATION OF GOD THE FATHER

Christ spoke of His authority as that of a shepherd over His sheep. Here Christ's authority with respect to the Church is entirely bound to His sacrifice as bridegroom and, as we shall see, it is this authority Christ entrusted to the Apostles. A description of the authority of Christ as Shepherd is given in the Gospel of John.

> The one who enters through the gate is shepherd of the sheep; the keeper opens the gate for him. The sheep hear his voice and he calls his own by name and leads them out. When he has brought out all those who are his, he walks in front of them, and the sheep follow him because they recognize his voice (John 10:2–4).
>
> I am the good shepherd; the good shepherd lays down his life for the sheep. The hired hand who is no shepherd nor owner of the sheep—catches sight of the wolf coming and runs away leaving the sheep to be snatched and scattered by the wolf. (John 10:11–13).
>
> I am the good shepherd. I know my sheep and mine know me in the same way that the Father knows me and I know the Father; for these sheep I will give my life. I have other sheep that do not belong to this fold. I must lead them too, and they shall hear my voice. There shall be one flock then, one shepherd.
>
> The Father loves me for this: that I lay down my life to take it up again. (John 10:14–17)

The role of the shepherd is to lead the sheep (vv. 3, 16). But the authority to lead is associated with the ability to give life as 10:10 states: "I came that they might have life and have it to the full." This leadership is marked by an intimacy between the shepherd and the sheep. The sheep hear and recognize the shepherd's voice (10:3, 4, 16). However, regarding Christ's own authority, the voice of the Good Shepherd is not His alone. Christ's authority and priesthood is entirely bound to His existence as revelatory of the Father. The voice of the Good Shepherd is the voice of the Father spoken through the Son and their authority is linked to their ability to give life.

> My Father is at work until now, and I am at work as well. . . .I solemnly assure you, the Son cannot do anything by himself—he can only do what he sees the Father doing. For whatever the Father does, the Son does likewise. For the Father loves the Son and everything the Father does he shows him. Yes, to your great wonderment, he will show him even greater works than these. Indeed, just as the Father raises the dead and grants life, so the Son grants life to those whom he wishes. The Father himself judges no one, but has assigned all judgement to the Son so that all men may honor the Son just as they honor the Father. He who refuses to honor the Son refuses to honor the Father who sent him. (John 5:17–23)
>
> Indeed, just as the Father possesses life in himself, so has he granted it to the Son to have life in himself. The Father has given over to him power to pass judgement because he is Son of Man. . . .I cannot do anything of myself. I judge as I hear, and my judgement is honest because I am not seeking my own will but the will of him who sent me. (John 5:26–30)

The above passage speaks of the greatest intimacy between the Father and the Son. Jesus is totally dependent upon the Father.[5] The incarnate Son of God exists as a type of sacrament of the Father's will and action.[6]

> Whoever has seen me has seen the Father. How can you say, "Show us the Father?' Do you not believe that I am in the Father and the Father is in me? *The words I speak are not spoken of myself; it is the Father who lives in me accomplishing his works.* Believe me that I am in the Father and the Father is in me, or else believe because of the works I do. I solemnly assure you, the man who has faith in me will do the works I do and greater far than these. (John 14:10–12) (Emphasis added.)

The passages in John's gospel that speak of Christ as revealing the Father are numerous.[7] Suffice it to say that Christ's salvific work reveals the Father's love and His authority cannot be disassociated from this work. Christ's salvific work flows directly from the will of the Father.

> Indeed, this is the will of my Father, that everyone who looks upon the Son
> and believes in him shall have eternal life. Him I will raise up on the last day.
> (John 6:40)

Christ's authority discloses the life-giving love of the Father. The question that concerns us at this point is why the Church and the salvation she brings to the world are bound to the masculine symbol of God as Father revealed in Christ as bridegroom and Son? Is *Father* merely a name for God or does the name *Father* reveal a truth about God that feminine symbolism does not disclose—a truth that is essential to the order of redemption?

THE FATHERHOOD OF GOD

For the answer let us first turn to the manner in which God has revealed Himself in the Old Testament. God is Father because He is the cause of His people and cannot be identified with His people. Yahweh remains the totally Other. Creation is from God and stands in relation to Him. Something that is not God is declared to be good as the Book of Genesis repeatedly testifies. There is an "I-Thou" relationship between God and what he has made in which creation can glorify Him and give Him praise (Pss. 145:10, 147:12). God and God alone is the founder of the Hebrew nation. The Hebrew people exist because they are in a covenant with Yahweh, a covenant He initiated. Christ states, "The words I speak are not spoken of myself; it is the Father who lives in me accomplishing His works" (John 14:10). The work of the Father is the work of salvation. This work began under the Old Covenant when God called the Hebrew people to be His own. He is the cause of their being liberated from slavery in Egypt to make a covenant with them at Mount Sinai. This covenant was the beginning of the fulfillment of the promise God gave to Abraham—a promise that has its first seed bestowed in the birth of Isaac. The Fatherhood of God is perhaps nowhere more vividly displayed than in the fact that it is He who opens the barren womb of Sarah, enabling her to be a mother—indeed the mother of a nation—and this when it was beyond all human power for her to conceive a child. God in Abraham and in Sarah engenders for Himself a people. The incident of the near sacrifice of Isaac further illustrates the power of God as Father. In Gen. 22 Abraham is called by God to sacrifice his only son—the son of promise—the son upon whom every hope of the Hebrew nation rests. When Abraham is ready to plunge his knife into the child, God intervenes again to give life (to actually re-engender) Isaac. Old Testament scholar Gerhard von Rad states that when Israel reflected on this story, it could only see itself in Isaac "laid on Yahweh's altar, given back to him, then given life again by him alone. That is to say, it could base its existence in history not on its own legal titles as other nations did, but only on the will of Him who in the freedom of His grace permitted Isaac to live."[8] God reveals Himself as Father time and again throughout the Old Testament. Life is *received* by creation, by Israel, and by women where there is no life. When Eve conceives Cain, she exclaims that the child is the result, not of Adam's power, but of God's: "I have produced a child with the help of the Lord" (Gen 4:1). There is a triumph between sterile women and God whenever they are finally blessed with a child such as Sarah, or Hannah, or in Luke's gospel, Elizabeth. The liberating paternity of God reaches its apex with the birth of Jesus who is God's own Son.[9]

The mother of seven sons in 2 Macc. 7:22–23 who watched the torture of her children proclaimed:

> I do not know how you came into existence in my womb; it was not I who gave you the breath of life, nor was it I who set in order the elements of which each of you is composed. Therefore, since it is the Creator of the universe who shapes each man's beginning as he brings about the origin of everything, he in his mercy, will give you back both breath and life, because you now disregard yourselves for the sake of his law.

God: "He brings about the origin of everything." It is important for us to notice that while these Old Testament women experience their power to conceive in relation to God—God does not substitute for them in their mothering function. He causes them to be mothers.

God reveals Himself as the Father of His people in Jeremiah 31:9–10 where the prophet speaks of the restoration of Israel following the Babylonian exile.

> I will lead them to brooks of water, on a level road, so that none shall stumble. For I am a Father to Israel, Ephraim is my first-born. Hear the word of the Lord, O nations, proclaim it on distant coasts and say: He who scatters Israel, now gathers them together, he guards them as a shepherd his flock.

That God is the one who has the power to scatter and the power to gather together takes us back to Gen. 22 and the sacrifice of Isaac. God commands Abraham to kill his only son from whom the nation of Israel will come, only to return the boy back to his father. The power of gathering and scattering is God's as He alone is the source of life and unity for His people. It is important to notice that fatherhood and the shepherding role are linked in the above passage and that Christ in the New Dispensation fulfills this role as the *arché* of the New Covenant. The authority of Christ the Good Shepherd is bound to the sacrifice He offers, and this sacrifice *gathers* together a people:

> . . . for these sheep I will give my life. I have other sheep that do not belong to this fold. I must lead them too, and they shall hear my voice. There shall be one flock then, one shepherd. (John 10:15–16)

The passage speaks of bringing together the Jews and the Gentiles and making them into one. This parallels exactly Eph. 2:13–16. Here, as we saw in chapter 2, Christ brings the Jews and the Gentiles together in one body through His Cross (v. 16). In John the death of Christ is explicitly the cause of a new people. In John 12:24 Jesus states: "Unless a grain of wheat falls to the ground and dies, it remains just a grain of wheat. But if it dies, it produces much fruit." The phrase "it remains just a grain of wheat" means the man remains alone and singular, but with death the Son of Man becomes the source of many—a new people.[10] In John 12:32 Jesus again tells the meaning of His death: "And I—when I am lifted up from the earth—will draw all men to myself." In addition to being the principle of unity, Christ's death paradoxically is a principle of scattering. Again joined together is Christ the shepherd and His death and all within the celebration of the First Eucharist: "Tonight your faith in me will be shaken, for Scripture has it: 'I will strike the shepherd and the sheep of the flock will be dispersed' " (Matt. 26:31).

The authority of God as Father vis-à-vis His people is that only through Him are they engendered into a people. God is their source of life and being. Consider the following passage from Ezekiel, which speaks of God as a true shepherd.

> Thus says the Lord God: Woe to the shepherds of Israel who have been pasturing themselves! Should not shepherds, rather, pasture sheep? You have fed off their milk, worn their wool, and slaughtered their fatlings, but the sheep you have not pastured. (Ezra 34:2–3)
>
> . . . For thus says the Lord my God: I myself will look after and tend my sheep. As a shepherd tends his flock when he finds himself among his scattered sheep, so will I tend my sheep. I will rescue them from every place where they were scattered when it was dark and cloudy. . . . In good pastures will I pasture them, and on the mountain heights of Israel shall be their grazing ground. (Ezra 34:11–12, 14)

Raymond Brown has commented, "The Patriarchs, Moses and David were all shepherds and so 'shepherd' became a figurative term for the rulers of God's people."[11] In Ezekiel 34, however, it is God who rules His people as a shepherd and His authority is rooted in the sort of care He has for His sheep. God restores them to life. This care is contrasted with how Israel's shepherds misuse authority. These shepherds exploit the sheep, lording their authority over the sheep "harshly and brutally" (Ezra 34:4). We can see clearly the meaning of authority. God's shepherding is not a despotism. His authority is not mere quantitative power. Authority is measured by life-giving power and care for others.

Christ is the Good Shepherd. And since the work of Christ is the work of the Father, the fatherhood of God to His people is revealed in Christ.

II. The Gender of God

Is God a Mother?

It is argued by many feminist theologians that fatherhood is only one expression of God in the Old Testament. There are places in Hebrew Scripture where God refers to Himself as a mother. The text most often cited to support God as a mother is Isa. 49:14–15:

> But Zion said, "The Lord has forsaken me; my Lord has forgotten me." Can a mother forget her infant, be without tenderness for the child of her womb? Even should she forget, I will never forget you.

First, we should notice that God is not called a "mother." Rather, His love is likened to that of a mother and actually far exceeds that of a mother. Manfred Hauke has rightly pointed out that the theological basis for Second Isaiah is marital.[12] God is described as the husband of Israel: "For he who has become your Husband is your Maker; His name is the Lord of hosts....The Lord calls you back like a wife forsaken and grieved in spirit" (Isa. 54:5–6). The economy of redemption pervading both the Old and New Testament is maritally ordered. Feminine images of God are aberrations that serve a particular crisis moment. These images have limited symbolic life in terms of Israel and the Church's relation to God.

Another passage often cited in an attempt to show God can be equally mother or father is Isa. 66:13: "As a mother comforts her son, so will I comfort you; in Jerusalem you shall find your comfort." This image is surely an aberration and even somewhat of a puzzlement. In all preceding verses it is Zion or Jerusalem who is the mother (vs. 7–12). It is stated of her "Oh, may you suck fully of the milk of her comfort, that you may nurse with delight at her abundant breasts" (v. 11). Such graphic maternalism is never applied to God. Indeed, His role is that of Father. In v. 9 He is the one who gives Israel the power to conceive: "Shall I bring a mother to the point of birth, and yet not let her child be born? says the Lord; Or shall I who allow her to conceive yet close her womb? says your God." When we come to the passage that compares God's comfort to that of a mother, this comfort of God *is through* Jerusalem—the mother. Hauke comments:

> The mother thus appears as a creaturely entity that is permitted, in a certain way, to transmit God's gifts of grace. Zion is a figurative type of the Mother of God and of the Church, similarly to the way in which the son, in Second Isaiah, is interpretable as a prefiguration of Christ.[13]

Christ compares Himself to a mother in His lamentation over Jerusalem. Matt. 23:37 reads: "O Jerusalem, Jerusalem, murderess of prophets and stoner of those who were sent to you! How often have I yearned to gather your children, as a mother bird gathers her young under her wings, but you refused me." It would appear that Christ is dispensing with His masculine role and taking on that of the feminine Jerusalem. But let us notice a few things about this passage. It is Jerusalem who is the mother. The children Jesus wishes He could gather are hers. She is spoken of as a *murderess* (ἡ ἀποκτείνουσα), a feminine killer of prophets sent to *her* (αὐτήν). Christ functions, not on the side of Jerusalem, but on the side of God's messengers sent to her. As they were rejected by her, Christ, too, is rejected by her. Christ's lamentation is a real one. It is as though He wanted to make up for Jerusalem's bad motherhood; as if a good husband and father wished to give to the children what the real mother will not. Because Jerusalem has been an unfaithful mother, her children are deprived of the truth of God and His saving action. Thus they are scattered because the mother rejected the husband sent to her. The punishment of the mother's rejection of Christ is for the Lord to abandon her: "You will find your temple deserted." This echoes the manner in which God dealt with Israel in the Book of Hosea for her infidelities to Him who was her husband as "he has withdrawn himself from them" (Hos. 5:6). Isaiah 54 also speaks of the Lord who is husband to Zion. In His wrath at her rejection of Him, He abandoned her and caused her to have no children: "For a brief moment I abandoned you, but with great tenderness I will take you back (v. 7). Again the abandonment of the temple by Christ finds its Old Testament parallel in Isa. 64:6b–10:

> For you have hidden your face from us and have delivered us up to our guilt. Yet, O Lord, you are our father; we are the clay and you the potter; we are all the work of your hands. . . .Your holy cities have become a desert, Zion is a desert, Jerusalem a waste. . . .Our holy and glorious temple has been burned with fire.

God is the father of His people—their maker. Christ relative to Jerusalem and the temple occupies the same position. He will abandon her, but He is not a substitute for her.

Often in the Old Testament, Israel is personified as a son in relation to God. This is found particularly in Second Isaiah where Israel is called Ephraim. Does this indicate that the Church could be represented by masculine symbolism and God by the feminine? In Isa. 46:6 and 49:6 Israel is is spoken of in masculine terms. These passages, however, do have a clear messianic prophetic theme. In Jer. 31:20 Israel, called "Ephraim," is God's "favored son." But, as Hauke explains, the son does not simply personify Israel, but the "son stands out from the people."[14] In other words, when "son" is used to personify Israel, he is in a representative role as well as communal. The son or servant figure "makes himself an offering for sin" (Isa. 53:10) and does so as the "representative of God before his people."[15] Thus, Hauke argues: "In the son, the two fundamental strands of priestly representation are prefigured that we will meet again in Christ; the concept of daughter, or bride, does not have this stamp."[16]

Finally, while God occasionally in the Old Testament is referred to as a mother, He is never directly called "Mother." God is, however, called "father." For example, Isa. 63:16: "Were Abraham not to know us, nor Israel not to acknowledge us, you, Lord, are our father." Other passages include Isa. 63:15, 64, 7; Pss. 68:6, 89:27, 103:13; and Jer. 31:9, 19. In Jer. 3:19–20 we find God as both father to sons (a symbol of His people) and lover to His bride, Israel.

One of the strongest arguments for the conclusion that God reveals Himself as a mother is that the Hebrew root word for mercy is *rehäm* (*rahamīm* pl.), which means maternal womb. Therefore the mercy of God is the "maternal mercy of God."[17] However, Hauke points out that the plural *rahamīm* designates not only feminine attributes but *all* the soft organs of the abdomen.[18] "These parts of the body, in a broader sense, appear 'as the organic site of the process that occurs in it' namely, 'sympathy' and, especially, 'mercy.'"[19] In the Old Testament this mercy is a paternal quality, and it is the Father God who expresses it: "Where . . . is your surge of pity and your mercy? O Lord, hold not back for you are our Father" (Isa. 63:15–16). Ps. 103:13 states: "As a father has compassion on his children, so the Lord has compassion on those who fear him."

WHY GOD IS FATHER

God is a father because He is completely differentiated from what He has made and yet stands in relation to creation as life-giving source. Cardinal Joseph Ratzinger states that relation is the ground of being—relation is the primordial reality.

Not only unity is divine; plurality is primordial and has its inner ground in God. Plurality is not just disintegration which sets in outside the divinity; it does not arise simply through the intervention of the "*dyas,*" of disintegration; it is not the result of the dualism of two opposing powers; it corresponds to the creative fullness of God, who himself stands above plurality and unity, encompassing both. So at bottom the belief in the Trinity, which recognizes the plural in the unity of God, is the only way to the final elimination of dualism as a means of explaining plurality alongside unity. . . .

To him who believes in God tri-une, the highest unity is not the unity of the inflexible monotony. The model of unity or oneness towards which one should strive is consequently not the indivisibility of the atom, the smallest unity, too small to be divided up; the authentic acme of unity is the unity created by love. The multiunity which grows in love is a more radical, truer unity than the unity of the "atom." . . .[20]

With the perception that, seen as substance, God is One, but that there exists in him the phenomenon of dialogue, of differentiation and of relationship through speech, the category of *relation* gained a completely new significance for Christian thought. . . .The experience of God who conducts a dialogue, of the God who is not only *logos* but also *dia-logos* not only idea and meaning but speech and word in the reciprocal exchanges of conversation—this experience exploded the ancient division of reality and substance, the real thing, and accidents, the merely circumstantial. It now became clear that the dialogue, the *relatio* stands beside the substance as an equally primordial form of being.[21]

St. Thomas Aquinas teaches the meaning of relation in the Trinity. In the *Summa* I, Q 28, a. 3 he asks "Whether the Relations in God Are Really Distinguished from One Another?" He answers:

Now by definition relation implies reference to another, according to which the two things stand in relative opposition to each other. Therefore since in God there is a real relation, as said above, relative opposition must also really be there. Now by its very meaning such opposition implies distinction. Therefore there must be real distinction in God, not indeed when we consider the absolute reality of his nature, where there is sheer unity and simplicity, but when we think of Him in terms of relation.[22]

Distinction in the Trinity involves "relative opposition." This relative opposition has to do with paternity and filiation. Aquinas goes on to state that relations are "opposed because of the procession of one thing from another."[23] Later, when Aquinas treats of the Divine Persons, the First Person is said to be the Father because He is a "principle" of the Son.

REPLY: The word "principle' means simply that from which another proceeds; we call "principle' everything from which another comes forth in any way at all, and vice versa. Since, then the Father is one from whom another originates, it follows that the Father is principle.[24]

The term *principle* can designate "a disparity based on perfection or power," but Aquinas clarifies that "we use the word 'principle' even in regards to matters wherein there is no such difference, but merely one based on some sort of order."[25] Aquinas even goes on to state that the term *principle*, which he has already applied to the Father, means *origin*.[26] Furthermore, the authority of the Father resides in the fact that He is "principle" of the Son.[27] Yet, Aquinas clarifies:

> ... to avoid even the chance of error we do not speak of the Son or the Holy Spirit in terms of suggesting subjection or inferiority. In this vein Hilary writes, *The Father is greater with the authority of a giver, but the Son to whom the same one being is given is not less.*[28]

Aquinas explains how paternity is more perfect in God than it is in human fathers. It is paternity that distinguishes the Father from all other persons; thus *Father* is God's proper name.[29] God is a father by the principle of generation: He is begetter of the Son and:

> ... clearly generation takes its species from its term and this is the form of the one begotten. Moreover the closer this offspring is to the form of the begetter, the truer and fuller is the generation. ... Hence that in divine generation the form of the begetter and begotten is the same numerically, but in creaturely generation, is not the same numerically but only specifically, makes plain that generation, and so fatherhood are present in God, and then in creatures. And the very fact that in God the distinction of begetter and begotten is based on the relation alone is part of the genuineness of the divine begetting and fatherhood.[30]

The authority of God the Father is also defined according to His existence as Unbegotten which is bound to what it means for Him to be an origin. Aquinas states (ST I, Q 33, a. 4):

> ON THE OTHER HAND there is Hilary, *The one differs from the other (i.e. the begotten from the unbegotten) by the properties respectively of not being born and of having origin.* REPLY: Even as among creatures we observe primary and secondary principles, so among the divine persons, while there is no first and second, there is a principle not from a principle, the Father, and a principle from a principle, the Son ... as he [the Father] is a principle

not from a principle, by his not being from another. That is what constitutes the property of not being born, to which the term "unbegotten' refers.[31]

Aquinas specifically links the authority of God the Father with His relation as origin: "in the godhead to be source or author means exactly the same as to be principle of origin."[32]

Aquinas then draws together two very important theological points regarding the relation of the Father and the Son to the world. The Son is the Word of God and as such is expressive of the Father and at the same time is the operative power by which creatures are known to God. God the Father has made the world through the Son, as Aquinas quotes Ps. 32:9: "He spoke and they were made."[33]

The Son, the Word of God, reveals the Father. Christ's headship, His authority, is entirely bound to what it means for Him to reveal the Father. What is revealed is the supreme creative love of the Father—definitively expressed in the sacrifice of Christ which is causative of the New Creation. The masculinity of Christ cannot be dissociated from the type of love He reveals. As in the Trinity, the love of Christ (as revealer of the Father) is relationally ordered: Christ as icon of the Father is the source of the Church. This order of love is marital. The Christian religion cannot exist outside of this marital order of love. The Father as principle of the Son is unique in His giving. The Father's place is not interchangeable. If the Father's love is unique, the symbol of its expression must likewise be unique. It is the marital order of creation and redemption that manifests the unique love of the Father to the world. And, furthermore, it is the femininity of the Church—caused by Christ —that expresses her own unique response—her sacrifice of praise which is not interchangeable with the sacrifice of Christ.

III. The Authority of the Apostles

THE APOSTLES—COMMISSIONED AND SENT BY CHRIST

The authority of Christ as shepherd and head revealing the love of the Father is the authority entrusted by Christ to the Apostles. This is made very clear in the commissioning of the Apostles. In Matt. 10 Christ instructs the Apostles on their mission and at the end states: "He who welcomes you welcomes me, and he who welcomes me welcomes him who sent me" (v. 40).[34] Christ's High Priestly Prayer in the Gospel of John repeats this formula of commissioning: "I solemnly assure you, he who accepts anyone I send accepts me and in accepting me accepts him who sent me"

(John 13:20). Later in the same Gospel Christ imparts to the Apostles His authority to forgive sins saying: "As the Father has sent me so I send you" (20:21).

First of all, these passages indicate clearly that Christ's own mission · of redemption entails that He was sent by the Father. This fact means Christ is outside the Church, in relation to the Church, and cannot be confused with the Church. The Apostles are likewise sent according to the very pattern of Christ's authority. As icons of Christ's salvific authority, the Apostles have a sacramental function. As Christ's representatives, they reveal sacramentally to the Church the love of the Father revealed by Christ. Authority and sacrifice are joined together. He is the Good Shepherd who will lay down His life for the sheep. This authority of the Shepherd is entrusted to the Apostles and their successors. The salvific authority of Christ, which they hold is an authority bound to their empowerment to offer the sacrifice of Christ that is the very cause of the Church, His body. Their authority is Eucharistic and the Eucharist is the celebration of the maritally ordered covenant between God and His people. Christ speaks of His leadership as that of the Good Shepherd who gives His life. Understood within the entire context of God's revelation to His people, this is the sacrifice of the bridegroom who espouses the Church in the shedding of His blood. For this reason the authority of Christ the Shepherd and thus priestly authority present in the Apostles and their successors is fundamentally male in character. It is male in character because this authority, rooted in the covenant between God and His people, reveals the Fatherhood of God and Christ as bridegroom of the Church.

As we pointed out in the beginning of chapter 2, the document *Inter Insigniores* teaches that the covenant between God and His people, even within the Old Testament, took on the "privileged form of a nuptial mystery."[35] The apostasy of the Jews in the Old Testament is repeatedly decried by the prophets as adultery because God has espoused Israel to Himself. The marital covenant between God and His people is further illustrated in the Book of Hosea.

> So I will allure her; I will lead her into the desert and speak to her heart. . . . On that day, says the Lord, she shall call me "my husband," and never again "my Baal."
>
> I will espouse you to me forever: I will espouse you in right and in justice, in love and in mercy. I will espouse you in fidelity, and you shall know the Lord. . . .
>
> Again the Lord said to me: Give your love to a woman beloved of a paramour, an adulteress; Even as the Lord loves the people of Israel though they turn to other gods and are fond of raisin cakes. (Hos. 2:16,18, 21–22, 3:1)

This nuptial mystery is fully consummated with the death of Christ. Christ is husband to the Church, the head, the New Adam. Marriage provides the model whereby Christ's saving mystery is revealed and understood. Christ's authority as head bound to His sacrifice is entrusted to St. Peter as recorded in John 21.

> Jesus came over, took bread and gave it to them, and did the same with the fish. . . .When they had eaten their meal, Jesus said to Simon Peter, "Simon, son of John, do you love me more than these?" "Yes, Lord," he said, "you know that I love you." At which Jesus said, "Feed my lambs."
>
> A second time he put the question, "Simon, son of John, do you love me?" "Yes, Lord," Peter said, "you know that I love you." Jesus replied, "Tend my sheep."
>
> A third time Jesus asked him, "Simon, son of John, do you love me?" Peter was hurt because he had asked a third time, "Do you love me?" So he said to him: "Lord, you know everything. You know well that I love you." Jesus said to him, "Feed my sheep." (John 21:13–17)

"Feed my lambs, tend my sheep, feed my sheep." As we saw in John 10, the authority of Christ over the Church is that of shepherd. It is specifically this authority of shepherding the flock that Christ passes on to Peter and to the other Apostles.

Christ's entrusting His authority to Peter is overlaid with Eucharistic significance. Jesus "took bread and gave it to them, and did the same with the fish" (John 21:13). This verse is a reminder of Christ's multiplication of the loaves and fishes in John 6, which is the introductory event to His discourse on the Bread of Life. The authority given to Peter is to feed the sheep of Christ—to give the sheep the food of eternal life. Christ proclaimed the meaning of such food in the Eucharistic discourse following the feeding of the five thousand in John 6.

> I myself am the Living Bread come down from heaven. If anyone eats this bread he shall live forever; and the bread I will give is my flesh for the life of the world. (John 6:51)

Here we have arrived at an apex in our argument. The Apostles are commissioned by Christ to carry on His authority—to be shepherds.[36] But this authority is none other than to feed the Church the Bread of Life as they stand in His place as shepherds. Christ's authority is bound to His sacrifice (John 10:15, 17), and the sacrifice is the giving up of His own body which is the cause of the Church. The Apostles are commissioned by Christ to offer this sacrifice, Eucharistically, sacramentally, whereby in the one act of true worship Christ and His people are constituted one flesh.

The source of hierarchical priestly authority is found at the institution of the Eucharist by Christ at the Last Supper.

> At the Last Supper on the night he was betrayed, our Savior instituted the eucharistic sacrifice of His Body and Blood. This he did in order to perpetuate the sacrifice of the Cross throughout the ages until he should come again, and so to entrust to his beloved Spouse, the Church, a memorial of His death and resurrection: a sacrament of love, a sign of unity, a bond of charity, a paschal banquet in which Christ is consumed, the mind is filled with grace, and a pledge of future glory is given to us.[37]

The institution of the Eucharist is recorded in all three of the Synoptic Gospels. The Gospel According to St. Luke provides the following account:

> When the hour arrived he took his place at table, and the apostles with him. He said to them: "I have greatly desired to eat this Passover with you before I suffer. I tell you, I will not eat again until it is fulfilled in the Kingdom of God."
>
> Then taking a cup he offered a blessing in thanks and said: "Take this and divide it among you; I tell you from now on I will not drink of the fruit of the vine until the coming of the reign of God."
>
> Then, taking bread and giving thanks, he broke it and gave it to them, saying: "This is my body to be given for you. Do this as a remembrance of me."
>
> He did the same with the cup after eating, saying as he did so: "This cup is the new covenant in my blood, which will be shed for you." (Luke 22:14–20)

According to Catholic sacramental doctrine, Eucharistic worship founded by Christ at the Last Supper is nothing less than the a true re-presentation of His sacrifice upon the Cross through which the New Covenant between Himself and the Church is established.[38] Christ willed "to perpetuate the sacrifice of the Cross throughout the ages." The authority of the priesthood is grounded in the will of Christ that through the Eucharist, his sacrifice, which is the cause of the Church, be perpetuated. The Eucharistic sacrifice and male ecclesial authority were instituted on the same night.[39] The authority of the priesthood resides in a sacramental power to effect the sacrifice of Christ which is entirely linked to His being head and shepherd. The encyclical *Mysterium Fidei* of Pope Paul VI teaches that the Eucharistic sacrifice and the institution of the priesthood are inherently connected.

> For, as the Evangelists narrate, at the Last Supper "He took bread and blessed

it and broke it, and gave it to them, saying: This is My Body, given for you; do this for commemoration of Me. And so with the cup, when supper was ended. This cup he said, is the New Testament, in My Blood which is to be shed for you." *And by bidding the Apostles to do this in memory of Him, He made clear His will that the same sacrifice be forever repeated.* (Emphasis added.)[40]

The words of Christ to the Apostles: "Do this in memory of me" constitute a sacramental commission. The Council of Trent affirms the teaching that when Christ instituted the Eucharistic sacrifice of His Body and Blood, he constituted the Apostles priests of the New Testament "commanding them and their successors in the priesthood to make the same offering."[41] The essence of Christ's headship is that He is the source of the Church's life and being through His death on the Cross. Priestly male authority is to stand in the place of Christ the head and shepherd. The power they have to perpetuate the sacrifice of the Cross is given to them by Christ. It is Christ's power.

THE AUTHORITY OF PRIESTS

Priestly authority is to engender the life of God within the Church and thus within the world. It is an authority that reveals the Father because priests represent Christ, who revealed the love of the Father through His sacrifice. The Vatican II decree on the pastoral office of bishops states:

Having been sent by the Father, he in turn sent his Apostles whom he sanctified by conferring on them the Holy Spirit so that they also might glorify the Father on earth and procure the salvation of men "for the building up of the body of Christ" (Eph. 4:12) which is the Church.[42]

The "building up of the body" is precisely the role of the head performed in His capacity as the New Adam. The Apostles and their successors have been entrusted with participation in Christ's headship. The Apostles are sent to carry on the salvific work of Christ, which is the work of the head to the body.[43] The divine mission entrusted to the Apostles by Christ was willed by Him to "last until the end of the world" (cf. Matt. 28:20). Therefore *Lumen Gentium* teaches that the Apostles, according to the will of Christ, appointed successors, namely bishops.

Amongst those various offices which have been exercised in the Church from the earliest times the chief place, according to the witness of tradition, is held by the function of those who, through their appointment to the dignity and responsibility of bishop, and in virtue consequently of the unbroken succession, going back to the beginning, are regarded as transmitters of the apostolic line. . . .In the person of the bishops, then to whom the priests render assistance, the Lord Jesus Christ, supreme high priest, is present in the midst of the faithful.[44]

The document goes on to explain that the authority of bishops and priests is sacramental. They share in Christ's consecration and mission. Priests by the sacrament of Orders are "after the image of Christ, the supreme and eternal priest" (Heb. 5:1–10, 7:24, 9:11–28).[45] A priest's authority is of a particular kind. His authority is grounded in a sacramental manifestation of Christ as priest, Christ as head, Christ as shepherd—meaning Christ as cause of the Church by His sacrifice. Priests are life-givers to the Body of Christ by sacramentally extending Christ's salvific work. Because they share in the headship of Christ, it is in the celebration of the Eucharist:

> . . . that they exercise in a supreme degree their sacred functions; there, acting in the person of Christ, and proclaiming his mystery, they unite the votive offerings of the faithful to the sacrifice of Christ their head, and in the sacrifice of the Mass they make present again and apply, until the coming of the Lord (cf. 1 Cor. 11:26), the unique sacrifice of the New Testament, that namely of Christ offering himself once for all a spotless victim to the Father (cf. Heb. 9:11–28).[46]

The priest's participation in the headship of Christ exists for the sake of worship—namely the Eucharist wherein the Church celebrates her union with Christ, a union caused by the head having given Himself up for her (Eph. 5:25). Priests sacramentally effect the personal, unique love of Christ—the love that is His own, the love of the bridegroom. De Lubac, quoting St. Cyril of Alexandria, expresses the marital nature of redemption made present in the Eucharist:

> "The participation of the Body and Blood of Christ effects nothing short of this, that we pass over unto that which we receive." The head and the members make one single body; the Bridegroom and the Bride are "one flesh." There are not two Christs, one personal and the other "mystical". *And there is certainly no confusion of Head with members; Christians are not the "physical" (or eucharistic) body of Christ, and the Bride is not the Bridegroom.* All the distinctions are there, but they do not add up to discontinuity; the Church is not just *a* body, but *the* body of Christ; man must not separate what God has united—therefore "let him not separate the Church from the Lord." (Emphasis added.)[47]

The marital structure of the Eucharist preserves what is unique in male and female responsibility. This responsibility is from the beginning of creation in which the man (Adam) is the source of Eve, and she confers on him his identity and purpose and is rendered mother of all the living. The worship of the Church is constituted by a marital/covenantal freedom and responsibility.

> This worship, centered on the eucharistic sacrifice, the *Christus totus* has therefore the structured, the qualified freedom, of the marital relation inherent in the New Covenant, in which the sacrifice offered *in persona Christi* by the priest is not competitive with the Church's sacrifice of praise, *but is creative of it, and qualitatively distinct from it.* Any ecclesiology which cannot accept this "model" of freedom in the Church has substituted an abstraction for the reality. (Emphasis added.)[48]

Vatican II is clear on the nature of the priesthood. The priesthood exists according to the authority and mission of Christ to offer sacrifice and to forgive sin.[49] By this authority Christ Himself "builds up, sanctifies and rules his Body."[50] Vatican II speaks of the "special character" conferred through the Sacrament of Ordination by which men are "configured to Christ the priest in such a way that they are able to act in the person of Christ the head."[51]

To act in the person of Christ the head is to stand in His place as *source* of the Church by offering His sacrifice. The offer of Christ's sacrifice is the salvific responsibility of the priesthood. Through the Eucharistic ministry of priests, the whole assembly of the Church is offered to God through Christ, the high priest who offered up Himself "that we might be the body of so great a head."[52]

Redemption springs from the truth that the righteous act of Christ (Rom. 5:18) *is His own.* Thus only Christ could commission His Apostles to "Do this in memory of me." The Apostles have received a real authority. Benoit explains they would never have dared to repeat Christ's action unless they had received authority from Christ to do so. The Last Supper is not a mere commemoration for a departed friend "but the renewal of a sacred action, by which the sacrifice of the Master, still living, was made present under the appearance of bread and wine."[53] Because the sacrifice *is Christ's own action*, it can only be offered *in persona Christi* "for in no other *persona* can the sacrifice be offered." Priests acting *in persona Christi* confirm the goodness of creation in that they sacramentally stand in the place of the New Adam to the New Eve. Here the meaning of masculinity and femininity knows its value, knows its goodness because it knows its differentiated responsibility in effecting the New Covenant. The society of Christ and the Church is marital, and it is at one with the Eucharistic sacrifice:

... in which the Bridegroom gives Himself totally to and for his bridal Church in the freedom of his mission from the Father, and receives from his immaculate Bride that which is indispensable to the New Covenant, all that she, in her created and covenantal and immaculately free dignity, has to give: the nuptial Body of which he, by her self-giving, her "sacrifice of praise," is the nuptial Head.[54]

The order of redemption is maritally structured, and it is this covenant of the One Flesh that is celebrated in the Eucharist by which the Church herself exists in true worship with her head. The very validity of this worship is attacked if a woman were to stand *in persona Christi*—not simply because Christ is a man—but rather because masculinity and femininity are the symbols by which the New Covenant lives—by which its truth is expressed. A female priesthood attacks the order of salvation, and thus any Eucharist offered by a woman would be invalid by its very nature because the marital symbols by which the New Covenant lives are themselves violated. Thus the internal truth of the covenant is not expressed. Some other reality is expressed, but not the Good Creation known by the One Flesh of Christ and His Church. A woman standing in the place of the head offering His sacrifice does not express the covenant because the covenant exists according to masculine and feminine responsibility for redemption. The issue here is not simply that a "woman priest" takes on an authority she does not possess—rather a female priesthood robs women of their own particular authority without which the covenant could not exist.

John Paul II draws together the relation between Eucharistic worship and male/female responsibility.

Since Christ in instituting the eucharist linked it in an explicit way to the priestly service of the apostles, it is legitimate to conclude that he thereby wished to express the relationship between man and woman, between what is "feminine" and what is "masculine." It is a relationship willed by God both in the mystery of creation and in the mystery of redemption. It is the eucharist above all that expresses the redemptive act of Christ, the bridegroom, toward the church, the bride. This is clear and unambiguous when the sacramental ministry of the eucharist, in which the priest acts *in persona Christi* is performed by a man. This explanation confirms the teaching of the declaration *Inter Insigniores*.[55]

THEOLOGY IN FAVOR OF WOMEN'S ORDINATION

If the marital order of the Eucharist is essential for the authentic liturgical expression of the New Covenant, then what is the underlying foundation of the theology that favors the ordination of women? The ordination of women is the fruit of a revisionist ecclesiology that leads to a revisionist notion of the priesthood and the Eucharist. This "new" approach was given sophisticated articulation by Edward J. Kilmartin, S.J., in his 1975 article "Apostolic Office: Sacrament of Christ."[56] The article did not directly treat the issue of a female priesthood. It provided the necessary theological basis upon which a female priesthood must rely. To say the least, in order for women to be "ordained" the very nature of the Catholic priesthood is entirely redefined. Kilmartin attacks the doctrine that the priesthood directly represents Christ the Head for the purposes of offering His sacrifice because he cannot accept that the priest's power to effect the Eucharist *in persona Christi* is a power distinct from the Church's faith. Apparently Kilmartin is trying to account for sacramental efficacy. If the Eucharist is the sacrifice of the whole Church, as the encyclical *Mediator Dei* affirms, then it is the Church's faith that causes this sacrament. The priest represents directly the faith of the Church and only secondarily does he serve as a transparency for Christ.[57] How is Christ present in the Church? Not by the Eucharist effected *ex opere operato* by a man who directly participates in the priesthood of Christ. Rather, Christ is present through the faith of of the Church.[58] According to Kilmartin, the priesthood is not the result of an apostolic succession in which authority was entrusted to the Apostles and then to bishops who carry on sacramentally the salvific work of Christ the head. Instead, those chosen to preside over the Eucharist receive the Holy Spirit bestowed by the community as it is a gift of the entire community.[59] The issue finally comes down to how Christ is personally present in the world and in the Church. Kilmartin's answer is that the Lord is not personally present except by faith.

> Without the exercise of faith no sacramental presence of Christ or the *passio Christi* is possible . . . and this means . . . that no word of God can be preached in the Church which is not derived from the exercise of faith in the Church.
>
> These considerations are germane to the question of the representative role of apostolic office. They point to the conclusion *that office directly represents the faith of the Church and only to this extent can represent Christ.* (Emphasis added.)[60]

Kilmartin goes on to say: "Because the office bearer represents the Church united in faith and love in his role as leader, he represents Christ."[61] According to Kilmartin, the Apostles were never commissioned to carry on Christ's salvific work at all. Apostolic authority has been reduced to the original faith experience of the Apostles regarding Christ's resurrection. It is this faith experience that is "represented" by apostolic authority.[62] Church leaders "objectify" to the Church her own faith or what Kilmartin calls "the common matter of the faith of the Church."[63] The Church's ministers are not *in persona Christi*, they are *in persona ecclesiae*. Essentially, Christ as the head of the Church is absent from history.[64]

> The radical consequence of [Kilmartin's] theology is that the Church is not caused by the sacramental historical event of Christ's sacrificial relation to the Church in and by which he is sacramentally present as at once priest and sacrifice. Rather, the Church is caused, created, by the presence of the Spirit sent by the risen Christ, who is "not here." The ontological Eucharistic presence is identified with faith.[65]

Because the minister represents, not Christ, but the faith of the Church, Kilmartin concludes logically that "the representative role of priest seems to demand both male and female office bearers in the proper cultural context: for the priest represents the one Church in which distinctions of race, class and sex have been transcended, where all are measured by the one norm: faith in Christ."[66] Instead of affirming the goodness and sacramental value of male and female sexuality, Kilmartin's theology makes Christianity mean virtually the leaving of one's body behind or at least, makes of the Church's central worship a reversion to an ancient pagan pessimisim in which the body is utterly insignificant to salvation.[67] Essentially, we are thrust into a nonhistorical Church, and also a nonhistorical salvation. The head/body relation by which the revelation is constituted has no intrinsic significance which might be uttered effectively in history.[68] Marriage is no longer the sign of the covenant, for the covenant can have no sign.

> As Kilmartin observes, his ecclesiology requires that the one Church "transcend all masculine-feminine distinction." Once the sacrifice of the Mass is dismissed by the reduction of the presence of Christ in the Church to a presence by faith, *all concrete qualification of historical human existence loses religious value* because every such qualification stands in contradiction to the ineffable *Una Sancta,* the Church which has no immanence in the historical humanity it utterly transcends: absent the Head, absent also the Body. The antihistorical cosmic salvation is restored, again androgynous, the nullification rather than the fulfillment of creation in the image of God. (Emphasis added.)[69]

At this point we can ask, if the priesthood does not directly represent Christ the head, what then does one make of Christ's masculinity—a male body that He bears even now in His resurrected-ascended state? Even St. Augustine, for all his Neoplatonism, affirmed that the human person will rise from the dead male or female. However, if the Church transcends sex, Christ's incarnation as a (male) has no meaning. His sex certainly does not speak a truth about His love. All one might say is that Christ's body shows that He chose to be one with the human condition—that He has radically and forever identified with man's lot. His body is a sign of His love. If God were to personally enter the world, He had to do so as one sex or another. He chose to be male because the historical circumstances demanded it.

However, Christ's Incarnation is not simply a sign of His love. God is not simply identifying with man. The Incarnation of God as a male means that He has forever identified with the created order of man and woman. It is this created order St. Paul declared, as a climax to all the Old Testament witness, to be the mystery of Christ's love for the Church. What is restored by the salvific work of Christ is creation maritally structured. This is what the Incarnation affirms—not merely mankind or *sarx* but the One Flesh that speaks the love of God and the world. The question we must answer is: How are women responsible for the One-Flesh order of redemption?

When Kilmartin says that priests represent the faith of the Church, we have entered into an antisacramental theology—a theology that does not understand the nature of sacraments or of the Church. We shall see in the chapters to come, which deal specifically with feminine authority, that to say the office bearer represents the faith of the Church is to say that the Church herself is not a reality that speaks herself. If she is really the Body of Christ, she is the expression of herself—particularly in the Eucharist. To say someone represents her or her faith is redundant and superfluous.

Ralph Kiefer begins where Kilmartin left off. He, too, justifies woman's ordination by stating that the priest represents the Church and acts as priest "only because he speaks in the name of the Church."[70] Woman's ordination is radically dependent upon a "theology from below." The priest does not act in the name of the Church because he is ordained but because he functionally "signs" the Church praying before God.[71]

Haye Van der Meer wrote one of the most comprehensive studies in favor of women's ordination. His work, first published in 1969, was one of the first to argue that the Church's ban on women priests was purely the result of historical conditioning.[72] Van der Meer's work leaves no doubt that justification for the ordination of women is built upon a denigration of the body flowing straight out of Gnosticism and Platonism. For example, Van der Meer gives his approval of St. Jerome's idea that a woman must shed (or at least go beyond) motherhood in order to be equal with men. In other words, Van der Meer seizes what is in fact a theologically faulty point of view in the Fathers in order to prop up an argument for women's ordination. Van der Meer interprets Jerome as saying that motherhood is not the defining characteristic of the female according to the spirit, and

Van der Meer then pushes the point. However, coming out of Platonism, the Fathers believed that a woman's spiritual value is noncorporeal. Only a man's body has spiritual value. We should be very leery of using the Platonic philosophy of the Fathers to say that they should have, after all, concluded women can be priests because the body is simply not important. Van der Meer places sexuality on the same level as being a slave, a Jew, or a Gentile. He reads Gal. 3:28 as rendering male and female sexuality completely insignificant to salvation. Van der Meer actually adopts the faulty thinking of the Fathers at this point.

> . . . when it is said that a Gentile can be a priest, it is true only because baptized Gentiles are the "new Israel according to the Spirit." *But is not the believing woman in the same way a man?* . . . if being a Gentile no longer matters for the question of whether someone can be a priest because the Gentiles are the new Israel, then also being a woman does not matter, because in Christ every woman is elevated to the masculine level.[73]

This thought does not represent the mind of St. Paul. In Gal. 3:28 St. Paul never meant to erase male and female sexuality as such. The issue for St. Paul is how baptism is the cause of unity. The letters of St. Paul, particularly Romans, demonstrate how conscious he was of religious division caused by the Old Law as opposed to the New Law of faith in Christ. The Jew/Gentile division represents the greatest social/spiritual enmity of a world divided. To know Christ is to bring an end to such division by being baptized into the one Body: "There is but one body and one spirit . . . there is one Lord, one faith, one baptism" (Eph. 4:4–5). I Cor. 12:13 teaches the same theme: "It was in one Spirit that all of us, whether Jew or Greek, slave or free, were baptized into one body." Gal. 3:28 should be interpreted by a hermeneutical method that applies the theology of St. Paul regarding baptism and unity. Hauke has rightly commented:

> . . . the Spirit of God does not do away with differences but makes possible their fruitful development. Galatians 3:28 does not, therefore, speak simply of "being equal" but rather of "being one" (εἷς ἐστε ἐν Χριστῷ ᾽Ιησοῦ) on the basis of a common Christian piety within the Holy Spirit.[74]

It is very important to keep in mind that the split between Jew and Gentile and the state of slavery are the result of the Fall. These conditions are the sign of sin in the world. Male and female sexuality is created by God in the beginning and is called "good." St. Paul knew this very well, and, therefore, in several places throughout his epistles, nuptial symbolism serves as the expression of the Christian's unity with Christ. This leads to the conclusion that Gal. 3:28 does not claim difference is insignificant, but rather that it is certainly no barrier to oneness or unity in Christ. And in the case of man and woman their "one flesh" is the very sign of redemption in the world—namely the unity between Christ and the Church.

Van der Meer puts forth a sacramental argument for women's ordination by failing to understand the reality that is signed by the male body in relation to Christ. He states that Christ has received life from the Father (the Father alone having nonreceived life) and quotes several Johannine texts to this effect. What Jesus passes on to priests is the life He has received.

> And what is true of the priest? He does not hand on nonreceived life, but he can act only insofar as he himself is empowered to do so. Once one begins to think in this direction, one can hardly avoid seeing here a parallel to woman instead of to man![75]

Since a woman receives from the man in order to conceive, Van der Meer can "discover no argument here for the male character of the priest." After all, a woman's receptive nature images Christ receiving life from the Father and thus her womanhood can serve as image of Christ breathing the Holy Spirit.[76]

Van der Meer has seized on one aspect of the Son—that He has received life from the Father—to justify females standing in the place of Christ. However, Christ has received a certain power, that of the Father who is unbegotten. Christ is the Word of God. If He has received anything, it is to serve as the very expression of what He has received. Christ reveals the Father as creator and as Son He has shared in the Father's creative action: "Through Him all things came into being and apart from Him nothing came to be" (John 1:3). The Son participates in and reveals the creative authority of the Father. He was sent for this reason in a way Mary was not sent. In turn, Christ sent the Apostles who received His authority. Yes, a priest does impart divine life of which he is not the source, but he does so by standing as the proper symbol of the Source whose life is not imparted: Christ's life may be imparted (as He is begotten) but He is icon of the Father (the nonimparted) and the priest is a sign of the Father because he stands *in persona Christi*. Van der Meer fails to appreciate what Jesus represents. He does not represent Himself (the Begotten) but the power and love of the Father toward and in relation to the world.

Male sexuality is the inherent symbol of this type of life-giving relation. This will become clear in the next pages. Suffice it for now to state that Christ is the begotten imaging the unbegotten, or as Aquinas would say, the Father as *principle* of the Son. It is this imaging of the Unbegotten Source of Life (the Father) by Christ (because He and the Father are one) that is also imaged by the male priesthood. That Christ has received His life and is sent demonstrates not that sexual difference is sacramentally insignificant but that subordination and ordering are not signs of injustice and inequality, but of difference.

IV. The Fatherhood of Bishops and Priests

St. Paul teaches that fatherhood is nothing less than a participation in the Fatherhood of God: "For this reason I bend my knees to the Father of our Lord Jesus Christ, from whom all fatherhood in heaven and on earth takes its name" (Τούτου χάριν κάμπτω τὰ γόνατά μου πρὸς τὸν πατέρα ἐξ οὗ πᾶσα πατριὰ . . . ὀνομάζεται) Eph. 3:14–15. Human fatherhood is patterned after the fatherhood of God, and, therefore, male sexuality discloses a truth about God in relation to the Church and the world. God the Father is the begetter of the Son and through the Son, source of all life. We have seen that Christ was sent by the Father to reveal the Father (John 14:7, 9–11). The Apostles likewise are sent (John 20:21). Because they stand in the place of Christ, they exercise a fatherhood to the Church's faithful that reveals the paternal nature of God's love as He exists as *source*. St. John Chrysostom teaches that a priest's authority is not His own—but is an authority received from a divine source.

> For indeed what is it but all manner of heavenly authority which he has given them when He says "Whose sins ye remit they are remitted and whose sins ye retain they are retained?" What authority could be greater than this? "The Father hath committed all judgment to the Son?" But I see it all put into the hands of these men by the Son.[77]

Priestly power is that of dispensing the sacraments. In other words, priests are an *arché* of divine grace. By their dispensing of the sacraments, we become members of the head.[78] For this reason priests are to be honored more than natural parents because they are "authors of our birth from God."[79] St. Paul understood his apostolic ministry as that of spiritual fatherhood.

> I am writing you in this way not to shame you but to admonish you as my beloved children. Granted you have ten thousand guardians in Christ, but you have only one father. It was I who begot you in Christ Jesus through my preaching of the gospel. (1 Cor. 4:14–15)

The fatherhood of the apostle is a participation in the fatherhood of God because it is a fatherhood in Christ. The paternal authority of the priest is derivative as male sexuality serves as a transparency of what is other than itself. If there is a grandeur in the hierarchical ministry, this grandeur is a reference to the mystery of Christ who represents the Father. God is the permanent source of a priest's fatherhood. But, as de Lubac notes, "This fatherhood of our pastors is nonetheless real, since it derives precisely from the one divine Fatherhood."[80]

The fatherhood of the priest involves actions sacramentally expressed by male sexuality: the gathering of the people of God and the engendering of the people of God. This gathering and engendering occurs most definitively through the priest's Eucharistic ministry.

The Second Vatican Council frequently spoke of bishops as shepherds of their people as they hold the authority of the Apostles.

> . . . with priests and deacons as helpers, the bishops received the charge of the community, presiding in God's stead over the flock of which they are the shepherds in that they are teachers of doctrine, ministers of sacred worship and holders of office in government. *Moreover, just as the office which the Lord confided to Peter alone, as first of the apostles, destined to be transmitted to his successors, is a permanent one, so also endures the office, which the apostles received, of shepherding the Church* a charge destined to be exercised without interruption by the sacred order of bishops. The sacred synod consequently teaches that the bishops have by divine institution *taken the place of the apostles as pastors of the Church, in such wise that whoever listens to them is listening to Christ and whoever despises them despises Christ and him who sent Christ* (cf. Lk. 10:16). (Emphasis added.)[81]

Lumen Gentium teaches that bishops are sent by the Father according to the pattern of the Good Shepherd.[82] Bishops are shepherds in the image of Christ the high priest. The passage calls Christ himself "shepherd and bishop of our souls."[83] According to Vatican II the bishop is both a father and a shepherd to his flock. Indeed, it seems the role of father and shepherd belong together and form the means by which apostolic authority is exercised and expressed.

> In exercising his office of father and pastor the bishop should be with his people as one who serves, as a good shepherd who knows his sheep and whose sheep know him, as a true father who excels in his love and solicitude for all, to whose divinely conferred authority all readily submit. He should so unite and mold his flock into one family, that all conscious of their duties, may live and act in the communion of charity.[84]

The bishop's fatherhood is rooted in his divinely conferred authority. He is to "unite" and to "mold" those over whom he has authority "into one family." In this way he is their *source* because he is their head. The authority he holds is not his own, nor does it come from the community of the faithful as Kilmartin and Van der Meer teach. The authority is Christ's, and He has entrusted it to the Twelve He chose to be the foundation upon which the New Israel stands.[85] The authority of the bishops is at the service of the Word and sacraments, and this is the meaning of ecclesial government. A bishop's authority is paternal. He is head because he is father.[86]

The governing function of the apostles, bishops, and priests is the result of their being at the service of the Word and sacraments. Their fatherhood exists in this: the ability to bestow the divine life of God. As Vatican II teaches, a bishop is head of his flock because bishops

> ... are the principal dispensers of the mysteries of God, and it is their function to promote and protect the entire liturgical life of the Church entrusted to them. They should therefore see to it that the faithful know and live the paschal mystery more deeply through the Eucharist, forming one closely-knit body, united by the charity of Christ; devoting themselves to prayer and the ministry of the word (Acts 6:4).[87]

The authority of the Apostles (and bishops) was described by St. Paul when he said: "Men should regard us as servants of Christ and administrators of the mysteries of God" (1 Cor. 4:1). Because their authority is *in persona Christi*, the bishops of the Church stand as cause of the "closely knit body," cause of the "one family." Their authority is entirely bound to their sacramental function as "administrators of the mysteries of God." The fatherhood of the priest derives from his standing *in persona Christi*. The Vatican II document *Presbyterorum Ordinis (On the Ministry and Life of Priests)* teaches that a priest's mission is in the service of the kingdom "and the task of heavenly regeneration." For this reason celibacy makes them "better fitted for a broader acceptance of fatherhood in Christ"[88] Archbishop Stafford in his pastoral letter "The Mystery of the Priestly Vocation" explained that Christ and his priests exercise a fatherhood.

> Since Christ himself was unmarried, we may find it strange at first that the council speaks of fatherhood in Christ. Yet the hymn "Summi Parentis Filio" speaks of Christ as the father of the world to come. If we bear in mind what St. Paul teaches us about the spousal love of Christ for his church (see Eph. 5:22–33), we will see that this world to come is nothing less than the child of that union, the fruit of that love. ...
>
> The priest, in union with Christ, takes the church for his spouse, to cherish

and to nurture. And from that union a true spiritual fatherhood ensues. It is not for nothing that the priest is addressed as "Father" by his people. As with the fatherhood of Christ, that of the priest points to the world to come.[89]

As we stated above, the shepherding and fathering roles exist together. The Old Testament already defined these roles as gathering a people together—causing the existence of a people, scattered and disunited (Jer. 31:10f). On priestly authority Vatican II teaches: "Exercising within the limits of the authority which is theirs, the office of Christ, the Shepherd and Head, they assemble the family of God as a brotherhood fired with a single ideal, and through Christ in the Spirit they lead it to God the Father."[90] *Presbyterorum Ordinis* also defines a priest's authority in terms of gathering a people: "Priests exercise the function of Christ as Pastor and Head in proportion to their share of authority. In the name of the bishop they gather the family of God as a brotherhood endowed with the spirit of unity and lead it in Christ through the Spirit to God the Father."[91]

Priests are true fathers because as they stand *in persona Christi* they are the means by which the divine life of grace is begotten among men. Because they participate in the fatherhood of God, they are a principle of regeneration. This regeneration is *to beget* life by dispensing the mysteries of God. Scripture often speaks of the new life of the Christian as being *begotten* whereby human beings are made the adopted children of God. Thomas E. D. Hennessy, O.P., wrote one of the few articles dealing directly with the fatherhood of priests. On the subject of God and regeneration he states that God is a father to human beings because he is the principle of supernatural life, the life of grace. There is a true generation of which natural fatherhood is the image. God's fatherhood brings true new life. By being conceived of God the person even participates in God's own nature. Thus we can say that human beings become the adopted children of God.[92]

I Pet. 1:3 teaches that the new life of the Christian has its source in God the Father.

> Praised be the God and Father of our Lord Jesus Christ, he who in his great mercy regenerated us (ἀναγεννήσας) unto hope which draws its life from the resurrection of Jesus Christ from the dead.

Christ, begotten by the Father, communicates, reveals, bestows the life of the Father. In baptism, the Father through Christ causes us to become His children.

> I solemnly assure you. No one can see the reign of God unless he is begotten (γεννηθῇ) from above. . . . I solemnly assure you, no one can enter into God's

kingdom without being begotten of water and Spirit. Flesh begets flesh, spirit begets spirit. Do not be surprised that I tell you you must all be begotten from above. (John 3:3–7).

The above word γεννηθῇ is rightly translated "begotten." It is true, as Raymond E. Brown explains, that:

> . . . the passive of the verb *gennan* can be either "to be born," as of a feminine principle, or "to be begotten," as of a masculine principle. . . . Despite the fact that the Spirit, mentioned in vs. 5 as the agent of this birth in begetting, is feminine in Hebrew (neuter in Greek), the primary meaning seems to be "begotten." In the Gospels there is no attribution of feminine characteristics to the Spirit and there are Johannine parallels that clearly refer to being begotten rather than being born (1:12; 1 John iii 9).[93]

The Christian is begotten of the Father after the fashion of the Son's having been begotten of the Father (and not born from the Father). The New Testament speaks of Christ as being the "only begotten of the Father" (John 1:14; 3:16, 18; Acts 13:33; Heb. 1:5; 5:5; 11:17). In 1 John 3:9 the adopted children of the Father achieve this status by also having been begotten: "No one begotten of God acts sinfully because he remains of God's stock; he cannot sin because he is begotten of God."

Other New Testament passages speak of the Christian as having been "regenerated" ἀναγεννήσας) as in 1 Pet. 1:3. In Titus. 3:5 this παλιγγεν-εσίας is specifically linked to baptism. This regeneration is the work of Christ, by it Christ functions as a true father. In baptism a generation occurs that produces a new living being (2 Cor. 5:17; Gal. 6:15). There is a communication of the same nature as the human being in baptism becomes a partaker in the divine nature of Christ (2 Pet. 1:4). The baptized person proceeds from Christ as from a conjoined principle. Thus Christ is a real father—human beings by the laver of regeneration become His sons and daughters.[94]

Christ's fatherhood to the individual believer flows from the fact that He is first bridegroom of the whole Church. Christ is not the Father of the Church. He is the Church's husband and not her father. Nonetheless, might it not be possible to say that, flowing from His headship, Christ does exercise, through the sacramental ministry, of which He is the source, a fatherhood to believers? Hennessy points out that Christ is a Father because He is first a priest, the High and Eternal Priest through whom the love of God the Father is communicated to men. Christ is the great high priest who participates in the divine paternity. By His sacrifice He has become the new father of the human race inasmuch as by His Cross He merited for human beings a participation in the divine nature. Christ thus shares in the divine paternity. He has a primary formal claim to supernatural fatherhood.[95]

The authority of the Apostles and derivatively that of bishops and priests is, of course, an authority that comes from sharing in the priesthood and thus the headship of Christ.[96] We saw earlier that the apostles were commissioned to be priests when they were entrusted with the priestly action of Christ to offer His sacrifice Eucharistically.

> Just as Christ is the image of the Father, so the priest is the image of Christ, because by the character of Sacred Orders the priesthood of Christ is impressed upon him, thus making him the minister of grace merited for men by the priestly act of Christ. By this character the priest is invested with divine authority and given the power to act in the very person of Christ. . . . Since, however, the fatherhood of Christ immediately flows from His priesthood, whoever shares in Christ's priesthood, by that very fact, participates in His divine paternity. . . . Thus St. Gregory, St. Jerome, and St. Alphonsus rightly call the priest "Father of Christians." [97]

By now it should be clear that male sexuality is sacramentally symbolic of the authority of the Son who mediates the love of the Father—a love which is causative of life. This priestly authority does not come from the Church—but is the *arché* of the Church's existence. We know both from the order of creation and the order of redemption that male and female sexuality is inherently nuptial. Christ by taking the sexual to Himself has made it forever the means by which the New Covenant is structured.

V. The Male Person as Symbol of God

Before we close this chapter it is important to explore how, according to the order of creation, the male body and sexuality serve as a symbol of God to the world. In other words, it is necessary to understand what there is about masculinity that reveals God that femininity does not. By this investigation we will see that masculinity (as well as femininity) are not arbitrary symbols of the covenant, but by their very nature they speak a truth about God and the world. Hans Urs Von Balthasar explains:

> The redemptive mystery "Christ-Church" is the superabundant fulfilment of the mystery of the Creation between man and woman, as Paul affirms very forcefully, so that the fundamental mystery of Creation is called "great" precisely in view of its fulfilment of the mystery of Redemption. The natural sexual difference is charged *as* difference, with a supernatural emphasis, of which it is not itself aware, so that outside of Christian Revelation it is possible to arrive

at various deformations of this difference such as, for example, a one-sided matriarchite or patriarchite, an underestimation of women or, finally, such a leveling of the sexes as to destroy all the values of sexuality. It is only from the indestructible difference between Christ and the Church (prepared, but not incarnate in the difference between Yahweh and Israel) that there is reflected the decisive light about the real reciprocity between man and woman.[98]

In all of Revelation, both in the Old and the New Covenants, God is the transcendent Other. He is not to be associated or confused with nature or creation. As God-Creator He stands apart from what He has made. He can look at something outside of Himself and call it "very good" (Gen. 1:31). Male sexuality stands as a sign of this type of creative action. To be male means to stand apart, over and against the world. Walter Ong, has provided one of the most insightful works on the meaning of male sexuality in his book *Fighting for Life*.

The adversary relationship with the environment, which has been seen to go back to the biological situation of the male embryo and fetus in the womb, would appear to serve as one basis for the male's tendency to fight. Human males tend to feel an environment, including other individuals of the species, as a kind of againstness, something to be fought with and altered. Environment is feminine, and women typically find they can rely on it as it is or comes to them. The received symbol for woman (Q), adopted by feminists apparently everywhere, signifies self-possession, gazing at oneself as projected into the outside world or environment and reflected back into the self from there, whole. The received symbol for man, Mar's spear (σ), signifies conflict, stress, dissection, division.[99]

What is pervasive in the world is not masculinity, but femininity. Nature, creation, and mother are everywhere. For a man to be a man he must claim his identity as apart from and other than this matrix. Ong states, quite contrary to Aristotelian philosophy, that "nature's primary impulse is to make a female."[100] "A woman is not a castrated male, a deficient man—rather a man is a female to which something has been added."[101] Surgeon James C. Neely provides scientific verification that between men and women the female is dominate and primary.

It is important to pause and realize how firmly based we are in our female nature since there is a predominance of three to one female sex chromosomes between XX woman and XY man. We do not have to study Amazon woman or go back to Nefertiti's matriarchy to establish the primacy of female sexuality. We don't even need the silvery moonlight of alchemy. *It is our natural state.*

We have it and live it everyday within ourselves. Let no one doubt that female is the foundation, the fundamental sex of humankind, for in order to make a male, you simply add a Y to the female configuration. Observed another way, a male is simply a differentiated female—a fact intuited and enjoyed to the hilt by many a poet. (Emphasis added.) [102]

Like God, a man is differentiated from creation. This is why male sexuality points to what is transcendent and beyond—what is other. To be different a man must *show* that he is different. His identity as male is therefore external and active—quantitatively measured. Ong explains that "woman is interiority, self possession." Her sexual organs are hidden and so her body is a mystery.[103] In contrast, a male's sexual organs are external to him. In this sense they are a witness to him—a witness to his power and his difference. As his sexual organs and his actions through them are external the man is directed outward. On the psychic level the male is focused on things outside of himself.[104] We can see how the man in this way is a symbol of God who comes to the world from the "outside." F. J. J. Buytendijk states that the difference of interiority for the woman and exteriority for the man manifests itself not merely in physical differences but on the psychological level as well. Women respond to situations more immediately and spontaneously and find it harder to distance themselves from the way they feel—while men have more distance from their emotions and a greater capacity to to remove themselves from immediate relations.[105] Moreover, there is a difference between male and female methods of cognition. Women tend to become one with the objects they relate to. Nothing is a mere thing—everything is a personal thing. Men, however, tend to know something by distancing themselves from it in order to understand it better so as to subject the objects to be known "to the tools of abstract thought."[106]

The fact that a man must show that he is different has great implications for the meaning of male ecclesial authority. Because his being must be confirmed from the outside, ecclesial authority must be received by him ritualistically—officially. This is why male ecclesial authority is that of public office. For him to be different means that he must stand out from the rest in some easily recognizable official capacity lest he fall back into and be absorbed by the feminine, in this case, the Church herself. Male sexuality is signified by representing what is apart in a confirmation of what it is to be male. Von Balthasar expressed clearly the difference between male and female authority:

While man, as a sexual being, only represents what he is not and transmits what he does not actually possess, and so is . . . at the same time more and less than himself, *woman rests on herself, she is fully what she is, that is, the whole reality of a created being that faces God as a partner, receives his seed and spirit, preserves them, brings them to maturity and educates them. . . .*

Restored nature would bring to light—within the parity of nature and parity of value of the sexes—above all the fundamental difference, according to which woman does not represent, but is, while man has to represent and, therefore, is more and less than what he is. (Emphasis added.)[107]

Ong observes that female authority is not ritualized because a woman has no need to prove herself sexually. Rather it is the man who must prove himself as different from her. A woman, because of her reproductive cycle, is constantly confirmed interiorly that she can give life. The fact that male ecclesial power is conferred externally, ritualistically, is consistent with the difference between male and female sexuality. A woman has no need to "earn" or have her authority conferred.[108] She possesses it in herself because, as Von Balthasar stated, "woman does not represent, but is." Masculinity has to be earned.

Masculinity for human males and . . . even for infrahuman males engenders agonistic activity because it is something to be won, achieved, "always in a state of being earned" . . . not at all simply something one is born with. The genetic determinants of masculinity, notably for human beings, establish not so much a state of being as a program. *A male finds his masculinity in some way outside of himself, especially in higher animal species and most especially among human beings.* (Emphasis added.)[109]

Because a man's identity is external, outside of himself, in some sense against the world, he can represent what he is not. Because his identity does not rest in himself (he is less than and more than what he is) a man is transparent—a symbol, a sign of what is beyond him and outside of him.[110] Priestly power will then be the result of an official public consecration. He will receive a power outside of himself. A woman's authority has no need for such a ritual.

Male sexuality represents God the Father. God is likened to the masculine because he is a source of life that is "other, different, separated (*kadosh* the Hebrew word translated *sanctus, hagios* holy, means at root "separated) from all his creation, even from human beings, though they are 'made in his image and likeness.' "[111]

It is then easy to see how male sexuality is a sign of this truth about God. A man, even if he is the most caring and tender of all fathers, still remains separate, apart from his children. He cannot know them physically, and thus psychically, with the same intimate bond that profoundly characterizes motherhood. First of all, in the act of procreation the male must deposit his life principle away from himself. Whatever effects come from the conjugal act, and particularly the conception of another human being, he is removed from it all. Everything is now the woman's. A man's explicitly sexual role in procreation is over with quickly, while the woman will experience its effects for months to come.[112]

> And so it is to our apparent misfortune that the male is somewhat distant or peripheral (not to say extraneous) to the reproductive process. The man sleeping with a pregnant woman feels the quickening inside her with excitement, but at a distance. His excitement is as much as anything else an excitement for her. The fetal kicks she feels he senses as part of her, even, indeed, as she feels them herself as integral and natural to herself. It is his child all right, but it is his child by proxy, because the child seems to be part of nature and nature is on her side.[113]

This is an essential difference between motherhood and fatherhood. Mothers are inherently *attached* to their children while fathers are physically detached and distant. Because there are no male umbilical cords, human beings do not have a comparable problem separating themselves from fathers. Nor do we have a problem separating ourselves from God.[114]

> We are distanced from God as from a father. We have never been physically and physiologically attached to God, yet Hebreo-Christian teaching insists that he loves us—hence he calls us, his children set off from him, and draws us near to him with love. In this sense, related to the biological sense though not entirely the same, God is male. He is not nature. . . .
>
> Always distinctive of God is that, with all his tenderness and concern and closeness . . . he is always also other, different, separated, as a father physically is, and not by becoming so but by simply being so.[115]

While a man is source of life that is apart and other, he is, nonetheless, the initiator of the procreative act and of conception. In this, male sexuality also images God—who alone actively initiated all of creation. The observation of Aristotle, also taught by Aquinas, that masculinity is active in relation to the female is essentially correct. The attribution of superiority to the active was, however, incorrect.[116] Aquinas defined fatherhood as "the relation of being the source of generation in the highest form of life."[117] Aquinas's notion of procreation was inaccurate in many respects, though consistent with the state of scientific knowledge of his time. The ovum of the woman as equally important in the conception of new human life was unknown as well as the XX and XY chromosomes. For Aquinas the male seed was the cause or organizing principle of the new human being. The woman supplied only the formless blood matter.[118] Inaccurate as Aquinas was about procreation we can say that he was more correct about the meaning of male sexuality than he was about the female. There is truth in his statement that the "relation of being the source of generation . . . is called 'fatherhood.' Fatherhood is to be a source of generation and even the 'active' principle of new life though not the sole principle or the more important."[119] A man is the source of generation and the more active principle of conception on a number of levels concerning masculine sexual behavior. First of all, in the sex act the woman must yield herself to the man and receive him. This surrender of herself is her giving as she allows herself to be penetrated by him. The man takes the initiative but only in response to her presence.[120] The marital act requires the free consent of both the husband and wife. However, in the act the male must truly "perform" in a way the woman does not have to. Ultimately, the accomplishment of the conjugal act will depend on the male's action. If he fails, there will be no act and no conception.

The act of conception itself teaches us something about masculine activity and female passivity. The male sperm must actively seek out the female ovum which waits motionless to be penetrated. The sperms actually compete for entrance. But female sexuality is not merely passive in the negative or inferior sense taught by Aristotle. The ovum preferentially *allows* access to only one sperm. In this there already exists a base for understanding feminine authority.

> Microscopy has shown that a number of sperms may cluster around a ripe egg, but only one is permitted access. And in that moment of access the sex of the zygote, the fertilized egg, is sealed by the addition of a Y or an X to what is already and always will be a firm female substratum.[121]

Male sexuality as active and initiating is a generating principle and stands in this way as an image of God who generates all of creation. The following observation will help us understand in what manner masculinity forms the proper image for God and Christ and in what manner femininity is related to this image.

> Ordained liturgical priesthood is the seedbed of union in, with and through Christ. It is rooted in the generative nature of God. It is from this life-initiating essence [of God] that all life and growth, spiritual *and* material, has its existence. . . .This generative initiative is the essence of masculine being, as germination is the essence of feminine being. . . .
>
> The Eucharist is Christ. It enters us as seed to quicken us, to conceive life

in us, to regenerate us.

Just so man enters woman to initiate life and growth and new being. Just so, the sperm penetrates the ovum to stimulate life and growth and individuation. If the sperm does not enter the ovum, the female cell remains closed upon itself. . . .

Generation is the ikon of God's transcendence. Germination is the ikon of his immanence.[122]

The generative quality of God and the germinative quality of that which He has conceived forms the covenantal structure of God's relationship to His people. It is a structure that is inherently marital. Christ spoke of His death in terms of a seed dying in relation to the earth which consumes it: "Amen, amen, I say to you, unless the grain of wheat falls into the ground and dies, it remains alone. But if it dies, it brings forth much fruit" (John 12:24–25). The death of Christ is essentially generative and marital in its order. In fact we should go so far as to say that His death is an essentially masculine death. It is the death of the man for the woman in which isolation is broken and a covenant formed. By dying the seed no longer remains alone. And it dies by falling into the feminine earth. The seed of the man will be absorbed into the woman, into her own life principle. The man will lose himself by being taken into her. As we stated earlier, femininity is pervasive. A man to be truly a man must declare his difference. A woman knows her power. She is the source of both men and women. She can produce a male who is totally dependent upon her "which is more than any male can do for either a male or a female."[123] A man must show himself worthy of the woman by external proof of his manhood in heroic contest against the world, in what Ong has described as agonistic activity.[124] A man will know his identity by what he achieves external to himself. If he fails in achievement, he cannot be consoled by saying to himself " 'I can still become a mother.' In his own mind his underpinnings are very weak, what he does is lonely and therefore heroic, because it is his daring against a cruel world."[125] A woman rests in herself through the bodily interiority of her own powers. But a man must *become* a man. In the lonely, heroic act of himself against the world the man is finally able to give something to the woman that is uniquely his own; something that she could not give to herself.[126] This is the male sacrifice that Christ fulfilled for His bridal Church. He dies *for her*. Because of this initiatory act neither remains alone. They are one flesh.

It is not an accident that feminist theologians destroy the Eucharist as a sacrifice and even empty the Passion of Christ itself of any sacrificial character. Because there is a connection between Christ's masculinity and His sacrificial act of love, feminists must render both insignificant. As we have seen, Ruether believes Christ's masculinity has no ultimate theological significance,[127] and His life and death (bound as it is by the limitations of history) is only one model of redemption.[128] Therefore, the Eucharist is not the Body and Blood of Christ given for the Church—the Eucharist is the Church, and she is able to give it to herself.[129] For Ruether there is nothing unique about Christ, neither his masculinity nor His sacrifice in relation to the Church. There is no need then for any unique sign to represent Him to mark Him off from the community and creation—namely a male priesthood. The Church, for the sake of feminine authority or power, must completely absorb Christ. And the absorption is effectively accomplished by a demolition of the nuptial order of redemption. Ironically, by absorbing or denying the meaning of Christ's masculinity, the feminine has truly become pervasive. Christ, the male, is born from a female. Christ received His masculinity from a woman. This shows the overwhelming femininity of the Church. By making women "priests," feminism will have fulfilled its goal by feminizing everything in the world. Notice, feminist theology never proposes that the Church be thought of or spoken of as male. The goddess will have conquered all.

VI. Christ and the Saving of Humanity

St. Athanasius stated "what was not assumed was not healed." This statement has proven problematic for many a feminist theologian. How are women saved if Christ's male sex is necessary for salvation? In what way is Christ the savior of women? Ruether's solution is to say Christ is only one model of redeemed humanity. She then proceeds to blame history for the unavailability of a full model: "The fulness of redeemed humanity, as image of God, is something only partially disclosed under the conditions of history. We seek it as a future self and world, still not fully achieved, still not fully revealed."[130] Here is the great flaw of feminist theology. Because Christ is a male He is only one model of redeemed humanity. In Himself He cannot sum up what it is to be redeemed. We must, therefore, cast about for other models (other monist paradigms) which, by the fact that they are monist, will always be partial. By such models we are forced to live in a fragmented world, forced to live in a world where "fulness of redeemed humanity is only partially disclosed." The fragmented partial model is the result of failure to accept that redemption is rooted in a marital covenant between Christ and His Church. There is no alternative model. This is *the* covenant itself.

Christ assumed human nature which both men and women share, but it is a differentiated nature. As one author explains:

If the Word has not assumed the differentiation of humanity as man or woman, then humanity which lives by this differentiation is not wholly re-deemed. But if it is assumed, then it is assumed *qua* differentiation, and it is the concrete essentiality of this differentiation in Christ which is inseparable from His universal mediation.[131]

As stated earlier, redemption rests on the sacramental order of creation. Males and females are not simply redeemed as separate human beings but creation itself is redeemed, which, from the beginning, is maritally ordered. Christ's Incarnation honors the marital difference of the sexes so that what is taken up is not simply human nature-flat and generic—but the nuptial order of the world. Christ's becoming male—born of a woman—did cause the salvation of all humanity because His Incarnation honored the nuptial meaning of human existence. What was not assumed was not healed. Christ's Incarnation as a man affirms an essential truth about humanity—that it is differentiated male or female. What was not assumed was not healed. Christ did assume all humanity as the nuptial order of the world is taken up in the Incarnation. Christ's masculine sexuality, far from being a stumbing block to redemption or insignificant to it, is actually essential if creation, nuptially ordered, is to be taken up and healed by the grace of Christ. The masculinity of Christ in relation to the bridal Church, rather than becoming a soteriological problem, is the very basis upon which His salvific work is effective.

If this is the truth about Christ, then male sexuality is integral to the sacramental worship of the Church by which the grace of the covenant is mediated. Within this covenant the male priesthood is the symbol of Christ the head whereby the mysteries of redemption flowing from the head are dispensed. The apostle, bishop, and priest carry a certain responsibility for the faith wherein is contained their authority in relation to the Church. The masculine sex of their office serves as sign of Christ's unique giving of self which reveals the love of the Father. But this responsibility, essential to the New Covenant, does not exhaust the covenant. This authority operates in relation to the feminine authority of the Church exemplified by Christian women. It is to this authority that we now must turn.

4

The Authority of Mary

I. Mary's "Fiat"—Source of the Incarnation

"Two parents have generated us for death, two parents have generated us for life."[1]

In this statement St. Augustine has bound together the original order of creation and the order of redemption in which both orders are founded upon the life-giving roles of man and woman. In the order of redemption the life of grace is given through the New Covenant created in the union between Christ and Mary—that is, the New Adam and the New Eve. Christ is the head of a New Humanity because He is the New Adam whose death is the foundation of the Church. This *is* His authority because this is how He is the *Source of Life*—the source of the New Creation. But women, too, possess authority insofar as they are source of life which is intrinsically constitutive of the New Creation. Feminine authority is derived from what women have been specifically entrusted with (according to the purpose and meaning of their gender) for the salvation of the world.

> Thus, at the time of the realization of the Redemptive Incarnation, just as at the beginning, man and woman are found face to face, and with very different functions. ... The role of Mary in relation to Christ, is in line with, even while transcending, that which the Creator assigned to Eve in the beginning. Mary, the woman par excellence of the new covenant, appears in the Infancy narratives of Luke and in the Fourth Gospel, first of all, as the one who says "yes" to the divine plan of salvation. Next *she is the mother without whose cooperation, this divine plan could not have been achieved.* (Emphasis added.)[2]

Because human sexuality is bound up with the order of redemption, the

115

Incarnation of Christ via a woman is not an arbitrary choice on the part of God but something that was necessary for the salvation of the world to be realized. It is here that creation grounded in the nuptial order of the First Adam and the First Eve is healed.

1 Cor. 11:11–12 declares an interdependency between the sexes:

> Yet, in the Lord, woman is not independent of man nor man independent of woman. In the same way that woman was made from man, *so man is born of woman;* and all is from God.

Within the order of redemption Christ is dependent on the life-giving power of woman to make Him physically present in history for the accomplishment of salvation. Indeed the only allusion to Mary found in St. Paul's epistles has to do precisely with the fact that Christ, the Savior, is *from her*:

> ...when the designated time had come, God sent forth his Son *born of a woman*, born under the law, to deliver from the law those who were subjected to it, so that we might receive our status as adopted sons. (Gal. 4:4–5)

Most exegetes agree that the statement "born of a woman" is simply St. Paul's way of affirming Christ's solidarity with the human race—namely, those under the law that He has come to save.[3] However, it is not possible to overlook the maternal source of this solidarity and the implications this has for the place of the feminine in the economy of salvation. We can become Sons (heirs) of the Father because Christ entered history through a woman. The primitive credal formula employed by St. Paul "born of a woman" is the forerunner of the credal statement "He for us men and for our salvation, came down from heaven and was incarnated by the Holy Spirit *from* the Virgin Mary."[4] There exists an intimate link between the maternity of Mary as Mother of the Savior and the rebirth of men within the covenant established between the New Adam and the New Eve.

Christ is from Mary due to her "yes," that is, her *"fiat mihi"* as it is recorded in Luke 1:38. Mary's "yes" is not only the beginning of her motherhood. Her "yes" actually effects, is the cause of the New Creation. Mary's effecting of redemption and the era of grace and mercy is often contrasted by the early Fathers with Eve's initiatory power in the effecting of the Fall—the era of sin and death. We cannot overestimate the importance of the witness of the Fathers regarding Mary's position in salvation. For them this woman is the Source of Life, the font of the New Covenant. The following works of the Fathers are a theological testimony to the life-giving power of Mary's *"fiat."*

St. Justin Martyr:

. . . he existed before all created things and came forth from the Father by his power and wisdom . . . and he has become man through the Virgin, so that by the very channel whereby disobedience from the serpent took its starting-point, by this same channel it should receive its destruction.[5]

Tertullian:

God recovered His own image and likeness, of which He had been robbed by the devil. For it was while Eve was yet a virgin, that the ensnaring word had crept into her ear which was to build the ediface of death. Into a virgin's soul, in like manner, must be introduced that Word of God which was to raise the fabric of life; so that what had been reduced to ruin by this sex, might by the selfsame sex be recoverd to salvation. As Eve had believed the serpent, so Mary believed the angel. The delinquency which the one occasioned by believing, the other by believing effaced.[6]

St. Irenaeus:

But Eve was disobedient. . . . And even as she, having indeed a husband, Adam, but being nevertheless as yet a virgin . . . having become disobedient, was made the cause of death, both to herself and to the entire human race; so also did Mary, having a man betrothed [to her], and being nevertheless a virgin, by yielding obedience, became the cause of salvation, both to herself and the whole human race. . . . For the Lord, having been born "the first begotten of the dead," and receiving into His bosom the ancient fathers, has regenerated them into the life of God, He having been made Himself the beginning of those that live, as Adam became the beginning of those who die. . . . And thus also it was that the knot of Eve's disobedience was loosed by the obedience of Mary. For what the virgin Eve had bound fast through unbelief, this did the virgin Mary set free through faith.[7]

And if the former did disobey God, yet the latter was persuaded to be obedient to God, in order that the Virgin Mary might become the patroness (*advocata*) of the virgin Eve. And thus, as the human race fell into bondage to death by means of a virgin, so it is rescued by a virgin; virginal disobedience having been balanced in the opposite scale by virginal obedience.[8]

St. Cyril of Jerusalem states: "Through Eve, yet virgin, came death, through a virgin, or rather from a virgin, must the Life appear."[9] That life comes from Mary is repeated by St. Ephrem Syrus: "Through Eve, the beautiful and desirable glory of men was extinguished; but it was revived through Mary."[10] St. Epiphanius declares this same truth: that life is from Mary because the Word is from Mary: "Eve became a cause of death to men. . . . *Mary a cause of life* . . . that life might be instead of death, life excluding death *which came from the woman,* viz. He who *through the woman has become our life.*"[11] By the time of St. Jerome, Mary as the source of life in contrast to Eve, cause of death, had become almost a type of slogan: "Death by Eve, life by Mary."[12]

These statements witness the fact that Mary is not a mere passive instrument whereby Christ may work His redemption. Mary is not an instrument. Rather she is *instrumental.* And she is instrumental in a personal way according to the meaning of her feminine life-giving powers. What the Fathers contrast between Eve and Mary is disobedience versus obedience. This means that Eve and Mary are real moral agents; they effect death or life. Mary's "yes" is an authoritative force that actually "undoes the knot of Eve's disobedience." It is through the authority of her "yes" that the "Word became flesh." Christ is the New Adam because he is "born of Mary." The entire order of redemption and Christ's redemptive work is bound up with this truth. It is as if the New Beginning is accomplished by reversing the order of the first. In the beginning Eve is taken from the First Adam. In the New Beginning the Last Adam is taken from the New Eve.[13] How clearly St. Paul's teaching on the order of the world is demonstrated by this and woman's place in this order: "In the same way that woman was made from man, so man is born of woman; and all is from God" (1 Cor. 11:12). Mary is a covenantal source—a real partner in the order of redemption and precisely as the integral expression of her integral femininity, her womanly nature, not despite it. And let us recall that Mary's role is not mere instrumentality. Rather her "yes" is the source of the New Beginning, marked by the Incarnation of God. Mary's adherence to the Word of God causes the redemptive Incarnation to happen. The starting point of the entire soteriological event is Mary's "yes."[14]

However, the New Beginning is not simply the Word becoming flesh. The New Beginning is the covenant effected by the oneness of wills and flesh between Christ, the New Adam, and His mother, Mary, the New Eve. The woman bears an authoritative function that actually constitutes the order of redemption. One scholar of the Eastern Church has noted:

> The Incarnation was not only the work of the Father and of His Virtue and His Spirit; *it was also the work of the will and faith of the Virgin.* Without the consent of the all-pure one and the co-operation of her faith, this design would have been as unrealizable as it would have been without the intervention of the three Divine Persons themselves. Only after teaching and persuading does God take her for his Mother and *receive from her* the flesh which she wills to offer

to him. Just as he voluntarily became Incarnate, so he willed that his Mother should bear him freely, with her own full and free consent.[15]

II. Mary's Word: The New Genesis

Mary's "*fiat mihi*" is a creative authoritative utterance that parallels and finally is the completion of the primordial "Let it be done" of God's creative word in Genesis 1. The scene of the Annunciation recorded in Luke incorporates elements of God's creative act in Gen. 1. The scene brings in the same divine Spirit that hovered over the primordial waters. Now the Spirit will come down upon Mary: "The Holy Spirit will come upon you and the power of the Most High will overshadow you" (Luke 1:35).[16] In Genesis God's all powerful Word, His divine "*fiat*," brings forth the creation out of nothing as He utters "Let it be done," and it is done. Psalm 33 states "He spoke, and it was made." At the Annunciation we are taken back to the First Creation in order to begin the New. Now the "Let it be done" is not God's, it is man's. More specifically, it is woman's.

It is through the power of the Holy Spirit that the Word will become flesh. But the Holy Spirit is made effective through the "Let it be done" of the New Eve, her word and her action. In the First Creation what is created by God is in relation to Him and it is good, as the text of Genesis 1 declares repeatedly. Now, in the New Creation this goodness of creation truly answers God. In this answer the New Covenant is born, and it is the woman's word that gives it life. E. L. Mascall states: "The creation of the world was brought about by the sole fiat of God; the re-creation of the world was, by God's dispensation, set in motion by the fiat of a young village girl who was engaged to a carpenter, *Fiat mihi secundum verbum tuum*."[17] In the beginning the Creator/Father calls being out of nothingness. At the Annunciation, creation calls its Creator into history.[18] And this call of God into concrete physical history by Mary has nothing to do with passivity. Mary is active and her activity is free.[19]

Because the Incarnation is the starting point of a new humanity, Mary is the New Eve, Mother of All the Living, in relation to Christ, the New Adam. At the Annunciation, Mary, the New Eve, brings forth the New Adam. In Luke's Gospel Christ is explicitly presented as the New Adam, as the first Adam is the original ancestor of Christ. Christ is the descendent of "Cainan, son of Enos, son of Seth, son of Adam, *son of God*" (Luke 3:37–38). Now Mary, the New Eve, will bring forth *the* Son of God in her maternal "yes" as the angel says to her: "the Holy offspring to be born will be called Son of God" (Luke 1:35). With the conception of this Son through the "*fiat*" of Mary a new aeon begins, the age of a new covenanted people.

She is the Mother of Christ, thus *the Eve* of this people who achieve grace through the Son conceived and born of her.

III. The Authority of Mary in the Mission of Christ

MARY AS THE SOURCE OF CHRIST

The authority of Mary does not end with her conceiving and giving birth to the Savior. Mary is the Mother of a New People because her "yes" to the Incarnation is a "yes" to the entire salvific mission of her Son—a "yes" to the Cross of Christ which is the consummation of the Incarnation's purpose. Mary's "yes" includes the Cross, and she, precisely in her maternity, is the source of the Cross. The Virgin of Nazareth, in total fulfillment of what it means for man to be from woman, conceives and bears the Son who will die upon it.[20] John Paul II in his encyclical *Redemptoris Mater*, quoting Vatican II, teaches that God willed that the consent of Mary precede the Incarnation and that this "*fiat*" was itself decisive "for the accomplishment of the divine mystery."[21] The mystery of redemption is entirely bound up with the man who is Christ, of whom Mary is the source. She makes Him historically present that He may accomplish the will of the Father. It is Mary's maternal authority that stands behind the New Covenant that is established through the true sacrifice of Christ, which is nothing less than the giving up of His flesh for the life of the world. The Letter to the Hebrews brings together all these theological truths:

> On coming into the world, Jesus said: " Sacrifice and offering you did not desire, but a body you have prepared for me; holocausts and sin offerings you took no delight in. Then I said, 'As written of me in the book, I have come to do your will, O God.' "
>
> First he says, "Sacrifices and offerings, holocausts and sin offerings you neither desired nor delighted in." (These are offered according to the prescriptions of the law.) Then he says, "I have come to do your will." In other words he takes away the first covenant to establish the second.
>
> By this "will," we have been sanctified through the offering of the body of Jesus Christ once for all. Every other priest stands ministering day by day, and offering again and again those same sacrifices which can never take away sins.
>
> But Jesus offered one sacrifice for sins and took his seat forever at the right hand of God. (Heb. 10:5–12)

Redemptoris Mater states that Christ's "will" was dependent upon Mary's:

The mystery of the Incarnation was accomplished when Mary uttered her *fiat*: "Let it be done to me according to your word," which made possible, as far as it depended upon her in the divine plan, the granting of her Son's desire.[22]

It is the "will" of Christ in the offering up of His body (that was prepared for Him) that inaugurates the New Covenant. The words of the Savior "I have come to do your will" were preceded by Mary's own "Let it be done to me"—namely the total surrender of her own will that parallels the will of Christ in the accomplishment of the world's salvation.[23] The New Covenant is through the sacrificed body of Christ. Christ is the head of the New Humanity, but Mary is also the source of this people because she is the source of the Incarnate God. She is a source in the way St. Paul understands it: Christ is *born* of her, he is *through* her as man is *through* woman (1 Cor. 11:12). The New Covenant is dependent upon the Incarnation of God and His bodily sacrifice, and this was achieved through Mary's maternity. The Incarnation of God took place through her "yes"—thus Mary is the Mother of the New Covenant.

We must draw out one other logical conclusion that the passage from Hebrews invites us to draw, namely, because she is the source of the Incarnation, Mary is the source of Christ's priesthood. René Laurentin explains:

> But our Lady not only gave her consent; she furnished the flesh whereby the Word might be grafted on the human race. And by virtue of this flesh God became not only man but priest and victim. Without that flesh He would not be a priest, for in order to be a priest it is first necessary to be a man, as we are told in the Epistle to the Hebrews (V, 1 and 7). Without that flesh he would not be a victim, for in order to be immolated it is necessary to be capable of suffering and death.[24]

Mary, because she is the mother (source) of Christ's priesthood, is by this fact also constituted Mother of the New Creation. Her motherhood is a redemptive responsibility. Not only is Mary entrusted with bringing Christ into the world, her maternity encompasses bringing Christ's priesthood to its supreme fulfillment as she leads her Son to the Cross. The Sacrament of Holy Orders is also in relation to and dependent upon the feminine responsibility for the faith. The sacramental priesthood is under the rule of women's responsibility for the faith as the sacramental order itself is ultimately realized through, centered in, and governed by the Marian maternal principle.

THE AUTHORITY OF MARY AT CANA

Mary's authority exists (as, in consequence, does all feminine authority within the covenant of God) in that she is an actual agent of salvation. Her role cannot be reduced to God's simply making use of female biology in order to "be made flesh." Mary's maternity consists in aiding her Son in His salvific work. In this she fulfills the meaning of "helpmate" in God's creation of woman (Gen. 2:18). As Mary opened her womb to Christ and gave birth to Him, so she gave birth to Him on the Cross. The account of the wedding at Cana reveals most clearly the authority of Mary as she instigates the mission of her Son and thus leads Him to His Passion.

> On the third day there was a wedding at Cana in Galilee, and the mother of Jesus was there. Jesus and his disciples had likewise been invited to the celebration. At a certain point the wine ran out and Jesus' mother told him, "They have no more wine." Jesus replied, "Woman, how does this concern of yours involve me? My hour has not yet come." His mother instructed those waiting on table, "Do whatever he tells you." (John 2:1–5)

The narrative indicates that it is Mary who takes the initiative in the situation. She makes the lack of wine her concern and the concern of her Son. She tells Jesus there is no more wine, and she expects that He will do something about it. The incident of Christ's first miracle, however, is not simply a matter of replenishing wine so as to rescue the bride and groom from embarrassment in the situation. The words of Christ to Mary "My hour has not yet come" are of very great theological importance. In John's gospel "the Hour" refers to Christ's crucifixion and to His eventual entering into His glory.[25] In John 12:23–25 some Greek-speaking Jews have come to see Jesus, and it is within the context of their presence that Jesus declares: "The hour has come for the Son of man to be glorified." This statement is followed immediately by Christ's discourse on the grain of wheat which must fall to the ground and die if it is to produce much fruit which is a direct reference to His own death (John 12:24). Jesus' words at Cana: "My hour has not yet come" connect His first miracle to His Passion. To perform this miracle is to usher in "the Hour," which is precisely the reason He was conceived and born "of woman." At Cana Mary is not only the "mother of Jesus," she is the mother of His mission in the sense that she is the source, the instigator, the principle agent in the initiating of Christ to His public ministry. Mary officiates at Cana in Christ's first miracle to help her Son accomplish the work of redemption for which He was conceived and born into the world. Andre Feuillet points out that the changing of water into wine is a messianic symbol tied to the fulfillment of Christ's mission: a sign of the wine He will offer the world once His Hour has come. But He offers this wine through the mediation of Mary's request.[26] That Mary's request has to to with the initiating of her Son's messianic mission is demonstrated by the quality and quantity of the wine produced by the miracle. The abundance of wine parallels the multiplication of loaves of fishes (John 6:11–13). The copiousness exists as a symbol of the superabundance of messianic times.[27]

At Cana, Mary actively serves as the catalyst of the salvific activity of her Son.[28] Furthermore she is the cause of the revelation of His glory which is the ultimate result of the miracle: "Thus did he reveal his glory, and his disciples believed in him" (2:11). She is not the cause of this glory in the sense that she gives Christ the power to perform the miracle. The power and glory of Christ belong to Him because He is God. But she is *source* in the sense of means or facilitator in the same way that Mary's authority is exercised in the Incarnation. As Mary brings Christ into the world, here she causes Christ's glory to be manifested to the world. And so she is also the source of the disciples' faith which comes as a result of the revelation of Christ's glory (2:11).[29]

Christ executes His first miracle because someone requests it. But this someone is not just anyone—it is His mother. And it is precisely because she is His mother, the source of His presence in the world for the purpose of redemption, that she has authority to ask Him for it and lead her Son to His mission. Mary and Mary alone possesses this authority because it is bound to her maternal role in the economy of redemption. Because she is the Mother of God she has been entrusted with aiding Christ in His work of salvation. She can send Christ to the Cross because she is the source of His priesthood and thus she has a maternal right to nourish its fulfillment. In fact, as the Mother of Christ she has, not just the right, but she has been given this responsibility. For Mary to be true to her motherhood she must be a true aid in the salvific work of Her Son. In this way Mary continues to undo the knot of Eve's disobedience. Eve led Adam away from what it meant for him to be a man and to be the head. Eve brought Adam under the power of her own whim. This was a misuse of her feminine authority which, as St. John Chrysostom in *Homily 9* stated, took Adam astray from the will of God. The New Eve uses her authority to lead her Son, not to do her will, but to accomplish the will of the Father who sent Him.[30] This is a key element in the meaning of feminine authority; this authority is meant to lead men to the accomplishment of what it means for them to be masculine and to fulfill the specific responsibilities and tasks that they are entrusted with in the order of creation and redemption.

Mary's statement to Christ: "They have no more wine" is met at first with a type of refusal on Christ's part, a refusal that even sounds harsh: "Woman, what is this to me and to you? My hour has not yet come" (τί ἐμοὶ καὶ σοί, γύναι οὔπω ἥκει ἡ ὥρα μου) 2:4.

Most commentators and biblical translations interpret the verse as Christ posing a separation between Himself and His mother. Her concern is not His. Strangely, Mary immediately turns to the servants in an action of taking charge and instructs them "Do whatever He tells you" (2:5). The instruction takes on the form of a command. Her words not only move the waiters but set Our Lord into action. What has Mary really done? Has she not actually answered Jesus' objection: "What is this to me and to you?" The miracle will have messianic import and thus the changing of water into wine has *everything* to do with her and her Son. Because Mary's maternity is bound to the Cross, she is ushering both of them to its Hour. Because the miracle has to do with the Hour and their parts in it, the Lord of the universe obeys her request. He subjects Himself to her in the accomplishment of His Father's business. Or perhaps we should say it is subjection to the Father's will through the mediation of Mary's maternal authority as she is the New Eve, true and effective helpmate to the New Adam.

At the wedding at Cana the co-redemptrix role of Mary is revealed in the manner in which Christ addresses His mother. He calls her *woman*. The theology of the Evangelist is very rich and very important here. The Woman of Cana is the Woman of Calvary where Mary accomplishes by her maternal authority the covenantal role of the New Eve whose work, united to the sacrifice of her Son, brings about the regeneration of all mankind.

MARY, WOMAN OF THE NEW COVENANT

The fall of the human race through the sin of Adam and Eve contains a promise that through the first mother of men a savior will be born. This promise is known from the earliest days of the Church as the Protogospel or the "first good news." After God confronts the first couple with their sin of disobedience, He turns to the serpent with these words:

> I will put enmity between you and the woman and between your offspring and hers; he will strike at your head while you strike at his heel. (Gen. 3:15)

The passage describes a serious struggle involving the woman, her offspring (or child), and the Evil One in which the triumph will ultimately be gained by the Offspring. St. Justin Martyr identifies the Offspring as Christ, who has come through the New Eve, whose life-giving obedience he contrasts with the death-producing disobedience of the old Eve.

> Christ came through the Virgin in order that disobedience which issued from the serpent might be destroyed in the same way in which it took its origin. . . . Thus through the intermediation of this Virgin He came into the world . . . through whom God would crush the serpent and others similar to him, angels and men, and who delivers from death those who return from their evil sentiments and believe in Him. (*Dialog with Trypho*, 100)[31]

The struggle of the Protogospel, whereby the world's redemption is won, does not place the primordial Adam at its center. As far as the first good news is concerned, he is peripheral. The drama of salvation involves the woman and her Offspring. It is she who having been seduced by Satan is most directly involved in the undoing of the Fall. But this undoing is possible through her because of her life-giving maternal position. The Redeemer who will strike at the heel of the Evil One *can* come from her as He comes from a Virgin by the power, not of man, but of the Holy Spirit. The encyclical *Redemptoris Mater* confirms that it is woman who is at the center of the redemptive struggle as Mary fulfills the prophecy of the Protogospel. The "enmity" of the Protogospel recurs again in the Apocalypse. This time the woman is "clothed with the sun" (Rev. 12:1). Here we see that Mary is placed at the very center of the enmity that marks the history of salvation itself.[32]

The very essence of woman is to have authority over the divine gift of life and because of this she is the source of the New Covenant, the New Beginning. This is what the Protogospel tells us about the meaning of the feminine. Woman as "mother of all the living" was indispensable to the beginning and indispensable to the initiation of salvation history, so, too, is woman the indispensable source of the New Beginning. John Paul II states this clearly in his apostolic letter *Mulieris Dignitatem* in his treatment of the Protogospel:

> It is significant that the foretelling of the Redeemer contained in these words refers to "the woman." She is assigned the first place in the Proto-evangelium as the progenitrix of him who will be the redeemer of man. . . . Mary is the witness to the new "beginning" and the "new creation" . . . since she herself, as the first of the redeemed in salvation history, is "a new creation": She is "full of grace." It is difficult to grasp why the words of the Proto-evangelium place such strong emphasis on the "woman," if it is not admitted that in her the new and definitive covenant of God with humanity has its beginning, the covenant in the redeeming blood of Christ. The covenant begins with a woman, the "woman" of the annunciation at Nazareth.[33]

The Protogospel teaches the most profound truth about feminine authority. Woman, even after the Fall, is still "source of life." The Savior will come from her. The Fall could not obliterate her power. Indeed, the maternity of Eve constitutes the vital factor in salvation history. The woman from the very beginning of history is identified with her power: she is "mother of all the living" (Gen. 3:20).

Joseph Cardinal Ratzinger comments:

In my opinion it is significant that her name is bestowed in Genesis 3:20 *after* the fall, *after* God's words of judgment. In this way the undestroyed dignity and majesty of woman are expressed. She preserves the mystery of life, the power opposed to death; for death is like the power of nothingness, the antithesis of Yahweh, who is the Creator of life and the God of the living. She who offers the fruit which leads to death, whose task manifests a mysterious kinship with death, is nonetheless from now on the keeper of the seal of life and the antithesis of death. The woman, who bears the key of life, thus touches directly the mystery of being, the living God, from whom in the last analysis all life originates and who, for that reason is called "life," and the "living one."[34]

The "Living One" and the "mother of all the living" possess a covenantal partnership as if humanity was produced between them. This covenantal relation and the maternal authority of the woman within this relation is scripturally affirmed when the first event of salvation history is declared by Eve: "I have produced a man with the help of the Lord" (Gen. 4:1).

The feminine authority of the first woman is definitively fulfilled by the Virgin Mary from whom comes the long awaited messiah. Eve's words of triumph literally apply to Mary. She can say "I have produced the God-man with the help of the Lord."[35] But the cooperation between woman and God does not end here. Because salvation is accomplished according to the marital/covenantal order of creation and redemption, Mary is entrusted not only with the birth of Christ; she also becomes "Mother of All the Living" by the birth pangs of a maternity that produce Christ on the Cross.

The woman of the Protogospel is the Woman who will stand at the foot of the Cross at Golgotha and become a true "mother of all the living" by the sacrificial offering she makes as the Second Eve, Mother of the Redeemer. The suffering of the woman is an essential part of the economy of salvation. "In pain shall you bring forth children" (Gen. 3:16) applies not only to Eve but also to the New Eve who in this pain becomes Mother of the Church and of Christians.

At Cana, Mary is entrusted with the task of ushering her Son to His Hour, but the Hour is also hers. The pain of Gen. 3:16, which belongs to the woman, is scripturally linked to the pain of the Cross. In the farewell discourse of John's gospel, Christ states:

> When a woman is in labor she is sad that her hour has come. When she has borne her child, she no longer remembers her pain for joy that a man has been born into the world. (John 16:21)

The drama of salvation is linked to the work of the woman. The woman who instigates Christ's first miracle is the same woman present at the hour of His death. The feminine life-giving power permeates salvation history, bringing it about from the very beginning in Genesis to the very end in the Apocalypse where the woman stands in relation to the headship of Christ as the source of a new people.

The primordial punishment Eve suffers, far from being the curse and the burden women must escape, is the means by which women are vessels of grace and thus effective of the order of redemption. The pain of bringing new human beings to birth, which is specifically feminine, is a redemptive suffering. Maternal suffering actually is constitutive of the New Covenant as it is in relation to the sacrifice of the Head. It is from the masculine sacrifice of the head and the feminine sacrifice of the body that a New Humanity emerges. As we stated earlier, Mary's "yes" to the Incarnation is productive of the entire mission of her Son. Archbishop Fulton Sheen once stated that Christ is the only man who was born to die.[36] As the Mother of God Mary is co-redemptress precisely in the agony of her Son. Christ and Mary are bound together by the suffering of the Cross.[37] Simeon's prophecy affirms their unified destiny: "This child is destined to be the downfall and the rise of many in Israel, a sign that shall be opposed, and you yourself shall be pierced with a sword—so the thoughts of many hearts may be laid bare" (Luke 2:34–35).

The interpretation provided by St. Paulinus of Nola, St. Augustine, and popularized in the Middle Ages, is that the sword that will pierce Mary is her participation in the Passion of her Son.[38] Furthermore, as Feuillet explains, v. 35 links

> ... the unveiling of the perverse designs of the wicked, the outcome or purpose of the Passion of Christ, directly to the compassion of Mary: "And thine own soul a sword shall pierce that out of many hearts thoughts may be revealed."[39]

Feuillet goes on to state that Mary is connected to the execution of the messianic judgment and then asks: "Could St. Luke more strongly have made the point that the suffering endured on Calvary by the Mother of Jesus constitutes, in its own way, an intrinsic part of the history of salvation?"[40]

With Feuillet we affirm that Mary is not the savior of mankind, but we cannot agree with him that her role in salvation is not redemptive. By *redemptive* we mean an actual cause of salvation that is necessary to the fulfillment of the covenant of salvation ordered as it is according to the meaning of male and female sexuality. The Hour of Christ is not simply His crucifixion— it is the Hour of the covenant actualized historically by the ways in which the man, Christ, and the woman, His mother, bring it about.

As we already indicated, Jesus describes His death in terms of a woman engaged in the painful labor of childbirth. The Protogospel is put at the center of Christ's Passion, where a woman gives birth to the Offspring that will crush the head of Satan. Thus the Hour spoken of at Cana is the Hour of the woman as well.[41] Mary's "*fiat*" has brought herself and her Son to the Cross as they both have accepted the meaning of the Incarnation.[42] And it is there that her maternity is ultimately fulfilled as she becomes the mother of all those reborn through the blood of the New Adam.

The Protogospel affirms that redemption is the work of the woman and her Offspring in their joint battle with the Evil One. The Apostolic Constitution *Munificentissimus Deus* (1950) eloquently teaches that Mary, in fulfillment of the Protogospel, had a share in the overcoming of the Adversary together with her Son.

> We must remember especially that, since the second century, the Virgin Mary has been designated by the holy Fathers as the New Eve, who, although subject to the New Adam, is most intimately associated with Him in that struggle against the infernal foe which, as foretold in the Protoevangelium (Gen. 3:15), finally resulted in the most complete victory over sin and death.[43]

The Gospel of John teaches that the crucifixion of Christ is the hour of the battle in which the Adversary is crushed.[44] Earlier we noted that the link between the hour and the death of Christ is made in John 12:23–24. Jesus goes on to say:

> "Now has judgment come upon this world, now will this world's prince be driven out, and I—once I am lifted up from the earth—will draw all men to myself." (This statement indicated the sort of death he had to die.) John 12:31–33

According to Gen. 3:15 the Adversary of the Offspring, the prince of this world, is also the enemy of the woman. Therefore the mother of the Offspring is not only present at the Cross, but she actually contributes to the overcoming of the Evil One whereby she is established for all eternity as Mother of All the Living. F. M. Braun states that the crucifixion is the great battleground in which all the traits of the Protogospel come together.[45] On Calvary the personages of the messianic drama meet each other for the final action. At Calvary Mary is again addressed by Christ as "Woman" and her womanhood is entirely bound to what it means for her to be the universal mother of all the disciples.

> Near the cross of Jesus there stood his mother, his mother's sister, Mary the wife of Clopas, and Mary Magdalene. Seeing his mother there with the disciple whom he loved, Jesus said to his mother, "Woman, there is your son."
> In turn he said to the disciple, "There is your mother." From that hour onward, the disciple took her into his care. (John 19:25–27)

The above passage states the central meaning of Mary's maternity and thus of her authority in the order of redemption. One might see in Christ's word's to His mother a desire to see that she is cared for following His death. However, such a narrow interpretation of Christ's last words from the Cross cannot be supported from the meaning of John's gospel as a whole and from the fact that it is extremely unlikely that John would include these words, spoken as they are by Christ in His Hour of glory from the Cross, spoken at the very climax of the Hour, unless they carried a truth that was integral to the meaning of what His suffering was accomplishing: namely the establishment of the New Creation.[46]

> The words of Christ to Mary and to the disciple constitute the supreme moment in the Crucifixion. Very shortly afterwards there is mention made of the Hour and the final fulfillment: 'From this very hour the disciple took her into his home after which, knowing from this moment all was accomplished, Jesus said, in order that the Scripture be fulfilled, I thirst' (19:27–28). Then He takes the vinegar and He says: 'It is finished: and bowing his head, he gave up the ghost' (19:30). The words of the Crucified to His mother and His disciple whom He loved are thus placed at the summit and the accomplishment of the redemption by Christ according to Scripture.[47]

Further Raymond E. Brown states that the sonship of John and the motherhood of Mary proclaimed from the Cross "are of value for God's plan and are related to what is being accomplished in the elevation of Jesus on the Cross. . . . The action of Jesus in relation to his mother and the Beloved Disciple completes the work the Father has given Jesus to do."[48]

At the Cross, Mary's universal motherhood is fulfilled. She is not only the mother of Christ, she is the mother of all the faithful whom John, the beloved disciple represents. Christ exercises His headship supremely from the Cross because it is from there that the Lord becomes *source* of a new people. Standing in direct relation to this headship of Christ is the New Eve, whom as the Protogospel indicates, and the New Testament theology of Mary affirms, is the active covenantal partner in the order of redemption. Mary has a role in the economy of the Cross that completes the sacrifice of her Son in the fulfillment of the covenant He was conceived by her to establish. The mystical body of Christ was already conceived by Mary, at least in promise, when she consented to become the mother of the Savior. Because Christ is *from her*, the body that comes from the Cross of Christ made up of all the faithful, that is, the Church, can also be said to be from her. Furthermore, the bride of Christ is made according to the Marian pattern as the Church is the feminine response to the creative action of God the Father in Christ. The words of Pope St. Pius X are insightful on this point:

Wherefore in the same holy bosom of His most chaste Mother, Christ took to Himself flesh and united to Himself the spiritual body formed by those who were to believe in Him. Hence Mary, carrying the Savior within her, may be said to have carried all those whose life was contained in the Savior. Therefore all we who are united to Christ, and as the Apostle says, are *members of his body, of his flesh, and of his bones*, have issued forth from the womb of Mary like a body united to its head.[49]

Mary is the mother of the head, but furthermore, when she conceived Christ, she conceived the faithful,[50] and in this way she is the mother of the whole body (composed of the disciples). This is why her maternity, declared by Christ on the Cross, is not merely a motherhood in the moral sense (as in the case of adoption) or simply symbolism. Mary's maternity over the disciples of Christ is a real motherhood and thus a real authority. And as the New Eve she gives birth in pain to those who will follow her Son. The Fathers of the Church call Mary the New Eve because by her obedience she is the mother of the Redeemer and thus the woman through whom the human race is regenerated. But the maternity does not end with Mary's giving birth to Christ. Vollert explains:

If Mary is mother of all the living, she is associated with her Son in his work of redemption. The consent which she freely gave at the annunciation to be the Mother of Christ and which was necessary for the carrying out of the recapitulation was enlivened anew at the crucifixion. By cooperating in the redeeming sacrifice, she is the New Eve in a heightened sense *source of our life*, mother of the body as she is mother of the Head. (Emphasis added.)[51]

When Jesus states "Woman behold thy Son," He is not creating a new reality or conferring a reality upon Mary that was not already in existence.[52] Mary is mother of the disciples because she is source of the head. Furthermore, her maternity over the faithful is manifested at Cana. It is through her that Christ's glory is revealed "and his disciples believed in him" (John 2:11).[53] Hanging upon the Cross, Christ reveals the mystery of Mary: the beloved disciple who stands for all the faithful is her Son.[54]

THE COMPASSION OF MARY

The woman is the covenantal partner of Christ in the order of redemption. Christ, priest, and victim offers the one sacrifice truly acceptable to the Father for the salvation of the world. Because this offering effects the covenant of the New People of God, its reality depends upon the response of creation to it. The response is not mere passivity, a reception of the gifts of grace, but rather the response is an active participation in the sacrifice that effects redemption. Mary is the Mother of Christ and the faithful because she gives this response. As her Son dies on the Cross, Mary, the New Eve, undergoes a Compassion with Him in fulfillment of the feminine responsibility for the New Covenant. Juniper B. Carol, well known in the field of Mariology, states that at Calvary Mary brought about the spiritual regeneration of the human race "by being a co-agent in Christ's redemption."[55] The maternity of Mary and her co-redemption are inseparable. Several popes have taught that the sufferings of Mary at Golgatha form part of the overall sacrifice of Christ by which redemption is won, e.g., Benedict XV taught:

> To such an extent did she suffer and almost die with her suffering and dying Son, and to such an extent did she surrender her maternal rights over her Son for man's salvation, and immolated Him, insofar as she could, in order to appease the justice of God, that *we may rightly say that she redeemed the human race together with Christ.*[56]

Pope Leo XIII states:

> . . . when Mary offered herself completely to God together with her Son in the temple, she was already sharing with Him the painful atonement on behalf of the human race . . . (at the foot of the cross) she willingly offered Him up to the divine justice, dying with Him in her heart, pierced by the sword of sorrow.[57]

Pope Pius XI, successor to Benedict XV, is the first pope to employ the word "co-redemptrix" as regards Mary's role in salvation. In a radio broadcast at the close of the Jubilee Year (29 April 1935), he prayed:

> O Mother of piety and mercy who, when thy most beloved Son was accomplishing the Redemption of the human race on the altar of the cross, didst stand there both suffering with Him and it as a Co-redemptrix; preserve in us, we beseech thee, and increase day by day, the precious fruit of His Redemption *and of thy compassion.*[58]

Pope Pius XII in the conclusion of his encyclical *Mystici Corporis* states:

> It was she, the second Eve, who, free from all sin, original or personal, and always most intimately united with her Son, offered Him on Golgatha to the eternal Father for all the children of Adam, sin-stained by his unhappy fall, and

her mother's rights and her mother's love were included in the holocaust. Thus she who was mother of our Head, through the added title of pain and glory became, according to the Spirit, the mother of His members.[59]

These papal statements teach that Mary's co-redemption is not that of a passive onlooker. The crucifixion of her Son is not something that simply "happens" to her. Mary participates in the sacrifice by offering up her Son. And it is a mother's sacrifice, the sacrifice of the New Eve, different from the sacrifice of the head, but in covenantal union with it. Without her sacrifice the New Creation would not be established. Mary's offering of Christ upon the Cross is the fulfillment of her "*fiat*" as the New Eve to the New Adam.[60] This offer is specific to feminine responsibility for the faith. The New Eve must hold Christ in her womb, but her motherhood in bringing forth the head resides equally in letting Him go. The Mother of Christ must let Him *be* the Savior. Mary must renounce possession of her Son. This means accepting that Christ should deliver Himself up to the Father's will—to die on a cross.[61]

The covenantal authority proper to the New Eve specifies the meaning of womanhood in general, and the means by which women exercise their authority. In Mary's offering up of her Son on the Cross, we are looking at the creative response to the redemptive action of the head, the response that is effective of the New Covenant in Christ.

As we stated previously, at the Annunciation Mary says "yes" to the entire salvific plan of God which includes the crucifixion of her Son. The Presentation of Christ in the Temple is the first "letting go" that Mary is called to fulfill according to the prophecy of Simeon. However, Mary does not simply "let him go," rather, she actually *presents* Christ in the temple. The presentation of one's firstborn in the temple within Jewish Law and custom was a liturgical action recalling the saving power of God in the Passover. Through the blood of the sacrificed lambs spattered on the doorposts, the firstborn are spared the judgment of God. The firstborn child of a Hebrew couple becomes a sign of the merciful deliverance of God.[62] Christ is this sign par excellence. He is the true Passover Lamb who will take away the sins of the world. When Mary presents her Son in the temple, she offers Christ up to His mission—in fact, as His mother she consecrates Him to it and with Him herself. Feuillet, as perhaps no other author, explains the Marian sacrificial aspects of the presentation of Jesus:

Of course, Mary is not a priest. But she is the Mother of the High Priest of the new covenant, of a priest whose essential characteristic is to be himself the victim of his own sacrifice. Now it is by the hands of Mary that Jesus is offered in Luke 2:22–23. The verb *to present (paristanai)*, which is applied to the presentation of Jesus in the Temple (2:22) has in the Pauline Epistles a distinctly sacrificial implication (Rom. 6:13–19; 12:1; 1 Cor. 8:8; 2 Cor. 4:14; 11:2; Eph. 5:27; Col. 1:28). The presentation of Jesus in the Temple thus appears as a prelude to the sacrificial offering of the Passion of which the Fourth Gospel speaks. And here already, Mary is associated with Jesus in his offering to God. . . . Together Mary and Jesus submit to a legal prescription not made for them (cf. the strange expression *their* purification in v. 22); together they are offered to God, but externally Jesus is offered through the mediation of Mary.[63]

Mary is a true associate of Christ in His salvific work. In this she accomplishes what the first Eve failed to do—namely, conduct Adam to do the will of the Father. Mary's offering of Christ in the temple is continued at the wedding at Cana. Herein lies her feminine authority—to lead her Son to be what He is called (or rather sent by the Father) to be. It is only by a real moral and spiritual sacrifice (and not simply being deprived of her Son by His death) that Mary, in truly offering up her firstborn, will become Mother (and that is the *source*) of a New Humanity.

Walter Ong, S.J., provides a beautiful interpretation of Michaelangelo's *Pietà* as a statue depicting Mary's total freedom in having offered up her Son to the will of the Father.

> In the Pieta the Virgin Mother has freed herself of possessiveness, transmuted all eros . . . into agape. . . . She has done so by lovingly acquiescing to her now adult Son's doing what He was called to do, His Father's will. She leaves her Son completely free, though doing so returns Him dead to her arms. And when she takes Him dead in to her arms, she does not clutch Him, but leaves her arms open. The statue tugs at the hearts of women and men alike, but its subject matter is supremely feminine. And it is supreme human freedom: Mary has deliberately chosen to let her Son be about His Father's business. . . . She is completely free, for she is fully aware of what she has chosen.[64]

The only thing analogous to Mary's suffering and sacrifice is on the side of God the Father as Scripture states: "For God so loved the world that He gave His only-begotten Son, that those who believe in Him may not perish, but may have life everlasting" (John 3:16). Mary is the handmaid of the Lord because her will is united to the Father's in the offering of the same Son for the salvation of the world. But Mary's offering is peculiarly feminine. Ong notes there are no male *Pietàs*. A child is separated from his father even before conception, and Christ has no earthly father. Christ, in the order of creation, must separate Himself from Mary if He is to be the head of the New Creation— the New Adam. He separates Himself from her care in order to fulfill His mission, and as Pope Pius XII stated in *Mystici Corporis*, Mary gives up her maternal rights of protection over Him when she offers Him upon the Cross.[65]

IV. The New Eve—Covenant Partner of Christ

THE NEW EVE—RESPONSE OF THE COVENANT

Salvation, because it is the reality of the New Covenant, exists not in Christ standing alone but in Christ standing in union with, in a complementary relation to His Bride, the Church, who is the New Eve of which Mary is the prototype. This is why the Compassion of Mary at the Cross, her co-suffering and essentially her co-offering of Christ is a salvific feminine action constitutive of the New Creation. God's sending of His only Son requires a response for the one flesh unity of the head and body to form that New Humanity that is the source of grace for the world.

The New Covenant could not be formed without cooperation coming from the side of humanity.[66] If nothing else, the *"fiat"* of Mary demonstrates this. The response that Mary gives at Calvary is the feminine response of God's graced creation to the sacrificial love of the New Adam. At Calvary, Mary, the Mother of God, is not simply a single person whose response to and participation in the Passion of her Son begins and ends with her. Mary represents the Church, the collectivity of the redeemed, which is the covenantal partner in redemption, the body and bride of Christ.

Because Mary gives her consent to the Cross and offers Christ upon it, the faithful are represented by her. In other words, Mary can really stand for them because she is their mother. The entire reality of the Church is present at Calvary in Mary. This is demonstrated by the woman of the Apocalypse. A continuity exists between the woman of Apocalypse 12:1–5 and that of verse 6. She is the beginning of the Christian Church as its mother, but also as its most preminent member. And it is during the Passion, when all others had lost their faith, that Mary turns out to be the single representative of the Church on Calvary.[67]

THE NEW EVE—SOURCE OF THE NEW HUMANITY

Because she is the New Eve of the Protogospel, the covenantal partner of Christ, Mary is the source of a New Humanity. Furthermore, this New Humanity, born from the covenant between Christ and Mary, has Mary as its model and mode of existence. The Apocalypse of John, chapter 12, teaches that Mary is a type of the Church. Indeed their reality is nearly indistinguishable.

A great sign appeared in the sky, a woman clothed with the sun, with the moon under her feet, and on her head a crown of twelve stars. Because she was with child she wailed aloud in pain as she labored to give birth. Then another sign appeared in the sky; it was a huge dragon. . . . Then the dragon stood before the woman about to give birth, ready to devour her child when it should be born. She gave birth to a son—a boy destined to shepherd all the nations with an iron rod. Her child was caught up to God and to his throne. . . .

When the dragon saw that he had been cast down to the earth, he pursued the woman who had given birth to the boy. But the woman was given the wings of a gigantic eagle so that she could fly off to her place in the desert, where far from the serpent, she could be taken care of for a year and for two and a half years more. Enraged at her escape, the dragon went off to make war on the rest of her offspring, on those who keep God's commandments and give witness to Jesus. (Rev. 12:1–5, 13–15, 17)

We are first struck by the fact that the woman here occupies an exalted position. She is "clothed with the sun" with the "moon under her feet" bearing a "crown of twelve stars" upon her head. The woman occupies an official position that is universally significant in dimensions. She is the center of cosmological focus as the cosmic elements adorn her and serve her. With a crown of twelve stars and the moon under her feet, the Woman rules over creation.[68] Her sovereignty springs from her life-giving powers; in bearing the Messiah who will crush the head of the dragon. Feuillet states:

> . . . the Virgin Mary is portrayed as crowned, it is because she has triumphed over the devil whose assaults fill chapter 12; her crown is made up of 12 stars, which call to mind the twelve tribes of the new Israel, because her triumph is in some way that of the Church. If the Woman of the Apocalypse is already crowned at the very time she is in pain giving birth to Christ (here, the metaphorical childbearing of the Passion), this astounding paradox is intended to highlight the fact that the Mother of Christ, through a quite extraordinary anticipation, participates in the victory of Christ over the powers of evil, even before the Passion and Resurrection of Christ.[69]

The woman gives birth to a single child. This is a compelling reason why the passage refers to Mary and not simply to the Church. The woman gives birth to a single child—to Christ, the Messiah-King.[70] It is important to notice that this king's authority is spoken of in terms of shepherding (v. 5). We are reminded here of John 10:11–18 and 21:15–19 and the significance of the priestly/shepherding function of apostolic authority in the Church.

Apoc. 12 parallels Gen. 3:15, the Protogospel. The Offspring of the woman is the seed that will crush the head of the serpent. The great prophecy finds its fulfillment here.[71] The entire chapter is filled with tension and struggle; the enmity between the woman, the child, and the serpent is portrayed with the triumph of the child over the forces of evil:

> Now have salvation and power come, the reign of our God and the authority of his Anointed One. For the accuser of our brothers is cast out. . . . They defeated him by the blood of the Lamb. (v. 10–11a)

The Woman who gives birth in Apoc. 12 is Mary.[72] Here we see the Johnannine theology of the birth Hour of pain that is the woman's participation in the Passion of her Son as stated in John 16:21. From the Cross Christ revealed the truth about His mother. She is "Mother of all the living" as John, who represents all the faithful, is her son. Apoc. 12 teaches the same truth. Mary is more than the Mother of Christ. She is the Church, mother and, universal sign of the New Humanity that is born of her. Le Frois points out that in the Apocalypse the male in 12:5 is an individual (the Messiah-King) and a collective (the sons of God) both born of the woman. The Woman, too, is both Mary and the Church.[73] Consistent with the universal motherhood of Mary at the foot of the Cross (her painful Hour of childbirth), Apoc. 12 states that when the dragon tries to devour the Woman, that is, the Church that successfully eludes him by hiding in the desert, the "dragon went off to make war on the rest of her offspring" (v. 17a). The motherhood of the Church and the motherhood of Mary partake of the same reality.[74] The Church comes from the maternal "yes" of Mary to the salvific mission of her Son and exists within this reality. Mary's graced response to Christ produces a new people. She has other children born in the likeness of the "first born of all creation." The order of redemption is the relation of the head to the body: their covenantal one-flesh union. Therefore, strictly speaking, the Church is not Christ. It is not a mere continuation, in a monadic mode of the Incarnation.[75] The Church is, if anything, the continuation of Mary—it is her feminine reality extended in history. This is because the Church lives in relation to Christ according to the Marian principles of maternity and brideship. To dismantle this relation, to tamper with its truth in any way, is in fact to dismantle the Christian faith and substitute some untrue and artificial structure in its place. What we are face to face with in the head/body, Christ–Mary/Church relation is the order of Christian worship itself; the covenant worship of the Eucharist that speaks its reality through the sacramental symbols of man and woman.

5

The Feminine Authority of the Church

I. Baptism and a Woman's Life-giving Authority

The salvation of the world is the result of the one flesh covenant that exists between Christ, the Head, and the Church, which is His Body. Within this covenant of redemption, authority, as such, is the power to give life together with the responsibility and rights that accrue to this power over the life which has been brought forth so that it may come to its proper fulfillment. Essentially God has authority over man because He is our creator. Why should one obey God at all? Because He is the *source* of our life. To obey Him is to live and know the source of human freedom.

Feminine authority resides in what the woman has been entrusted with in the covenant of redemption. In the Incarnation, God instituted the New Covenant by and through a woman, and Christ saved us through the Church. The dignity, beauty, and order of the human person and the world resides in the reality of this partnership between God and what He has created. Human sexuality, which the human race created as male and female, is the symbol whereby this partnership of redemption is expressed and made real in the world, and this by the design of God from the beginning. The unity of man and woman is the first and irreplaceable religious symbol. A secular society that wishes to banish all symbols of God will eventually, whether at the beginning or at the end of its program, deny the significance of gender.

But, of course, in the Christian faith, the dignity of the human race as male and female is forever confirmed because man and woman are taken up into the order of redemption and form the language of God by which His love and His authority are made known. In this language we are concerned for what the woman speaks. What is her word in the accomplishment of

137

salvation? Hearing it we begin to know and appreciate what is woman's task without which salvation would not exist.

The order of redemption was frequently expressed by the Fathers of the Church as a birth of the human being through God the Father and Mother Church. Frequently St. Augustine expressed this rebirth from our spiritual parents with a startling literalism.

> Love your father but not more than the Lord. Love the one who has given you life but not more than your creator. . . . Love your mother, but not more than the Church who has given birth to you unto eternal life. That is to say, as love is given to your parents, it must be given to God and the Church. If love is to be given to those who engendered you to death what love must you give those who have engendered you for eternity, and to last eternally![1]

> Let us love our Lord God, let us love His Church: Him as a Father, Her as a Mother: Him as a Lord, Her His Handmaid, as we are ourselves the Handmaid's sons. But this marriage is held together by a bond of great love: no man offends the one and wins the favor of the other. Let no man say, "I go indeed to the idols, I consult possessed ones and fortune-tellers: yet I abandon not God's Church; I am a Catholic." While you hold to your Mother you offend your Father. Another says, Far be it from me; I consult no sorcerer, I seek out no possessed one, I never ask advice by sacrilegious divination . . . though I am in the party of Donatus. What does it profit you not to have offended your Father, if he avenges your offended Mother? . . . Does not the analogy of human marriage convince you? Suppose you have some patron that you court every day . . . if you utter one calumny against his wife, could you reenter his house? Hold then, most beloved, hold all with one mind to God the Father, and the Church our Mother.[2]

> You have the parents of your flesh, or at least you had in the world those who brought you forth to suffering, to punishment, and to death. But because each one of you, by reason of a blessed bereavement, can say of such parents: "My father and my mother have left me," acknowledge, O Christian, that Father who, when they abandoned you, received you from your mother's womb and to whom one of the faithful says faithfully: "From my mother's womb you are my protector." *Your Father is God; the Church is your Mother. Far otherwise will you be generated by them than when you were begotten by your physical parents.* No labor, no misery, no weeping, no death will attend these parturitions, but only ease, blessing, joy, and life. Generation through human instruments was full of sorrow; through these, it is desirable. They, in giving us life, generated us unto eternal punishment because of the longstanding guilt; these, in regenerating us, bring it about that neither fault nor punishment remain. (Emphasis added.)[3]

St. Augustine makes a clear parallel between our earthly parents who have given us life and the parenthood of God the Father and Mother Church. Indeed, the latter are even more our parents to whom we ought to turn our love because the life we have received from them is more perfect. Earthly parents are really only an imperfect sign of the perfect reality that resides in Father God and Mother Church. They are the true parents. This is why Edith Stein could say that the call of the woman is "to embody in her highest and purest development the essence of the Church—to be its *symbol*." The symbol of what? The symbol of the Church's own life-giving power—life which is bestowed according to the very meaning of maternal truth that the Church herself contains.

Second, St. Augustine teaches that it is by this joint parenthood that life is brought forth. The Father is not a father alone—but a father in union with the Church. We are her (children) sons. Everlasting life is gained by being begotten by the parentage of both. Furthermore, in Augustine's thought, the fatherhood of God and the motherhood of the Church exists in a marital union: "this marriage is held together by a bond of great love." And it is extremely important not to overlook the intimacy of this love. Father God and Mother Church are so united in their life-giving covenantal bond that to offend against the Church is to offend against God. The status of this mother is such that to offend her is to offend God Himself. It is, of course, Christ, and not the Father, who is the spouse of the Church. Nonetheless, when St. Augustine teaches that Father God and Mother Church enjoy a marital unity, his thought illustrates an important point, namely, the covenantal unity of God and the Church.

The motherhood of the Church is, of course, located in her power to give life. We must ask ourselves at this point whether the motherhood spoken of is merely a poetic metaphor or if it defines the very essence of the Church's existence. De Lubac states:

> When the Christian who knows what he is saying speaks of the Church as his mother, he is not giving way to some sentimental impulse; he is expressing a reality. "The motherhood of the Church," wrote Scheeben, "is not an empty title; it is not a weak analogy of natural motherhood. It does not signify only that the Church acts like a tender mother towards us. . . . *This motherhood is as real as the presence of Christ is real in the Eucharist*, or as real as the supernatural life that exists in the children of God." (Emphasis added.)[4]

Mathias Scheeben's words, quoted by de Lubac, are extremely bold. The motherhood of the Church is as real as the presence of Christ in the Eucharist. The Church is a true mother because it is from her and within her that the life of Christians is maintained in the world.

The most famous passage on the motherhood of the Church was penned by another great African bishop, St. Cyprian of Carthage. In his work *On the Unity of the Church*, probably composed to refute the Roman schism of Novatian, Cyprian first of all states that the Church is the bride of Christ— she cannot be adulterous to her Lord, and it is through this one exclusive bride that men enter the Kingdom of Heaven.

> Whoever breaks with the Church and enters an adulterous union, cuts himself off from the promises made to the Church; and he who has turned his back on the Church of Christ shall not come to the rewards of Christ: he is an alien, a worldling, an enemy. *You cannot have God for your Father if you have not the Church for your mother.* (Emphasis added.)[5]

The realism expressed by St. Augustine quoted earlier is matched by Origen of the school of Alexandria.

> The *Church* too *is our Mother*, whom God the Father through the Holy Spirit took unto Himself as Spouse. *Through her He begets sons and daughters* for Himself. And such as are reared in knowledge and wisdom *are the joy* of both God the Father and *of Mother Church*; but *she is smitten with bitter pain and grief* over their stupidity—when we refuse to repent, remaining attached to our depravity.[6]

The fatherhood of God and the motherhood of the Church is realized in the sacrament of baptism. Several Church Fathers speak of this reality. In *Of Baptism*, which is addressed to catechumens, Tertullian writes:

> Therefore, blessed [friends], whom the grace of God awaits, when you ascend from that most sacred font of your new birth, and spread your hands for the first time in the house of your mother, together with your brethren, ask from the Father, ask from the Lord, that His own specialties of grace [and] distributions of gifts may be supplied you.[7]

Joseph C. Plumpe in his magnificent study *Mater Ecclesia* comments on the above passage. In baptism the catechumens receive a *novus natalis*, and they are admonished to pray to the Father while they are with their mother. Mother Church and Father God are the principles of new life—they are the parents of the catechumens.[8]

The prayer uttered by the newly baptized Christians was the Lord's Prayer and "in the administration of baptism itself they would hear the *Ecclesia* mentioned along with the Trinity, as we know again from Tertullian. 'In baptism she became their mother in truth; she presented them as children to the Father.'"[9]

St. Optatus in 365 wrote a treatise refuting the Donatist errors of Parmenianus. He states that it is through the "sacramental womb"[10] of the Church that God becomes the Father of men. The womb of the Church is baptism itself.[11]

This imagery is very bold in a passage from Didymus the Blind (died ca. 398). In baptism, God is the Father of men through the baptismal font which is the mother of Christians.

> The font is the workplace of the Trinity for the salvation of all men who believe, and those who are washed in it are set free from the Serpent's sting, and *it becomes the mother of all through the Holy Spirit, while remaining a virgin. . . .* But why not briefly mention its special greatness? It teaches us who we are on earth fearlessly to call Him Father whom the heavenly beings dare not call thus. And this is what is sung in the Psalm: "My Father and my mother have forsaken me," meaning Adam and Eve did not remain immortal, "but the Lord hath taken me up," *meaning He gave me for mother the font, for father, the Most High God, for brother the Saviour.* (Emphasis added.)[12]

Again we see very clearly, the rebirth of the Christian occurs by a collaboration between God and Mother Church. The holy partnership of baptismal regeneration is likewise very strongly expressed by St. Augustine.

> "Our Father who art in heaven." This shows you are beginning to have God for father. And you will have Him when you are born. However, *even now before you are born, you have been conceived of His seed, for you are about to be brought forth in the font, the womb of the Church.* (Emphasis added.)[13]

In another place Augustine, when speaking to catechumens, again refers to the baptismal font as the Church's "womb" or "uterus," by which persons are "born of God." [14]In *Sermon 216*, also addressed to those about to be baptized, Augustine states:

> O you who are being born [to the faith], whom the Lord has made, strive to be born in sound and healthful fashion, lest you be prematurely and disastrously delivered. *Behold the womb of your mother*, the Church; behold how she labors in pain to bear you and to bring you forth into the light of faith. Do not, by your impatience, disturb your mother's body and make narrow the passage of your delivery. (Emphasis added.)[15]

According to de Lubac, the above words "Behold the womb of your mother" is a reference to the font as the Church's uterus. Augustine "develops the image with a sustained realism."[16]

The above passages show that the Christian life of grace is the result of being reborn of God through our Mother the Church. It is not only the action of the Father— but also the action of the Mother that is vital. There exist in the writings of the Fathers numerous references to the fact that Christians are born through Mother Church and that the baptismal font is her womb. These references indicate that the early Church was very conscious of the life-giving power of *Mater Ecclesia*. The term"Mater Ecclesia" occurs with great frequency and spontaneity which indicates that the practice had entered the mainstream of tradition well before the close of the second century.[17]

Frequently in his letters St. Cyprian indicates the maternal Church simply with the unmodified word *"Mater."*[18] Such simplicity would infer that by the middle of the third century his readers had no difficulty understanding that the *"Mater"* was indeed the Church.

The womb of the Church brings life to human beings. This was clearly the teaching of St. Augustine in *Sermons 216, 119,* and *56* quoted above. In the Eastern Church, Clement of Alexandria (died ca. 215) teaches, "For this was what was said, 'Unless you be converted, and become as children,' pure in flesh, holy in soul by abstinence from evil deeds; showing that He would have us to be such as also He generated us from our mother the water."[19] Our rebirth is from the baptismal womb of the Church and again St. Clement shows that this birth is through the unity of God the Father and Mother Church. He has begotten us through her.

St. Ephrem, a fourth-century Eastern writer, equates baptism with the womb of the Church in which children are conceived bearing the image of Christ. In baptism they come up pure children who went down into the water with defilements. Baptism is "another womb" that has the power to make young people out of the old.[20] St. Methodius in his work *The Banquet* also teaches that in baptismal rebirth the Christian takes on the image of Christ. The character Thecla comments upon the woman of the Apocalypse. The woman is Mother Church who brings about this marvelous rebirth of men. This rebirth indeed is her unique and definitive task.

> Thus the Church stands upon our faith and our adoption—signified here by the moon— *until the fullness of the Gentiles shall come in,* and under this aspect is she indeed their mother. For just as a woman receives the unformed seed of her husband and after a period of time brings forth a perfect human being, so too the Church, one might say, constantly conceiving those who take refuge in the Word, shaping them according to the likeness and form of Christ, after a certain time makes them citizens of that blessed age. Hence it is necessary that she should stand over the laver [baptismal font] as the mother of those who are washed.[21]

The Church's conception of Christians is compared to the activity of an earthy woman who conceives and brings forth a man. In this we see that the Church's life-giving activity is inherently feminine. A woman's procreative powers is the way the Church's own power to conceive and give birth is described. St. Zeno, bishop of Verona in northern Italy from 362 to 372, also employs what is by now a conventional theme in his baptismal writings, that the baptismal font is the womb of the Church.

> Why do you tarry, you who differ in class, age, sex, and condition, you who are soon to be made one? Hasten to the font, to the sweet womb of your ever-virgin Mother. . . . O wondrous and truly divine and sacred birth.[22]

In this passage St. Zeno teaches that the Church's womb by which men are reborn is also the source of ecclesial unity. Maternity is the means by which men are gathered and made one. This feminine unitive power is intrinsic to the meaning of feminine authority.

Finally, Louis Ligier has noted that in the baptismal liturgies of Syria and Antioch, in addition to the theme of the Church as the bride of Christ, "the theme of motherhood is insisted upon: the font is a 'maternal womb'; like the Church, it is given the noble name of 'mother of life.'"[23]

The Gospel of John 3:5 teaches that to enter God's kingdom one must be "begotten of water and the Spirit." As we have seen, great stress has been given by Church Fathers to the maternal role of the font and the water. But water is not enough. There must be also the Spirit. We are reborn by the covenant wherein the love of the Father is mediated through Mother Church. The necessary role of the Spirit in baptism is stressed by the blessing of the water as Theodore of Mopsuestia explains:

> You are not baptized in ordinary water, but in the water of second birth. . . . Consequently the bishop beforehand pronounces a perscribed form of words, asking God to let the grace of the Holy Spirit come upon the water and make it capable of begetting this awesome birth, making it a womb for sacramental birth. For when Nicodemus asked: "Can a man enter a second time into his mother's womb and be reborn?," our Lord replied "Unless one is born of water and the Spirit, he cannot enter the Kingdom of God." He means that just as in natural birth the mother's womb receives a seed, but it is God's hand that forms it according to his original decree, so too in baptism the water becomes a womb to receive the person who is being born, but it is the grace of the Spirit which forms him there for a second birth and makes him a completely new man . . . so here too: the one baptized settles in the water as in a kind of womb, like a seed showing no sign of an immortal nature; but once baptized and endowed with the divine grace of the Spirit, his nature is reshaped completely.[24]

The passage is rich in sexual symbolism. A human being's new life in God is accomplished by the paternal and maternal powers of God and the baptismal font. Here we see the active, forming masculine power of the Spirit. Theodore's imagery of the womb evokes comfort. The catechumen settles himself in the water "as in a kind of womb," and the water has become a womb that receives the person. Indeed, Nicodemus was not so far off. Yes, to be reborn, one must reenter his mother's womb. He does so by entering into the welcoming maternal waters of the font.

MARY, BAPTISM, AND THE CHURCH

This rebirth of the Christian through the baptismal womb is, of course, linked to the fact that Christ is born from the womb of the Virgin. Regarding the birth of Christ St. Augustine states:

> Our life himself came down into this world and took away our death. He slew it with his own abounding life, and with thunder in his voice he called us from this world to return to him in heaven. From heaven he came down to us, entering first the Virgin's womb, where humanity, our mortal flesh, was wedded to him so that it might not be forever mortal.[25]

George Maloney comments that for Augustine we must reenter the first virginal womb as well if we are to be made God as Christ was made man and "this virginal womb of Mary, where is it found, if not in the Church?"[26]

We need to pay attention to the fact that it is the bishop who invokes the Spirit. The prayer is appropriate to his office—standing as he does as God's representative to the Church. In another of St. Theodore's baptismal homilies, the bishop's role is connected with the Spirit: "The pontiff uses consecrated formulae and blessings; he asks that the grace of the Spirit may come down on the water and make it perfect in view of all this."[27]

In the discourses of Narsai (400-503), the priest, standing in the place of God, is the covenant partner of the waters. "The power of the creator (the priest) buries the dead and quickens the dead; and so from the womb he begets men spiritually."

> And of the Church's children he says: "The womb of the waters has brought them forth spiritually." Referring to the voice of the priest, he indicates somewhat of a parallel between Mary and the font: "The dumb (elements) hear a new utterance from rational beings, like that utterance which Mary heard from Gabriel."[28]

The creation of a new man from the power of the Spirit and water is accomplished according to the original creation of the world. In Gen. 2:2 the "mighty wind (or spirit) swept over the waters" bringing forth the life of the world. Tertullian in *On Baptism* teaches, as in the beginning the baptismal waters are made fecund by the action of the Holy Spirit.[29]

> Therefore all water, from the prerogative possessed from its origin, receives at the invocation of God the power of sanctifying the mystery. For there immediately comes down the Spirit from heaven who is upon the water sanctifying it from Himself, and thus sanctified, it imbibes the power of sanctifying.[30]

The covenant quality of regeneration exists in the relation of the Spirit to the baptismal womb of the Church. The Spirit hovering over the maternal waters in baptism, in the manner by which the world was first created, is also the manner by which Mary conceived the Logos in her womb. As we saw in chapter 4, Luke's account of the Annunciation brings in the same divine Spirit that hovered over the primordial waters. St. Ambrose, in his commentary on the second chapter of St. Luke's Gospel, states that Mary is a type of the Church because both she and the Church conceive by the power of the Holy Spirit.

> Rightly is Mary called espoused though a virgin (Luke 1:27) because she is a type of the Church who is immaculate though wedded, who as a virgin conceives us of the Spirit, who as a virgin gives us life without groaning.[31]

In his work *On the Mystery* Ambrose even more explicitly connects Mary, the Spirit, and the Church's own baptismal maternity:

> For Mary did not conceive of man, but received of the Holy Spirit in her womb.... If, then, the Holy Spirit coming upon the Virgin effected conception, and effected the work of generation, surely there must be no doubt that the Spirit, coming upon the Font, or upon those who obtain baptism, effects the truth of regeneration.[32]

The Spirit by which Mary conceived the Son of God is the Spirit invoked by the Church's priestly minister over the baptismal waters of the Church's sacramental womb. The Church's life-giving powers, and thus the locus of her authority, exists according to the pattern of Mary's own maternity and covenant partnership with God. This is why the motherhood of the Church is as real as the Real Presence of Christ in the Eucharist. The Church is a mother because she carries on the truth about a person: the New Eve, mother of all the living.

The ancient liturgy of the Mozarabic Rite of the Spanish Church announces clearly that the maternal powers of the Church first existed in the Mother of God.

> The one gave salvation to the nations, the other gives the nations to the Savior. The one carried Life in her womb, the other carries it in the sacramental font. What was once accorded to Mary in the carnal order is now accorded spiritually to the Church. She conceives the Word in her unfailing faith, she gives birth to it in a spirit freed from all corruption, she holds it in a soul covered with the Virtue of the Most High.[33]

In St. Leo the Great's baptismal doctrine we find that the reality of Mary and the Church have nearly blended into one another—to form almost one single reality. The baptismal font possesses the same power as the womb of Mary, overshadowed as she was (as the Lucan account records) by the power of the Holy Spirit.

> In this Offspring of the Blessed Virgin only produced a seed that was blessed and free from the fault of its stock. And each one is a partaker of this spiritual origin in regeneration; and to everyone when he is re-born, the water of baptism is like the Virgin's womb; for the same Holy Spirit fills the font, Who filled the Virgin, that the sin, which that sacred conception overthrew, may be taken away by this mystical washing.[34]
>
> He placed in the font of baptism the origin He took in the Virgin's womb. *He gave the water what He gave His mother.* The power of the most High and the overshadowing of the Holy Spirit (Luke 1:3), which had Mary bring forth the Saviour, also has the water give rebirth to the believer.[35]

The Church is the true mother of Christians because they are born of her—born of her according to the pattern of Christ's birth from Mary. What is worked in us by baptism had for its intitial model the life-giving feminine truth of the Virgin Mary. As the feminine was indispensable to the Incarnation of Christ, the feminine is indispensable to the rebirth of the human being in the image of Christ whereby we become sons and daughters of God. St. Hippolytus, in his work *The Antichrist*, develops the image of the maternity of the Church in connection with his christology of the Logos; it is especially manifested in his theology of baptism. The birth of the Logos from the womb of the Virgin Mary is considered in connection with the rebirth of believers from the maternal womb of the Church. That his passage refers to baptism is guaranteed by explicit reference to the καινὴ γέννησις of baptism.[36] Furthermore, the interpretation is supported by another passage in Hippolytus that states only those can find themselves near to the Father who are born "from the Spirit and from the Virgin." And he adds explicitly that the Virgin is the Church.[37]

In one of his sermons St. Augustine confirms that the Church is a virgin and yet a mother and that in this she imitates Mary who gave birth to the Lord: and no one denies that Mary gave birth and yet retained her virginity. Augustine explains that the Church, like Mary, gives birth to Christ "for those who are baptized are the members of Christ. 'You are, says the Apostle, the body of Christ and his members' (I Cor. 12:27)." Augustine then goes on to make this remarkable statement: "So then, if she [the Church] gives birth to the members of Christ, she is *absolutely the same as Mary* "[38] (Emphasis added). The theology here is based upon a reference to St. Paul that Christians are the members of Christ. A parallel exists between Mary who gave birth to Christ and the Church who, through baptism, gives birth to Christ again in producing His members. The Church continues Mary's life-giving activity. Augustine's statement that the Church is "absolutely the same as Mary" means that the Church possesses a life-giving authority patterned on Mary—a life-giving authority that is constitutive of the order of redemption. Christ's redemption is accomplished within the maternal Marian power of the Church to produce His members—those who are saved in Him. As God could not be made man without the cooperation of woman so man cannot be saved apart from the maternal activity of the Church. Hugo Rahner climaxes a long examination of the Fathers' teachings on the maternity of the Church in baptism by declaring "The womb of Mary is the womb of the Church."[39]

II. The Biblical Testimony

One of the strongest testimonies concerning the motherhood of the Church is found in St. Paul's letter to the Gal. 4:21-31. Here the Apostle contrasts the Old and the New Covenant. Christians are "children of the promise" (v. 28) because they are born of the new Jerusalem—"of a mother who is free" (v. 31).

> You who want to be subject to the law, tell me: do you know what the law has to say? There it is written that Abraham had two sons, one by the slave girl, the other by his freeborn wife. The son of the slave girl had been begotten in the course of nature, but the son of the free woman was the fruit of the promise. All this is an allegory: the two women stand for the two covenants. One is from Mt. Sinai, and brought forth children to slavery: this is Hagar. The mountain Sinai [Hagar] is in Arabia and corresponds to the Jerusalem of our time, which is likewise in slavery with her children. But the Jerusalem on high is freeborn,

and it is she who is our mother.

"Rejoice you barren one who bear no children; break into song, you stranger to the pains of childbirth! For many are the children of the wife deserted—far more than of her who has a husband."

You, my brothers are children of the promise, as Isaac was. . . .

Therefore, my brothers, we are not children of a slavegirl but of a mother who is free. (Gal. 4:21-31)

The two women represent the two covenants. Here we see that Hagar and Sarah possess a significance larger than themselves. They are signs; Hagar of the Jews bound to the law, and Sarah of the New Jerusalem—namely the Church, the mother who gives birth to freeborn sons who will inherit the promises of God. A woman is the sign of the Church, and specifically in her procreative life-giving powers, as Sarah gave birth to Isaac. Furthermore, she is barren, but God has made her fruitful. Her barrenness is a sign of the New Covenant. The passage from Isa. 54 is significant in this regard. It is the barren one God will make fruitful. Plumpe comments that "the Jerusalem on high":

. . . has always been interpreted in the light of the Church's ministrations as a mother; and added impetus was given this personification of the Church when the Apostle continued (27) by speaking of the fecundity of the Heavenly Jerusalem, applying to her, identified as the Mother of Christians, the Messianic verse of Isaias (54:4) concerning the barren and rejected woman.[40]

Gal. 4:46: "the Jerusalem on high which is freeborn and it is she who is our mother," more than any other Scripture passage served to promote the idea of the Church as a mother, especially in the East.[41]

The passage is significant for a number of reasons. First, as we have already noticed, it is women who personify the covenants and specifically in their ability to bear children. Second, the promises are inherited by those who are born of this second mother. It is interesting that St. Paul does not say the New Jerusalem is like a mother, or can be compared to a mother, but he says *she* is *our mother*. The terminology is personal and real, evoking sentiments of affection, gratitude, and allegiance. Christians should not at all be indifferent to the fact that the New Jerusalem is their mother to whom they owe their life. Third, as God made Sarah fruitful, so likewise the Church in her covenantal relation to God is made fruitful by His power. Furthermore, the Isaiah passage leads to the conclusion that God has become the husband of this fruitful new Jerusalem. She was deserted,[42] but now through the intervention of God, she has many children—more children than of the wife who has a husband. Indeed, Isa. 54:4 specifically states God is the husband of this barren woman: "The shame of your youth you shall forget, the reproach of your widowhood no longer remember, for He who has become your Husband is your Maker; his name is the Lord of Hosts."

St. Paul's teaching on the motherhood of the New Jerusalem exists in the same chapter 4 of Galatians where he teaches that Christ is born of a woman (4:4). The same theme of freedom is at work here. The human race is made free because Christ was "born of a woman, born under the law, to deliver from the law those who were subjected to it, so that we might receive our status as adopted sons." Christ's being "born of a woman" is the source of his historical messianic mission of salvation. It is by this birth from Mary that now these adopted sons can cry out with the Son "Abba!" ("Father!"). We can become the children of God because Christ was the child of Mary. In other words, Gal. 4 teaches that God's fatherhood over us can be traced back to the maternal role the woman played in salvation: that Christ was "born of a woman." Her role is not irrelevant to the achievement of redemption's goal which is to make God the father of men, but in fact it is a necessary element in the economy of salvation itself. Later, the same chapter again takes up the theme of motherhood: Christians become children of the New Covenant (with God as our Father) because they are born of "a mother who is free." St. Cyril of Jerusalem used St. Paul's teaching from Gal. 4:21-31 in direct reference to the Catholic Church. Addressing catechumens he states: "the Catholic Church. For this is the peculiar name of this Holy Church, the mother of us all, which is the spouse of Our Lord Jesus Christ . . . and is a figure and copy of Jerusalem which is above, which is free, and the mother of us all; which before was barren, but now has many children."[43]

The Jerusalem above who has God for her husband spoken of by St. Paul is also found again in Rev. 21. She is the new Jerusalem "from on high. . . coming down out of heaven from God, beautiful as a bride prepared to meet her husband" (21:2). The nuptials between Christ and the Church fulfill the covenant of redemption: "This is God's dwelling place among men. He shall dwell with them and they shall be his people and he shall be their God who is always with them" (21:3).

In 2 John 1 and 5 the local Church is personified as a woman and a mother. The epistle is addressed "The elder to a Lady who is elect and to her children." F. J. Dolger has argued from contemporary inscriptural evidence that the "Elect Lady" (ἐκλεκτή κυρία) is a Christian community or church and not a particular woman.[44] De Lubac notes that Clement of Alexandria and Tertullian (among others) both understood the "Elect Lady" to refer to a local community as well.[45] He states Tertullian was inspired to call the Church *Domina Mater Ecclesia* in his work *To the Martyrs* because of the usage of the expression in the Second Epistle of John.[46]

The epistle not only calls the local church an "elect Lady" but in doing so brings in all of the covenantal themes that flow from such an image. Max Thurian comments that the epistle completes the "image of the Christian family community, which finds its principle of unity in the fraternal and maternal care of the Church." Concerning the Lady and her children the epistle states:

> It has given me great joy to find some of your children walking in the path of truth, just as we were commanded by the Father. But now, my Lady, I would make this request of you . . . let us love one another. (4-6)

We find in v. 13 that the church from which the elder is writing is also referred to as a woman who has children: "The children of your elect sister send you their greetings."

> The head of a church writes to another church. He calls this church "the elect lady" and he thinks of her as the mother of her faithful ones some of whom he actually knows. He invites her to share in mutual charity between their neighboring churches, charity which flows from the truth, the possession of the Father and the Son. Finally he sends her the greeting of the Church over which he is head and in which he dwells; he speaks of this church as the "elect sister" of which the faithful are his children. Here the personification of the local church, by the title of "elect lady" (Eklekte Kyria) derived from the title of Christ, "elect, Lord" (Eklektos, Kyrios), and her motherhood, emphasized by the title of "children" (Tekna) . . . are clearly indicated. God is the Father of the believers who confess "Jesus Christ came in the flesh," his Son, the Elect, the Lord; the local churches, the Elect Ladies, are sisters one with another and each are mothers of their faithful members.[47]

The "elect Lady" exists alongside of her "elect Lord." She has a status worthy of Him. In no sense is this Mater Ecclesia degraded but everything about her is exalted, dignified, and worthy of reverence.

Finally, we look again to St. Paul who likened the local Church to Eve in 2 Cor. 11:3. The passage in which this appears is filled with marital imagery.

> I am jealous of you with the jealously of God himself, since I have given you in marriage to one husband, presenting you as a chaste virgin to Christ. My fear is that, just as the serpent seduced Eve by his cunning, your thoughts may be corrupted and you may fall away from your sincere and complete devotion to Christ.

Fiorenza believes this passage represents a patriarchalized corruption of the genuine Pauline statement of Gal. 3:28. When Paul must deal with concrete pastoral situations, his original ideal teaching on the equality of the sexes becomes modified. Gal. 3:28 was further qualified "in a patriarchal direction by the Pauline 'school.'"[48] The position of Eve in 2 Cor. 11:3 appears unflattering; Fiorenza points out Eve is the one whom the devil successfully seduced thus she is used by St. Paul to "stress the gullibility of the Corinthian community."[49] However, to say that this is the central thrust of the comparison between the community and Eve is to miss the entire marital context of the passage (11:2-3) which makes the reference to Eve appropriate and intelligible in the first place. The Church here is the virgin bride of Christ. As we pointed out at length in Chapter 2, St. Paul in Romans refers to Christ as the New Adam. Here the Church is to be wedded to Him, the New Eve to the New Adam. The Church's chaste virginity resides in her uncorrupted doctrine; this is indicated by vs. 3-4. The point is not that the Church is like the old Eve, but that she is meant to be a true virginal, uncorrupted Eve, unseduced by the devil and thus maintaining her "sincere and complete devotion to Christ" (v. 3c). Concerning this passage Plumpe comments that it "assumes a double significance" for a study of the early Church. Not only is it concerned about the virginal (i.e., doctrinal) integrity of the Christian community, "but the idea of her motherhood is also present. The Church as the second Eve and our second mother is a notion that we shall meet repeatedly farther on; she must not be vitiated, like the first Eve, but remain a *virgin mother—παρθένος μήτνρ.*"[50]

Not only is the New Eve, the Church, to be the antithesis of the first Eve as St. Paul teaches, but the model of the kind of fidelity he is talking about, namely, "sincere and complete devotion to Christ" (1 Cor. 11:3c), was fulfilled in Mary. It is Mary who exemplifies absolute fidelity to the will of God and is *the* New Eve of the New Covenant. St. Irenaeus taught that Mary undid the knot of Eve's disobedience. The feminine Church of Corinth in her own "sincere devotion" is called to manifest this reality in her nuptial union with Christ.

III. The Church Feeds Her Children

The Fathers of the Church, as we saw, understood baptism to be intrinsic to the maternal function of the Church. Also intrinsic to the Church's motherhood is the nourishment she gives her children in the form of doctrine, Scripture, and the sacraments, especially the Holy Eucharist. The Church does not simply give birth to the children of God, but as a mother she is responsible for sustaining their life. As we shall see, her responsibility to provide nourishment to the faithful is accomplished in relation to the hierarchy. Priests, acting *in persona Christi*, are the official dispensers of the sacraments—but the sacraments can only be dispensed through Mother Church.

St. Hippolytus teaches that Eve has become the Church. God has:

> ... raised Eve who is not seduced.... O blessed woman who does not desire to be apart from Christ. Accept this Eve, she who does not engender us in sorrow. Accept the New Eve, the Living One upon whom one can rely.... After her union with the Incorruptible One she wishes to provide nourishment by which human nature will no longer have to hunger or thirst. Henceforth Eve is a true companion for Adam. O what admirable aid—she brings Him to us by the proclamation of the Gospel.... Her children drink from the milk of her breast, each one drinks from the law of the Gospel, harvesting food for eternity.[51]

Here the Church's bridehood and motherhood are linked. She is the true companion of the New Adam, and by her union with Him she can feed her children from the "milk of her breast." As the companion of Christ the Church is the mediatrix of life, the nurturing mother.[52] The Church feeds her children by the Gospel preached within her.

St. Irenaeus, of whom Hippolytus was a disciple, speaks of the Church as a "precious vessel" who holds the faith within herself.

> For this gift of God has been entrusted to the Church ... for this purpose, that all the members receiving it may be vivified; and [the means] of communion with Christ has been distributed throughout it, that is, the Holy Spirit. ... For where the Church is, there is the Spirit of God; and where the Spirit of God is, there is the Church.... Those, therefore who do not partake of Him, *are neither nourished into life from the mother's breasts*, nor do they enjoy that most limpid fountain which issues from the body of Christ; but they dig for themselves broken cisterns ... and drink putrid water out of the mire, fleeing from the faith of the Church lest they be convicted. (Emphasis added.)[53]

The Church is a mother because she is the repository of Christian faith and the Holy Spirit. The image here is one of fullness and abundance. To partake of the Spirit immanent within her is "to feed at the mother's breasts." Those who refuse to partake of her "limpid fountain" of faith and the Holy Spirit drink instead of some contaminated counterfeit, a beverage without nourishment. Regarding the authority of the *Mater Ecclesia* it is important to appreciate that access to God, life, truth, the Gospel, the Holy Spirit, and grace is possible only through the Church. Because she is the repository of faith, men have life only when they are connected to her and allow themselves to be fed by her upon the true doctrine of God that has been entrusted to her and the living presence of God, i.e., the Holy Spirit who dwells within her. St. Irenaeus's description of Mother Church is quite earthy and graphic. She nourishes her children (*nutriri, enutriri*). She is the source of their continued life and growth which they receive at her bosom (*in eius sinu*), "taking in their nourishment through her breasts (*mammillis*)."[54] And she feeds them *lac* (milk) that comes from the *corpus Christi*.[55] This *body of Christ* is synonymous with herself, the Second Eve, of whom, the Christ, the Second Adam, is the head.

St. Clement of Alexandria also teaches that the "Virgin Mother," the Church, nurses her children with the holy milk of the Logos. In *The Instructor* he comments upon 1 Cor. 3:2 where St. Pauls says: "I fed you with milk, not with solid food, for you were not yet ready for it." For Clement "the milk is the Word (Logos), Christ, rained down, like manna, by a loving Father. This milk offered us by the Church in the preaching of the Gospel becomes solid food—our faith."[56] St. Cyprian in his work *The Unity of the Catholic Church* speaks of the Church as a mother who nourishes her children by the milk of her breasts:

> [the Church] spreads her branches in generous growth over all the earth, she extends her abundant streams even further; yet one is the headspring, *one the source, one the mother* who is prolific in her offspring, generation after generation; *of her womb we are born, of her milk we are fed*, of her Spirit our souls draw their life-breath. (Emphasis added.)[57]

St. Cyprian's words are powerful in their stark simplicity: "of her womb we are born, of her milk we are fed." It is important to notice that the mother here is a *source*—a source in the sense of being an *origin of life* from which her maternal authority flows as from a "headspring." A little later in the same passage Cyprian will warn that one must stay connected to the *Mater Ecclesia*, the origin of life, as he says: "You cannot have God for your Father if you have not the Church for your mother."[58] To perish is to withdraw oneself from the bosom of the Church: "For my part I hope, dearest brethren . . . if possible, not one of the brethren should perish, but that our Mother should have the happiness of clasping to her bosom all our people in one like-minded body."[59]

St. Augustine even repeats St. Cyprian's famous phrase in connection with the Church's ability to nourish her children.

> Love the Lord because He loves you, go often near your mother who has engendered you. See what this mother gives you: she has united the creature with the creator, of servants she has made sons of God, of slaves of the devil

brothers of Christ. For these great blessings you will not be ungrateful if you render to Him the homage of your presence. *No one can have God for a benevolent Father if he despises the Church, his Mother.* This holy and spiritual Mother each day prepares for you a spiritual nourishment, by which she replenishes not your body but your soul. She gives you the bread from heaven, she presents to you the cup of salvation. She does not desire that any of her children should suffer from this hunger. Take care, my brothers not to abandon such a Mother. (Emphasis added.)[60]

The food that Mother Church gives to her children is the "bread from heaven" and the "cup of salvation," namely, the Holy Eucharist. The Church is not the source of the Eucharistic Body of Christ in the sense that this sacrament is caused by the faith of the community. The Eucharist is caused by the apostolic authority of the priesthood to offer the one sacrifice standing in the person of Christ. How then can St. Augustine say that it is Mother Church who feeds us upon the "bread from heaven"? Have we not already argued that it is Christ Himself who is feeding us through His priesthood? To answer the question is to get at the heart of how feminine authority functions in the Church. We are fed upon the Eucharist (and nourished by the other sacraments as well) in the same way, or (we should say) according to the order of salvation in which Christ became a man. The Church, like Mary, is a concrete historical entity called by God to be the repository of His grace. God became man through a woman—she has given the Second Person of the Trinity His historical *real presence*. We receive *the Body of Christ* from the Church that exists according to the Marian maternal principle. As Mary gives us Christ—the Church gives us Christ. As Christ was nursed at Mary's breasts so those reborn as "other Christs" in the baptismal womb of the Church are nursed at her breasts. The Church, bride of the New Adam, is New Eve to us: mother of all the living. The Holy Eucharist comes through the Church as she is united to Christ as Bride—and is simultaneously a mother.

Let us furthermore recall the Christ "born of a woman" is the Christ born to "give His life as a ransom for many" (Matt 20:28, Mark 10:45). His being born, in other words, the Incarnation itself, is from the beginning irrevocably connected to the sacrifice of Christ. And, of course, this sacrifice is one and the same with the Eucharist. To appreciate the Eucharist is to be brought back to the maternal principle upon which it is based. The Body of Christ Christians eat is the broken body of Christ born of Mary. St. Augustine taught that the Body of Christ in the Eucharist was the same body conceived by the Blessed Virgin.

In hesitation I turn to Christ, since I am herein seeking Himself; and I discovered how the earth may be worshipped without impiety. For he took upon him earth for earth; because flesh is from earth, *and He received flesh from the flesh of Mary. And because He walked here in very flesh, and gave that very flesh to us to eat for our salvation.* (Emphasis added.)[61]

This theme has been carried over the Christian centuries and today even finds a voice in Pope John Paul II.

"Ave verum Corpus natum de Virgine"!
Hail true Body born of the Virgin Mary!
On the feast of the Most Holy Body and Blood of Christ, our grateful thanks is raised to the Father, who has given us the Divine Word, the living Bread come down from heaven, and our thanks is joyfully raised to the Virgin, who offered the Lord his innocent Flesh and his precious Blood which we receive at the altar. "Ave verum Corpus": true body, truly conceived through the work of the Holy Spirit, borne in the womb with ineffable love . . . born for us of the Virgin Mary.

That divine Body and Blood, which after the consecration is present on the altar. . . . *preserves its maternal origin from Mary.* She prepared that Body and Blood before offering them to the Word as a gift from the whole human family that he might be clothed in them in becoming our Redeemer, the High Priest and Victim.

At the root of the Eucharist, therefore, there is the virginal and maternal life of Mary . . . which through the work of the Holy Spirit made her flesh a temple and her heart an altar . . . And if the Body that we eat and the Blood that we drink is the inestimable gift of the Risen Lord to us travelers, it still has in itself, as fragrant Bread, the taste and aroma of the Virgin Mary.[62]

The covenantal partnership between God and Mary is brought out in this passage. Thanks is to be given not only to the Father who sent the Son into the world, but also to Mary by whom Christ became man. The words of John Paul II bring out very beautifully the maternal origin of the Eucharistic Lord. He is Eucharistic Lord because His presence on the altar rests on the maternal "yes" of His mother in the Incarnation. The Church standing as the New Eve continues to make Him present. Thus she is our mother who, continuing the truth about Mary, gives the "bread from heaven" upon which her children are to feed.

The spiritual nourishment the Church provides to the faithful within the sacramental system is intrinsic to the motherhood of the Church. It is part of the feminine responsibility for the faith. For now it is important at least to make clear how sexual symbolism is connected to this issue. It is not mere poetic metaphor to say of the Church that she is a mother who feeds her children through the sacraments of the Church (and also via Scripture and doctrine). This nourishing is a free maternal activity because the spiritual sustenance provided by the Church is *her own food.* Grace and the Holy Spirit are intrinsic to the Church's nature as milk is to a nursing mother. The Lord is within her as he dwelled in the womb of the Virgin. In the words of John Paul II above: "the Holy Spirit made her flesh a temple." The person born of Mary was God Most High—but He was yet the fruit of her womb! And thus we are fed by what comes through and is of the Body of Christ, the Church, His bride, our mother. A male, on the other hand, has no food within him by which others may be fed. A man feeds others by foreign substances he must acquire outside of himself. This is not so for the pregnant mother or new birth mother. But let us not make the mistake of saying that the Church is the source of the sacraments of herself as if to turn the Church into some humanist project. The sacraments are obtainable through the Church within the covenantal relationship that exists between her and Christ. In the following passage from St. Augustine, the creation of the Church and the sacraments are intimately associated.

> But where did [Christ] sleep? On the Cross. When He slept on the Cross, He bore a sign, yea, He fulfilled what had been signified in Adam: for when Adam was asleep, a rib was drawn from him, and Eve was created; so also while the Lord slept on the Cross, His side was transfixed with a spear, and the Sacraments flowed forth, whence the Church was born. For the Church the Lord's Bride was created from His side, as Eve was created from the side of Adam. But as she was made from his side no otherwise than while sleeping, so the Church was created from His side no otherwise than while dying.[63]

In St. Augustine's commentary on Psalm 41, in a similar passage, he states that Eve was called "mother of all living" precisely in view of the fact that she signified the Church sprung from Christ's side.[64] Tertullian, in *On the Soul,* also sees the sleep of Adam as a prefiguration of Christ's death and the creation of the Church from his side.[65] Plumpe, commenting upon the passage from Tertullian, states:

> The implication is clear: as our physical life is from Adam *through our first mother, Eve,* so our entire spiritual life is derived ultimately from Christ, the Second Adam, *through our Second Mother, the Church.* She gives us birth and life through the water of baptism, presignified by the blood and water that flowed from Christ's side, *giving life to our Mother herself.* (Emphasis added.)[66]

As we saw in the above quotation from St. Augustine, the sacraments, signified by blood and water flowing from the side of Christ, bring the Church into being: "the Sacraments flowed forth, whence the Church was born." However, the Sacraments that give life to the Church are also distributed through her as it is through her intimate union with Christ the head that she becomes the true "Mother of All the Living." From within Christ "rivers of living water shall flow" (John 7:38). These living waters are the Holy Spirit (John 7:39). The Church, the bride of Christ, sprung from His side, is the place where the living waters of Christ flow in the world—making her a fertile mother.

One has access to these living waters by maintaining union with Mother Church. Certainly this was the teaching of St. Irenaeus when he taught that one partakes of God by taking nourishment at the breasts of Mother Church.

The Christian never actually outgrows Mother Church. Indeed, the entire Patristic witness declares that those who do leave her risk their eternal salvation. In the words of St. Cyprian, quoted earlier, "She it is that keeps us unharmed for God, she appoints the sons she has begotten to His kingdom." Salvation is dependent upon remaining in the womb of Mother Church wherein the Christian has access to the food of God.

> The Church is not a mother "in the way Eve was"; she does not give birth to a people "whose birth would be a tearing away and the source of innumerable oppositions." . . . Quite the contrary, through childbirth, her goal is to react tirelessly against this misery that is so congenital to our sinful race and to "gather into a single body the dispersed children of God." That is what is expressed in a paradoxical image: whereas, in the physical order, *the child leaves the womb of his mother, and withdrawing from her, becomes increasingly independent of her protective guardianship as he grows . . . the Church brings us forth to the new life she bears by receiving us into her womb, and the more our divine education progresses, the more we are intimately bound to her.* St. Irenaeus was already saying "one must cling to the Church, be brought up within her womb and feed there on the Lord's Scripture." (Emphasis added.)[67]

IV. Mother and Teacher

The Church, because she gives birth to the children of God is also, as a mother, entrusted with the godly education of these children. The educative task of the Magisterium is accomplished within the Church as mother. She, too, is *teacher*—guiding, directing, protecting, educating the faithful unto eternal life via Word and Sacrament. While the clergy as fathers feed the flock under their care, the whole Church as mother is entrusted with the spiritual upbringing of her children. For Tertullian, the Church was not only a mother in baptism, but in the education of her children afterwards as well.[68] To fall into heresy was to be "motherless."[69] St. Hippolytus connects even the preaching task of the Church to her maternal power: "the church will not cease to bear from her heart . . . the Word . . . by which is meant that the church, always bringing forth Christ . . . becomes the instructor of all nations."[70]

The Church existing as both mother and teacher was confirmed by Pope John XXIII in his famous encyclical *Mater et Magistra* .

> The Catholic Church has been established by Jesus Christ as Mother and Teacher of nations, so that all who in the course of centuries come to her loving embrace, may find salvation as well as the fullness of a more excellent life. To this Church, "the pillar and mainstay of the truth," her most holy Founder has entrusted the noble task of begetting sons unto herself, and *of educating and governing those whom she begets,* guiding with maternal providence the life both of individuals and of peoples. (Emphasis added.)[71]

Max Thurian suggests that Mary served as a teacher to the Apostles following the resurrection of her Son. The Acts of the Apostles 1:12-14 records her presence in the midst of the Eleven in the Upper Room. At the foot of the Cross she was declared "Mother of All the Living" and was given John as her son. For this disciple and for all the disciples Mary is a type of Mother Church. She will be able, in the power of the Spirit, to transmit to the disciples and the early Church all that she knew about her Son—everything that she had guarded and pondered in her heart (Luke 2:19, 51). In this she is a spiritual mother to the disciples, recalling for them what Christ did and said.[72]

According to the model of the Blessed Virgin Mary, the Church is a teacher by disclosing the mystery of her Son. This is the fundamental educative task with which she has been entrusted by God. The Church who educates as Mother is not simply she who tenderly guides her children submissively receiving whatever comes from the hand of the bishop. Rather, she is an educator who fights for the proper food for her children—the food that her spouse, the Lord, wills her to have and of which she refuses to be deprived. Thus the Church as Mother contains within herself an authority to admonish bishops to be true and faithful Fathers. The Church as Mother *calls them* to fatherhood. She is their teacher.

When one enters into the bosom of Mother Church one enters into the school of divine life. Taken into the Church is to be taken into *her life* —fed upon her breasts, through her intimate maternal care one is taken into the practice of the faith. Might this not be what Paul Claudel meant concerning his own conversion: "Praised be this great majestic Mother, at whose knees I have learned everything!"[73]

V. The Feminine Side of Worship

Christ's death on the Cross is the supreme act of the head as *source* of the body, which is His bride, the flesh that completes Him. The order of redemption that exists within this "one flesh" covenant is made real in history through the true worship of the Church, namely, the Holy Eucharist. Where this worship exists there is the Church. The Church continues the reality of Mary, as Mary, *plena gratia*, conceived the Son, the Church achieves her own self-realization in the Eucharist. It is here that the Lord is covenantally present to her. "In this event the holy society which is the good creation, the covenant and the sacrifice, the '*Christus totus*,' has its foundation and central expression."[74]

This worship is not simply a monist re-presentation of Christ—rather the worship is effected by (and effects the Church through) the covenantal union of Christ and His people. As we saw, Christ's redemptive role is an inherently masculine one; the Church's redemptive function, in relation to Him, is no less inherently feminine. The Christian woman possesses authority to be the sign of the fullness of covenantal response to the initiative of Christ—a response that *completes and fulfills the covenant* by which the world is saved.

We can return for a moment to an earlier passage from John Paul II.

> Born of the Virgin to be a pure, holy and immaculate oblation, Christ offered on the Cross the one perfect Sacrifice which every Mass, in an unbloody manner, renews and makes present. In that one sacrifice, Mary, the first redeemed, the Mother of the Church, had an active part. She stood near the Crucified, suffering deeply with her First-born; with a motherly heart she associated herself with His Sacrifice; with love she consented to his immolation (cf. "Lumen Gentium," 58; "Marialis Cultus," 20) *she offered him and she offered herself to the Father*. Every Eucharist is a memorial of that Sacrifice and that Passover that restored life to the world; every Mass puts us into intimate communion with her, the Mother, whose sacrifice "becomes present" just as the sacrifice of her Son "becomes present" at the words of consecration of the bread and wine pronounced by the priest.[75]

Mary, in her "*fiat*," in her offering up of Christ on the Cross, stands for the entire human race. Woman confirms the goodness of creation.

Mary appears as the prototype of a creation which is . . . called to respond; she manifests the freedom of the creature, a freedom which is not dissolved, but comes to its fulfillment, in love. *But it is precisely as a woman that she exemplifies saved and liberated mankind,* that is, in the physical specificity which is inseparable from the human being: "Male and female he created them." (Emphasis added.)[76]

Creation, coming from the hand of God, is capable of life; restored in grace it can give its own response in love.[77] Yves Congar explains that, contrary to Protestantism, and to Luther in particular, this cooperation of the creature in redemption is fundamental to Catholicism. "Our Lady in the redemptive work of the Incarnation stands for the part of humanity and of the Church."[78]

Lack of appreciation for feminine authority comes from a monism—by definition radically one-sided—which cancels out the covenantal order of redemption. Consider Luther's statement: "Just as Christ was conceived by the Holy Spirit, so anyone who has faith is justified and reborn by the operation of the same Spirit, *quite apart from any work of man.*"[79] Congar explains that for Luther salvation "is an *opus Dei,* God's work not ours; and therefore God's *only.* He says for instance: 'It is not ourselves who perform the good works we do, it is he.'"[80] Man's response of faith to God is solely God's action also.[81] Karl Barth, in total agreement with Luther on this point, writes that not only is it God who speaks to us, but he who hears in us as well.[82] Congar comments, "no activity on our part is needed to make fruitful what Christ has done."[83] He goes on to draw the ultimate conclusion from Luther's position. If redemption is the action of God solely, according to a monist principle, in which man and creation have no active constitutive role, then the very humanity of Christ has no salvific function. There is nothing from the side of creation, from the side of man that is actively involved in the work of salvation. The Incarnation itself is all God's work. This means woman in Mary, as sign of the whole human race, is utterly insignificant. But to cancel Mary is to cancel the Incarnation.[84] It has been said of Luther that he invented a radically masculinized Christianity;[85] masculinized by rejecting any goodness of creation that stands in relation to God and can respond to Him in praise—the Church, Mary, and all mankind.

In the Eucharist, Christ comes to us. But the Eucharist is not only Christ coming to us. It is also the response of the bride—in that joyous covenantal one flesh unity with Him. This is the teaching, moreover, of Vatican II: "Christ, indeed, always associates the Church with himself in this great work in which God is perfectly glorified and men are sanctified. The Church is his beloved Bride who calls to her Lord, and through Him offers worship to the eternal Father."[86] The one-flesh marital order of creation protects against a dry and stunted Christo-monism, or as Congar stated, the "disastrous adjective *sola gratia, sola fide*"[87] in which the Church, as man's response, is absorbed into the uniqueness of Christology.[88] It is good to remind ourselves at this point that:

> In Paul's usage . . . the "Body of Christ" (which we are) is always to be understood against the background of Gn. 2:24: "The two became one flesh" (cf. I Cor 6:17). The Church is the body, the flesh of Christ, in the spiritual tension of love in which the conjugal mystery of Adam and Eve is fulfilled, in the dynamism of unity which does not eliminate reciprocity. This means that the very eucharistic-christological mystery of the Church which is proclaimed in the term "Body of Christ" can only keep its proper proportions if it includes the marian mystery, namely, that of the Virgin who hears the word and—having been liberated by grace—utters her "Fiat" and thus becomes the Bride and the Body.[89]

In the Eucharistic worship Christ offers Himself up for the Church. In relation to Him the Church offers herself in a sacrifice of praise. This reality, and no other, is the foundation of the New Covenant. The center of the economy of salvation is the *Christus totus*—the head and body.[90] Women are the sign of the total self-offering of the body whereby, through feminine symboling power, the covenant of salvation is made real in history. Christ is born of a woman (Gal. 4:4). Grace is mediated to the world *through* Mother Church. Every Christian woman, according to the meaning of female sexuality, is the concrete historical reality of what the Church is as a whole.

In Eucharistic worship it is the woman, as the locus of everything good about creation, who provides the necessary sacramental response by which the "one flesh" unity of Church and Christ is expressed historically. Without the feminine response to God Christian worship would be meaningless— indeed, Christianity would be some other religion. If the symbols of human sexuality by which the Church worships are changed, the religion itself collapses. The order of redemption is bound up with marital freedom by which all of creation is affirmed as good.

THE PRIESTHOOD OF THE FAITHFUL AS FEMININE

Lumen Gentium teaches: "Though they differ essentially and not only in degree, the common priesthood of the faithful and the ministerial priesthood are none the less ordered to one another; each in its own proper way shares in the priesthood of Christ."[91] The ministerial priesthood is rooted in the meaning of male authority—definitely exercised in the offering of the One Sacrifice by the Incarnate Son of God. The Eucharistic sacrifice can only be offered by one who can rightfully express this kind of life-giving authority—namely, another male "who has been made sacramentally one with [Christ] so as to be able to say in all sacramental truth: this is my body, this is my blood."[92] If the ministerial priesthood is rooted in the meaning of male authority then one can say, particularly when it comes to Eucharistic worship, that the sacrifice of praise offered by the common priesthood of the baptized has a distinctly feminine character—even though this priesthood is exercised by men as well as women. Again, we are asking whether women exemplify "the sacrifice of praise," made by the common priesthood of the faithful—that this sacrifice, whether offered by males or females, finds its deepest, truest meaning expressed within feminine sexuality. Throughout the history of the Church, the Fathers, theologians, and especially mystics like Bernard of Clairvaux spoke of the human soul as female in relation to the redemptive grace of God.[93] C. S. Lewis defended the all male priesthood by stating that outside of the sacrament of orders "we are all, corporately and individually, feminine [to God]."[94] This point of view attempts to express the truth about the feminine, that woman, as the perfection of the creature *as creature*[95] is the full symbol of openness and reciprocity to God. However, we must be careful not to dissolve masculine sexuality into the feminine, thus rendering it theologically and sacramentally insignificant. Men worship by and through the feminine Church whereby access to God is made possible. And they worship *in ecclesia*, according to the feminine paradigm of openness and reciprocity of which women are the full sacramental reality. But as sons of this mother their masculinity is not erased and made sexually insignificant to the order of redemption.

Feminists charge the Church Fathers with teaching that faith turned women into men. Let us not make the comparable mistake and say Catholic worship turns men into women. Yes, the Church in relation to Christ is feminine. The unordained male's sexuality serves as the covenantal sacramental symbol whereby women, as sign of the Church in worship, can be recognized, appreciated, and understood as such—within family life, within the workplace, as well as within Eucharistic worship.

Once again, however, the priesthood of the faithful is definitively expressed by Christian women as they stand over and against the ordained priesthood according to the marital structure of redemption. This is so because the feminine is associated with creation—with what the Father has brought forth in his creative act and in woman (as in Mary) creation makes its response of praise.

The Eucharistic sacrifice is offered by the whole Christ—head and body. The priesthood of the faithful is most definitively engaged when participating in the Eucharist to which all other works of charity are ordered. As *Lumen Gentium* states: "Taking part in the eucharistic sacrifice, the source

and summit of Christian life, they offer the divine victim to God and themselves along with it."[96] The offering of the whole Christ is accomplished
according to the symbols of male and female sexuality that express the
"one flesh" unity of the covenant that is brought about and perpetuated by
the Eucharist.

> It is the meal in which the Church responds to his love by making his
> sacrificial act her own. Thus *Christ and the Church* return to the Father in a
> sacrificial worship that expresses their union as Bridegroom and Bride. . . .[97]
> Just as Christ, the New Adam, offered His sacrifice on Calvary, and Mary, the
> New Eve and figure of the Church, united herself with his offering, so in the
> Eucharist the ordained priest makes Christ's offering present and the Church
> throughout history continues to unite herself with that offering . . . a woman
> cannot be the sacramental image of Christ in the act that is proper to him
> precisely as the New Adam. The symbolism of the New Adam and the New
> Eve expresses the relation between Christ and the Church which is profoundly
> involved in the Eucharistic celebration. . . .[98] And if it is proper to a woman
> to be a sacramental representation not of Christ but of the Church, does it not
> follow that she could not represent any offering *other than the offering of the
> Church* ? In that case she would represent the Church as principle offerer in an
> offering distinct from that of Christ. (Emphasis added.)[99]

Many who favor women's ordination believe that the presence of the
male priest acting *in persona Christi* is a sign that the Eucharist is male
dominated and male centered. This is the reason why in certain liturgical
circles concelebration is discouraged. It means that men will outnumber
women on the altar—and in the feminist mind the sanctuary is the domain
of power. However, Eucharistic worship is not dominated by male power,
rather it is permeated by and ultimately entered into by way of femininity—
by the totally indispensable role women play in the Church's worship. The
Eucharist is the celebration of the beloved's love for the bride. Women are
the concrete, historical expression of this Bride. Indeed, the entire priestly
office exists to serve, not itself, but the life-giving authority of the Church,
at once Wife and Mother.

VI. The Church—Mother of Priests

The Church is the mother of the faithful—giving birth to sons and daughters
of God in baptism. In doing this she is also the source (or mother) of
bishops and priests that come from her body through the power of the Holy
Spirit. De Lubac strongly acknowledges that clergy do not receive authority

from the Christian community, rather "they are given to the Church by the Father. They are not delegates of the community, but Christ's delegates within it."[100] Nevertheless, it is because of the Church's maternal role that priests are nurtured within her. They are dependent upon her for their very purpose and being. Consider the words of St. Augustine:

> Where in fact did these bishops come from who are all over the world today? The Church calls them fathers, *she who gave birth to them, who placed them in the sees of their fathers.* Do not, therefore, consider yourself abandoned because you no longer see Peter in person, or Paul, or because you no longer see those to whom you owe your birth: a fatherhood has arisen for you from among your own children. . . . Such is the Catholic Church. *She has given birth to sons* who, through all the earth, continue the work of her first Fathers. (Emphasis added.)[101]

The teaching of 1 Cor. 11:12 "In the same way that woman was made from man, so man is born of woman; and all is from God" is confirmed by the relation of the clergy to Mother Church. In the Church's perpetual principle of renewal, she never ceases to give birth to her fathers.[102] We are at the heart of the meaning of Sacred Tradition itself. It is not enough that God wills the Church have fathers. Sacred Tradition and also Apostolic Succession have life within the concrete reality of the Church as she exists in relation to Christ as wife and mother. It is *Mater Ecclesia*, imbued with all feminine life-giving principles, who extends Christ into the world. This is because it is woman who secures history, confirms its validity, and carries it into the future.

Hans Urs Von Balthasar has provided a wonderfully insightful explanation of the dependency of the apostolic-Petrine office on the bridal Church of whom Mary is the archetype. He states:

> This Marian profile is also—even perhaps more so—fundamental and characteristic for the church as is the apostolic and Petrine profile to which it is profoundly united. . . . The Marian dimension of the church is antecedent to that of the Petrine, without being in any way divided from it or being less complementary. Mary Immaculate precedes all others, including obviously Peter himself and the apostles. This is so, not only because Peter and the apostles, being born of the human race under the burden of sin, form part of the church which is "holy from out of sinners," but also because their triple function has no other purpose except to form the church in line with the ideal of sanctity already programmed and prefigured in Mary. A contemporary theologian has rightly stated that Mary is "queen of the apostles without pretensions to apostolic powers: She has other and greater powers."[103]

It is important again to mention that the authority of the clergy as fathers to the Church is derivative. It is not theirs—it is Christ's.[104] But the authority of the Church's motherhood is indeed her own.

VII. The Divinization of Woman

The Church possesses authority as the covenantal partner of Christ standing in relation to Him as bride and mother. Her authority, and the authority of women who exemplify the Church in the world, stands, not on the side of divinity but on the side of creation. Women are creation's authoritative life-giving voice. Nothing more severely attacks the covenantal order of redemption and thus the authority of women within this order, particularly their sacramental role in the Eucharistic celebration, than the disastrous notion that women must stand on the side of God in order for them to possess power and be equal with men. But this is precisely the theology of liberation theologian Leonardo Boff regarding Mary in his book *The Maternal Face of God*. Boff asks two very important theological questions about women: 1) To what extent is the feminine a path to God for humanity? and 2) Conversely, to what extent is the feminine a path to humanity for God?[105] In answering these questions Boff, however, commits the fatal error common to nearly all feminist theology. In order for women to have dignity, equality, and authority, somehow you have to get women up into God. As long as woman stays on the side of matter and creation, she is nothing, or at least she remains victim to the dominance of the masculine. The way to overcome this inherently unjust situation of women is to feminize God in her: "the feminine would have a divine depth, and God would have a feminine dimension."[106] Boff's theology proceeds from a flawed critique of the Christian religion itself:

> Judeo-Christianity is an eminently masculine religious expression. God is a Father, God has an eternal Son, that Son is born in time, of a virgin. In its institutional presentation, Judeo-Christianity is a religion of males. Theirs is the monopoly of the means of symbolic production. They are the ones who organize and preside over the Christian community. Women's place is marginal. Jesus Christ's masculinity has attained its divinization, while his feminine aspect, according to common tradition, has remained in its creaturely state. . . . The Old and New Testaments are books about men in a society of men. Women are merely "ancillary."[107]

Such a vision of the Judeo-Christian religion can only be arrived at by examining the Church through a monist lens. However, the faith of

Christ is covenantally, maritally based, to which the feminine has always been indispensable. To be on the side of creation (rather than divinized or made into a god according to the feminist program of equal rights) is woman's glory, not her denigration, because in her Christ and the covenant of salvation is complete.

Boff's basic thesis states that each human being possesses a masculine and feminine side.[108] Even Christ is put together according to Jungian psychology.[109] This masculinity and femininity adheres imperfectly in human beings, but perfectly in God.[110] In God, Christ represents the masculine principle and the Holy Spirit the feminine.[111] Of course Boff does not fail to quote Carl Jung and on the Assumption of Mary:

> P erhaps this definition may lead the Church to a deeper consideration and the ultimate formulation of the mystery of God's motherhood: in her Assumption Mary returns to her source. Not she but God is the ultimate prototype of motherhood and femininity, even materially. . . . Just as Christ, in ascending to heaven, carried us to the arms of God our eternal Father, may it not be that Mary, assumed into heaven, means to lead us to a deeper knowledge and love of God our eternal Mother?[112]

This position is extremely dangerous to the significance of women, not merely to that of Mary. If God is the ultimate prototype of motherhood, this means women are not. Boff, in attempting to secure the dignity of women, has in effect robbed them of their dignity because he has taken away their reality. Women will not be the fullness of what they are—but will become sacramentally transparent as men—representing what they are not. Boff empties femininity of its own meaning and gives the ultimate reality to God. In this all the ancient pagan pessimisms are reinvented. Creation has no reality or goodness of its own. It can make no response to God that is not already God. For justice to exist God must swallow everything. In Boff's theology Mary as woman is not the perfection of creation, over and against God, who gives a sacrifice of praise in a graced freedom that is her own. Here the Lutheran dictum finds its radicalized fulfillment. God not only speaks to us—He really *does hear* in us as well!!! Boff, standing on Jung's foundation, agrees that "God, the eternal Mother, the absolute feminine, is totally historicized in the life of Mary."[113]

Mother God becomes historicized in Mary by the Holy Spirit "hypostatically divinizing the feminine, directly and explicitly, and divinizing the masculine implicitly—just the converse of the divinization of the male human being Jesus by the eternal Word."[114] Mary is "hypostatically united to the Third Person of the Blessed Trinity."[115]

The conclusion to this is that because of "the equal dignity of the masculine and the feminine, both have the same mission—that of being a sacrament of God within creation."[116]

Both have the same mission. Gone is what is unique to male and female sexuality that is constitutive of the covenant between God and creation. God alone speaks. Creation is silent. Boff's thesis is stated quite clearly: "Mary is raised to the level of God in order to be able to engender God. . . . Mary is assumed by the Holy Spirit, and thus elevated to the level of God."[117] This elevation occurred when Mary uttered her *"fiat."*[118] From then on "The Spirit began to assume in her everything that would ever happen in her life."[119]

Since this spiritualization of Mary does not occur until the Annunciation, one can assume that Mary was her own person until that point. But what happens to the person of Mary after this? Who is acting? Who is speaking? Who responds to God? Undoubtedly Boff would not deny that the person of Mary still exists. But she has had her entire person united to the Holy Spirit—*hypostatically* united. Certainly the significance of Mary's personhood as a created creature is diminished—the part that a human person *qua* creature could ever play in the drama of redemption has been obliterated. It is no longer a creature, a woman, standing for all humanity, who conceives Christ within the covenantal freedom of a graced human will. Rather, even the Mother of God who should be the pinnacle of creation's response to the creator, must be raised to the level of God before God can be brought into the world. Ironically, in Boff's admirable attempt to secure feminine authority, he actually ends up, by turning women into God, emptying woman of what is basic to her authority—her ability to give life *in a motherhood* that *is hers* in the order of redemption, and not God's. This does not mean that women have not received their power to give life from God. They have received it as gift. But as gift it is truly theirs. Eve is taken from the side of Adam. He, as symbol of God's generative power, is her *source* as head to body. This marital/covenantal order rests on the reality of male and female sexuality as irreducible to each other. The problem with Boff's theology is that God essentially takes over Mary's role, and thus women's role in salvation.

Boff goes so far as to say that because the Holy Spirit assumes the person of Mary: "God the Mother engenders the humanity of the eternal Son."[120] If it is God the mother who engenders Christ, what then is left for Mary who is called Mother of God? Of course, Boff solves the dilemma on the basis that the Holy Spirit is hypostatically united to Mary—thus Mary's maternity is that of the Holy Spirit within her. But this leads to the conclusion that as a mere creature in relation to the Spirit, Mary is not the mother of Christ. Her motherhood is God's motherhood.

Regarding Mary's motherhood of Christ Boff states that: "Only the divine can engender the divine."[121] Because Mary was lifted to the level of divinity what she bears is holy.[122] The first statement robs woman of her true creaturely maternal role in the Incarnation. The second statement gives the distinct impression that had Mary remained a mere woman her offspring would somehow have been tainted, left unholy by her creatureliness. But it is Mary, not as hypostatically united to to the Holy Spirit who is holy, but *the female person herself* who, full of grace as a human being, gives herself to God completely. This is the true meaning of her existence as the New Eve—that creation, *qua* creation, can be holy and respond to God—*without being God.*

Boff tries to secure the Good Creation not by simply filling it with God—but by making it God.[123] In terms of covenantal response nothing is offered by this Good Creation that God does not already give to Himself. This means that the Good Creation, as such, does not exist. In the end everything will be God.[124]

VIII. The Feminine Response to the Covenant

The covenantal love between Christ and His people is made present sacramentally in the Eucharist. The Eucharist functions as a sign of what it means to be male and female in Christ and here the Good Creation is itself affirmed. It is affirmed by the fact that Christ died for His bridal Church—it is affirmed in that unity of the one flesh by the fact that the Church responds to His love. Women are the full sign of this response in the world. Absent this feminine response, rooted in the concrete reality of feminine sexual symbolism, and not only the Church, but the world itself is plunged into chaos and dissolution. Regarding the authority of women, we quote again Von Balthasar:

> While man as a sexual being, only represents what he is not and transmits what he does not actually possess, and so is . . . at the same time more and less than himself, *woman rests on herself, she is fully what she is,* that is, the whole reality of a created being that faces God as a partner, receives his seed and spirit, preserves them, brings them to maturity and educates them. . . . Restored nature would bring to light—within the parity of nature and parity of value of the sexes—above all the fundamental difference, *according to which woman does not represent, but is,* while man has to represent and, therefore, is more and less than what he is. . . .
>
> It should give woman a feeling of exaltation to know that she—particularly in the Virgin Mother Mary—is the privileged place where God can and wishes to be received in the world. Between the first Incarnation of the Word of God in

Mary and its ever new arrival in the receiving Church, they must participate—whether they have an office or not—in this comprehensive femininity of the Marian Church. (Emphasis added.)[125]

The Adam/Eve, Christ/Church one flesh unity is not wiped away even in the eschatological order. Indeed, the Book of Revelation affirms the nuptial structure of redemption wherein God and His creation are perfectly fulfilled.

> Then I saw a new heavens and a new earth. The former heavens and the former earth had passed away, and the sea was no longer. I also saw a new Jerusalem, the holy city, coming down out of heaven from God, beautiful as a bride prepared to meet her husband. I heard a loud voice from the throne cry out: "This is God's dwelling among men. He shall dwell with them and they shall be his people and he shall be their God who is always with them." (Rev. 21:1-4)

To the very end the words of Scripture testify to the glorious marital order of redemption—in which Christ, the New Adam, is not alone—but is with His bride in the completion of His redemptive work. Woman's place is forever affirmed as "The Spirit and the Bride say, 'Come!'" (Rev. 22:17).

6

The Authority of Women

I. Woman—Center of the World's Moral Order

WOMAN—CENTER AND SOURCE OF LIFE

Pope John Paul II stated in his apostolic letter *Mulieris Dignitatem* that what is human has been entrusted to women. "The moral and spiritual strength of a woman is joined to her awareness that God entrusts the human being to her in a special way . . . precisely by reason of her femininity."[1] This is why the Church, rooted in feminine life-giving principles, is bride of Christ and mother of the faithful. These feminine life-giving principles are true, concrete historical realities. We are not talking about merely imaginative metaphors, poetic metaphors, or some abstract ideal of the feminine. We are concerned at this point with the historical significance of the female human being, thus with her inherent life-giving powers within which the covenant of salvation resides and achieves its historical expression alongside the masculine.

Within the covenant of salvation woman is the life-giving center to which male authority is ordered. Male authority is in service to the feminine as Christ "gave himself up" for the Church. The moral order of the world is centered upon women's life-giving powers because what is human has been entrusted to her. The authority of woman is that she is "the keeper of the seal of creation."[2] Walter Kasper explains this feminine authority by saying:

> Woman's vocation, in accordance with creation, is the vocation to the service of life. She is Eve, that is to say, the mother of all the living (Gen 3:20). This vocation to motherhood can be fulfilled in different ways: in marriage and the

170

family, but also in celibacy, which frees people to devote themselves in another way to the service of the coming generation. . . . Responsibility for life and for humane conditions of life constitute the vocation of woman.[3]

The woman is the helpmate to man in that she has been "entrusted with the birth, nurture and care of life, that is, the concrete life of this unique individual person with his countless needs. . . .The woman possesses the special talent to nurture an individual life into its full development."[4] Through woman, life is preserved and perpetuated.[5]

According to anthropologist Ashley Montagu, women are actually superior to the male in terms of the necessary contribution the female sex makes to the survival of the human species. Superiority in any trait is measured by the extent to which that trait confers survival benefits upon the person and the group.[6] This corroborates the meaning of authority we have expressed in this work, namely, that authority, whether of God or man, has to do with conferring life—it is not the exercise of raw power. Montagu states that women are more valuable to the survival of the human race because of their stronger constitution. Prior to birth more male unborn children experience death than do females. And infant mortality rates are also higher for male neonates.[7] Woman also have a longer life expectancy than men.[8] Montagu notes that the male is more active, the female more quiescent, the male more katabolic, the female more anabolic. Woman is thus preserver of energy; she stores it rather than dissipates it. Montagu explains why this is significant in the relation between men and women in the service to life:

Undoubtedly there is a profound phylogenetic basis for this difference between the sexes. Geddes and Thomson were the first to offer the hypothesis that the female organism is characterized by a predominance of constructive utilization of energy, by *anabolism* as compared with *katabolism* or destructive utilization of energy. This hypothesis has been widely adopted. It is a useful and an interesting hypothesis, but actually it doesn't go far'enough in explaining the differences between the sexes with reference to the differences in the ends which they function to serve. The ends which both sexes serve is reproduction of the species. But reproduction of the species is not enough; the species must be maintained. And this is where the difference between the sexes expresses itself, for while it is the function of the male to produce fertilization, it is the function of the female to be fertilized and in the mammals to maintain the uterine developing organism and see it through not only to successful birth but through infancy and childbirth. . . .One may readily see, then, why the female is likely to be anabolic and the male katabolic. From the standpoint of survival the female is vastly more important biologically than the male, and it is therefore important that she be a conserver rather than a dissipater of energy.[9]

The woman is the "principal maintainer and protector of the species."[10] When Montagu says that men utilize energy destructively, this ought not be understood in any disparaging sense. In the act of conception, for example, a man loses what he possesses. All his sperm, passed over to the woman, will die except one alone. What a man earns or makes is consumed for life, "given up"—given away. In relation to the man, woman conserves, preserves, maintains what has been given to her. Indeed, only through the feminine can the male find himself extended into the future through her maternal life-bearing powers. The dissipating, conserving principles of male and female can readily be applied to the covenantal relation between Christ and the Church. Christ, the head, is the uncreated dispenser of grace—but this grace is given over to the Church, and within her womb, as within a reservoir, the faithful are maintained, preserved, and nurtured.

From the perspective of the social sciences, George Gilder has provided the key to understanding the authority of women and how men are ordered toward this authority. Otto Weininger remarked toward the end of the previous century, "Men possess sex; women are possessed by it." But, as Montagu himself noted, the very opposite is true.[11] Gilder's work supports Montagu's observation. Gilder's thesis states that when male sexual behavior is no longer placed in the service of the familially centered reproductive powers of the woman, the primary means by which social and also moral order in the world is maintained collapses and male energy, instead of being put to the service of life (because now disassociated from the feminine cycle of reproduction), serves only chaos and death in a reversion of civilization in which women end up, no longer honored, but used and then abandoned.

Gilder provides a stinging critique of our modern moral culture in which the sexual relation, by female capitulation to male demand, is temporary. It is the maternal life-giving powers of women that gives the male sex its actual significance whereby male sexuality, instead of dissipating in the burn-out of fleeting sexual encounters, is extended into the future, into history itself, with creative purpose. Thus women *do* possess sex—men are possessed by it.

> The divisions are embodied in a number of roles. The central ones are mother and father, husband and wife. They form neat and apparently balanced pairs. But appearances are deceptive. In the most elemental sexual terms, there is little balance at all. In most of those key sexual events, the male role is trivial, even easily dispensable. Although the man is needed in intercourse, artificial insemination has already been used in hundreds of thousands of cases. Otherwise the man is altogether unnecessary. It is the woman who conceives, bears, and suckles the child. Those activities which are most deeply sexual

are mostly female; they comprise the mother's role, defined organically by her body.

The nominally equivalent role of father is in fact a product of marriage and of other cultural contrivances. There is no biological need for the father to be anywhere around when the baby is born and nurtured. In many societies the father has no special responsibility to support the specific children he sires. In some societies paternity is not even acknowledged. The idea that the father is inherently equal to the mother within the family, or that he will necessarily be inclined to remain within it, is nonsense. In one way or another the man must be made equal by society.

In discussing the erotic aspects of our lives, we must concern ourselves chiefly with women. Males are the sexual outsiders and inferiors. A smaller portion of their bodies is directly erogenous. A far smaller portion of their lives is devoted to sexual activity. Their own distinctly sexual experience is limited to erection and ejaculation. Their rudimentary sexual drive leads only towards copulation. The male body offers no sexual fulfillment comparable to a woman's passage through months of pregnancy, to the tumult of childbirth, and on into the suckling of her baby. All are powerful and fulfilling sexual experiences completely foreclosed to men.[12]

We accept Gilder's thesis up to the point where he looks upon men as inferior. According to the Christian covenantal truth about men and women, all language about superior versus inferior must be eliminated. What we are concerned with is *difference*. Nonetheless, Gilder provides considerable insight into the ordering of the sexes. A woman is constantly affirmed in her sexuality by the reproductive cycle of her body "in a long unfolding process.... Whatever else she may do or be, she can be sure of her essential nature. Women take their sexual identity for granted."[13] As Von Balthasar said, a woman "is fully what she is." However, male sexuality on the level of bodily function is limited, thus male sexuality must be extended in action. But this action cannot be mere arbitrary exercises in freedom and power in what Gilder calls "undefined energies."[14] Gilder says these energies must be guided by culture. But not simply any culture will do, only one ordered around the life-giving powers of women.

The crucial process of civilization is the subordination of male sexual impulses and psychology to long-term horizons of female biology. If one compares female overall sexual behavior now with women's life in primitive societies, the difference is relatively small. It is male behavior that must be changed to create a civilized order. *Modern society relies increasingly on predictable, regular, long-term human activities, corresponding to the female sexual patterns. It has little latitude for the pattern of impulsiveness, aggressiveness, and immediacy, arising from male insecurity without women. . . . This is the ultimate and growing source of female power in the modern world. Women domesticate and civilize male nature. They can destroy civilized male identity merely by giving up the role.* (Emphasis added.)[15]

It is not necessarily the economy of the marketplace that women control—rather what they have authority over is "the economy of eros: the life force in our society and in our lives."[16] Because women are the keepers of the mystery of life, a woman's authority "over" a man lies in calling the male to the service of life and family of which she is the center. Gilder states it this way:

> Love performs its most indispensable role in inducing males to submit to female cycles of sexuality. In a civilized society men must ultimately overcome the limited male sexual rhythms of tension and release, erection and ejaculation, and adopt a sexual mode responsive to the extended female pattern—proceeding through pregnancy, childbirth, and nurture. By involving the long period of bearing and nurturing children, the female pattern entails a concern for the future.[17]

Because the male finds his identity and purpose in response to feminine life-giving powers that call him to lasting future-oriented commitment it is not difficult to see how it is that women can be called the heart of the family and of the home. Those who desire to free women from what they perceive to be the shackles of marriage and childbearing so that women may compete with men as "equals" in the public workplace fail to realize that all work, male or female, ought to be at the service of the home. Gilder stated, "The woman's place is in the home, and she does her best when she can get the man there too, inducing him to submit most human activity to the domestic values of civilization."[18]

THE MEANING OF FEMININE SURRENDER

When we say woman is the heart of the family, we need to dismiss any sense of heart in terms of mere soft, mushy, sentimental, emotional pietism. Heart must be understood in terms of that which places moral order in the world because it orders human relationships. Pope Pius XI wrote in *Casti Connubii*, "For if man is the head, the woman is the heart, as he occupies the chief place in ruling, so she ought to claim for herself the chief place in love."[19] Traditionally *ruling versus love* has been understood in terms of the rational versus the emotional—the former being male, the latter female. But we must come to a new deep conscious appreciation of the purpose to which the "ruling" authority of the male is put. Within the covenantally based union of man and woman perhaps we ought to dispense with such words altogether. Rulership connotes an extrinsic force for the sake of giving order to what would otherwise be in chaos. One cannot speak of the male-female relation in this sense. One cannot say that the male rules the female—rather they both are ruled by the covenant of the marriage to which their lives are both submitted. The authority is that of the One Flesh:

> . . . in the New Covenant, the Head, the Body and the One Flesh of their sacrificial union are constituted by their interrelation, and their mutual authority is qualitatively differentiated without subjugation: the Head gives himself totally to the Bridal Church, who gives herself totally in reply, and both are under the authority, the irrevocability of their union in One Flesh.[20]

Keeping in mind that within Christian marriage the husband represents Christ to his wife, he has authority to rule only in the sense that he can require of her what is essential to the life and meaning of the sacramental covenant they have been called to live. His "rulership" exists to bring her to sanctity, and when it is exercised in this way, she has an obligation, rooted in the will of God, to respond. His "rulership" is at the service of life. Feminine authority exists to bring the male to the fulfillment of his masculinity—and thus to sanctity as we will see more clearly below.

At this point we need to look at the much discussed (and nowadays derided) theological and psychological issue of feminine surrender. The paradigm of feminine surrender is, of course, the *"fiat"* of Mary—the total "yes" of her life to God which is the foundation of the Church's worship.[21] In terms of secular morals surrender to another is deemed as weakness. In the kingdom of God, however, it is the source of life-giving powers of which woman is the exemplar. Von le Fort states:

> Surrender to God is the only absolute power with which the creature is endowed. To bring about his salvation, all man has to contribute is his readiness to give himself up completely. The receptive, passive attitude of the feminine principle appears as the decisive, the positive element in the Christian order of grace. The Marian dogma, brought down to a simple formula, means the cooperation of the creature in the salvation of the world. . . . *In woman's constitutive desire to surrender, to give herself, rests the very depth of life.* (Emphasis added.)[22]

It is not independence, isolation, and autonomy, so cherished by the woman's movement, that causes life—but the very opposite. It is the willingness to be connected by a responsive receptivity and yielding of the woman to the man that life can be conceived into this world. Certainly the surrendering nature of the woman is revealed in the human act of procreation. The woman must literally open herself to the man and allow herself to be penetrated and filled by him. In her very yielding her authority is expressed. The man remains in isolation unless she does so. Indeed, feminine surrender to the male life-giving authority is the cause of human unity as it was in Mary the cause of humanity's union with God. When woman refuses to be united to God and to others, achieved ultimately through a willingness to give of herself, the moral order of the world, of which she is the heart, knows its dissolution. This is the true meaning of Eve's sin.

> The most profound surrender has as its opposite the possibility of utter refusal, and this is the negative side of the metaphysical mystery of woman. It is because, according to her very being, and her innermost meaning, she is not only destined to surrender, but constitutes the very power of surrender that is in the cosmos, that woman's refusal denotes something demonical and is felt as such.[23]

Feminine surrender is tied to life. When Eve refuses to receive God as God—indeed wills to take His place—she falls as does her husband with her. Adam, as a male, was tied to her destiny and to her refusal. This is why it is false to say that woman is the weaker sex. The Bible story clearly shows that while the man stands in the foreground of strength, woman dwells in its deeper realms. Woman is suppressed, not because she is weak, but because she is recognized and feared as possessing power. And when the stronger power refuses to surrender but looks for self-glorification, only catastrophe follows.[24]

A woman's very being reflects in its psychophysical nature openness and receptivity to others. "In the act of sexual union the male organ is convex and penetrating and the female organ is concave and receptive."[25] Even the action of the sperm cell in relation to the immobility of the female ovum indicates that this feminine "passivity" is at the service of receptivity.[26]

> The man's initiative and the woman's opening are not merely physical but also psychological. The man's dominance in penetrating and taking possession is an attitude of mind and heart, not mere bodily power. The woman's gift of herself to the man, his gift of himself to her, are spiritual and psychological as well as physical. His aggressive giving of his substance to her, her yielding of her substance, hidden deep within, to him, describe spiritual realities no less than biological ones.
>
> The woman shows submission and responsiveness, an unfolding, a centering of her attention upon him. She seeks, as an abiding psychological attitude, to

draw forth what is best in him, not just from his body but from all levels of his being.[27]

Psychologist Judith Bardwick provides a definition of "passivity" that will be helpful here:

> Passivity can be conceived as receptivity, as the vaginal tract is receptive. But the contractility of the tract is alive. This is an internal, nonobservable, active taking within oneself and is not a withdrawal from activity. Receptivity can be similar to Erikson's concept of activity directed inward within oneself, and is normal and observable in girls and women. This intraceptive tendency can mean a rich inner life.[28]
>
> Passivity in the sense of indrawing, of elaborating and evolving a rich, empathic, intuitive inner life—in contrast with activity directed outward—may be a necessary part of the personality equipment of healthy women. It is also probable that this tendency is a preferred coping technique at particular times such as during pregnancy or in those years when one is nurturing very young children.[29]

This kind of passivity is not to be confused with helplessness or preferring domination or a device for manipulation.[30] A woman's passivity is her peculiar ability to be internally open for another which is the precondition for love and for life. Her motherhood and her ability to mother depends on it. God has endowed women with an inward space for others, namely her womb, and whether she ever physically bears children or not, the womb is the feminine characteristic that dominates the meaning of her life. A woman has an empty space within her that only another human being can fill. It is an inner space open to the mystery of a new person. Thus a woman's interiority is not primarily of the mind, though she may be brilliant. Rather, her interiority is *rooted in her womb* and is open for the seed of her husband and for a child.[31]

WOMAN—CENTER OF HUMAN RELATEDNESS

The woman is the heart of the home and family because it is from the nature of her sexuality that human beings become bound together. In short, the moral and social center of human relatedness begins with the woman and has its perpetual anchor there. If we are trying to understand the true power of women, here is where it lies. And here, too, lies the correlation between what the concrete historical woman is and the motherhood of the Church. Both, in the deepest sense of what is feminine, are the source of human unity.

From the very beginning, the man for whom solitude was "not good"

(Gen. 2:18) was ordered toward completion in the woman—the "suitable partner." We are told in Gen. 2:24 that it is the male who *leaves* father and mother and *clings* to his wife. The directionality here is very instructive. The woman brings an end to the "frontier of solitude"[32] both for the man and for herself. It is the man's relation *toward the woman* that establishes the "communion of persons."[33]

In the ancient Hebrew worldview "aloneness" is the antithesis of authentic living. True life is not individual, not monadic, but corporate. In Gen. 2:18 the Hebrew word for "alone" carries an overtone of separation, even alienation.[34] Woman emerges not simply as the helpmate of man (in the traditional sense that Adam is primary and Eve secondary) but as a kind of savior to him. The word "helper" of Gen. 2:18 does not mean that the woman's presence is ancillary to the man's as if she were simply "his helper." The noun *ezer* is derived from the verb *azar* which means "to succor" (at the existential level of being), or to "save from extremity, to deliver from death." In other semitic languages the word refers to the action of giving water to a person dying of thrist or the placing of a tournaquet on the arm of someone bleeding to death. This does not describe the activity of someone subordinate or in a menial position. Woman, rather, is man's savior. The "helper" is source of hope, salvation, health, peace, and life.[35]

The woman provides for the man a deliverance from his void of alienation.[36] Because of this she is the queen of the created order.[37] If we can agree that woman is the "savior of the man," it is not in the sense that she is the head. She is his flesh and "saves him" in the sense that she completes him.

The woman's authority to be the source of human relatedness only begins with the companionship she provides to the man. Because woman is the bearer of life, based on Gilder's observations, she gives the male purpose and identity in his work. But her authority as the source of human unity goes beyond the husband. The one flesh unity of husband and wife gives way to the maternal unity of mother and child. Life, the acquisition of human identity and the meaning of human relatedness, is found here as nowhere else. Here we are not dealing with simply a theological question but a most fundamental anthropological question. The meaning of being human is resolved in appreciating what it means to be begotten by a father in the womb of a woman, nurtured within her, and born from her. Personhood is directly connected with how one is *personally* brought into existence and *personally* related to the *origins* of one's existence.[38] Fatherhood already, by definition, involves a distancing in this relation. Because motherhood, on the other hand, is by definition an intimate connectedness to another, it is woman who provides physically and psychically the paradigm and center of human relatedness.[39] We are *from* our mothers in a way we are not from our fathers. Psychologist Helene Deutsch describes the intimacy between mother and child before birth:

> Mother and child are an absolute organic unity, and the same biologic process governs the needs of both. This unity is expressed with regard not only to the positive life processes but also the destructive ones. Within the framework of the biologic process, disturbances in the organic functions of the one are also disturbances in those of the other, the well-being of the one is the well-being of the other, and the death of the one frequently involves the death of the other.[40]

The mother-child relation is life determining for each. The woman, entrusted with the human in pregnancy, experiences the most profound changes of her entire being geared toward fostering of the child.

> The genital processes enormously influence the woman's whole organism through a number of physiologic phenomena, so that it is completely mobilized to serve the reproductive task. Each cell participates more or less in this task; gradually the whole physical personality of the woman becomes the protector of the fetus.[41]

The observation of the psychologist finds corroboration from the philosopher. Edith Stein writes that a woman's soul is present and lives more intensely in all parts of the body while a man uses his body more as an instrument in the accomplishment of tasks with a certain detachment. Stein argues that the relation of a woman's soul to her body is related to the unity experienced by a woman in relation to her child in pregnancy.

> The task of assimilating in oneself a living being which is evolving and growing, of containing and nourishing it, signifies a definite end in itself. Moreover, the mysterious process of the formation of the new creature in the maternal organism *represents such an intimate unity of the physical and spiritual that one is well able to understand that this unity imposes itself on the entire nature of woman.* (Emphasis added.)[42]

Motherhood, and the maternal feeling itself, turns women toward what is weak, helpless, and dependent. Gertrude von le Fort observes that motherhood concerns itself not simply with giving birth to one's own but to the nuturing of whatever has been born. "The child that breaks through the mother's womb, breaks through her heart also, opening it to all that is small and weak."[43]

In her life-bearing, life-giving powers the woman is inclined to what is personal and interrelated. One might say that femininity is that power in the world that holds things together, always against the threat of some contrary raw force that seeks the destruction, thus the separation of things. The passage below from Edith Stein is instructive on this point:

> Woman naturally seeks to embrace that which is *living, personal, and whole.* To cherish, guard, protect, nourish and advance growth in her natural, maternal yearning. Lifeless matter, the *fact*, can hold primary interest for her only insofar as it serves the living and the personal, not ordinarily for its own sake. Relevant to this is another matter: *abstraction in every sense* is alien to the feminine nature. The living and personal to which her care extends is a concrete whole and is protected and encouraged as a totality; this does not mean that one part is sacrificed to another, not the mind to the body or one spiritual faculty at the expense of the others. She aspires to this totality in herself and in others. Her theoretical and practical views correspond; her natural line of thought is not so much conceptual and analytical as it is directly intuitively and emotionally to the concrete.[44]

For the woman, knowledge and her overall perception of the world is related to what is human and personal—what connects her to others and human beings to one another. The lifeless *fact* can only hold her interest when placed at the service of the personal, as Stein states so well. In order to know an object the man must remain separate from it and then once separated proceed to know by taking apart. A woman's cognitive skills involve giving herself over to the object, taking it whole within herself in relatedness.[45] Men disassemble and classify. Women relate personally to objects "as individuals whose response is more integrated."[46] "A man, with his abstract reason, is able to distance himself rather far from the concrete things around him, and he often adopts the same attitude toward his own body (and himself)."[47] Bardwick concludes:

> Men live in an impersonal world, women, in their domestic role, live in a very personal world. The female world is *autocentric*, which Gutman defines as one where the individual has recurrent experiences of being the focus, the center, of communal events and ties. In the *allocentric* world of men, the individual, has the feeling that the centers and sources of organization, social bonds, and initiatives are separate from him. In the perceptual world of women there is the feeling that she is a part of all that is worth being a part of, and the sense of self includes all of those others that persistently evoke action and affect from oneself. Whereas for men success depends upon the ability to perceive the world objectively, women can personalize the world, perceiving it without boundary.[48]

The woman is the center of communal events and ties. How well this supports Gilder's thesis! Regardless of the male tendency to be apart, he is united to the whole and his work placed at the service of life and the whole insofar as he is attached to the woman. "Women continue to perceive the world in interpersonal terms and personalize the objective world in a way that men do not."[49] While women may excel in occupational goals, their true talent and ability lies in the area of interpersonal relationships.

How clearly this shows itself in the area of sexual activity itself! Men tend to focus upon the pleasure involved in the sex act with a woman. Women find it more difficult to participate in a sexual relationship without becoming emotionally attached to their partner. Sex is eminently personal for them. The identity of their partner is more important than sexual pleasure. The pleasure is contingent on the personal nature of the relationship. A man is sexually aroused usually by some physical stimuli. A woman is stimulated by some expression of personal attention. Furthermore, men are more capable of disengaging themselves personally from their sexuality while women are more invested personally and emotionally in their sexuality.[50]

In 1968 Bardwick conducted a study on women, mostly college students who were taking oral contraceptives. The study revealed that even when "liberated" from past sexual mores, it is not pleasure that is the prime motivator in lovemaking for women. Though disappointed that pleasure is usually not achieved, what is most "important is the feeling of closeness in the relationship, which they ensure by their sexual participation."[51] Bardwick reports "Perhaps the most frequent response was the perception of sex as an important technique for communicating love in a relationship which they hoped was mutual."[52]

The person-oriented nature of women is illustrated even when women engage in work outside the home. Montagu states that it is not by chance that in the field of medicine women favor pediatrics, psychiatry, obstetrics, and anesthesia. Women appear happier

> when they can give the support of their personalities, their sympathy and understanding, as well as their wisdom and skill to their patients. The technical accomplishment of a cure or a surgical procedure does not constitute their greatest reward, as seems to be the case with the male. The male is interested in the performance of a task, in the solving of a problem; the female is concerned with its human meaning and with administering to the need in terms of that meaning.[53]

In a 1966 study of adolescent girls quoted by Bardwick, their career and vocational plans "were infused with the feminine needs of wanting to help others."[54] Stein acknowledges the many professional accomplishments of women and notes that there is such a thing as a "feminine profession." This profession would expand upon and be fundamentally rooted in the natural maternal, care-giving, person-oriented abilities of women such as doctor, nurse, teacher, and so on. "Basically the same spiritual attitude which the wife and mother need is needed here also, except that it is extended to a wider working circle and mostly to a changing area of people; for that reason, the perspective is detached from the vital bond of blood relationship and more tightly elevated on the spiritual level."[55]

The authority of women as the center of human unity is not derived from the accomplishment of external tasks and achievements. Montagu has rightly noted, and is in complete agreement with Walter Ong on this point, that the self-identity and self-esteem of men is far more bound up with their occupational and career goals. Both agree with Bardwick who comments that masculinity has to be earned.[56] The feminine difference, as Montagu states, is that women create naturally—from themselves—while men create artificially. And the woman's creative power is to bring human beings into the world as was first expressed primordially "I have made a man with the help of Lord" (Gen. 4:1). What we need to understand is that fundamentally feminine creativity is inherently bound up with human relatedness. When she creates, she gives life to people; they are bound to her and she to them personally. As Montagu states, in a woman's fundamental maternal power to create "Her medium is humanity, and her materials are human beings."[57]

II. The Church and Women—Source of Human Unity

The Church is feminine because her union with Christ and her maternity make her the source of human unity in the world. Human beings are bound together as one people of God through Mother Church. St. Augustine teaches this when comparing the Church to Mary. As Mary gave birth to the head, the Church gives birth to us. In this birth of peoples the Church joins us to the unique and only Son of whom she is the one body and the one spouse and thus she is the mother of unity.[58] Elsewhere Augustine states that those in the Church are brothers because they were all engendered by the same Church.[59] Unity is the result of the same birth experience of baptism that causes all men, otherwise separated, to be made into one people for they all have one mother. This reality is the means by which the fertile mother reconciles heretics and schismatics. Because they were all originally born of her they must be brought back to her.[60] Indeed Gal. 3:8, most frequently quoted by feminist theologians to show that in baptism sexual differences are erased, is a most powerful illustration of the unifying aspect of baptism. The maternity of the Church in baptism is indeed inclusive, not exclusive, reconciling into one body what would otherwise remain alienated and apart.

St. Clement of Alexandria speaks of the Church saying: "The Mother draws the children to herself; and we seek our Mother the Church."[61] The Church is also a loving mother "calling her children to her."[62] We are reminded here of Christ's desire to gather the children of Jerusalem "as a mother bird gathers her young under her wings" (Matt. 23:37). Christ's longing is fulfilled through the New Jerusalem, his bride, who in accepting Him becomes mother of a people gathered to Him.

The maternal power to gather in a people is expressed very poignantly by St. Cyprian. In contrast to the disruptive power of the Decian persecution, Cyprian hopes for the time when "we have begun to be gathered again into the bosom of Mother Church."[63] The unitive force of the Church's very catholicity is bound to the maternal authority of the Church. St. Cyprian teaches that regardless of the number of children this mothers bears, she knows no division of her body.

> . . .the Church forms a unity, however far she spreads and multiplies by the progeny of her fecundity; just as the sun's rays are many, yet the light is one, and a tree's branches are many, yet the strength deriving from its sturdy root is one. So too, though many streams flow from a single spring, though its multiplicity seems scattered abroad by the copiousness of its welling waters, *yet their oneness abides by the reason of their starting point.* . . . So too Our Lord's Church is radiant with light and pours her rays over the whole world, but it is one and the same light which is spread everywhere, and the unity of her body suffers no division. She spreads her branches in generous growth over all the earth, she extends her abundant streams even further; *yet one is the head-spring, one the source, one the mother who is prolific in her offspring, generation after generation; of her womb we are born, of her milk we are fed, of her Spirit our souls draw out their life-breath.*[64]

The unity of the Church exists in the reality of the children remaining united to their *source*—their *source* of life—namely, their mother from whom they are born. How intimate is the mother-child bond! As it exists between any human mother and her babe, so does it exist between the child of faith and Mother Church. Cyprian portrays the beauty of this intimate life-giving unity when, speaking of the Church, he says, "of her Spirit our souls draw their life-breath."

Separation from the Church is separation from Mother for she clasps to "her bosom all our people in one like-minded body."[65] Schism is an attempt to tear apart the unity of Mother Church, but "That unity cannot be split;

that one body cannot be divided by any cleavage of its structure, nor cut up in fragments with its vitals torn apart. Nothing that it separated from the parent stock can ever live or breathe apart; all hope of salvation is lost."[66]

Death is the result of being torn from one's origin; the womb of the mother, in this case, Mother Church.[67] The language here carries the imagery of abortion—that which is outside of the womb cannot live, the dissident dooms himself to die.[68] Let us recall a passage we quoted earlier from de Lubac in which the Christian's life depends, not upon leaving the womb, but always remaining within the womb of the Church.[69] "The maternal action of the Church towards us never ceases, and it is always in her womb that this action is accomplished for us."[70]

Tertullian illustrated the maternal unity of the Church when he spoke of the fate of heretics who separate from Mother Church: "A great many of them do not even have churches; motherless, orphans in the faith and driven into exile, left to their lone selves—so to speak—they rove afar."[71] The result of being motherless is to find oneself abandoned into a horrifying loneliness in a complete breakdown in human relatedness. The alienation of such frightening individualism is brought out by the words "driven into exile, left to their lone selves. . .they rove afar," meaning without a mother one is disconnected and thus doomed to wander aimlessly without ties to home and what brings about human identity.[72]

The feminine concern for what is whole and what is personal is the antidote to human solitude and deadly isolation. We have discussed at some length the unique life-giving intimacy that exists between mothers and their children. This type of unity exists in the Church and so it is the Church as mother who safeguards our personal character.

> In the Apocalypse, it is again said that the "victor" will receive a white stone upon which his name, a new name will be written. In proportion to our faith, the Church, this "family" into which baptism has introduced us, preserves the consciousness of our personal identity with this symbolic name. She furnishes us with the environment in which this consciousness can flourish. She maintains among us those things that are so endangered: respect for life and death, the sense of fidelity in love, the sacred character of the family; she maintains them as only a mother can.[73]

Woman is entrusted with the human. What does this really mean but that women will preserve the personal identity of the individual from being lost and effaced by all that is not human—all that, especially in our modern technological age, would reduce a man to a thing.[74] And the first way to treat a man as a thing is to make him unrelated to everything else that is human—to place him outside the family of man. The feminine concern for the personal is the primary bulwark against such dehumanization. The Church as a mother tells us who we are. Our identity is known by being in relation to this mother through whom the Father has made us His beloved children.

> From birth to the grave she envelops us in her vast sacramentary structure. Through her, we learn that something in us, what is most ourselves, escapes all deterioration as it does all constraint. Through her, owing to the demands she reveals to us on behalf of the Lord, we obtain and strengthen the sense of our own responsibility. And we do so first of all by "recognizing that we are sinners": in fact, nothing testifies to the essential dignity of our existence more than this recognition of our sinfulness. Through her, we have fathers and brothers—we have a mother! Through her, a dizzying opening that is obscure but unfailing raises us up to a Father, "our Father in heaven." We are taken into this community of life as into a net.[75]

It is through the feminine that we overcome our deadly isolation. A truly loving mother saves our personal life by placing us in relation to others— to our brothers and sisters and to our father. Indeed, motherhood is the teacher of charity. If woman is the source of human relatedness, then it is the mother as source of a family who teaches us to love our neighbor. The first lesson in this kind of love comes through the woman because it is from woman that human beings know their human unity and bonding to one another. It is through the life-giving powers of woman that the meaning of neighbor is known. To be a neighbor is to know one's radical dependency and relation to another of which the bond of the mother with the child-in-utero is the prime instance.

Once severed from others the human being alone is no longer at the service of other human beings but—because he is now alone he can be placed at the service of mechanization. The curse of the modern age is the philosophy that human beings are first individuals isolated one from another in pursuit of freedoms.[76] Motherhood is the antidote to such isolation. But we ought to notice in the age of individualism it is, not coincidentally, motherhood that is held in such low esteem. Nothing could serve as a more frightening illustration of the present fragmentation of human relatedness than the modern phenomenon of legalized abortion. If the authority of women resides in their power to be the center of communal ties and human relatedness, then surely abortion, which feminists cling to as the source of true female power and liberation, is ironically the definitive threat to authentic female authority. Abortion does not simply kill the child-in-utero. Abortion dismembers human beings from each other, and thus it is the antithesis of feminine power. As Stein mentioned earlier, the woman embraces that which is living, personal, and whole. If woman is the center of life and human relationships, then surely nothing could plunge the world into chaos, disintegration, and hostile conflict more thoroughly than the practice of abortion.[77] If *Mater Ecclesia* taught us how much we are truly in relation to each other, the killing of abortion would be unthinkable.

"He made war upon the woman" states Rev. 12:37. Because woman is the keeper of the seal of creation and the moral order of the world grounded in human relatedness, the disintegration of moral order is accomplished by attacking the feminine.[78] Feminist ideology rests on the principle that women's dignity depends on the autonomy of her being, upon an isolated independence by which women can assert control over their own lives and power over the lives of others.[79]

When we say the disintegration of moral order is accomplished by attacking the feminine, the attack we are speaking of is aimed precisely upon the life-giving powers of women entirely bound up with the meaning of human relatedness. Once the feminine is attacked as the center of life and communal ties, the relationships of human beings one to the other crumble into the disorder and alienation of unrelated atoms. Order is then achieved, not through the intrinsic authority of the life-giver, but through sheer extrinsic force that must in the end crush difference and individuality in an attempt to provide justice for all.[80]

Not only does the dragon make war upon the woman, the one who gave birth to the Son, but in the Apocalypse it is a woman who serves as the epitome of corruption and disorder under the sign of the whore. Here woman is not the partner of God, but of the Beast—she is the sign of sheer power, who, in her very use of sex, bursts asunder all ties of human relatedness as "the kings of the earth committed fornication with her" (Rev. 17:2). She, too, is a mother, but she only gives birth to others like herself, to other harlots; those outside of any covenantal union in whom copulation speaks only alienation. Instead of giving life this mother is the devourer of men "drunk with the blood of God's holy ones and the blood of those martyred for their faith in Jesus" (v. 6). Of this woman von le Fort said:

> Only a woman who has become unfaithful to her destiny can portray that absolute unfruitfulness of the world which must inevitably cause its death and destruction. . . . She serves but as a thing, and the thing avenges itself through domination. Over the man who has fallen under the dominion of dark forces she rises triumphantly, the enslaver of the passions. The whore as utter unfruitfulness denotes the image of death. As mistress she is the rule of utter destruction.[81]

As sign of the destroyer of the world's order, the mother of Babylon is found, of course, in no other than "a desolate place" (v. 3).

The attack upon woman as the center of human relatedness results in the depersonalization of the human. This is true in society as well as in the Church. Because we are born from Mother Church, she summons us to a most personal life—a life inextricably bound up with our neighbor in which acts of charity are performed for a concrete person who has a name and a face. The Church in her feminine power to bind men together:

> . . . resists all attempts—which are so consistent with one of the inclinations of our intelligence, but so destructive of our personal existence itself—to transform the faith addressed to the person of Jesus Christ into a clever gnosis, an impersonal gnosis. It is indeed supremely desirable that the consciousness of this personalizing force which was given to her forever not be blunted by contact with the depersonalizing forces which are at work everywhere around her. Teilhard de Chardin observed once that the Christian sometimes needs courage to "overcome the antipersonalist complex" which paralyzes so many of our contemporaries by preventing them from attributing a "face and a heart to the divinity."[82]

When the Church is no longer embraced as the mother of Christians, faith becomes ideology—something im*personal*, in the true sense of that word, and charity is reduced to a cause. An ideology has no need of a mother because it is a rootless abstraction. It is interesting to note that in his anger and dissent against the Church, Hans Küng refuses to love the Church as a mother.[83] His dissent is facilitated by first denying the personal relation and further by denying the authority this mother has over him. The rejection of the Church as mother is linked to the widespread rejection and lack of appreciation for the essential role Mary plays in the order of redemption.

> The Church takes on the character of a human, rational construction, which arises from the desire and the effort of men. Such a Church lacks any grace-filled, mystical basis. It is no longer the maternal womb, from which, in a grace-filled mystical way, supernatural life arises and which in itself carries the mystery of divine fulness. This sociological-humanistic misunderstanding of the Church goes hand in hand with faith in the divine maternity of Mary becoming ineffective. The statement that we today can no longer love the Church as "mother" has as its background the forfeiture of the mystery of the divine maternity of Mary, because where Mary is no longer in a salvific way acknowledged as Mother, the Church then loses its maternal, salvific characteristics and becomes an organization of human interests and rational purposefulness.[84]

The feminine/maternal/Marian nature of the Church is the way all people within her know their interrelatedness as "the protection, security, and the familiarity which flow from a maternal-virginal being. The post-Counciliar Church is in danger of losing these characteristics and becoming an apparatus of masculine intellectuality, which despite the greatest efforts is unproductive."[85] A healthy devotion to Mary keeps the Church from becoming inhuman. Without the feminine Marian element the Church becomes functionalistic—a souless, hectic enterprise. In the masculine world ideology is preeminent and one ideology simply replaces another where everything becomes humorless, bitter, polemical, and finally boring. Such a Church is deserted in droves.[86]

Karl Rahner once remarked that the decrease in Marian piety was linked to the tendency among Christians to "make an ideology, an abstraction, out of Christianity. And abstractions have no need of a mother."[87] We may add that they have no need of a father either. Let us not lose sight of the truth that human personal identity is bound to one's being from a mother and a father who are joined in a covenant within which their authority functions. As St. Cyprian so wisely stated, "You cannot have God for your Father if you have not the Church for your Mother." Denial of one's bond to the authority of *Mater Ecclesia* is at the same time to lose the personal love of the Father. Without allegiance to the Church the love of the Father becomes increasingly distant and unreal. De Lubac notes that in addition to the refusal to accept the Church as our mother another factor of impersonalism is at work. The personal headship of a bishop to his people, by which the paternal love of God is revealed and known, is frequently replaced by rule-making and decision making by bishops' committees. When the Church is ruled by committees, the bishop loses the paternal character of his authority. There is the danger that collegiality reduces the personal responsibility and thus the personal obligation of each pastor. In its place we find a bureaucratic organization that increasingly removes the pastor from his flock. His personal authority is replaced with an abstraction. The fatherly authority of the bishop and thus the maternal countenance of the Church is hidden.[88]

De Lubac goes on to affirm that human unity is maintained in the unique, particular authority of woman to bind together. His own words are worth repeating in their totality.

> The relationship of father to son, which is deeply rooted in the gift that has come from the Father, which is maintained in the Mater Ecclesia and established within her fraternal relationships across time and space, is in itself very different from what any psychological investigation would reveal in it. Neither is it just some obsolete relic of a paternalistic age studied by historical soci-

ology. It provides us with the necessary, blessed and irreplaceable expression of the mysterious reality which constitutes the dignity of Christians just as it constitutes today even to saving the dignity of man.[89]

The Church is a mother because those born of her share a common identity and history—and her children, as members of a family, all participate in the same mystery of relation. This is why when a Catholic severs himself from the Church it is always disruptive and devastating to the Church. It is the severing and denial of a true bond, a wrenching away felt very deeply in the consciousness of Catholics themselves, that the body of the Church has truly suffered a painful tear.[90]

III. The Woman as Teacher

Female sexuality is the prime symbol of human receptivity to the offer of God's grace in the world. Because of her unique powers of receptivity women can best transmit spiritual and moral values to others, in particular to husbands and children. In chapter 1 we already provided an expanded and detailed discussion of female teaching authority, with many examples taken from the writings of the Church Fathers. Furthermore, we have seen the teaching authority of Mary at Cana in relation to Christ and the inauguration of His public mission. As His mother, Mary helped to prepare Christ to fulfill His salvific mission. Now we need to examine more closely the manner in which feminine teaching authority flows from the woman as center of communal ties and human relatedness.

The intimate psychophysical bond between a mother and her child makes her the first natural educator of her child. Of course, we are not talking about education in the narrow sense of the dispensing of information or only intellectual formation—but education in the sense of a full communication of the world to the child and the child to the world in which the child's very sense of self and the world is obtained. Karl Stern has remarked that the intimate mother-child relationship makes of "every mother a natural mediatrix of faith."[91] Abandonment to God, so necessary in a mature spiritual life, is learned first in the trust the child knows in his relation to mother. The profound dependency the child has upon his mother makes her the child's proper teacher. Von le Fort sees in women the continuance of the Church's maternal teaching role. The Christian woman who conceives and gives birth allows the child, indeed gives up the child, to be born of the Church.

The second birth of the child is concluded in its religious education. The woman, who as mother stands for a part of nature, represents as a Christian mother a portion of the Church. In the religious training of the child, the Church acts through the mother as through one of her members, while the mother functions consciously as a member of the Church. This means from the mother of the baptized child a light falls once more upon nature as the first step toward grace. For the mother the natural process of expecting the child repeats itself as a spiritual process. Again the same stream of life circulates through mother and child; but instead of the shared physical space they have entered a spiritual area, and the forces of blood have given way to the powers of the spirit.[92]

We have seen in this chapter the unique concern women have for what is whole and personal wherein dwells the moral order of life. Edith Stein states that there is a connection between a woman's sensitivity to moral values and the education of children.

A quality unique to woman is her singular sensitivity to moral values and an abhorrence for all which is low and mean; this quality protects her against the dangers of seduction and of total surrender to sensuality. This is expressed by the mysterious prophecy, become legendary, that woman would be engaged in a battle against the serpent; and this prophecy is fulfilled by the victory over evil won for all humanity through Mary, queen of all women. Allied closely to this sensitivity for moral values is her yearning for the divine and for her own personal union with the Lord, her readiness and desire to be completely fulfilled and guided by His love. That is why, in a rightly-ordered family life, the mission of moral and religious education is given chiefly to the wife.[93]

The woman is the chief moral educator of the man. This is ultimately the conclusion of George Gilder when he states that women from within the meaning of their own life-giving powers teach men the long term purposefulness of their own sexuality. Women's life-giving powers bring men into the bonds of human relatedness in which male occupational tasks become full of moral meaning put to the service of the familial order upon which civilization is based.[94] This is the fundamental moral education provided by the woman to the man. Ultimately, when we speak of feminine authority, we speak of her right to guide men to be men—to fulfill the masculine life-giving task in relation to her that means, on a spiritual level, women lead men to fulfill what it means for them to image the fatherhood of God—whether the man is lay or cleric.

Montagu states that in the sex act itself it falls to the woman to teach the man the person-oriented as opposed to the goal-oriented aspect of this kind of sexual closeness.[95] The survival of the human species is more dependent upon feminine capacity for cooperativeness (another word could be *receptivity*) more than upon male aggressiveness. Montagu states that the woman's task is to teach men how to be human. If a woman's place is "in the home," this place is not subservient to the man. The home provides the foundation for the kind of world we live in. So, in a sense it is true that the hand that rocks the cradle rules the world. Woman's task is to raise men who will make a world fit for human beings to live in.[96]

Montagu states that "A good husband is the workmanship of a good mother."[97] We would agree, but a good husband is the result of a good father as well. In fact even a cursory sociological observation discloses that boys who do not have a good father to serve as an example of masculine caring and commitment grow up without assuming the responsibilities of husband and father though they may in fact "father" a number of children with women to whom they refuse to maintain any long-term commitment. It is not enough to be raised by a loving mother. The loving mother is a moral cripple if she has failed to demand commitment of the man who has fathered her children. And here is where good motherhood begins. The good mother is the good wife who has required from the man a permanent commitment out of which he is able to exercise the duties of true fatherhood.[98]

John Paul II in *Mulieris Dignitatem* confirms that women are the chief educators of their children. This education is entirely bound up with the woman's intimate link to the child.

> Motherhood involves a special communion with the mystery of life and "understands" with unique intuition what is happening inside her. In light of the "beginning," the mother accepts and loves as a person the child she is carrying in her womb. This unique contact with the new human being developing within her gives rise to an attitude toward human beings—not only toward her own child, but every human being—which profoundly marks the woman's personality. It is commonly thought that women are more capable than men of paying attention to another person and that motherhood develops this predisposition even more. The man—even with all his sharing in parenthood—always remains "outside" the process of pregnancy and the baby's birth; in many ways he has to learn his "fatherhood" from the mother. . . . The child's upbringing, taken as a whole, should include the contribution of both parents: the maternal and paternal contribution. In any event, the mother's contribution is decisive in laying the foundation for new human personality.[99]

Feminine authority shows itself distinctly in the fact that the male's role in parenting is dependent upon the woman's mediating the reality of his parenthood to him. Woman is the keeper of the seal of creation and the man will remain outside the reality of his child unless the woman lets him in on the mystery of life and of his own human relatedness to the child. The man will learn of his fatherhood from the woman. As Mary mediated the presence of Christ to the world so this authority is repeated in every woman who bears a child. The man will know of life through the feminine. Paternity is a precarious thing. A man might be nagged by doubts that the sperm that produced the child was indeed his. The chastity of the woman in her commitment to him is what provides the male with security in his fatherhood.[100] As Gilder states: "Only the woman has a dependable and easily identifiable connection to the child—a tie on which society can rely. The maternal feeling is the root of human community."[101] The male, so organically separate from his offspring, "is introduced to the children by the mother."[102] Sociologically, a man's paternity is dependent upon the woman naming him as the father of her child. To learn from the woman is to learn within the school of human relatedness. This is her first educational purpose. Even her role as the chief religious educator has to do with gathering men together for God, leading men and children to the Father.[103]

IV. The Mediatorial Authority of Women

Woman is the mediator of life to men, as she mediates the child to the father and to the world. We need look no further than to the salvific role of Mary who in her *fiat* joined God to the earth within her divine maternity. St. Augustine saw this mediatorial role within the Church. He exhorts those listening to him whom he calls his brothers and sons to love the Lord and to come often to the Church who has engendered them—it is she who has united the creature to the creator.[104] Edith Stein states that "the feminine sex is ennobled by virtue of the Savior's being born of a human mother; a woman was the gateway through which God found entrance to humankind."[105] De Lubac, in his commentary upon the work of Teilhard de Chardin, writes:

> At the very beginning the essential Feminine, starting its career in the most material and ill-defined forms, said: " 'In me is seen that side of beings by which they are joined as one, in me the fragrance that makes them hasten together and leads them, freely and passionately, along their road to unity.'" And now we find her who is finally about to pronounce her name, the woman blessed among women, explaining her unitive function in the same words:
>
> "If God, then, was to be able to emerge from himself, he had first to lay a pathway of desire before his feet, he had to spread before him a sweet savour of beauty. . . .

"Lying between God and the earth, as a zone of mutual attraction, I draw them both together in a passionate union."[106]

Women are the sign of creation's response to God in the covenant of salvation. The *fiat* of the woman is preceded and made possible by the fact that she is *full* of grace—all in response to the initiative of God. That the woman is the sign of creation's response makes her the link, the bridge, the human locus of communication between God and the world. The teaching authority of the woman is bound up with her ability to mediate—to gather together what would otherwise be dispersed. As the woman in her life-giving powers mediates the child to the father, so, too, does the Church gather together a people for God and joins them to God. This truth is frequently taught by the early Church Fathers. St. Hippolytus speaks of Christians gaining access to the Father through baptism—those born of the Spirit and the Virgin.[107] Tertullian teaches the same thing when he states that the neophytes, only after receiving baptism from within the house of their Mother, will for the first time open their hands to pray to the Father.[108] About this passage Plumpe states, "In baptism she became their mother in truth: she presented them as children to the Father."[109] Clement of Alexandria compares the Church to a school wherein Jesus is the master teacher. It is through this school that the Christian comes to know on earth the Father God they will fully receive in heaven.[110] St. Irenaeus states that the Father only "meets and touches us through his two infinitely holy hands which are the Son and the Spirit."[111] De Lubac comments that these two hands of the Father are given only through the "two maternal arms of the Church."[112]

The mediatorial power of women (and thus their authority in relation to men) is clearly illustrated in the accounts of the resurrection of Christ. The first glorious news of the resurrection was entrusted to female disciples. The Gospels record the faithful presence of women at the foot of the cross, including Mary Magdelene (Matt 27: 55-56; Mark 15:47; Luke 23:49; John 19:25). We are told in Matt 27:55 that the women followed Jesus from Galilee "to attend to his needs." This attending to his needs is a sign of motherly attention to Him. It is interesting to note that the maternal care of these women is extended to Christ even in his death while the male disciples appear frightened and confused. Mary Magdelene and the women come to the tomb as recorded in Mark 16:1 with "perfumed oils with which they intended to go and anoint Jesus" (also Luke 23:56-24:1). It is their desire to "mother" Christ that brings them to the tomb of this outcast man. And they are rewarded with being the first to know the good news of his triumph. In Mark 16:6 they are addressed by an angel:

You are looking for Jesus of Nazareth, the one who was crucified. He has been raised up; he is not here. See the place where they laid him. Go now and tell his disciples and Peter, "He is going ahead of you to Galilee, where you will see him just as he told you."

The women receive a definite commissioning. They are to tell the news of the resurrection to the Apostles and give instructions to them (also Matt. 28:5–7). In John 20:17b the commission to Mary Magdelene is from Christ Himself: "Go to my brothers and tell them, 'I am ascending to my Father and your Father, to my God and your God!'" Matt 28:10 records that the women as a group receive a direct commission from Christ.

The women are envoys of Jesus' word to the Apostles. John Paul II states that Mary Magdelene came to be called "the apostle to the apostles."[113] The women at the tomb become teachers and mediators between Christ and those He chose to be the shepherds of the Church. One may ask at this point why then should it be inappropriate for women to preach the Word of God within the formal liturgy of the Church? If women could bear witness to the Apostles of the Lord's resurrection is it not inconsistent for them to be banned from formal preaching and the reading of the Gospel? First it must be noted that Mary Magdelene and the women are commissioned to announced the resurrection *to the Apostles*. They do not receive a commissioning in the same sense that the Apostles are *sent by Christ* as Christ was sent by the Father. They have not received a commissioning within the sacramental order whereby a priest *in persona Christi* speaks the Word of God to the Church and to the world.

Again, it is interesting to note that the women are sent to the Apostles. And this is entirely in keeping with the meaning of feminine authority. Their task is to cause the Apostles to realize their own mission more fully—to give them the news of the resurrection upon which their own authority to act in the place of Christ depends. Thus the proper response of the Apostles to these women, who were entrusted with the mystery of Christ in relation to the Apostles' own sacramental ministry, is obedience.[114]

Within in the covenant of Christ-and-the-Church, the One Flesh of the New Creation, we have tried to show from a number of perspectives how women, from within the nature of their own God-given sexuality, exist sacramentally as a sign of the Church—the response of creation to God. It should be clear by now that if authority has to do with the power to give life and the responsibilies over life, authority cannot be reduced to mere juridicism. What we are talking about is a fundamental mystery of sexuality which gives not only the Church, but creation itself, its meaning and order. To undo the order of the sexes, one to another, is to undo the world. When we talk of feminine authority, an anxiousness underlies the question that can be articulated impatiently and crudely: "Well, so who in the end do women get to boss around?" Posing the question this way is still to understand authority as power to control and be above and outside of a free covenantal order whether we are talking about male or female authority. The "bossing around" can only be rightly understood within the matrix of responsibility that flows from giving life. To make demands and order others to do something is only authentic authority insofar as it is in the service of life. It is interesting to note that frequently it is children and those most dependent who seem to have the most authority as they are the ones most frequently calling men and women to assume responsibilities for life.

An understanding of feminine authority depends upon moving from the abstract to the concrete. We say that the Church is bride and mother with the authority to complete Christ as head of the Church. But we need to see how this authority actually exists in the particular; how it is actually exercised in the lives of Christian women themselves. Though we have examined closely the authority of one particular woman, namely Mary, it will be helpful to now examine briefly how other women have fulfilled their authoritative role in the history of the Church and the world.

7

Women,
The Covenant Partners of Christ

I. Women of the Old Testament

JUDITH

In the covenant between Christ and the Church women, exemplify and make real the responsibility for the faith that has been entrusted to the Church, bride and flesh of Christ. The Fathers of the Church taught that Christian women have the God-given responsibility (and thus the authority) to call their husbands to moral rectitude. Indeed, the moral virtue men expected their wives to practice was something Christian women had a right to expect from their husbands—and the authority was theirs to admonish and instruct their husbands on matters of right conduct and the spiritual life. This is, of course, a strong example of feminine authority.

When we examine the lives of women in the Old Testament, we are confronted by the fact that the covenant of salvation, salvation history itself, would not be possible without the cooperative partnership of women. Eve hardly bears mentioning, but we must not overlook figures such as Sarah, mother of the son of promise; Miriam, the preserver of Moses; Rachel and Leah, mothers of a nation; the mother of Samson; Hannah, the mother of Samuel; Deborah, Ruth, and Esther.

Judith stands as a fine example by which the authority of women is revealed. Judith, a holy and pious widow, becomes the source of encouragement and hope for the entire Hebrew nation. By her courage and confidence in the face of the Assyrians, she reinvigorates the Hebrew nation, and in particular the army, rulers, and military leaders. Judith's piety is directly related to her living out the vocation of widowhood in which she turns to an intense life of prayer, penance, and fasting (Judith 8:4-8). She, of course, holds no formal office, either by election of the people or by ritual consecration, yet because of her piety she emerges as the teacher of the nation. Judith harshly reprimands the leaders for their cowardice and provides them with spiritual guidance when she says they should not have made a deal with God by telling Him that they would surrender to the Assyrians in five days unless God provided the the Jews with water.

> When you promised to hand over the city to our enemies at the end of five days unless within that time the Lord comes to our aid, you interposed between God and yourselves this oath which you took. Who are you then, that you should have put God to the test this day, setting yourselves in the place of God in human affairs? It is the Lord Almighty for whom you are laying down conditions; will you never understand anything? You cannot plumb the depths of the human heart or grasp the workings of the human mind; how then can you fathom God, who has made all these things, discern his mind, and understand his plan? (8:11b-14)

Judith, by the power of her prayers, becomes an intercessor between God and the Hebrew people (Judith 9). When she prepares herself to go out and meet the Assyrian enemy, Judith takes on the appearance of a bride: "She took off the sackcloth she had on, laid aside the garments of her widowhood . . . and put on the festive attire she had worn while her husband Manassah was living" (10:3). St. Ambrose saw in this action the imagery of one who has become Christ's bride as one who intended to please, not her dead husband, but a Man who has priority over her husband.[1] Ambrose states clearly that widows are figures of the Church. He gives as an example the widow of Sarepta in which he states that the whole story of Elijah and this widow speaks of the mystery of Christ and the Church.[2] The moral courage of the widow is shown in the fact that though she has been forsaken she keeps her chastity, which is the moral sign of an enduring faith even in adversity.[3] The Church at various times is a "a virgin, married, and a widow." Here it is important to note that Ambrose teaches that all women who occupy these various states of life "have an example to imitate," namely, the Church, who possesses in relation to Christ these feminine realities.[4]

The chastity of the widow is part of Judith's moral superiority over Holefernes and his men. Indeed, Ambrose links Judith's victory over Holefernes to her ability to maintain her chastity which is bound to bridal imagery: "And she did well in resuming her bridal ornaments when about to fight, for the reminders of wedlock are the arms of chastity, and in no other way could a widow please or gain the victory."[5] St. Ambrose already sees chastity as the living expression of an enduring faith in a time when one experiences spiritual desolation. Thus Judith is the sign, and even the reality, of Israel's fidelity. It is her faith that enables her to conquer Holefernes. Moreover, St. Ambrose attributes Judith's victory to her sobriety and temperance, which were precisely the areas of virtue where Holefernes and his men failed.[6] Judith's virtue is the cause of male bravery "And so the temperance and sobriety of one widow not only subdued her own nature, but, which is far more, even made men more brave."[7]

DEBORAH

St. Ambrose sees Judith the widow as an example of virtue to be imitated by other widows. After his treatment of Judith, St. Ambrose turns to another widow, Deborah, who served as a judge of Israel in the capacity of a mother to her people (Judg. 5:7). He cannot say enough on her behalf "A widow, she governs the people; a widow, she chooses generals; a widow, she determines wars and orders triumphs."[8] Ambrose then states something one would not expect to read in a Church Father: he says that weakness cannot be attributed to sex. Moral strength is a question of a valor which makes one strong regardless of sex.[9] In the Book of Judges Deborah provides wisdom and military leadership by which the Hebrews overcome Jabin, the Canaanite king who had oppressed them for twenty years. Ambrose interprets Barak to be Deborah's son by whom Jabin's general Sisera is routed. The mother is teacher of her son, (4:6–7) and Barak is totally dependent upon her, so much so that he will not go into battle unless she is with him (4:8). St. Ambrose comments:

> ... this widow, before all others, made all the preparations for war. And to show that the needs of the household were not dependent on the public resources, but rather that public duties were guided by the discipline of home life, she brings forth from her home her son as leader of the army, that we may acknowledge that a widow can train a warrior; whom as a mother, she taught, and, as judge, placed in command, as, being herself brave, she trained him, and as a prophetess sent to certain victory.
>
> And lastly, her son Barak shows the chief part of the victory was in the hands of a woman when he said: "If thou wilt not go with me I will not go, for I know not the day on which the Lord sendeth his angel with me." How great then was the might of that woman to whom the leader of the army says, "If thou wilt not go I will not go."[10]

The phrase "public duties were guided by the discipline of homelife" describes well the nature of feminine authority that Deborah exercises. St. Ambrose sees that her public authority is not something apart from her domestic authority, but, indeed, flows from it and derives its authenticity from the discipline Deborah exerts on the homelife of herself and her son out of which he was trained to become a warrior.

For St. Ambrose, Deborah is the one who leads her son to fulfill his destiny and mission for Israel: "How great, I say, the fortitude of the widow who keeps not back her son from dangers through motherly affection, but rather with the zeal of a mother exhorts her son to go forth to victory, while saying that the decisive point of that victory is in the hand of a woman."[11] In this Deborah prefigures Mary who at Cana directs Christ to the Cross—to the attainment of His victory and the fulfillment of His glory.

When St. Ambrose says above "the decisive point of that victory is in the hand of a woman," he is referring to Deborah's words to Barak that it is not he but a woman who will actually attain the final triumph: "for the Lord will have Sisera fall into the power of a woman" (4:9). The woman Deborah refers to is Jael. Sisera flees to her tent hoping to gain refuge from Barak's assault. Jael allows him to think that he will have refuge with her, but while he is asleep, she drives a tent peg through his temple and kills him. Her action is very reminiscent of Judith who, in a tent, cut off Holofernes's head while he was unconscious, "sodden with wine" (Jth. 13:2).

St. Ambrose has a very interesting interpretation of Jael's victory. Jael is not an Israelite but a member of the Gentile race. In this Ambrose sees in her a type of the Church as the Church had arisen from among the Gentiles.[12] The story of Sisera's defeat is understood as an allegory foretelling the Church's own triumph among the Gentiles. Barak represents the Hebrew people who were the first to put to flight the enemy in the form of sin or the devil. But because they did not accept Christ, the Jews could not finish the victory. Thus Ambrose concludes: "So the commencement of the victory was from the Fathers, its conclusion is in the Church" of which Jael, the Gentile woman, is the prototype.[13] Ambrose also sees in the exercise of Deborah's authority the faith of the Church in battle against evil.

> And so according to this history a woman, that the minds of women might be stirred up, became a judge, a woman set all in order, a woman prophesied, a woman triumphed, and joining in the battle array taught men to war under a woman's lead. But in a mystery it is the battle of faith and the victory of the Church.[14]

Both Jael and Judith, because of their triumph over the enemies of Israel, share in the same formula of blessing that ultimately belongs to Mary, the New Eve. Regarding Jael we read: "Blessed among women be Jael, blessed among tent dwelling women" (Judg. 5:24). The words of Elizabeth to Mary at the Visitation strongly echo the blessing for Judith: "Blessed are you daughter, by the most High God, above all women on earth, and blessed be the Lord God, the creator of heaven and earth, who guided your blow at the head of the chief of our enemies" (Jth. 13:18). We hear in these words, do we not, the ancient song of feminine triumph that pervades all salvation history, that the woman shall overcome the evil one by a mortal blow struck to his head (Gen. 3:15).

SUSANNAH

In his *Commentary on the Book of Daniel,* St. Hippolytus also sees the Church in the character of Susannah. Susannah's chastity is again a sign of the Church's faith that Hippolytus equates with fidelity to God as opposed to the sin of adultery of which Susannah is not guilty. To show that Susannah's chastity stands for the faith of the Church, he calls her God's "pure bride."[15]

Susannah upholds the chastity (faith) of the Church against the seduction and persecution of the two men who represent Jews and Gentiles who reject her faith.[16] The following passage illustrates that the woman's sexual fidelity is sign of the Church. Lack of faith is identified with adultery which brings death to the soul.

> In an evangelical sense Susannah despised them who kill the body, in order that she might save her soul from death. Now sin is the death of the soul, and especially (the sin of) adultery. For when the soul that is united with Christ forsakes its faith, it is given over to perpetual death, viz., eternal punishment. And in confirmation of this, in the case of the transgression and violation of marriage unions in the flesh, the law has decreed, the penalty of death.[17]

II. Early Christian Women

SS. PERPETUA AND FELICITY

One of the most compelling stories of early Christian martyrdom is that of the passion of Saints Perpetua and Felicity during the reign of Septimus Severus in A.D. 202. What strikes one immediately is the manner in which they exercised their motherhood toward their own children while suffering the deprivations of prison life. Literally mothers in the flesh, by having kept the faith during persecution, they are mothers of the Church as well.

The narrator of their martyrdom describes Perpetua as a young twenty-two year old with "an infant son at the breast."[18] She dutifully nurses her son while in prison and must suffer the constant pleadings of her father to give up the Christian faith and win her freedom. The aged father's persistent argument is that Perpetua should do this for the sake of the family. Although Perpetua is the one thrown into a dungeon, she comforts and supplies encouragement to her family when she, of course, is in need of such things from them.[19] As long as she has her child with her, Perpetua considers the dungeon her true home: "Forthwith I grew strong, and was relieved from distress and anxiety about my infant; and the dungeon became to me as it were a palace, so that I preferred being there to being elsewhere."[20]

Perpetua's fidelity to the faith causes her to become the superior of her father. Once again he tries to persuade her to give up the Christian faith. He is her chief tempter. His attempts to persuade her are even described by Perpetua as his "seeking to turn me away and cast me down from the faith." For her to be "cast down" would place her on the same level as her father. Even the father recognizes that Perpetua's fidelity to Christ has caused a dramatic shift in their relationship. He must appeal to her no longer as "daughter"—which was his chief weapon against her— but now acknowledges her as "lady."[21] The father cannot manipulate the affections of his daughter, but must appeal to her as a woman with authority to say "Yes" or "No." Ironically, her refusal to deny Christ causes her father to suffer the persecution Christians undergo. While trying to "cast down" Perpetua from the faith, he is seized at the prison by Hilarianus, the procurator, and beaten with rods.[22]

St. Felicity is in prison while eight months pregnant, and there, in the dungeon, she delivers a baby daughter. In giving birth to a child she gives birth to her own martyrdom. As long as she remained pregnant, her persecutors spared her life for "pregnant women are not allowed to be publicly punished."[23] She longed to give birth so that she might join in the martyrdom of her fellow prisoners. Her martyrdom is specifically understood in terms of a second birth: "Felicity was there, rejoicing that she had safely given birth, so that she might fight with the wild beasts; from the blood of the midwife to the blood of the gladiator, to wash after childbirth with a second baptism."[24] Not only is Felicity's martyrdom a chance for her to give birth a second time but it should be noted that both births are understood in terms of struggle and combat—contests with blood. Her martyrdom is seen in terms of feminine power to undergo travail and give life.

How interesting that it is precisely the feminine nature that Perpetua and Felicity's captors seek to ridicule. Stripped naked and placed on ex-hibition before the people they are threatened with death by a "very fierce cow" the devil had prepared for them "mocking their sex in that of the beasts."[25] Felicity faces this beast "with breasts still dropping from her recent childbirth."[26] A more compelling image of feminine martyrdom does not exist in Christian writing. Earlier, Perpetua had a vision in which she was stripped "and became a man" wherein her spiritual battle of martyr-dom in the arena is likened to a gladiatorial contest.[27] But, when the actual martyrdom is described, any sense of it being a masculine battle is entirely absent. Instead we have a portrait of feminine suffering in which Perpetua, far from being a strong male gladiator, a body rubbed with oil, comes before her torturers as a "woman of delicate frame" while Felicity's breasts are weighted with the milk of her motherhood.

Perpetua's vision in which she is a gladiator doing battle in the arena would seem to be fulfilled at the end of the passion narrative. She indeed does do "battle" with a young gladiator who is actually afraid to kill her because of her purity and womanly authority:

> ... Perpetua, that she might taste some pain being pierced between the ribs, cried out loudly, and she herself placed the wavering hand of the youthful gladiator to her throat. Possibly such a woman could not have been slain unless she herself had willed it, because she was feared by the impure spirit.[28]

We see the captors are not in control of the women, but the women are in control of the captors. Furthermore, women serve as the spiritual leaders of the other Christians, both men and women, who are also awaiting martyrdom. Just prior to her own death Perpetua encourages the others and is their spiritual teacher: "Stand fast in the faith, and love one another, all of you, and be not offended at my sufferings."[29]

The passion of SS. Perpetua and Felicity has stood in Christian tradition as a paradigm of feminine courage through which the faith of the Church has been fostered.

The Motherhood of Blandina

The martyrdom of Blandina and her companions under Marcus Aurelius in A.D. 177 is recorded by Eusebius in his *Ecclesiastical History*.[30] Again we are presented with a woman of rare courage who is the chief spiritual leader of the martyrs of Vienne and Lyons. Eusebius describes her many tortures and her remarkable ability, despite a weak body, to endure it all.[31] One of her tortures was to be hung on a cross and:

> ... by her firmly intoned prayer, she inspired the combatants with great zeal, as they looked on during the contest and with their outward eyes saw through their sister Him who was crucified for them, that He might persuade those who believe in Him that everyone who suffers for the glory of Christ always has fellowship with the living God.[32]

Since none of the wild beasts touched her, Blandina's martyrdom was postponed. She took a fifteen-year-old boy under her care, Ponticus, also in prison for being a Christian. Together they were forced to watch the torture of others as their captors hoped this would force them to deny their faith. Blandina, however, gives the boy the necessary support and consolation he needs to undergo the tortures himself: "For Ponticus was encouraged by his sister, so that even the heathen saw that she was urging him on and encouraging him, and after he had nobly endured every torture he gave up the ghost."[33]

Blandina's part in this martyrology is described as that of a mother who has successfully seen to it that not one of her children perished in the sense that all the imprisoned Christians maintained their faith in Christ despite the awful trials they had to suffer. In this sense, Blandina as a mother brought her children to life. And as a good mother she shared in the trials of her children:

> But the blessed Blandina, last of all, like a noble mother who has encouraged her children and sent them forth triumphant to the king, herself also enduring all the conflicts of the children, hastened to them, rejoicing and glad at her departure, as if called to a marriage feast and not being thrown to the beasts.[34]

Blandina is a living sign of the Church's own reality. Blandina has brought all of God's children safely to Christ, which was precisely the desire of Virgin Mother Church described earlier in Eusebius's narrative. Mother Church experienced great anxiety that not all her children would be born—in other words—that some would deny Christ and thus be stillborn from her.

> Through the living the dead were made alive, and martyrs gave grace to those who failed to be martyrs, and there was great joy in the Virgin Mother, as she received back alive those who had been brought forth as dead. For, through them, most of those who had denied were restored [to their Mother] again and were conceived again and were made alive again and learned to confess; now alive and strong, as God made them happy, who desires not the death of the sinner but is kind towards repentance.[35]

Blandina is the reality of Mother Church, causing those children of the Church who fail in the faith to be "conceived again" and made "alive again."

In Eusebius we see again the partnership of parenthood between God the Father and Mother Church. In a kind of afterword to the martyrdom of the Christians in Vienne and Lyons, Eusebius tells of those called "confessors"—those who suffer for the faith but are not crowned with the glory of martyrdom though they desire to give their lives for Christ. These confessors pray to God the Father "shedding many tears" and "Always loving peace, and commending peace to us, they went to God with peace, leaving behind no sorrow for their mother."[36]

The epistle from which Eusebius gained his material was written in A.D. 177 or 178. According to Plumpe it contains perhaps "the earliest preserved instances of 'Mother' as a direct appellative for the Church."[37] Plumpe finds it significant that the word is used with a great deal of spontaneity and familiarity. This is evidence that the title "Mother" for the Church predates the letter and had been presented to the Christians of Vienne and Lyons often before. Furthermore, the theology of the Church as mother in the letter is quite well developed.[38]

Blandina's prototype exists in the mother of the Maccabees.[39] This valiant woman of the Old Testament is the primary religious teacher and source of courage for her seven sons. She exercises her maternal authority in leading her seven sons to martyrdom for the sake of fidelity to God's law. When all but one has yet to suffer cruel torture and be put to death, Antiochus, the pagan king, hopes to win this youngest son away from the Hebrew faith. He entices him with promises of riches and power. But the boy's mother instructs him to be strong. She makes her appeal to him precisely from her maternal authority, as she (with God, 2 Macc. 7:22-23) is the source of his life.

> In derision of the cruel tyrant, she leaned over close to her son and said in their native language: "Son have pity on me, who carried you in my womb for nine months, nursed you for three years, brought you up, educated and supported you to your present age. I beg you, child, to look at the heavens and the earth and see all that is in them; then you will know that God did not make them out of existing things; and in the same way the human race came into existence. Do not be afraid of this executioner, but be worthy of your brothers and accept death, so that in the time of mercy I may receive you again with them." (2 Macc. 7:27-29)

If the mother of the Maccabees is the prototype of Blandina, she is also the prototype of Mary. The mother of the seven sons aids them in achieving their ultimate destiny as did the mother of Christ. The death of the seventh son is even described in terms of a saving sacrifice: "I offer up my body and my life for our ancestral laws, imploring God to show mercy soon to our nation, and by afflictions and blows to make you confess that he alone is God. Through me and my brothers, may there be an end to the wrath of the Almighty that has justly fallen on our whole nation" (7:37-38).

After the death of her last son the mother, too, was finally killed. We see here, what was repeated in Blandina, that the mother, after encouraging her children to be true to the Lord, has willingly shared in their suffering.

MONICA, MOTHER OF THE SAINT

St. Monica is a good example of a woman who personified the maternal authority of the Church. St. Augustine himself attributes his own conversion to Catholicism to the example, prayers, and pious sacrifices of St. Monica. In the *Confessions* Augustine writes: "Out of the blood of my mother's heart, through the tears she poured out by day and night, a sacrifice was offered up to you in my behalf, and you dealt with me in a wondrous way."[40] In another passage the tears of Monica for her son's conversion are likened to the waters of baptism through which Augustine would later be reborn. Addressing God Augustine states: "you preserved me, all full of execrable filth, from the waters of the sea and kept me safe for the waters of your grace. For when I would be washed clean by that water, then also would be dried up those rivers flowing down my mother's eyes, by which, before you and in my behalf, she daily watered the ground beneath her face."[41]

It is clear that Monica's influence over her son, and especially her prayers, are the source of Augustine's rebirth in the waters of baptism. As Monica is his physical mother she is also his spiritual mother. Augustine states: "I have no words to to express the love she had for me, and with how much more anguish she was now suffering the pangs of childbirth for my spiritual state than when she had given birth to me physically"[42] Let us recall how frequently Augustine understood the Church to be a mother giving birth to her children in the waters of baptism, etc. Certainly the powerful role Monica played in the development of his spiritual life would make it easy for him to develop a theology of the Church as mother.

There is a stern and harsh motherhood in Monica that reflects a truth about the Church's own maternity. The Church as the bride of Christ and mother of God's children "being without stain or wrinkle" refuses to be tainted with corrupt doctrine. When Augustine becomes a Manichee, Monica shuts him out of her house.[43] Because he has embraced heresy Augustine is excommunicated from her presence. As long as he continues in this error the son is no longer part of her home. The mother of Augustine is for him what the *Mater Ecclesia* is for all those who choose to be apart from her. The Church is not only gentle but terrible and demanding so that souls steeped in error may realize the seriousness of their sin and come back to her heart. De Lubac comments:

> A truly loving mother, she saves our personal life, not by flattering our instincts, but by calling us back to both the gentleness and the strictness of the Gospel. We must place ourselves, not on the psychological level, but on the spiritual ("pneumatic") level in order to judge this. It is at the moment when her countenance seems perhaps austere to us that she is best fulfilling her maternal function.[44]

It is particularly interesting to note that Monica consents to live with Augustine after she has a dream concerning his conversion. In the dream Monica lamented for her son's perdition. A young man in the dream reassures her "that she should attend and see that where she was, there was I also," the "I" being her son Augustine. In the dream Monica is standing on a wooden measuring rod which is a symbol for the "rule of faith."[45]

This dream provides Monica with great consolation. She was able to see in her son the future son of the Church, and thus, though Augustine was still a Manichee, Monica was able to "share the same table" with him in his home.[46]

St. Monica not only exercised authority over her son, but she also was responsible for bringing her pagan and unfaithful husband, Patricius, to baptism. Augustine reports:

> She never ceased to try and gain him for you as a convert, for the virtues with which you had adorned her, and for which he respected, loved, and admired her, were like so many voices constantly speaking to him of you.[47]

Augustine speaks of Monica's patience regarding Patricius's unfaithfulness to her, but Monica brings him to fidelity when she brings him to the faith,[48] though this was at the end of his life.

> In the end she won her husband for you as a convert in the very last days of his life on earth. After his conversion she no longer had to grieve over those faults which had tried her patience before he was a Christian.[49]

In addition Monica's maternal authority is seen in that she was a peacemaker "between souls in conflict over some quarrel."[50]

Monica is loved and cherished by Augustine as a life-giver to him and to others.

> She had brought up her children and had been *in travail afresh* each time she saw them go astray from you. Finally, O Lord, since by your gift you allow us to speak as your servants, she took care of us all when we had received the grace of your baptism and were living as companions before she fell asleep in you. She took good care of us, as though she had been the mother of us all.[51]

"She took care of us all when we received the grace of your baptism." Monica lived the vocation of the Church—she who cares for her children born in baptism. Monica is the center of Augustine's postbaptismal communal life, and her role is not simply to look after physical needs. Augustine relates how she served even as a spiritual guide within the realm of her maternal position.

> I also heard that one day during our stay at Ostia, when I was absent, she had talked in a motherly way to some of my friends and had spoken to them of the contempt of this life and the blessings of death. They were astonished to find such courage in a woman . . . and asked whether she was not frightened at

the thought of leaving her body so far from her own country. "Nothing is far from God," she replied.[52]

St. Monica's final request before she died was to be remembered at the altar during the sacrifice of the Eucharist.[53] We can be quite sure that Augustine, the priest, did not neglect to fulfill his mother's wish himself. In this we see the life of Mother Church, who Augustine himself said was the mother of her fathers entrusted with the Church's sacramental life, fulfilled in Monica.[54] Because Monica is the spiritual mother of Augustine—son of the Church, she is also responsible for leading Augustine to the fatherhood he will exercise on her behalf and on behalf of the whole Mother Church from whom he was born.

III. St. Catherine—The Pope's Guide

The fourteenth century provides us with a paradigm of the Church as mother through the life and work of St. Catherine of Siena. Her entire life exudes authority as Catherine in her maternal role acts to bring about a restoration of the Church marred by confusion, disunity, and corruption. Teacher, preacher, reformer, and envoy of Christ, Catherine's God-given vocation was to mediate between Christ and the pope and between the pope and the faithful. Her lifelong task was to call human beings back to the pure love of Christ. Often her message was directed at bishops with the intention of reforming those who represent the headship of Christ—the hierarchy.

> In a letter to the bishop of Florence, Angelo Ricasoli, surrounded by numerous prelates immersed in politics and wordly affairs, Catherine recalls the obligations of charity and of courage in the ministry, the duty of conferring spiritual and temporal goods for the good of the brethren . . . not engaging in financial speculations, not squandering in riotous living the patrimony of the Church, which belongs to the poor, but rather honoring God and serving their brethren. This is the job of pastors![55]

Catherine is known for her part in the restoration of the papacy to Rome after its seventy-year exile in Avignon, France. She alone is responsible for instilling in Pope Gregory the courage necessary to make the move. Catherine was always confident that she spoke God's will, and she broke the pope's indecision and overcame the host of opposition to Gregory—opposition composed of leaders of the Church and the papal states.[56]

Later in the struggle between Pope Urban VI and the antipope, Catherine valiantly rises to the defense of the true papacy.

> It is she who gives the Pope courage, *who reminds him of the high dignity and the authority of his office and exhorts him to take up again the tradition of irreproach which had always characterized the Vicars of Christ*, surrounding himself with counselors and functionaries of unsustained lives, now that he was freed of traffickers in blood. *Only Catherine would dare to advance this sort of advice, to make such suggestions to a Pope. . . .* Pope Urban . . . was the target of all sorts of threats from kings and powerful rulers; but he did have on his side a pure and invincible power: Catherine of Siena. (Emphasis added.) [57]

Not only does Catherine give courage to Urban VI, but she severely reproaches those Italian cardinals who dared to rise up against him. The election of the antipope aroused in her a great anger, and she wrote to three Italian cardinals, upbraiding them for their hypocrisy and fickleness in first putting forth Urban VI as the authentic pontiff only to repudiate him later as illegitimate. She does not even hesitate to call them stupid, blind, liars, and idolators.[58]

What we see in St. Catherine is the image of the Church as teacher desperately trying to restore order among her children. Her children include not only children and the unlearned but priests, bishops, cardinals, and even the pope! She does not will to take over the authority of the hierarchy, specifically the authority of the pope. Rather her authority is exercised precisely to enable *the pope to be pope*! Catherine continues the role of Mary at Cana. As Mary provoked Christ to His public life—to His salvific mission, Catherine provokes and exhorts His vicar on earth to fulfill his mission as head of the Church.

IV. St. Margaret Clitherow

On 25 March 1586 St. Margaret Clitherow of York was martyred for the Catholic faith during the reign of Queen Elizabeth I. Alongside Edmund Campion and John Fisher this woman's heroic life and death during the first half century of the English Reformation contributed to the survival of the Catholic faith in her native country. It would be impossible to examine the many ways she served as a true mother of the Church and bride of Christ.

A convert to Catholicism, even under the threat of persecution she took the necessary risks to see to it that her children were given a proper religious education.

When she returned to the Castle in 1580, a well-educated gentleman, Brian Stapleton, was among the prisoners on the men's side; he was to spend several years there, but eventually escaped. By 1586 he was hidden in Margaret's house and employed as tutor to her children and others. (Margaret 'prayed God that her children might have virtuous and Catholic education, which only she wished to be their portions').[59]

Not only does she see to the responsibility of her children's education "and others" as well, but Margaret exercises her wifely authority in regard to her husband's spiritual well being A recent biography of her states "The problem of her husband touched her at every level."[60] Margaret had promised to obey him as her marriage vows required and did so except regarding the affairs of God which occupied a great deal of her life.[61]

> John was a human soul in danger of damnation, one of those 'with whom she might safely deal' in discussing religion, *a soul entrusted to her just as much as her children were, and to him she felt the same responsibility for instruction and conversion.* (Emphasis added.)[62]

Margaret personified and made real in her own life the maternity of the Church by her zeal and heartfelt concern for the conversion of souls: "One of the few things that had the power to depress Margaret was the 'trouble of God's Church, and loss of souls.' When she heard of Catholics living 'in folly' or apostatizing—falling 'from the unity of Christ's Church'— or dying outside the Church 'she were cast thereby into some anguish of mind.'"[63] In this Margaret is a living sign of the Church's own maternal care and solicitude. Recall how the martyrs of Vienne and Lyons spoke of the sorrow of the Virgin Mother whenever her children gave up the faith of Christ.[64]

Margaret's primary "crime," for which she was tried and executed, was the harboring of a priest, Francis Ingleby, in her own home "to set forward God's Catholic service."[65] Her decision to perform this dangerous gesture was motivated by her concern for the work of the Church itself—to see that the sacraments of grace were celebrated even though prohibited. Again, her action exemplified the maternal nature of the Church. Margaret made her own home an *ecclesia* wherein the priesthood itself could function and have its place as it does in the universal Mother Church. Ultimately, Margaret gave her life for the sacrament of the Eucharist. It is interesting to note that it was in the home of another English woman that the Jesuit priest St. Edmund Campion was given refuge for the celebration of Mass.[66] Fr. Mush (whom Margaret also hid in her home) while regarding Margaret as his "virtuous daughter" also called her "my blessed mother."[67]

Also to Margaret's maternal authority can be credited the fact that her daughter entered religious life. Indeed, she sent her son Henry to France to study for the priesthood (though he was never ordained), and this "without the knowledge of her husband."[68]

> It is a comment on the strength of her faith and her detachment from purely human considerations that Margaret should be willing to part with her son Henry, who was only twelve years old, and anxious for him to receive the priesthood which could only be exercised in England at great personal danger.[69]

Margaret behaved toward her son as Mary behaved toward Christ. As mothers they had to experience a parting—indeed a parting that they both initiated (i.e., Mary at Cana)—that their flesh and blood may walk the path God had called them to.

Margaret shared in the Hour of Mary who had to give up her Son upon the Cross. She shared in it because she, too, has her own Hour of martyrdom. If there was one thing that would cause her to deny the faith and save herself from execution, it was the love she had for her children and the keen motherly duty she held for them. In martyrdom she had to give up her children as Mary had to give up Christ.

> She had . . . offered her son Henry freely to God when she sent him abroad, and she well knew that her children's constancy in the Faith depended upon her own. . . . If ever a woman loved her children *in Christ* it was this one, and two at least did their utmost to follow the example of her life. It had been the will of God that she should bear them; now he had expressed his will in another way. He had an even higher task for her than their upbringing: to die for him.[70]

St. Margaret understood her own martyrdom as a ceremony in which she would be wedded to Christ. In martyrdom she is the bride of Christ prepared to meet her husband. In this she is *in persona ecclesiae*, a living symbol of the Church's own reality. In Margaret's response to Christ the response of the Church is made manifest in the world. She made plans to die in a white linen smock which she most deliberately intended to be her wedding gown.

> She occupied herself in these last days with an important piece of needlework. She must have asked Mrs. Vavasour to obtain a piece of linen for her . . . and with it she who had always been 'quick in the dispatch of business' made 'a linen habit like to an alb . . . to suffer martyrdom in.'

Margaret had two purposes in view in making this garment; one was symbolic, for her mind at this time dealt in symbols. The making of this white garment reveals her heart more clearly than words can say. Another Yorkshire martyr, the great St. John Fisher, had taken the same action fifty years earlier. On the morning of his execution he asked his manservant 'to lay him out a clean white shirt, and all the best apparel he had as cleanly brushed as might be, and to his enquiry replied, 'Dost thou not mark that this is our marriage day, and that it behooveth us therefore to use more cleanliness for solemnity of that marriage?'

It is the symbolism of the Apocalypse: 'For the marriage of the Lamb is come: and his wife hath prepared herself. And it is granted to her that she should clothe herself with fine linen, glittering and white. For the white linen is the justification of the saints. And he said to me: Write: Blessed are they that are called to the marriage supper of the Lamb.' (Apoc. 19, 7-9).[71]

What St. John Fisher was by imitation, St. Margaret Clitherow, by virtue of her sex, was in reality: the covenantal partner of Christ as sign of the bridal Church. Her biographer says of her: "It was as a bride that she stepped out of the New Counter prison."[72]

Before leaving our study of Margaret, it is important not to overlook Mrs. Vavasour's role in this persecution drama. A soul equally as stalwart as Margaret, Mrs. Vavasour exercised her feminine authority in relation to her husband; she serves as the spiritual guide of her husband when she sees him faltering in faith.

... she 'encouraged much her good and virtuous husband to be constant in the Catholic faith,' for 'seeing him somewhat careful [i.e., worried]' 'she did desire him cast away all care and fear for her and his children, and to do that constantly and nobly in God's cause which his conscience did teach and move him to do. Herewith, he ... did take heart ... and prepare himself, with God's grace, to suffer what persecution soever God should suffer to fall upon him.'[73]

Mrs. Vavasour, prior to her arrest, was "the chief matron and mother of all the good wives in York."[74] It was from Mrs. Vavasour's home that Margaret secretly received instructions in the Catholic faith. Interestingly, Mrs. Vavasour operated a maternity ward from her home—where not only were children safely born, but were also safely baptized.[75] Furthermore, Mrs. Vavasour gave refuge to priests including St. Edmund Campion.[76] Again we see in Mrs. Vavasour a figure of the Church as she took care to see that sacramental grace was available to the people of York.

Mrs. Vavasour's house had been recounted the principal Mass-centre in York, 'a house of refuge for all afflicted Catholics, of what state, degree or calling soever, resorting thither. There God's priests, wandering in uncertain places for fear of imminent danger, had harbour and the best entertainment that she could make them. There gentlemen and poor men too, so that they were honest and Catholics, were all accepted. . . . All good Catholics resorting thither had free access, with her good will, unto divine service and sacraments.'[77]

These words give the clearest description possible of a woman who, as symbol of the Church, is the gatherer of men, a means whereby their unity is possible focused upon sacramental worship.

Mrs. Vavasour, arrested in a raid upon her house (perhaps by information given by St. Edmund Campion under torture), spent the rest of her life in prison.[78]

V. The Authority of Consecrated Virgins

In the covenant between Christ and the Church women personify the relation of the Church to Christ whereby the worship of the one flesh actually has a concrete historical manifestation. In terms of the issue of authority male and female persons exercise a responsibility for the faith by which the covenant is made real and expressed.

Virginal consecration is a form of feminine authority. In this consecration the woman speaks a truth about redemption that builds up and advances Christ's salvation. The consecrated virgin utters the response of the Church to Christ as the Church herself is the virgin bride of her Lord. De Lubac states:

> This maternal virginity, or this virginal maternity, which the Second Vatican Council was to bring to mind again, is affirmed in many ways, notably in the works of Origen, Ambrose and Augustine. "All the Church," explains the latter, "is called virgin. The functions of her members are various, but altogether they form one unique virgin. This virginity is one of thought. In what does it consist? In an upright faith, a firm hope, a sincere charity."[79]

Lumen Gentium, to which de Lubac refers above, teaches that the Church herself is "rightly called mother and virgin" and that the Blessed Virgin Mary is the exemplar of the Church's maternity and virginity.[80] We have seen that the Church is built upon the reality of a woman, indeed Mary *is the Church*, the fullness of creation's response to the salvation wrought by Christ. Thus we can see that the Church cannot ever be understood apart from the meaning of feminine authority. When we examine consecrated virginity, we are looking at how women, besides Mary, but in the pattern of Mary, continue to exercise authority by which the covenant of the one flesh is constituted and made real.

In the Church, of course, motherhood and virginity are linked:

> The Church indeed contemplating [Mary's] hidden sanctity, imitating her charity and faithfully fulfilling the Father's will, by receiving the Word of God in faith becomes herself a mother. By preaching and baptism she brings forth sons, who are conceived of the Holy Spirit and born of God, to a new and immortal life. She herself is a virgin, who keeps in its entirety the purity of faith she pledged to her spouse. Imitating the mother of her Lord, and by the power of the Holy Spirit, she keeps intact faith, firm hope and sincere charity.[81]

Pope Pius XII in his encyclical letter *On Holy Virginity* teaches clearly that consecrated virginity contains symbolic, one might even say sacramental, value.

> Worthy of special consideration is the reflection that the most delicate fruit of virginity consists in this, *that virgins make tangible, as it were, the perfect virginity of their mother, the Church and the sanctity of her intimate union with Christ.* . . .
>
> The greatest glory of virgins is undoubtedly to be the *living images* of the perfect integrity of the union between the Church and her divine Spouse. For this society founded by Christ it is a profound joy that virgins should be the marvelous *sign* of its sanctity and fecundity, as St. Cyprian so well expresses it: "They are the flower of the Church, the beauty and ornament of spiritual grace, a subject of joy, a perfect and unsullied homage to praise and honor, the image of God corresponding to the sanctity of the Lord, the most illustrious portion of Christ's flock. In them the glorious fecundity of our mother, the Church, *finds expression* and she rejoices; the more the number of virgins increases the greater is this mother's joy." (Emphasis added.)[82]

Earlier in the document Pius XII called consecrated virginity an "office."[83] While men may occupy this office as well as women, the sacramental aspect of male virginity is not the same. Indeed, male virgins are called disciples of Christ, not spouses.[84] A male cannot be a consecrated virgin in the way a woman can and with the same meaning that a woman's feminine sexuality lends to her consecration. In terms of consecrated virginity the preeminence of office lies with women. As St. Cyprian said, consecrated virgins are "the most illustrious portion of Christ's flock." In terms of "office" the formally vowed and consecrated woman exercises an authority for the covenant that cannot simply be taken over by men. Indeed, male vowed virginity is understood as celibacy, as a way of exercising spiritual fatherhood in Christ.[85]

St. Cyprian spoke of virgins as signs of the Church in her fruitfulness. The total consecration of a woman to Christ shows the fruitfulness of the Church's faith in producing virtue in the birth of full response to Christ without which the Covenant of Salvation is not complete. Virginity was understood by the Fathers as a true marriage of the woman to Christ.[86] In their consecration the one flesh unity of the Church with Christ is historically spoken.

The parallel between the virginity of Mary and that of the Church is total devotion to Christ.[87] Feminine virginity is the sexual sign of the Church's devotion. In faith Mary and the Church "commit themselves unreservedly to Christ and to no other. In this exclusivity of devotion to Christ they are, in the christological sense, fruitful."[88] As one author explains, since Mary is the true physical sign of what the Church holds on a spiritual level, "Spiritual and physical virginity are fully inseparable from one another in this concrete-symbolic way of looking at things."[89] St. Augustine points out that the material-physical virginity of the Church is limited to a small number of members. But these consecrated women physically exemplify the virginal faith of all. For Augustine, because of the Church's Marian character, "the Church stands in need of people of a special state, who in the sense of a concrete way of living actualize virginity."[90] Virgins actualize, not simply virginity, but sacramentally, the Church's virginity.

In a sermon Augustine teaches that virgins are the mothers of Christ. "They fructify the life of faith of the Church, they give birth to new faith and new believers."[91] St. Jerome also spoke of virgins as the mothers of Christ. First the virgin is Christ's mother whom he makes into His bride:

> And He whose name you have so recently inscribed upon the table of your heart, and have written with a pen upon its renewed surface—He, after He has recovered the spoil from the enemy, and had spoiled principalities and powers, nailing them to His cross—having been miraculously conceived, grows up to manhood; and, as He becomes older, regards you no longer as His mother, but as His bride.[92]

The virgin is Christ's mother in that she must first give birth to Christ in herself. Once this is accomplished, she is mature enough to be His bride. However, the reality could just as easily work the other way around. Taken as His bride, once she is spiritually mature she becomes His mother, and really the mother of others in that, as the fruit of a womb, faith is perfectly formed in her. In any case we see that the consecrated virgin occupies an ecclesial office that manifests the spiritual realities of the Church.

The consecrated virgin is that sign of the Church's own full response of worship to her Lord. This sense of total response to the covenant is seen in the fact that virginity is likened to martyrdom.

> For virginity, according to St. Ambrose, is a sacrificial offering, and the virgin "an oblation of modesty, a victim of chastity." Indeed, St. Methodius, Bishop of Olympus, compares virgins to martyrs, and St. Gregory the Great teaches that perfect chastity substitutes for martyrdom: "Now, though the era of persecution is gone, yet our peace has its martyrdom, because though we bend not the neck to the sword, yet with a spiritual weapon we slay fleshly desires in our hearts."[93]

The authority of consecrated virginity also exists in that it is a sacramental sign of the eschaton. Such self-offering points to the time when all will be consummated in Christ. It is the reminder to the world that it is passing away and that there is something beyond history as we know it that is worth giving up everything for—namely the author of history, Christ Himself.

Finally, holy virginity, as Pius XII had stated, allows women to become mothers to the poor and the outcast.[94] How clearly we see this to be true when we look at the life of Mother Teresa of Calcutta! She is truly a mother because in her life she has made concretely real the universal love of Mother Church. She is a life-giver to others as a woman faithful to the covenant. For this reason, morally speaking, Mother Teresa is the most influential and powerful woman in the world.

VI. Modern Examples of Women's Ecclesial Authority

THE AUTHORITY OF ADELE NATHANSON

We need not confine ourselves to the past in order to discover women who exercise the bridal and maternal authority of the Church. Our own time, despite its many moral and spiritual conflicts, is full of instances of feminine authority. One may begin to examine how feminine authority is exercised by looking at the Right-to-Life movement in the United States and Europe. In terms of a social/moral phenomenon there is perhaps no other social justice movement in this century that contains as many woman leaders. National, state, and local organizations are more frequently headed by women, not to mention the numerous female legislators who champion this cause. The women leaders include Nellie Gray of the March for Life; Dr. Mildred Jefferson of the Crusade for Life; Judie Brown, director of the American Life League; Louise Summerhill, foundress of Birthright; Juli Loesch Wiley, foundress of Pro-lifers for Survival; Molly Kelly, Kathleen Sullivan, and Colleen Kelly Mast are active in promoting and teaching chastity to young people; Barbara Wilke, coauthor with her husband of the most popular prolife manual *The Handbook on Abortion* and a spokeswoman for the rights of the unborn; Carolyn Gerster and Jean Doyle, both past presidents of the National Right to Life Committee; as well as Marie Dietz and Rita Marker, leaders in the antieuthanasia movement. Among these female prolife leaders are the women activists Christy Ann Collins, Ann O'Brien, Lynn Mills, and Marjorie Reed. This list does not include the many women who have founded and run prolife pregnancy help centers and the many others who are engaged in other aspects of right-to-life work. The list could go on and on.

The story of Adele Nathanson provides us with a true and extremely powerful instance of feminine authority. Her husband, Bernard Nathanson, in the middle and late 1960s, was one of the key promoters of legalized abortion in the United States. A gynecologist/obstetrician, he directed the busiest abortion clinic in the world in New York City when the state of New York legalized abortion through the sixth month of pregnancy in 1967. In November 1974 Nathanson shocked the proabortion community when in *The New England Journal of Medicine,* he publicly confessed that he was responsible for killing over sixty thousand human lives by abortion. That was the beginning of a moral and spiritual trek that would eventually bring Nathanson from avowed atheism to a faith in the Christian God. In *Aborting America* Nathanson attributed his new-found respect for human life to his having become aquainted with the science of fetology. Nathanson again and again insisted that it was pure science that caused his dramatic moral shift. But there was far more to his conversion than pure "objective" science could offer. Science may be able to determine whether the unborn are human, but it cannot determine the *value* of human life, and Nathanson's change was not simply the product of further pragmatic information, but had occurred on the plane of morality.

The making of an abortionist who killed over sixty thousand human beings into one of the most articulate, intelligent, and tireless champions of the unborn child's right to life is the result of his wife Adele's moral instruction to him in the years prior to his public confession. Adele Nathanson herself revealed this fact during a speech she delivered 1 May 1988 at a rally for Operation Rescue in New York City. What we are faced with here is one of the most powerful instances of a wife's authority over her husband. She called her husband to be a righteous man, and did so completely in keeping with everything the Fathers of the Church have to say on the subject of a woman's rights over her husband. Adele spoke of her long, difficult, and painful ministry to her husband in order to convince him that his killing of unborn children was immoral. One can say that Bernard's Nathanson's conversion was not caused by his fidelity to pure science, but by his wife's pure fidelity to him.

THE AUTHORITY OF JOAN ANDREWS

Finally, when we seek a modern example of feminine authority, we must stop and ponder the life of Joan Andrews, who is, without question, the most powerful woman in the Right-to-Life movement. Her power is, again, not one of office in the strict and formal sense of that word. Rather her power flows directly from her womanly faithfulness to God and to his creation by which she is a true mother, though at the time of her greatest persecution she was unmarried and had no children of her own. She is a true mother because of her uncompromising sacrifices for the outcast children of other mothers who seek to undo their lives in the coldness and human alienation of the abortion chamber.

In March 1986 Joan Andrews entered a Pensacola, Florida abortion center and attempted to pull the plug of a suction machine from its wall socket.

> Andrews was charged with burglary, malicious mischief, resisting arrest and assault—which latter charge in Florida carries a life sentence. When she refused not to engage in even legal actions against abortion ("I couldn't promise not to save a child's life," she told the Judge, "to me, that's scandalous"). Bail was denied. For four months she remained in prison under a life sentence until the assault charges were dropped because they were false.[95]

She was convicted by Judge William Anderson in a nonjury trial. Because of her "nonrepentant" attitude, refusing to promise to cease her "illegal" defense of unborn children in the future, on 24 September 1986 Anderson sentenced her to a five-year jail term, far beyond the Florida sentencing guidelines that recommend a year to thirty months maximum for convicted burglars.[96] In jail Andrews refused to cooperate with the prison system because she believed God called her to be a witness for the unborn. Her conviction required a firm resolve not to give in to anything designed to make her participate in reparation for having tried to protect His children.[97] Thus her motherhood took her to the Broward Correctional Institute, which houses Florida's most dangerous female prisoners. There she spent twenty-one months in solitary confinement.

Because of her courage and love Joan inspired hundreds of others to understand prolife work not simply on the level of political strategy but on the level of spiritual sacrifice in which the prolifer erases all distinctions between himself and the unwanted unborn child.[98] In this sacrificial love of the Cross God's graces are multiplied.

The authority of such a woman as Joan is the covenantal authority of Mary who offered herself with her Son at the foot of the Cross. In a letter written from prison addressed to all those who wrote to her or prayed for her during her time of incarceration, she states:

> Could I ask something more of you—something far more important than any aid you could ever give me directly or materially, but which would benefit me and yourselves, our Holy Faith, the nation, and all people beyond any ability to estimate? Would you spend some time with the little babies in your own neighborhood before they die? Maybe you'll even be able to directly save some lives, maybe not. What's even more important, you'll be there. In a sense it may be a way to redeem the abandonment of Jesus by his apostles, when they refused to be with Him at His death—too often, we refuse to be with Jesus for fear of the Cross, do we not?
>
> These little ones dying today are indirectly connected with the sufferings and the death of Our Savior. There is a bond here that must not be overlooked. All the political action, educating, donation of funds, demonstrations, alternative work, important and necessary as these are, do not make up for an absence at the death scene. Thus, let me beg you to view your presence at the killing center in your area as the place where God wants you to be. Grab your rosary, pick up your Bible, bring your devotionals, and go out to the Calvary not far from you—where Christ is being crucified today in your midst.[99]

Matt. 12:46-50, Mark 3:31-35, and Luke 19-21 all relate a story about Mary and Christ's brothers who come to see Him. When Jesus hears that they are outside, he responds:

> "Who is my mother? Who are my brothers?" Then, extending his hand toward his disciples, he said, "There are my mother and my brothers. Whoever does the will of my heavenly Father is brother and sister and mother to me." (Matt. 12:48b-50)

Mary was never more the mother of Christ when she stood with Him on Calvary. A woman *mothers* Christ when she becomes, like Mary, the covenantal partner of redemption, when she exercises motherhood toward those who suffer, particularly when this entails becoming poor and outcast herself. Replicated in her life is the maternal solicitude of the Church in union with the sacrificed Son of God.

A well known prolife leader tried to persuade Joan that she should try to get out of prison as soon as possible because he believed being in jail was of no practical service to the prolife movement. Joan shunned the "practical" stategist's way of doing things precisely to illustrate that the value of human beings was something that could not be compromised. She stated:

> The world always wants to slaughter Jews or Arabs, or the bourgeoise, or "uppity" blacks, or preborn children, or the "unfit" as Margaret Sanger considered them and her Planned Parenthood still does—as a practical measure to make things easier on a more privileged group of people. And it has always been the Church, sometimes more bravely, sometimes less, that has stood in the path of this "practical" approach. . . . I think it may be true that the world in a particular way needs the Church—needs Christians—to be especially brave today, in order to rescue the world once again from its maniacal understanding of "practicality." Needs this more than even the shrewdest practical, political calculation . . . I do believe that faithfulness is . . . the shrewdest practical, political calculation.[100]

Joan, from an exercise of her own motherhood to Christ and to the (literally) outcast unborn children, articulates the motherhood of the Church who, in this age when human beings everywhere are sacrificed to what is practical and utilitarian, stands up to protect the inherent, God-given dignity of each person. This kind of defense comes from the nature of motherhood. On this the words of Karl Stern are instructive:

> Whenever individuals become ciphers, the feminine is wounded. For on the purely natural level—apart from the question of Grace, or even apart from all theological or philosophical reflection—the sense of the individual importance of the single individual is rooted in the experience of pregnancy, birth, and nursing. Scripture and theology teach us that the world has been created for Man to dwell in. But while someone is reading this line, a woman gives birth, with that immediate sense of certainty that the world has been created for this particular new human being. This certainty is not the result of abstraction. It arises out of an irreducible fusion with creative being. Hence the calculus of human logistics, that horrid concept of the human "material," which can be thought of as usable and as expendable, is forever inimical to the feminine.[101]

The woman is the force in the world who stands as the bulwark against everything in this technological era that threatens to reduce a person to a thing.[102] A woman knows she has given birth to a man, not a thing, whose life has been entrusted to her protection in a special way—that the bond between her and the life she has created cannot be reduced to serving mere practical societal goals.

The authority of Joan Andrews is clearly seen in the fact that her example helped cause auxiliary Bishop Austin Vaughn of the Archdiocese of New

York also to risk arrest for defending the unborn. Vaughn, in a speech first delivered 1 May 1988 at an Operation Rescue rally in New York City, publically credited Joan with showing him the value of her type of sacrifice for life.[103] We see here the authority of a woman who called a head of the Church to give a deeper witness to the truth of Christ's Church, making him thus a more faithful pastor of the flock of Christ.

VII. Some Final Words

This examination of authority in the lives of Christian women could go on indefinitely. Absent from our discussion is St. Joan of Arc, Mother Seton, Dorothy Day, and Mother Cabrini whose lives would certainly illuminate the feminine authority of the Church. Also pertinent to this study are undoubtedly the millions of modern Christian women, who are not famous or well known in any way, but whose domestic authority is the concrete spiritual backbone of the covenant of salvation as it must be made real in the world today and until the day of the Lord's return.

It is clear that authority, whether male or female, cannot be reduced to sheer holding of power for the sake of dominating the direction or order of the group. Authority is not extrinsic organizational force.[104] The authority of the covenant of redemption is certainly not this. When we talk about the authority of Christ, the head, and his bride, the Church, we are really speaking at the edge of a mystery, which, because this covenantal authority is the basis of creation and redemption, must be lived as a mystery—a living and an understanding only made truly possible by grace.

The greatest spiritual danger for the Church aimed at collapsing her covenantal authority is the desire of women to either destroy or possess and own what the man has. This is, of course, the essence of the push for female priests. For the woman to own what the man has will not result in simply exercising an authority that has been "reserved" to him but to destroy this authority—and to destroy this authority is to destroy him. Karl Stern gives us a picture of this kind of destruction and what is at its roots in his examination of Ibsen's character Hedda Gabler:

> Women like Hedda seem not to be created for the polarity of love. They waver between either pole. They are often attracted to sensitive men like Lovborg. Most of George Sand's lovers were Ejlert Lovborgs. The artist's soul is a lock to which this women wants to be key—and to be key, not lock, is the leading phantasy of her life. *But whether she plays at key or lock she can never fit because she lacks complementariness. The only form of union of which her feelings are capable is not the union of love but the union of "power over," of ownership.* (Emphasis added.)[105]

If we look at Mary, we see that the mystery of feminine authority lies precisely, not in the Promethian lust to take power for oneself, but in the power to receive and be filled; to be the absolute antithesis of the modern curse of man's refusal to receive help from above.[106]

In the above quotation Stern hits upon a fiundamental basis for male and female authority, namely, the order of complementarity. The first thing that must go is the idea that authority has to do with competition between beings who are different. Stern comments:

> Only complementariness can make us self-less. This self can only be lost in the *other*, in something which is not self. It is complementariness which mobilizes our generousity. Hence the phallic woman who denies otherness cannot love. All she can do is compete, and this often in an illusory way. If the male partner is weaker, things don't work out *because* he is weaker. If he is stronger, they don't work because he is stronger. He cannot win, neither can she. In the first case it is disdain that prevents her from loving, in the second it is envy. . . . She cannot be helpmate. . . . It is a beautiful expression, and it pertains equally to man and woman. For just as woman for her greatest creative act needs to conceive from the male, man, for his creative activity, is in need of a mysterious "conception" from the female.[107]

This brings us back to the major principle of our thesis on the subject of male and female authority. Authority is linked to being an *origin*, a *source* of life and to appreciate the meaning of covenantal authority is never to steer from from the words of St. Paul: "Yet in the Lord, woman is not independent of man nor man independent of woman. In the same way that woman was made from man, so man is born of woman; and all is from God" (1 Cor. 11:11-12).

The very order of redemption is bound to this interdependency and mystery of the sexes. Scripture attests that woman is the place where God dwells—the new Jerusalem come down from heaven, beautiful as a bride: "This is God's dwelling among men" (Rev. 21:3). The Covenant rests within this mystery of sexual interdependency. God saves the world through *His relation* with the Church. By this relation the Scriptures can testify "He shall dwell with them and they shall be his people and he shall be their God who is always with them" (Rev. 3b). In this covenant it is the authority of the woman who holds the Almighty One bound to the earth. The Scriptures say, "Come I will show you the woman who is the bride of the Lamb" (Rev. 21:9c). When there is neither death nor mourning and the "former world has passed away," she will still reveal the splendor of God.

Notes

Abbreviations

AEW   *Augustine: Earlier Writings, Library of Christian Classics*, vol. 6. Ed. and trans. J.H.S. Burleigh (Philadelphia: The Westminster Press, 1953).

ANF   *The Ante-Nicene Fathers*, ed. Alexander Roberts and James Donaldson (Edinburgh: Wm. B. Eerdmans, American Reprint of the Edinburgh edition, ed. A. Cleveland Coxe).

CCL   *Corpus christianorum series latina. Turnhout.*

CSEL   *Corpus scriptorum ecclesiasticorum latinorum.*

FC   *The Fathers of the Church* Vols. 1-82 (New York: Fathers of the Church, Inc.; Washington, D.C.: Catholic University of America Press, 1946-90).

MA   *Miscellania Agostiniana*, vol. 1, *Sancti Augustini Sermones*, ed. D. Germani Morin, et. al. (Rome: Typis Polygottis Vaticanis, 1930).

NPNF   *Nicene and Post-Nicene Fathers*, ed. Philip Schaff and Henry Wace (Grand Rapids, Mich.: Wm. B. Eerdmans).

PG   J. P. Migne, *Patrologia Cursus Completeus*, Series Graeca.

PL   J. P. Migne, *Patrologia Cursus Completeus*, Series Latina.

WAH   *The Works of Aurelius Augustine, Bishop of Hippo*, vols. 1-12, ed. Rev. Marcus Dods (Edinburgh: T & T Clark, 1871-1984).

Chapter 1. Feminine Authority and the Conventional Order of Salvation

1. Edith Stein, *The Collected Works of Edith Stein*, vol. 2: *Essays on Woman*, ed. Dr. L. Gebler and Romaeus Leuven (Washington, D.C.: ICS Publications, 1987), 230.

2. Edith Stein was a Jewish convert to the Catholic faith. Also known as Sister Benedicta of the Cross of the Discalced Carmelites, she was killed in the Auschwitz concentration camp in 1942.

3. Elizabeth Schüssler-Fiorenza, "Breaking the Silence—Becoming Visible," in *Women Invisible in Church and Theology*, eds. Elizabeth Schüssler Fiorenza and Mary Collins, *Concilium*, 182 (Edinburgh: T & T Clark, 1985), 4.

4. Ibid., 5

5. Ibid.

6. Ibid., 6.

7. Elizabeth Schüssler-Fiorenza, *In Memory of Her* (New York: Crossroad, 1983), xx–xxi.

8. Ibid., 28–29.

9. Feminist theology is rooted in a particular anthropological presupposition and world-view which is used to judge and then, if necessary, alter the Christian Revelation. The Revelation is subservient to feminist theology. Platonism and Aristotelianism also made the Revelation subservient to its influence. The misogynist and therefore radically un-Christian view of women one finds frequently in the Fathers of the Church is the result of their uncritical acceptance of philosophical positions derived from a pagan worldview which obscured the authentic Revelation. This is not to say that philosophy cannot be used in the service of the faith; nevertheless, it needs to be recognized that such pagan philosophical systems rest upon presuppositions that are incompatible with the faith. These principles may need to be nuanced or radically altered when placed at the service of the Church.

10. The Second Vatican Council in the Dogmatic Constitution on the Church (*Lumen Gentium*) refers to the Church under the various titles: "Kingdom of Christ" (art. 3), "Temple" of God (art. 3), a "Sheepfold" (art. 6), the "Body of Christ" (art. 7), and the "People of God" (art. 9). In article 7 the Church is called the "Bride of Christ." Above all other titles of the Church, bride of Christ stresses that she is the object of His love. Whatever else the Church may be she is loved by God as His bride. The love of Christ for the Church is expressed nuptially. As *Lumen Gentium* states:

"Christ loves the Church as his bride, having been established as the model of a man loving his wife as his own body (cf. Eph. 5:23–28); the Church in her turn, is subject to her head (Eph. 5:23–24). 'Because in him dwells all the fulness of the Godhead bodily'(Col. 2:9), he fills the Church, which is his body and his fullness, with his divine gifts (cf. Eph. 1:22–23) so that it may increase and attain to all the fulness of God (cf. Eph. 3:19)."

11. Rosemary Radford Ruether, *Sexism and God-Talk: Toward a Feminist Theology* (Boston: Beacon Press, 1983), 12.

12. Ibid., 12–13.

13. Ibid., 13–14.

14. Mary Jo Weaver, *New Catholic Women: A Contemporary Challenge to Traditional Religious Authority* (San Fransisco: Harper and Row, 1985), 184.

15. Ibid., 185.

16. Naomi Goldenberg, *Changing of the Gods: Feminism and the End of Traditional Religions* (Boston: Beacon Press, 1979), 5.

17. Ruether, *Sexism*, 14.

18. Schüssler-Fiorenza, *In Memory of Her*, xv.

19. Ibid., 60.

20. Ibid., 53.

21. Ruether, *Sexism*, 22–23.

22. Ibid., 18–19.

23. Mary Daly, "The Qualitative Leap Beyond Patriarchal Religion," *Quest*, 1 (1975), 33.

24. Ruether, *Sexism*, 114.

25. Ibid., 115.

26. Ibid., 114.

27. Ibid., 137.

28. Ida Raming, *The Exclusion of Women from the Priesthood: Divine Law or Sex Discrimination?* (Metuchen, N.J.: The Scarecrow Press, 1976), 128–29.

29. Ruether, *Sexism*, 136–37.

30. Ibid., 157.

31. Ibid., 158.

32. Ibid.

33. Ruether states that role differentiation is the work of culture and is not biologically dictated:

Maleness and femaleness exist as reproductive role specialization. There is no necessary (biological) connection between reproductive complementarity and either psychological or social role differentiation. These are the work of culture and socialization, not of "nature." (*Sexism*, 111)

34. A very strong case can be made that today the preeminent symbol of an oppressed human being is an unborn child, killed as they have been and by the millions, under legalized abortion laws. The feminist movement in the United States and in Europe is committed to the advocacy of abortion. With regard to the killing of the unborn, women stand in the place of the oppressor. In no sense does womankind have exclusive claim to "victim status." Recent years have shown that women can perpetrate injustice against the weak and helpless as much as be recipients of it.

35. Fiorenza, *In Memory of Her*, 130.

36. Ibid., 135.

37. Marie Zimmerman, "Neither Clergy nor Laity: Women in the Church," in *Women Invisible in Church and Theology,* eds. Elizabeth Schüssler Fiorenza and Mary Collins, *Concilium*, 182 (Edinburgh: T & T Clark, 1985), 33.

38. Ibid., 32.

39. Ruether, *Sexism*, 138.

40. Ibid., 211.

41. Ibid., 208–9.

42. The widespread acceptance of female (usually young girl) acolytes indicates that a great many Catholics believe that the issue of women's rights and equality in the Church is a matter of clericalization. Office should be open to anyone, male or female. Most Catholics are simply unaware that admitting women to the ministerial priesthood entails an entire alteration of the meaning of the Church's sacraments and worship.

43. *The Constitution on the Sacred Liturgy (Sacrosanctum Concilium)*, 47, *The Documents of Vatican II*, ed. Austin Flannery (Collegeville, Minn.: The Liturgical Press, 1975), 16

44. Ruether, *Sexism*, 34; Fiorenza, *In Memory of Her*, 107, 120.

45. Fiorenza, *In Memory of Her*, 76–84.

46. Ibid., 84.

47. Ibid., 78.

48. Ibid., 265.

49. Ibid., 263–64.

50. Ibid., 286.

51. Ibid.

52. Ibid.

53. Ibid., 286–87. The "institutional consolidation" Fiorenza refers to—namely ecclesial authority centered on the bishop—is much earlier than the second century in which she places its appearance. The authority of the bishop as head of the local church was well established by the end of the first century as we see from the letters of St. Ignatius of Antioch and St. Clement of Rome. Indeed, even the New Testament itself provides evidence that very early the Church was centered in episcopal authority as is seen in the First and Second Letters of St. Paul to Timothy and St. Paul's Letter to Titus.

54. Ibid., 289.

55. Ruether does not explain the reasons why the bishops "felt the need" to cut off and suppress the charismatic/prophetic sector of the Church with any scholarship of her own. She does not cite any early Church documents or historians in support of her thesis. If this early Church crisis existed as she states with the theological implications for the faith which she describes, one would expect sources to exist for a scholar to rely upon. At best her argument is plausible speculation.

56. This move from a nonhierarchical/charismatic Church to the institutional Church is likened in feminist theology to a fall similar to the Platonic fall of pure spirits into matter. Structure, hierarchy, and institutionalization represent a corruption of the original Christian community imbued with the Spirit "blowing where it will."

57. Ruether, Sexism, 124.

58. Ibid., 125.

59. Ibid., 16–17.

60. Ibid., 12.

61. Carolyn Osiek, "The Ministry and the Ordination of Women According to the Early Church Fathers," in Women and Priesthood: Future Directions, ed. Carroll Stuhlmueller (Collegeville, Minn.: The Liturgical Press, 1978), 60.

62. Ruether, Sexism, 21–22. Ruether makes it very plain in Sexism and God-Talk that she does not accept the Judeo/Christian theological tradition or the Hebrew and Christian Scriptures as standing in a "privileged relation to God." Because of Ruether's adherence to the principle of egalitarianism and nonexclusiveism no one religion or religious tradition can claim to have a more truthful understanding of God than any other. For feminist theology the Christian Revelation is not important except insofar as the "Revelation" can be placed at the service of feminist theological principles. Any religion may be a "useable tradition" for feminism. These traditions may be "1) Scripture, both Hebrew and Christian . . . (2) marginalized or 'heretical' Christian traditions, such as Gnosticism, Montanism, Quakerism, Shakerism; (3) the primary theological themes of the dominant streams of classical Christian theology—Orthodox, Catholic, and Protestant; (4) non-Christian Near Eastern and Graeco-Roman religion and philosophy; and (5) critical post-Christian world views such as liberalism, romanticism, and Marxism" (pp. 21–22).

63. F. M. Cornford, From Religion to Philosophy: A Study in the Origins of Western Speculation (New York: Harper and Brothers, 1957), 67.

64. Ibid., 68.

65. Ibid., 71.

66. Ibid., 180.

67. Ibid.

68. Ibid.

69. Ibid., 181.

70. Ibid., 246.

71. Richard A. Baer, *Philo's Use of the Categories Male and Female* (Leiden: E. J. Brill, 1970), 20.

72. Ibid., 16.

73. Ibid., *De Opificio Mundi*, 134, p. 121 of Baer.

74. Ibid.

75. Baer, 34.

76. Ibid., 36.

77. Philo, *De Opificio Mundi*, 151–52, p. 36 of Baer.

78. Ibid.

79. Baer, 37.

80. Ibid., 39.

81. Baer, 42.

82. Ibid., 45, 49.

83. Mary Daly, *Beyond God the Father: Toward a Philosophy of Women's Liberation* (Boston: Beacon Press, 1973), 114–22. Here Daly describes in detail the "Most Unholy Trinity" of men: rape, genocide, and war.

84. Mary Daly, *Gyn/Ecology* (Boston: Beacon Press, 1978), 317. Below is a list which represents, according to Daly, the many ways male corruption infects the lives of women. This corruption from Daly's point of view is like an invisible gas of whose deadly effects its victims may not even be aware.

> Women are spooked by patriarchal males in a variety of ways; for example, through implicit messages of their institutions, through body language, through the silences and deceptive devices of their media, their grammar, their education, their professions, their technology, their oppressive and confusing fashions, customs, etiquette, "humor," through their subliminal advertising and their "sublime" music (such as Christmas carols piped into supermarkets that seduce the listener into identifying with the tamed Goddess who abjectly adores her son).

85. Daly, *Beyond God the Father*, 172–73.

86. Daly, *Gyn/Ecology*, 2.

87. Ibid., 338.

88. Ibid., 340.

89. Ruether, *Sexism*, 231.

90. Ibid.

91. Ibid., 85–86.

92. Ibid., 257.

93. Ibid., 258.

94. Cornford, *From Religion to Philosophy*, 180.

95. Ibid., 179.

96. St. Ambrose, *De Paradiso* 3.12, 15.7 (CSEL 32,1–2.272, 331); St. Paulinus of Nola, *Epistula 23* 24 (CSEL 29.181–82); St. Augustine, *Epistula 127* (CSEL 44.28–29); St. Augustine, *De Trinitate* 12.7.10 (CCL 50.364–65).

97. St. Augustine, *Epistula 127*, St. Ambrose, *De Paradiso* 3.12, 4.24, 12.56, 15.73 (CSEL 32,1–2.272, 280–81, 316, 331); St. Ambrose, *Exp. Evang. Sec. Luc.*, 10.161 (CSEL 32.517); St. Jerome, *Comm. in epis. ad Ephes.*, 3.5 (PL 26.567); St. Gregory the Great, *Moral, lib.* 28.3 (CCSL 143b.1402–1403); St. Cyril of Alexandria, *In Johannia evang.*, 12.20.15 (PG 74.691).

98. St. Augustine, *De Genesi ad Litteram* 11.42.58 (CSEL 28.377–78).

99. St. John Chrysostom, *Homilia 9*, "In Epist. i ad Tm." (PG 62.544–45); St. Clement of Alexandria, *Paedagogus* 2.2 (PG 8.430); Tertullian, *De Cultu feminarum* 1.1 (CSEL 70.59–60).

100. Paulinus of Nola, *Epistula 23* 24 (CSEL 29.182); St. John Chrysostom, *Homilia 9* (PG 62.544).

101. St. Augustine, *De Genesi ad Litteram* 9.5 (CSEL 28.273).

102. St. Clement of Alexandria, *The Instructor*, 3,3, *The Ante-Nicene Fathers*, vol. 2, eds. Alexander Roberts and James Donaldson (Grand Rapids, Mich.: Wm. B. Eerdmans, 1962), 276 (PG 8.582).

103. St. Augustine, *On the Trinity*, 12, 7, 10, trans. Authur West Haddan, *The Works of Augustine of Hippo*, vol. 7, ed. Rev. Marcus Dods (Edinburgh: T & T Clark, 1873), 292 (CCL 50.364–65). St. Augustine makes the same statement in his treatise *De Opere Monachorum* 32.40 (CSEL 41.594).

104. St. Augustine, *De Trinitate* 12.7.12 (CCL 50.367).

105. *On the Trinity*, 12,7,10, WAH, 292 (CCL 50.364–65).

106. Ibid., 12,7,12, p. 294 (CCL 50.367).

107. Ibid.

108. *De Trinitate* 12.7.12 (CCL 50.366).

109. St. Augustine, *On the Work of Monks,* 32, 40, trans. Sr. Mary Sarah Muldowney, *Fathers of the Church*, vol. 16 (New York: Fathers of the Church, 1952), 393 (CSEL 41.594).

110. St. Augustine, *Faith and the Creed*, 4, 9, trans. John H.S. Burleigh, *Augustine: Earlier Writings, Library of Christian Classics*, vol. 6 (Philadelphia: The Westminster Press, 1953), 358.

> Detestandi autem etiam illi sunt, qui dominum nostrum Iesum Christum matrem Mariam in terris negant habuisse, cum illa dispensatio utrumque sexum, et masculinum et femininum, honorauerit et ad curam dei pertinere monstrauerit non solum quem suscepit, sed illum etiam, per quem suscepit, uirum gerendo, nascendo de feminia. (CSEL 41.12)

111. Ibid.

112. *De Fide et Symbolo* 4.9 (CSEL 41.13).

113. *Faith and the Creed*, AEW, 4, 10, p. 359. The phrase "a woman's internal organs" in the Latin: "muliebrium uiscerum" (CSEL 41.13).

114. Origen, *Hom. in Jos.*, 9.9, and *Hom. in Ezech.* 3.3 (PG 13.689–90.

115. Origen, *Sel. in Ex.*, 23.17 (PG 12.296).

116. St. Jerome, *Letter 22 to Eustochium*, 19, trans. W. H. Fremantle, *Nicene and Post-Nicene Fathers*, vol. 6, eds. Philip Schaff and Henry Wace (Grand Rapids, Mich., Wm. B. Eerdmans), 29 (CSEL 54.169). The phrase "no germ of life from without but fruitful

in singleness like God himself" in Latin: "nullo extrinsecus germine cohaerente et ad similitudinem dei unione fecunda."

117. *Epistula 22 ad Eustochium*, 18 (CSEL 54.167).

118. St. Augustine, *Enarr. on the Book of Psalms*, 127,4, *Nicene and Post-Nicene Fathers*, vol. 8, ed. Philip Schaff (Grand Rapids, Mich., Wm. B. Eerdmans, 1956), 607, (CCL 40.1862, Ps. 126.7).

119. Ibid., 5, p. 608 (CCL 40.1863, Ps. 126.8).

   Quasi quaereres iterum: Quibus dilectis? *Ecce hereditas Domini, filii, merces fructus uentris.* Quando dicit: *fructus uentris,* parturiti sunt filii isti. Est quaedam mulier, in qua spiritaliter ostenditur quod dictum est Euae: *In gemitu parturies.* In cuius figura etiam Eua *mater uiuorum* appellata est. In membris parturientis erat ille qui dicebat: *Filioli mei, quos iterum parturio, denec Christus formetur in uobis.* Sed non frustra parturiuit, nec frustra peperit; erit semen sanctum in resurrectione mortuorum; abundabunt iusti, qui diffusi sunt modo toto orbe terrarum. Gemit illos ecclesia, parturit illos ecclesia: in illa autem mortuorum apparebit partus ecclesiae, transit dolor et gemitus.

120. St. Irenaeus, *Contra Haereses* 22.1 (PG 7,1.255–56).

121. Ibid., 22.2 (PG 7,1.256–57).

122. Ibid., 22,4, *The Ante-Nicene Fathers*, vol.1 (Grand Rapids, Mich.: Wm. B. Eerdmans, 1967), 455 (PG 7,1.258–59).

123. Ibid.

124. Rosemary Radford Ruether rejects the teaching of the Fathers on Mary as the New Eve because she believes it is a theology on male terms. She states that this theology sunders Mary from her body—spiritualizing her in a dualism of body and spirit—in which the spirit (as it was prior to the sin of Eve) dominates and orders the flesh. The New Eve theology scapegoats women for the cause of the world's evil in Eve's disobedience rooted in her sexuality which is then overturned by Mary whose body is ruled by the spirit (*Sexism and God-Talk*, 151–52.).

125. St. Justin Martyr, *Dialogus cum Tryphoe Jud.* 100 (PG 6.710).

126. Prudence Allen, *The Concept of Woman: The Aristotelian Revolution* (Montreal: Eden Press, 1985), 213.

127. Ibid.

128. St. Augustine, *City of God*, 22,17, trans. Marcus Dods, *The Works of Aurelius Augustine, Bishop of Hippo*, vol. 2 (Edinburgh: T & T Clark, 1878), 509–10 (CSEL 40.625–26). The word in the Latin text for "built up" ("the sacraments by which the Church is built up") is "aedificauit." The Latin word for "edification" in the phrase "the edification of the body of Christ" is "aedificationem."

129. St. Augustine in *De Trinitate* 12.7.12 rejects the notion that the body is in the image of God. The image refers only to man's rational mind. In this Augustine does not allow for any sacramental dimension to the body—male and female—in image of the Trinity. However, in other works such as *De Sancta Virginitate,* one finds in Augustine an appreciation for the sacramental value of sexuality. Here he sees a woman's childbearing function as an image of the Church.

130. St. Jerome, *Letter 22 to Eustochium*, 21, NPNF, vol. 6, p. 30 (CSEL 54.173).

131. Ibid., 23, p. 31. The Latin reads: "[N]eque enim aureum vas et argenteum tam carum deo fuit, quam templum corporisvirginalis. praecessit umbra, nunc veritas est" (CSEL 54.175–76).

132. Ibid., 38, p. 39 (CSEL 54.204). "[D]omine concepimus et dolumus et peperimus; spiritum salvationis tuae fecimus super terram."

133. Ibid. (CSEL 54.205).

134. St. Augustine, *On Holy Virginity*, 2, 2, trans. John McQuade, S.M., *Fathers of the Church*, vol. 27 (New York: Fathers of the Church, 1955), p. 145 (CSEL 41.236). The phrase "preserve in their very flesh" in the Latin: "quae hoc custodiunt etiam in ipsa carne."

135. St. Ambrose, *Concerning Virgins*, 1, 6, 31, trans. H. De Romestin, *Nicene and Post-Nicene Fathers*, vol. 10, second series, eds. Philip Schaff and Henry Wace (Grand Rapids, Mich.: Wm. B. Eerdmans, 1955), 368 (PL 16.208).

136. St. Jerome, *Comm. in epist. ad Eph.*, 3.5 as quoted by Mary Daly, *The Church and the Second Sex* (New York: Harper and Row, 1968), 43 (PL 26.567).

137. The following references from the Fathers treat the woman's childbearing ability as purely functional: St. Jerome, *Comm. in epist. ad Eph.*, 3.5 (PL 26.567); St. Augustine, *De Trinitate* 12.7,10; St. Augustine, *De Genesi ad Litteram* 9.5 (CSEL 28.273); St. Ambrose, *De Paradiso* 10.47 (CSEL 32,1.305); St. Ambrose, *Exp. evang. sec. Luc.*, 10.161 (CSEL 32,2.517); St. Paulinus of Nola, *Epistula 23* 25 (CSEL 29.182).

138. St. Jerome, *Letter 22 to Eustochium*, 27, NPNF, vol. 6, p. 34 (CSEL 54.184).

139. Jo Ann McNamara, "Equality in the Cult of Virginity in Early Christianity," *Feminist Studies* 4 (1976), 153.

140. Alice Zimmern, *The Home Life of the Ancient Greeks* (New York: Cooper Square Publishers, 1906), 135; Frank Gardner Moore, *The Roman's World* (New York: Columbia University Press, 1936), 183–85. On the role of the *paterfamilias*: both sons and daughters were under his absolute authority. Upon marriage the daughter passed under the *manus* (the hand) or authority of her husband. However, as Moore indicates, Roman law provided women with some privileges and freedom not accorded to women living in Greek antiquity.

141. St. Clement of Alexandria, *De Stromatatum* 2.23 (PG 8.1087).

142. St. Ambrose, *De Virginibus ad Mar.*, 1.10.58 (PL 16.216).

143. *Concerning Virgins* 1,10,56, NPNF, vol. 10, p. 372 (PL 16.215, 1,9,56).

144. Ibid., 1,12,63, p. 373 (PL 16.217).

145. St. Jerome, *Letter 22 to Eustochium*, 20, NPNF, vol. 6, p. 30 (CSEL 54.170). The phrase "now the mother-in-law of God" in the Latin: "grande tibi beneficium praestitit: socrus dei esse coepisti."

146. St. Augustine, *On Holy Virginity*, 4, 4, FC, vol. 27, p. 147 (CSEL 41.238).

147. Ibid.

148. St. Augustine, *Sermon on the Mount*, 1, 16, 43, trans. Denis J. Kavanagh, *Fathers of the Church*, vol. 11 (New York: Fathers of the Church, 1951), 65 (CCL 35.49). The term "put away" means separation but not divorce and remarriage. St. Augustine taught that divorce and remarriage was contrary to the Law of Christ. See *De Bono Conjugali* 7.

149. St. Augustine "Ad Conjugatos," *Sermo 392* (PL 39.1711–1712).

> Concerning the equality and place of wives Augustine states: "In all other things, [outside your husband's morality] be a maidservant to your husband, prone to his every wish. Do not be wanton, or haughty or quarrelsome, or disobedient. Attend to him as though you were his maidservant. There is one matter in which the blessed Apostle made you equal, saying, *Let the husband render to his wife her due, and likewise the wife to the husband* (1 Cor. 7:3). Upon saying this, he adds: *The wife has not authority over her body, but the husband. . . . The husband likewise has not*

authority over his body, but the wife." ("To the Married," *Sermon 392*, trans. Quincy Howe, Jr., *Selected Sermons of St. Augustine* [New York: Holt, Rinehart and Winston, 1966], 32.)

150. St. Augustine, *De Bono Conjugali* 6 (CSEL 41–42.195).

151. St. Augustine, "Ad Conjugatos," *Sermo 392* (PL 39.1711–1712).

152. Ibid., "To the Married," *Sermon 392*, *Selected Sermons of St. Augustine*, 32–33.

153. St. Caesarius of Arles, *Sermon 42*, 3, trans. Sr. Mary Magdelene Mueller, *Fathers of the Church*, vol. 31 (New York: Fathers of the Church, 1956), 211 (CCL 103.187). His use of the Pauline formula "with God there is no distinction of male or female" (et non est apud deum discretio masculi et feminae) is not meant to erase sexual difference. Caesarius uses the phrase to declare that there can be no double sacramental or moral standards in Christianity between men and women.

154. Ibid., *Sermon 43*, FC, vol. 31, p. 215 (CCL 103.191).

155. St. Paulinus, of Nola *Epistula 23* 24 (CSEL 29.182); St. Ambrose, *De Paradiso* 12.56 (CSEL 32,1.316); St. Augustine, *Epistula 127* (CSEL 44.28–29). This letter of St. Augustine is a good example of the ambivilance and conflict in this Church Father between a Platonic/monist philosophy of sexuality and the teaching of Christianity. He says mutual consent must be made by both spouses before one or the other undertakes a vow of continence. In other words, a husband was subject to his wife's authority on this issue. Indeed, he recognizes that the wife has rights in this matter that the husband could not violate. God forbids such violation. However, in the letter it is the wife who is ready to live a life of sexual abstinence, not the husband. She is only prevented from doing so because spouses are to render the debt to one another as St. Paul teaches in 1 Cor. 7:4. St. Augustine, however, encourages the husband to consent to his wife's desire for continence. He calls the wife the "weaker sex," yet she is more ready to practice virtue which is from *vir*, "man." As a man, the husband should not allow the woman, the "weaker sex," to show him up.

156. St. John Chrysostom, *Homily 61*, trans. Sr. Thomas Aquinas Goggin, *Fathers of the Church*, vol. 41 (New York: Fathers of the Church, 1960), 161–62 (PG 59.340–41).

157. St. John Chrysostom, *Homily 9*, trans. Philip Schaff, "Homilies on Timothy," *Nicene and Post Nicene Fathers*, vol. 13, ed. Philip Schaff (Grand Rapids, Mich.: Wm. B. Eerdmans, 1962), 435 (PG 62.544).

158. St. Paulinus of Nola, *Letter 44* 94, trans. P.G. Walsh, *Letters of St. Paulinus of Nola* (Westminster, Md.: The Newman Press, 1976), p. 237. The phrase "to become the bones of her husband" in the Latin: "in ossa uiri sui" (CSEL 29.372).

159. St. Augustine, *De Sancta Virginitate* 44.45 (CSEL 41.289–90).

160. St. Cyprian, *De habitu virginum* 6 (CSEL 3.192).

161. St. Ambrose, *De Virginibus ad Mar.* 2.4.22 (PL 16.224).

162. Eusebius, *Historia ecclesiastica* 5.1 (PG 20.426).

163. St. Paulinus of Nola, *Epistula 23* 39 and 42 (CSEL 29.195, 197).

164. Feminist theology seeks to advance the equality of women but does so by abolishing the significance of gender. Fiorenza states:

> The remembrance of women's sufferings in religious patriarchy must be explored structurally in order to set free the emancipatory power of the Christian community which is theologically rooted neither in spiritual-sexual dimorphism nor in patriarchal ecclesial dominance, but in an egalitarian vision and in altruistic social relationships that may not be "generalized." (*In Memory of Her*, 92)

Chapter 2. The Authority of Christ

1. *Declaration on the Admission of Women to the Ministerial Priesthood (Inter In-signiores)*, 5, Sacred Congregation for the Doctrine of the Faith, in *Vatican Council II: More Postconciliar Documents*, vol. 2, ed. Austin Flannery O.P. (Collegeville Minn., The Liturgical Press, 1982), 339.

2. Ibid., 339–40.

3. Ibid., 341. That the priest stands in the place of Christ as head is also taught in the Vatican II documents: *Lumen Gentium*, 28, and *Presbyterorum ordinis*, 6.

4. Ibid. This phrase "in which the whole Church offers and is herself wholly offered" is a quotation from *Mysterium Fidei*, the encyclical letter of Pope Paul VI (3 September 1965). Here the document relies on St. Augustine, *City of God*, 10, 6 which states: "And this also is the sacrifice which the Church continually celebrates in the sacrament of the altar, known to the faithful, in which she teaches that she herself is offered in the offering she makes to God" (trans. Marcus Dods). The phrase indicates that the Church as Christ's body offers the Eucharist in union with her head as *Mysterium Fidei* states the Mass "is an act of Christ and the Church. In offering this Sacrifice, the Church learns to offer herself as a sacrifice for all" (Boston: St. Paul Editions, 14–15).

5. It is not our purpose to enter into the issue of whether Ephesians is a pseudepigraphic composition, an issue that is much debated among New Testament scholars. We will assume its authenticity. In any case the letter represents a development of Pauline theology found in the earlier epistles.

6. J. P. Sampley, *And the Two Shall Become One Flesh* (New York: Cambridge University, 1971), 2.

7. Ibid.

8. L. Cerfaux, *The Church in the Theology of St. Paul* (New York: Herder and Herder, 1959), 339.

9. Ernest Best, *One Body in Christ* (London: SPCK, 1955), 146–47.

10. Stephen F. Miletic, *"One Flesh": Eph. 5.22–24, 5.31 Marriage and the New Creation*, Analecta Biblica, 115 (Roma: Editrice Pontificio Istituto Biblico, 1988), 74. Why Miletic states that the term "head" connects Christ to both the cosmos and the Church without drawing any distinctions between the two is not entirely clear. The headship of Christ to the cosmos is exercised differently than it is to the Church which in itself denotes a distinction.

The scholars cited by Miletic in support of a double meaning for "headship" are: Schlier, H. *Der Brief an die Epheser* (Düsseldorf: Patmos-Verlag, 1957), 89, 200, 253–54; Cambier, J. "Le Grand mystère concernant le Christ et son Église," *Bib* 47 (1966): 49, 59; Gnilka, J. *Der Epheserbrief.* HTKNT 10.2 (Freiberg: Herder, 1971), 276–77; Barth, M. *Ephesians, Anchor Bible*, vols. 34–34A (Garden City, N.Y.: Doubleday and Company, Inc., 1974), 614.

11. Miletic, *One Flesh*, 74.

12. S. Bedale, "The Meaning of κεφαλή in the Pauline Epistles," *Journal of Theological Studies* 5–6 (1954–55): 212–13.

13. Ibid., 213.

14. Miletic, *One Flesh*, 84–85.

The use of δίδωμι in the Greek scriptures indicates that this verb was used at critical points in the sacred history of Israel. For example, at Gen. 9.2 God makes an important promise to Noah and his sons. God will "place" all the animal kingdom under their hands or in their control (ὑπὸ χεῖρας ὑμῖν δέδωκα).

At v. 12 we learn that the rainbow in the sky is a sign of the covenant that God "gives" (δίδωμι) to Noah. The very same action characterizes covenantal action between God and Abram at 12.7. God will "give" (δώσω) the land to Abram. The use of δίδωμι to express divine activity in connection with covenantal narratives indicates the theological significance this verb has within the Greek scriptures.

15. Ibid., 85.

16. Ibid., 75.

17. Marcus Barth, *Ephesians, Anchor Bible*, vol. 34 (Garden City, N.Y.: Doubleday and Company, Inc., 1974), 271.

18. J. Armitage Robinson, *St. Paul's Letter to the Ephesians* (London: James Clarke and Co. Ltd., 1922), 68.

19. Joseph Huby, *St. Paul: Les Épistres de la Captivité* (Paris: Beauchesne et ses fils, 1935), 187.

20. Ibid.

21. M. Barth, *Ephesians*, 318.

22. Ibid.

23. Ibid., 319.

24. J. Paul Sampley, "The Letter to the Ephesians," in *Ephesians, Colossians, 2. Thess., the Pastoral Epistles, Proclamation Commentaries*, ed. Gerhard Krodel (Philadelphia: Fortress Press, 1978), 19.

25. Huby, *St. Paul*, 216.

26. Bedale, "The Meaning of κεφαλή," 214.

27. J. Armitage Robinson, *St. Paul's Letter to the Ephesians*, 62–63.

28. Ernst Käsemann, *Leib und Leib Christi* (Tübingen: J. B. C. Mohr (Paul Siebeck), 1933), 168.

29. Some authors do collapse the Church into Christ in which there is almost no distinction between them. For example, Ernest Best in his work *One Body in Christ* (London: SPCK, 1955), 76 states regarding 1 Cor. 6:15:

> The believer is also a member of Christ. This suggests that it is not each believer with Christ forming a single person but that the whole group of believers with Christ forms a single person—and this person is Christ, whose members are the bodies . . . of the believers.

On p. 78 he states:

> The phrase "members of Christ" suggests, however, a very close identity between Christ and the community of believers; if they are his members, then together they form him. The Church, or the community of believers, is thus identical with Christ; the Church is Christ.

J. A. T. Robinson also virtually collapses Ecclesiology into Christology. In his work *The Body: A Study in Pauline Theology* (Naperville, Ill.: Alec R. Allenson, 1957), p. 71 he states regarding Eph. 1:9:

> Just as it was the good pleasure of the Father that the whole expanse of the Divine fulness should settle down in the one man, Christ Jesus, so now that fulness is to be extended to incorporate every man, till all are brought within the One.

The deficiency in their interpretation of St. Paul is that they have not maintained the distinction between Christ and the Church. Indeed, Robinson's phrase is an utterly Platonic formula. Instead of Christians leaving the body to be united with the One, the One becomes the body which absorbs everything. Best and Robinson would have the Church absorbed into Christ, which is contrary to the marital covenant between them.

30. Joseph Huby, *St. Paul*, 287.

31. Ibid.

32. Ibid., 293. Also F. W. Grosheide, *Commentary on the First Epistle to the Corinthians* (Grand Rapids, Mich.: Wm. B. Eerdemans, 1953), 292. Grosheide states that the phrase "So also is Christ" means:

> Christ is also one body that has many members. This cannot be applied merely to the body of our Savior. Paul does not make mention of Him either in this verse or in the following. This statement concerning Christ does not fit in with what is revealed to us in the Scriptures. For that reason we understand "Christ" as having reference to the body of Christ, in accordance with vs. 27 (cf. Eph. 1:22,23), it is Christ *with His church* (cf. [1 Cor.] 6:15).

33. See Paulus Andriessen, "The New Eve, Body of the New Adam" in *The Birth of the Church* (Staten Island, N.Y.: Alba House, 1968), 11-39.

34. Those scholars who collapse ecclesiology into Christology are cited in footnote 28 in a discussion of this subject.

35. Andriessen, "The New Eve," 112.

36. Ibid., 114.

> It was natural that the specific word signifying the flesh became the usual term for expressing blood relationship. *Basar* is a principle of solidarity rather than of individuation. This is why we like to point out the relationship we have with someone by identifying his body with our own. Judah dissuaded his brothers from killing Joseph "for he is our flesh" (Gn. 37:27). Similarly in Isaiah 58:7: "When you see a naked man cover him up, and do not despise your flesh." Laban says to his nephew Jacob: "Truly you are flesh of my flesh and bone of my bone," an expression which in this sense is met with at least eight times in the Old Testament and which brings us back to the account of the formation of Eve, the root of all kinship.

37. Ibid., 114-15.

38. Pierre Benoit, "Corps, tête et plérôma dans les épîtres de la captivité," *Revue Bibl.* 63 (1956), 13.

39. Andriessen, "The New Eve," 126.

40. Ibid., 138.

> It has been asked what the reasons are that brought Paul to use this body metaphor. These solutions have been proposed: the Stoic theme of the cosmic body or the body politic, the Gnostic myth of the heavenly *Anthropos*, the Old Testament notions of corporate personality, the rabbinical speculations on the first man, the preponderant role of the crucified body of the Lord in the redemption mystery, the very special capacity of his glorified body, the equation: Body of Christ=temple of the new covenant, the institution of the Eucharist, the very important place occupied by the vine metaphor in Judaism. We think that all of these may have influenced the Apostle. Yet Paul has clearly shown what the chief source of this metaphor was, namely the account of the formation of the first human couple to which he refers us several times.

41. The comparison between Adam and Christ can be found in the following exegetes: Francois Amiot, *The Key Concepts of St. Paul* (New York: Herder and Herder, 1962), 71-72; Karl Barth, *Christ and Adam* (New York: Octagon Books, 1956), 29, 31-32, 89; C.K. Barrett, *From First Adam to Last* (New York: Charles Scribner's Sons, 1962), 110;

Lucien Cerfaux, *Christ in the Theology of St. Paul* (New York: Herder and Herder, 1959), 232–35, 348; C.E.B. Cranfield, *The Epistle to the Romans*, vol. 1 (Edinburgh: T & T Clark, 1975), 291; S. Nowell Rostron, *The Christology of St. Paul* (London: Robert Scott, 1912), 71–72; William Sanday and Arthur Headlam, *The Epistle to the Romans* (Edinburgh: T & T Clark, 1960), 139; Robin Scroggs, *The Last Adam: A Study in Pauline Anthropology* (Philadelphia: Fortress Press, 1966), 83–84, 88, 106.

42. Scroggs, *The Last Adam*, 106–7.

43. Cranfield, *The Epistle to the Romans*, 283.

> The word τύπος [type] denotes a mark made by striking (it is cognate with τύπτειν), an impression made by something, such an impression used in its turn as a mould to shape something else ... hence a form, figure, pattern, example, and—a specialized use in biblical interpretation—a type in the sense of a person or thing prefiguring (according to God's design) a person or thing pertaining to the time of eschatological fulfilment.

44. Scroggs, *The Last Adam*, 21.

45. Ibid., 99.

46. K. Barth, *Christ and Adam*, 58–59. Concerning the relation between Adam and Christ, Barth states:

> On both sides there are the same formal relationships between the one and the many, so that both sides have the same ordering principle. But within that formal identity, Adam is subordinate, because he can only be the forerunner, the witness, the preliminary shadow and likeness, the *typos* (type) [v. 14] of the Christ who is to come. Because he is that, because he is really like Christ, vv. 18–19 and 21 can go on to draw a valid and significant parallel between the two. The *pollo mallons* (much more of vv. 15, 17), in its first meaning, has already made it clear that the two sides do belong together in that way. But within this belonging together there is a disparity. For Christ who seems to come second, really comes first, and Adam who seems to come first really comes second. In Christ the relationship between the one and the many is original, in Adam it is only a copy of that original. Our relationship to Adam depends for its reality on our relationship to Christ. And that means, in practice, that to find the true and essential nature of man we have to look not to Adam the fallen man, but to Christ in whom what is fallen has been cancelled and what was original has been restored.

We are essentially in agreement with Barth's theology here. Adam is created in the image of Christ. In this way Christ is the head of all males as archetype to symbol according to 1 Cor. 11:3 f. We will deal specifically with the sacramental nature of the male body as taught by this passage later in this same chapter.

47. John G. Gibbs, *Creation and Redemption: A Study in Pauline Theology* (Leiden: E. J. Brill, 1971), 48. Some exegetes interpret Christ's one righteous act and obedience as not specifically a reference to the crucifixion but rather the character of Christ's whole life before God, i.e., C.E.B. Cranfield, *Romans: A Shorter Commentary* (Grand Rapids, Mich.: Wm. B. Eerdmans, 1985), 122. However, Rom. 5:18–19 refers to a singular act of righteousness and certainly Christ's Passion is His definitive act of obedience to the Father. Moreover, the sacrifice of Christ is mentioned earlier in the chapter (vs. 6–10) as the source of salvation and the act of righteousness of v. 18 is also identified as the source of salvation.

48. Scroggs, *The Last Adam*, 89–90. The scholars cited by Scroggs are Cullmann, *Christology of the New Testament*, 174–81; P. Bonnard, *L'Epître de Saint Paul aux Philippiens* ('C.N.T.'; Neuchatel, 1950), 43; Ch. Guignebert, "Quelques remarques d'exegese sur Phillipiens," 2, 6–11, *Revue d'Histoire et de Philosophie Religieuses* III (1923), 522f.

49. Miletic, *"One Flesh"*, 83. His full exegesis of the parallels between 1 Cor 15: 20–28 and Eph. 1:19–23 is from 79–83.

50. Karen Armstrong, *The Gospel According to Women: Creation of the Sex War in the West* (Garden City, N.Y.: Doubleday, 1987), 17–18; Denise Lardner Carmody, *Biblical Woman: Contemporary Reflections on Scriptural Texts* (New York: Crossroad, 1988), 128–30; Georgia Harkness, *Women in Church and Society* (Nashville/New York: Abington Press, 1972), 68–69; Virgina Ramey Mollenkott, *Women, Men and the Bible* (Nashville: Abington Press, 1977), 97–99; Schüssler-Fiorenza, *In Memory of Her*, 46. Carmody is particularly explicit in her hostility toward St. Paul regarding 1 Cor. 11:13. She accuses him of being simplistic, unreflective, rooted in social convention, and possessing a warped sense of what leadership means.

51. Earl Muller, *Trinity and Marriage in Paul: The Establishment of a Trinitarian Analogy of the Trinity Grounded in the Theological Shape of Pauline Thought* (New York: Peter Lang, 1990), pp. 160–97.

52. C. K. Barrett, *A Commentary on the First Epistle to the Corinthians* (New York: Harper and Row, 1968), 248–49.

53. Ibid., 248.

54. Ibid., 249.

55. Andriessen, "The New Eve," 128. The passages Andriessen cites are: 2 Cor. 4:4: "Their unbelieving minds have been blinded by the god of the present age so that they do not see the splendor of the gospel showing forth the glory of Christ, the image of God."

Col. 1:15: "He is the image of the invisible God, the first-born of all creatures."

Heb. 1:3: "This Son is the reflection of the Father's glory, the exact representation of the Father's being."

Muller, *Trinity and Marriage in Paul*, 171.

Also Manfred Hauke, *Women in the Priesthood* (San Francisco: Ignatius Press, 1988), p. 349. Regarding the issue of subordination Hauke states:

> Even when woman is regarded as "the glory of man" and not, directly, as "the image and glory of God," a lesser degree of being-in-the-image-of-God is not thereby asserted of her. Christ, too, is described in the Pauline letters as "image" or "glory" of the Father, yet that in no way diminishes his equality with God. The same applies in the subordinate position of Christ to the Father.

Hans Conzelmann, *1 Corinthians: A Commentary on the First Epistle to the Corinthians* (Philadelphia: Fortress Press, 1975), 186.

56. Muller, *Trinity and Marriage in Paul*, 171.

57. Bedale, "The Meaning of κεφαλή," 214–15.

58. St. Thomas Aquinas, *Summa Theologica*, I, Q 93. a. 5, trans. Edmund Hill, *Blackfriars*, vol. 13 (New York: McGraw-Hill; London: Eyre and Spottiswoode, 1964), 61.

59. Ibid.

60. Andre Feuillet, "La dignité et le rôle de la femme d'apres quelques textes Pauliniens: Comparaison avec L'Ancien Testament," *New Testament Studies* 21 (1975): 161.

61. R. St. John Parry, *The First Epistle of Paul the Apostle to the Corinthians* (London: Cambridge University Press, 1937), 159.

62. Muller, *Trinity and Marriage in Paul*, 196.

63. Barrett, *A Commentary on the First Epistle to the Corinthians*, 251. Hauke, *Women in the Priesthood?*, 348: "Paul's declarations have, above and beyond their changeable

aspects, a thoroughly paradigmatic meaning. The covering or uncovering of the head is only an expression of the underlying difference between the sexes. For Paul, this difference has its foundation in creation, and its effects extend all the way to the divine service."

64. Feuillet, "La dignitié et la rôle de la femme," 160.

William Ramsay, *The Cities of St. Paul: Their Influence on His Life and Thought* (Grand Rapids, Mich.: Baker, 1949), 202ff.

65. Parry, *The First Epistle*, 159–60.

66. Barrett, *A Commentary*, 254–55: According to Paul . . . it is man, and not woman who is the glory of God, and who will therefore naturally play the active role in worship. . . . Yet now woman, too, speaks to God in prayer and declares his word in prophecy; to do this she needs authority and power from God. The headcovering which symbolizes the effacement of man's glory in the presence of God also serves as a sign of that which is given to the woman. . . . That is, her veil represents the new authority given to the woman under the new dispensation to do things which formerly had not been permitted her."

Muller, *Trinity and Marriage*, 187.

67. Ramsey, *The Cities of St. Paul*, 202–3.

68. Ibid.

69. Muller, *Trinity and Marriage*, 187.

70. Ibid., 302.

71. John Paul II, *The Original Unity of Man and Woman* (Boston: St. Paul Editions, 1981), 78–79.

> Let us recall the passage of Genesis 2:23: "Then the man said, 'This at last is bone of my bones and flesh of my flesh; she shall be called Woman, because she was taken out of Man." In the light of this text, we understand that knowledge of man passes through masculinity and femininity, which are, as it were, two "incarnations" of the same metaphysical solitude, before God and the world—two ways, as it were, of "being a body" and at the same time a man, which complete each other—two complementary dimensions, as it were, of self consciousness and self- determination and, at the same time, two complementary ways of being conscious of the meaning of the body.

72. Scroggs, *The Last Adam*, 13.

73. The same could be said for Eph. 2:14–16, 20–22, and 4:16. Regarding Eph. 2:11–22 Miletic explains: "a careful analysis of the imagery and language in 2:11–22 will show that here Christ's death must be understood in terms of Adamic Christology and that understanding 5.23c in light of *both* 5.25b and 2.11–22 will lead us to detect the Adamic Christological character of in σωτήρ in 5.23c" (p. 56).

74. Huby, *St. Paul*, 177–78; J. A. T. Robinson, *The Body*, 69; Wilfred X. Knox, *St. Paul and the Church of the Gentiles* (Cambridge: Cambridge Univerity Press, 1961), 186; Best, *One Body*, 147. Best argues that *plērōma* in Eph. 1:23 does not teach that the Church completes Christ. His argument, however, contains a theological contradiction. He states:

> The principal idea here is not the direction of the Head by the Body but the unity of both in love; and this unity comes from the Head who contributes the love to the Body. εδωκε must not be weakened but given its full sense: God *gave* Christ to the Church as Head above all; this is an act of grace. *In no sense is the Church necessary to Christ*; he is always and in all respects necessary for it.

Best states that the "unity of both in love . . . comes from the Head." This is correct in so far as Christ is the source and initiator of this unity. But Best would turn the Church into a completely passive vessel; a vessel that contributes nothing to the covenant unity. The doctrine of Ephesians teaches that according to the order of redemption founded on the "one flesh" of marriage, the Church *is necessary to Christ*. There is no way that there can be a real *covenantal* "unity of both in love" if the Church is not necessary to Christ in this unity; a unity upon which the world's salvation itself depends. Again, we emphasize with Best that Christ is the initiator of this unity and its sole source of grace.

75. Pope Pius XII, *Mystici Corporis*, 77, 29 June 1943 (Boston: St. Paul Editions), 46–47.

76. J. Armitage Robinson, *St. Pauls's Letter to the Ephesians*, 255–59; Ferdnand Prat, *The Theology of St. Paul* vol. 2, trans. John L. Stoddard (Westminster, Md.: The Newman Bookshop, 1927), 283.

77. Huby, *St. Paul*, 176. While Huby admits the strength of the position of those exegetes who interpret *plērōma* as the Church being the completion of Christ, he does not accept this view. He prefers an interpretation that states that Christ *fills* the Church with his "plenitude" and his "puissance de sanctification," 177.

Huby, like most authors who reject the Church as the fullness of Christ, such as Best and J.A.T. Robinson, is eager to protect Christ's primacy in salvation. He states on p. 177 that Eph. 1:23 and 5:23–24 declare "l'absolute suprématie du Christ." He interprets these passages in light of Eph. 4:13, 15–16 where Christ is spoken of as the "principe vital" of the Church. In other words, the rejection of the Church as the completion of Christ, is born from a doctrinal anxiousness—that to say the Church completes Christ threatens the truth that He is the source of the Church and of the world's salvation. However, the Church completes Christ because she is His covenantal partner in redemption. That she is so, according to the marital order of authority, in no way threatens Christ's divinity or His primacy in salvation—Christ is the *head* of the Church.

78. George S. Hitchcock, *The Epistle to the Ephesians* (London: Burns and Oates, Chicago: Benziger Bros., 1913), 133–35; E.L. Mascall, *Christ, the Christian and the Church: A Study of the Incarnation and Its Consequences* (London: Longmans, Green, 1946), 120; Prat, *The Theology of St. Paul*, 283–84. Pratt states:

> The Church is the 'complement of Christ' as the trunk is the complement of the head and as the limbs are the complement of the organism. The head is helpless without the body; the organism can function normally only if it possesses every one of its organs. So Christ without the Church would be an incomplete being; incomplete as a Redeemer, since the grace which he possesses for the purpose of bestowing it would remain inactive; incomplete also as the second Adam, because he is so only by his representative character; incomplete even as Christ, for Christ is also, in St. Paul a collective personality.

79. J. Armitage Robinson, *St. Paul's Letter to the Ephesians*, 43; Bedale, "The Meaning of κεφαλή," 214. Bedale states that while headship means *source* it is still possible to interpret *plērōma* as the fulfillment of the head as Robinson has done.

80. L. S. Thornton, *The Common Life in the Body of Christ* (London: Dacre Press, 1942), 222.

81. Miletic, *"One Flesh"*, 97.

82. Ibid., 93.

83. John Paul II, *Mulieris Dignitatem (On the Dignity and Vocation of Women)*, *Origins* 18 (6 October 1988): 278.

84. Rosemary Radford Ruether, *Sexism and God-Talk* (Boston: Beacon Press, 1983), 257–58.

85. Emmett Cardinal Carter, *Do This In Memory of Me: Pastoral Letter on the Sacrament of the Priesthood* (Archdiocese of Toronto, Can., 8 December 1983), 44–45.

86. Hauke, *Women in the Priesthood?* 353. Hauke's thesis that male headship and female subordination rests on an "ontological and functional differentiation" (p. 354) is quite correct. However, the weakness in Hauke's argument is that while headship defines the salvific functional role of husbands, to define women simply in terms of subordination leaves undefined the equal role and value of the woman in relation to the head. In other words, the constant formula of Hauke: "headship of the husband and subordination of the wife" (p. 355) leaves unindicated what the feminine contribution to the covenant is meant to be expressed by her "subordination." It would probably be more fruitful to speak not so much in terms of "headship and subordination" but of "head" and "body."

87. Miletic, *"One Flesh,"* 94.

88. *Mulieris Dignitatem*, 277–78. Regarding the issue of subjection John Paul II states:
> ... the husband is called the "head" of the wife as Christ is the head of the church; he is so in order to give "himself up for her" (Eph. 5:25), and giving himself up for her means giving up even his own life. However, whereas in the relationship between Christ and the church the subjection is only on the part of the church, in the relationship between husband and wife the "subjection" is not one-sided but mutual.

Christ is not subject to the Church in the sense that he "owes" her His obedience. The Church is obedient to Christ in gratitude for the salvation He wrought in His blood. Nevertheless, one can legitimately speak of Christ as having "subordinated" Himself to the Church. In fact, He performed the radical subordination by dying on the Cross for her. Therefore, even on the level of Christ and the Church there is a "mutual" subordination. Both Christ and the Church must "give themselves over" to one another. His sacrifice enables the Church to give a sacrifice of praise. It is this kind of covenantal subordination between Christ and the Church that forms the ground of all marital subjection of husband and wife. It must be noted that when John Paul II stated in the above quotation that a mutual subjection exists between husbands and wives he made a statement that has the power to profoundly affect Catholic thinking on the meaning of authority.

89. Gertrud von le Fort, *The Eternal Woman: The Woman in the Timeless Woman* (Milwaukee, Wisc.: Bruce Publishing, 1954), 103.

Chapter 3. The Meaning of Male Escclesiastical Authority

1. Emmett Cardinal Carter, *Do This in Memory of Me: Pastoral Letter on the Sacrament of the Priesthood*, 8 December 1983 (Archdiocese of Toronto, Can.), 41.

2. The scholarly work of Joachim Jeremias is invaluable for the evidence it supplies for the historical authenticity of Christ's institution of the Eucharist in *The Eucharistic Words of Christ* (Oxford: Basil Blackwell, 1955). Particularly helpful is his exegesis of the institution narrative in Mark and the Pauline text 1 Cor. 11: 23–25, pp. 118–32. He concludes:
> Of the traditions which have come down to us, Mark's is the nearest to the primitive Aramaic account of the Last Supper. ... That in the remaining space of at most a decade after the death of Jesus the Eucharistic rite should have been freely created, and the account of the Lord's Supper invented as an aetiological legend, is as much incapable of proof as it is improbable. It is even

improbable that in the first decade after the death of Jesus the tradition should be in any essentials obscured; against that we have to set the complete unanimity in content of the mutually independent reports of Mark and Paul which came from different sections of the Church. Since the tradition of Mark, besides its material indications of a very early age, possesses a further guarantee of trustworthiness in its Palestinian origin (Semitisims), we have every reason to conclude that it gives us absolutely authentic information. (p. 132)

On whether the command of Christ "Do this in memory of me" is authentic, J. Tixeront in *Holy Orders and Ordination* (St. Louis, Mo.: Herder, 1928) pp. 35–36 responds:

Now it is true that the words in question are not to be found in the accounts of St. Matthew and St. Mark. . . . However, the present text of St. Luke—as I have remarked before—can be well defended; also we have to admit that the contested words were to be found in at least one of the Gospels as early as the second century, since St. Justin says that he read them in the *Memoirs* of the Apostles "which are called Gospels." For the rest, the authority of St. Paul would suffice to establish the authenticity of the τουτοποιειτε, even though we had no other. There is no basis for the assumption that the tradition of St. Paul is posterior to that of S.S. Matthew and Mark. The first Epistle to the Corinthians was written in the year 56 or 57, and may antedate the final draft of the first Gospels. The words of institution which it contains would therefore be chronologically the first words of Our Lord related in the New Testament. As to the theory that St. Paul was influenced by the practice of the celebration of the Eucharist already in use, how explain the existence of this practice without some preliminary command and institution of the Savior? (p. 36)

3. Henri de Lubac, *The Splendour of the Church* (Glen Rock, N.J.: Paulist Press, 1956), 84.

4. Elizabeth Schüssler Fiorenza, *In Memory of Her* (New York: Crossroad, 1988), 146–47, 150–51.

Fiorenza makes it quite clear that God the Father can have no concrete effective expression in the world. But even more than this, fatherhood as such does not exist in the community Christ has founded. She treats the New Testament passages that state the disciples of Christ form His true family: "Whoever does the will of God is brother and sister and mother to me" (Matt. 12:46–50; Mark 3:31–35; Luke 8:19ff). Fiorenza takes note that there are no fathers within this circle that she claims forms a "discipleship of equals" (147). She explicitly states "this new 'family' of equal discipleship . . . has no room for 'fathers.'" While "fathers" are those left behind in discipleship (Matt. 19:29; Mark 10:29) "they are not included in the new kinship which the disciples acquire" (147).

Fiorenza ensures that God the Father will be absent by using Christ's words "Call no one father" (Mark 10:29–30) against the Church's sacramental priestly system (150–51). She states: "The kinship relationship in the discipleship of equals does not admit of 'any father' because it is sustained by the gracious goodness of God whom the disciples and Jesus call 'father.' . . . The 'father' God is invoked here, however, not to justify patriarchal structures and relationships in the community of disciples but precisely to reject all such claims, powers, and structures" (150). She states that the disciples of Jesus were enjoined by Him "from recognizing *any* father authority in their society, because there *is* only one father" (151). In Fiorenza's theology this "father" God, however, is utterly transhistorical. Nothing and no one can speak for Him or represent Him. In effect this "father" God has no sign and no expression in the world and gone with Him is any notion of fatherly authority in the world. In the end male authority does not exist because the very thing upon which it depends (the Fatherhood of God) cannot be spoken in the world. Fiorenza has not rid the universe of patriarchy, rather she has committed patricide. In the feminist world of equality there are no fathers in the Kingdom of God.

5. R. H. Lightfoot, *St. John's Gospel* (London: Oxford University Press, 1957), 138–45. In these pages Lightfoot treats the issue of unity between the Father and the Son and the Son's dependency on the Father.

> In 5:17 the Lord had expressed, in a positive form, the complete union in action between the Father and Himself. He now in 5:19 shows that the union is due to the absolute dependence, in all things, of the Son upon the Father; and this is expressed first negatively and then positively. His actions, we read, have their origin, not from Himself, but from His sight of the actions of the Father; and all that the Father does is done also by the Son. The union, therefore, is absolute. It is not, for instance, as though the Son reveals the Father in certain particular ways or in certain remarkable actions; no moment of His life, and no action of His, but is the expression of the life and action of the Father [12:45, 14:9]; and we may add, the same is true of His words [3:34, 8:26, 12:49]. (p. 141)

C. K. Barrett's exegesis of 5:26 corroborates that of Lightfoot. He states that the central theme of the discourse is "the complete continuity between the work of the Father and the work of the Son. The life, however, of the Son is dependent upon that of the Father." *The Gospel According to John* (Philadelphia: Westminster Press, 1978), 262.

6. C. K. Barrett, *The Gospel According to John*, 259. Regarding 5:19–20 Barrett states:
> "The activity of Jesus the Son . . . can only be claimed as a revelation of the Father on the ground that Jesus never acts independently of him. What he does is always a refection of the Father's own work." The activity of the Father and the activity of the Son are identical."

7. See p. 48 of chapter 2 for a list of Johannine passages.

8. Gerard von Rad, *Genesis: A Commentary* (Philadelphia: Westminster Press, 1961), 239–40.

9. Juli Loesch, "God the Father," *The National Catholic Register* (26 February 1984), 5.

10. Joseph Cardinal Ratzinger provides an insightful treatment of this passage from John 12:24 in his work *Introduction to Christianity* (New York: Herder and Herder, 1969), 189–91. Christ's death means that He lives *for others* in a giving up of self that breaks all human isolation.

11. Raymond E. Brown, *The Gospel According to John: I-XII, Anchor Bible*, vol. 29 (Garden City, N.Y.: Doubleday, 1966), 397.

12. Manfred Hauke, *Women in the Priesthood?* (San Francisco: Ignatius Press, 1988), 230.

13. Ibid., 233.

14. Ibid., 231.

15. Ibid.

16. Ibid., 231–32.

17. Ibid., 233. Phyllis Trible provides a feminist exegesis of the Hebrew word for "inner parts" and the Hebrew root word for mercy (*rhm*). Since "inner parts" sometimes parallels "womb" in various Old Testament passages she concludes that the word applies to the mercy of God; God has "motherly compassion" or a *womb*. See pp. 45–71 for her full discussion in *God and the Rhetoric of Sexuality* (Philadelphia: Fortress Press, 1978).

For a response to Trible, see John W. Miller, "Depatriarchalizing God in Biblical Interpretation: A Critique," *Catholic Biblical Quarterly* 48 (Oct. 1986): 609–16. He argues that simply because the root meanings of certain words are feminine such as *raham* meaning "mother compassion" in Jer. 31:20, does not mean God can be referred to as feminine. It is not inappropriate for a father to yearn for and have compassion upon his children: "As a matter of fact, *rahum* occurs frequently in Canaanite texts as a characterization of the Canaanite father deity *El*" (613). Miller concludes:

> Not once in the Bible is God addressed as mother, said to be mother, or referred to with feminine pronouns. On the contrary, gender usage throughout clearly specifies that the root metaphor is masculine-father (614). . . . Yahweh, then, is not simply male, but father to his worshippers as the name Yahweh itself may imply ("he causes to be"). (615–16)

18. Hauke, *Women in the Priesthood?*, 234.

19. Ibid.

20. Joseph Cardinal Ratzinger, *Introduction to Christianity* (New York: Herder and Herder, 1969), 128.

21. Ibid., 131.

22. St. Thomas Aquinas, *Summa Theologica*, I, Q 28, a. 3, trans. Edmund Hill, *Blackfriars*, vol. 6 (New York: McGraw-Hill; London: Eyre and Spottiswoode, 1964), 35.

23. Ibid.

24. ST, I, Q 33, a. 1, *Blackfriars*, vol. 7, p. 5.

25. Ibid.

26. Ibid., ad. 3, p. 7.

27. Ibid., ad. 2.

28. Ibid.

29. ST, I, Q 33, a. 2, p. 9.

30. Ibid., ad. 4, p. 11.

31. Ibid., ST, I, Q 33, a. 4, pp. 17,19.

32. Ibid., ad. 1, p. 19. In Latin: "Nam fontalitas et auctoritas nihil aliud significant in divinis quam principium originis."

33. Ibid., ST, I, Q 34, a. 3, p. 39.

34. Matt. 10:40 is addressed exclusively to the 12 Apostles. This is confirmed in Matt. 11:1 which states: "Now it came to pass when Jesus had finished giving instructions to his twelve disciples."

35. *Declaration on the Admission of Women to the Ministerial Priesthood (Inter Insigniores)*, Sacred Congregation for the Doctrine of the Faith, in *Vatican Council II: More Post Conciliar Documents*, vol. 2, ed. Austin Flannery, O.P. (Collegeville, Minn.: The Liturgical Press, 1982), 340.

36. *Dogmatic Constitution on the Church (Lumen Gentium)*, in *Vatican Council II: The Conciliar and Post-Conciliar Documents*, ed. Austin Flannery, O.P. (Collegeville, Minn.: The Liturgical Press, 1975), 375.

"The Lord made Peter alone the rock-foundation and the holder of the keys of the Church (cf. Matt. 16:18–19), and constituted him shepherd of his whole flock (cf. John 21:15ff.). It is clear, however, that the office of binding and loosing which was given to Peter (Matt 16:19), was also assigned to the college of the apostles united to its head (Matt 18:18; 28:16–20). This college, in so far as it is composed of many members, is the expression of the multifariousness and universality of the People of God; and the unity of the flock of Christ, in so far as it is assembled under one head."

37. Ibid., *Constitution on the Sacred Liturgy (Sacrosanctum Concilium)*, 47, p. 16.

One of the earliest records of the historical institution of the Eucharist by Christ comes from St. Paul in 1 Cor. 11:23–27:

> For I myself have received from the Lord (what I also delivered to you), that the Lord Jesus, on the night he was betrayed, took bread, and giving thanks broke, and said, "This is my body which shall be given up for you; do this in remembrance of me." In like manner also the cup, after he had supped, saying, "This cup is the new covenant in my blood; do this as often as you drink it, in remembrance of me." For as often as you shall eat this bread and drink the cup, you proclaim the death of the Lord until he comes."

M. E. Boismard, O.P. comments:

> The expressions "to receive . . . to deliver (to hand on)" are technical expressions, frequently found in the writings of the rabbis, to denote the unbroken chain of the "traditions" handed down from generation to generation in the rabbinic schools. . . . St. Paul simply wants to make it understood that the traditions he is handing on have their origin in the teaching of Christ himself, as it was preserved in the Christian communities. So the teaching on the institution of the Eucharist by Christ was part of the early Christian catechesis, just as much as the statement of the central mystery of the death and Resurrection of Christ. . . . To be quite accurate, this statement concerns above all the actual account of the institution of the Lord's Supper by Christ ["The Eucharist According to St. Paul," in *The Eucharist in the New Testament* (Baltimore and Dublin: The Helicon Press, 1965), 138–39].

38. Pope Paul VI, *Mysterium Fidei*, 3 September 1965 (Boston: St. Paul Editions, 1965), 12.

39. Council of Trent, Sess. 22, Chap.1

> [A]t the last supper , on the night He was betrayed, wishing to leave His beloved Spouse, the Church, a visible sacrifice such as the nature of men requires, that would re-present the bloody sacrifice offered once on the cross, and perpetuate its memory to the end of time, and whose salutary virtue might be applied in remitting those sins which we daily commit . . . offered His body and blood under the species of bread and wine to God the Father, and under the same species allowed the apostles, whom He at that time constituted the priests of the New Testament, to partake thereof; commanding them and their successors in the priesthood to make the same offering.

The above quotation is taken from Francis J. Wengier, *The Eucharistic Sacrifice* (Milwaukee: The Bruce Publishing Co., 1955), 241. See also H. J. Schroeder, *Canons and Decrees of the Council of Trent* (St. Louis, Mo.: B Herder, 1941), 144–45; Council of Trent, Sess. 23, chap. 1, Schroeder, *Canons and Decrees of the Council of Trent*, 160; *Instruction on the Worship of the Eucharistic Mystery (Eucharisticum Mysterium)*, 103, Flannery.

40. *Mysterium Fidei*, 12.

41. Council of Trent, Sess. 22, chap. 1., Schroeder, 145.

42. *Decree on the Pastoral Office of Bishops in the Church (Christus Dominus)*, 1, *Documents of Vatican II*, ed. Austin Flannery, O.P. (Collegeville, Minn.: The Liturgical Press, 1975), 564.

43. *Lumen Gentium*, 18, Flannery, 370.

44. Ibid., 20, p. 371–72.

45. Ibid., 28, p. 384.

46. Ibid., 28, p. 384–85.

47. De Lubac, *Splendour*, 91–92. The quotation "let him not separate the Church from the Lord" is from Origen, *In Matt.* 14.17.

48. *Do This in Memory of Me*, 26.

49. *Decree on the Ministry and Life of Priests (Presbyterorum Ordinis)*, 2, Flannery, 864–65.

50. Ibid., 865.

51. Ibid. In art. 12 this document states: "By the sacrament of Orders priests are configured to Christ the priest as servants of the Head, so, that as co-workers with the episcopal order they may build up the Body of Christ, the Church" (p. 885).

52. Ibid. This section of the document relies on St. Augustine's *The City of God*, 10, 6.

53. Pierre Benoit, O.P., "The Accounts of the Institution and What They Imply," in *The Eucharist in the New Testament* (Baltimore and Dublin: Helicon Press, 1965), 82.

54. Donald Keefe, S.J., "Gender, History, and Liturgy in the Catholic Church," *Review for Religious* 46 (November-December 1987): 876.

55. John Paul II, *Mulieris Dignitatem (On the Dignity and Vocation of Women)*, *Origins* 18 (6 October 1988): 279.

56. Edward J. Kilmartin, S.J., "Apostolic Office: Sacrament of Christ," *Theological Studies* 36 (1975): 243–64.

57. Ibid., 248.

58. Ibid., 250. ". . .the minister represents Christ in representing the Church and represents the Church in representing Christ. However, this is only possible if the minister directly represents the Church in a special way and so serves as transparency for Christ."

59. Ibid., 252.

60. Ibid., 255. At this point one might ask of Kilmartin what would prevent simply anyone in the Church from exercising apostolic office if such office represents the faith of the Church?

61. Ibid., 258.

62. Ibid., 257.

63. Ibid., 261.

64. Edward Schillebeeckx built his theology of the Church as the sacramental extension of Christ upon the premise that Christ is empirically absent from history [see *World and Church* (New York: Sheed and Ward, 1971), 123–24]. Because Christ is absent from us, Schillebeeckx therefore makes the Church the extension of Christ to the point of asserting that the Church *is Christ*. There is insight in Schillebeeckx's position but I don't think ultimately it is the most fruitful theological understanding of how Christ is still visibly present in the world. Basically Schillebeeckx suffers from a weak Eucharistic theology and from an almost nonexistent Mariology as does Kilmartin. Christ *is not* absent from the world. He remains historically-physically present as risen, as triumphant grace in the Eucharist—sacrament of the Real Presence upon which the Church is grounded. Furthermore, the Sacrament is over—against the Church. It is Christ's objective presence to her and cause of grace in her. The response to this presence is the graced response of a free other—different from Christ. Salvation is not summed up in Christ monistically. In a real sense Christ does not respond for us as Schillebeeckx teaches in *Christ the Sacrament of the Encounter with God* (New York: Sheed and Ward, 1963), 18.

The world, and more specifically the Church, has her own response, yes, created in Christ but still distinct from Him.

Because Schillebeeckx has formed such an emphasis on the Church as the extension of Christ and even the sacraments as an extension of the Church—it is not entirely a puzzlement how in his more recent theology [see *Ministry: Leadership in the Community of Jesus Christ* (New York: Crossroad Press, 1981] church ministers are appointed and thus accredited by the community "from below" and thus represent the community. Marquette University Theology professor, Fr. Donald Keefe, S.J., observes in an unpublished review of Schillebeeckx's book that Schillebeeckx's approach is marked by an historical pessimism peculiar to the Reformation which cannot attribute to any discrete historical event the actual mediation of the risen Christ ("The Recoil From History: Schillebeeckx on the Priesthood").

For a full critique of Schillebeeckx's *Ministry*, see *Review of Contemporary Perspectives on Ministry*, Committee on Doctrine, National Conference of Catholic Bishops (Washington, D.C.: United States Catholic Conference, 1983). This booklet contains articles by Henri Crouzel, Walter Kasper, and Albert Vanhoye, S.J.

65. Donald Keefe, S.J., "Sacramental Sexuality and the Ordination of Women," *Communio* 5 (Fall 1978): 237.

66. Kilmartin, "Apostolic Office," 263.

67. Keefe, "Sacramental Sexuality," 238.

68. Ibid., 240.

69. Ibid., 240–41.

70. Ralph Kiefer, "Christ in Liturgical Prayer," in *Women and Priesthood*, ed. Carroll Stuhlmueller, C.P. (Collegeville, Minn.: The Liturgical Press, 1978), 110.

71. Ibid.

72. Haye Van der Meer, S.J., *Women Priests in the Catholic Church?: A Theological-Historical Investigation* (Philadelphia: Temple University Press, 1973), 25, 68–69. Note especially Van der Meer's treatment of St. Paul (pp. 10–39) and early Church Fathers (pp. 46–86).

73. Ibid., 142.

74. Hauke, *Women in the Priesthood?*, 346.

75. Van der Meer, *Women Priests*, 146–47.

76. Ibid., 147.

77. St. John Chrysostom, *On the Priesthood* 3, 5, trans. Rev. W. R. W. Stephens, *Nicene and Post-Nicene Fathers of the Christian Church*, vol. 9 (Grand Rapids, Mich.: Wm. B. Eerdmans, 1956), 47 (PG 48.643).

78. Ibid.

79. Ibid., 47–48.

80. Henri de Lubac, *Motherhood of the Church* (San Francisco: Ignatius Press, 1982), 120–21.

81. *Lumen Gentium*, 20, Flannery, 372.

82. Ibid., 27, p. 383.

83. Ibid., 41, p. 398.

84. *Christus Domimus*, 16, Flannery, 572.

85. Galot, *Theology of the Priesthood*, 73. The author explains that Christ exercised a creative action in the choosing of the Twelve:

> Mark takes pains to emphasize that there is something of a creation in the initiative of Jesus. He says: "He made Twelve of them . . . He made the Twelve" (3:14;16). The event that happens here is not, then, only the choice of twelve men one by one; it is the constitution of the group, a group that bespeaks a new creation. The verb "to make" suggests by association the verb that

appears in the Genesis account of the first creation, and again in Isaiah (43:1; 44:2) with reference to the establishment of God's people.

86. De Lubac, *Motherhood*, 104–5.

87. *Christus Dominus*, 15, Flannery, 571–72.

88. *Preysbyterorum Ordinis*, 16, Flannery, 893.

89. Archbishop J. Francis Stafford, *The Mystery of the Priestly Vocation*, Origins 18 (10 November 1988): 357.

90. *Lumen Gentium*, 28, Flannery, 385.

91. *Preysbyterorum Ordinis*, 6, Flannery, 872.

92. Thomas E.D. Hennessy, "The Fatherhood of the Priest," *The Thomist* 10 (July 1947): 278.

93. Raymond E. Brown, *The Gospel According to John: I–XII*, 130.

94. Hennessy, "The Fatherhood of the Priest," 286.

95. Ibid., 289.

96. Ibid.

97. Ibid., 202. Christ is the source of the priesthood. For this Hennessy relies on Aquinas, S.T. III, Q 22.a.4. In this question of the *Summa* Aquinas treats of whether Jesus was the recipient of the effect of His priesthood. His answer is no. Rather, Christ communicates His priesthood to others: "Christ is the fountain-head of the entire priesthood; for the priest of the Old Law was a figure of Him; while the priest of the New Law works *in His person*." (Emphasis added.)

98. Hans Urs von Balthasar, "The Uninterrupted Tradition of the Church," *L'Osservatore Romano* (24 February 1977): 6.

99. Walter Ong, *Fighting for Life* (London: Cornell University Press, 1981), 77.

100. Ibid., 113. Also p. 65: "the male still needs a feminine environment for development in early postuterine life. This poses psychological problems. From carefully analyzed case histories Robert Stoller has concluded contrary to 'Freud's position that masculinity is the natural state' of which femininity is a modification, the male child has 'a task in developing his gender identity [sense of masculinity as against simple biological sex] that does not burden the female.'"

See Robert Stoller, M.D., *Sex and Gender: On the Development of Masculinity and Femininity* (New York: Science House, 1968), 263–64, 265–68.

101. Ong, *Fighting for Life*, 113. See also James C. Neely, M.D., *Gender: the Myth of Equality* (New York: Simon and Schuster, 1981), 28. We should also notice that the female chromosome is larger that the male.

102. Neely, *Gender*, 26–27.

103. Ong, *Fighting for Life*, 90.

104. Paul Quay, S.J., *The Christian Meaning of Human Sexuality* (San Francisco: Ignatius Press, 1985), 25.

105. Stephen B. Clark, *Man and Woman in Christ* (Ann Arbor, Mich.: Servant Press, 1980), 382.

106. Ibid., 385. In this section Clark relies on the following works of Edith Stein and Karl Stern: Edith Stein, *The Writings of Edith Stein* (London: Peter Owen, 1956); Karl Stern, *The Flight from Woman* (New York: Farrar, Straus and Giroux, 1965).

107. Von Balthasar, "The Uninterrupted Tradition," 7.

108. George F. Gilder, *Sexual Suicide* (New York: Quadrangle/The New York Times Book Co., 1973), 16–20. The major thesis of Gilder's book is that women are sexually superior in the sense that it is around the female life-giving ability that the world itself is ordered and to which the male—to be fulfilled—must submit.

Later Gilder revised and expanded this book published under the title *Men and Marriage* (Gretna: Pelican Publishing Co., 1986).

109. Ong, *Fighting for Life*, 62. Ong explains that female aggressiveness is realistic as opposed to male combat, strength, and aggressiveness which is often ceremonial and ritualized (61–62).

110. Ibid., 98.

111. Ibid., 174–75.

112. Quay, *The Christian Meaning*, 26. Clark, *Man and Woman in Christ*, 388.

> "[S]exuality is more diffused in time and space for the woman. It is spread throughout her body and her life and is thus more fully a part of her personality, rather than being more of a distinct, localized sense datum specified in space and time, as it is for the man. A man tends to consider sexual activity as another element in his life, something he can more easily detach from himself and compartmentalize."

113. Neely, *Gender*, 16.

114. Ong, *Fighting for Life*, 175.

115. Ibid., 175–76.

116. Prudence Allen, *The Concept of Woman: The Aristotelian Revolution 750 BC-AD 1250* (Montreal: Eden Press,1985), 89–92.

117. Aquinas, *Summa Theologica* I, Q 28, a. 4, *Blackfriars*, vol. 6, 37.

118. Allen, *The Concept of Woman*, 91, 387.

119. In defense of Aristotle Hauke writes:

> Modern observers find these assumptions so shocking that they decidedly reject any and every connection between the metaphysics of matter-form and the duality of the sexes. This sort of relation seems to go too far. For it is not because Aristotle proceeds from false scientific assumptions that he sees a connection between hylomorphism and the polar-opposition male-female. The Philosopher was a very exact student of nature, and of biology in particular. His writings on natural science have been generally admired right up to modern times and long remained unsurpassed. It was in nature that Aristotle was able to discover the same sort of thing that, in our time, Philip Lersch has described: namely that, female creatures, including the human female, behave differently from their male counterparts. He recognized that the behavior of men was more strongly formative, while that of women was more strongly receptive, and that there was an analogy here to his contrasting concepts matter-form.
>
> Even today, the metaphysics of matter and form would seem, despite the varying ways in which it can be concretely developed to have lost none of its relevance (*Women in the Priesthood?*, 112–13).

120. Quay, *The Christian Meaning*, 31. Quay rightly points out that the male and female physiology of giving and receiving in the sex act possesses meaning on the psychological and spiritual levels as well.

121. Ibid., 27.

122. Marie P. Brown, "The Fallacy of the Fempriest," *Homiletic and Pastoral Review* (October 1981): 20–21.

123. Ong, *Fighting for Life*, 113.

124. Ibid., 43–44.

125. Neely, *Gender*, 52.

126. Ong, *Fighting for Life*, 113; Margaret Mead, *Male and Female* (New York: Dell, 1949), 104–5. Mead states:

> In every known human society, the male's need for achievement can be recognized. . . . The recurrent problem of civilization is to define the male role satisfactorily enough—whether it be to build gardens or raise cattle, kill game or kill enemies, build bridges or handle bank-shares—so that the male in the course of his life reach a solid sense of irreversible achievement, of which his childhood knowledge of the satisfactions of childbearing have given him a glimpse. In the case of women, it is only necessary that they be permitted by the given social arrangements to fulfill their biological role, to attain this sense of irreversible achievement.

Mead's anthropological observations fully support the theological truths of Von Balthasar quoted earlier. A man must earn his masculinity by outward achievement while a woman rests in herself.

127. Rosemary Radford Ruether, *Sexism and God-Talk: Toward A Feminist Theology* (Boston: Beacon Press: 1983), 137. See chapter 1, p. 17.

128. Ibid., 114–15. See chapter 1, pp. 15–16.

129. Ibid., 208–9. See chapter 1, p.24.

130. Ibid., 114.

131. Steven A. Long, "The Metaphysics of Gender and Sacramental Priesthood," *Faith and Reason* 10 (Fall 1984): 217.

Chapter 4. The Authority of Mary

1. St. Augustine, *Sermo* 22.10 (CCL 41.300). The full quotation reads:

> Quia duo parentes nos genuerunt ad mortem, duo parentes nos genuerunt ad vitam. Parentes qui nos genuerunt ad mortem, Adam est et Eva. Parentes qui nos genuerunt ad vitam, Christus est et ecclesia. Et pater meus qui me genuit Adam mihi fuit; et mater mea mihi fuit. . . . Deus autem pater et mater ecclesia non ad hoc generant. Generant autem ad vitam aeternam, quia et ipsi aeterni sunt.

2. André Feuillet, *Jesus and His Mother* (Still River, Mass.: St. Bede's Publications, 1984), 205.

3. Joseph Cardinal Ratzinger, *Daughter Zion* (San Francisco: Ignatius Press, 1983), 38–39. "When in Galatians 4:4 Paul says of Jesus that he is "born of woman" he is simply concerned to show that Jesus participated in complete ordinariness of being human, that he entered fully into the human condition."

4. Bertrand Buby, *Mary, the Faithful Disciple* (New York, Paulist Press, 1985), 35; *Lumen Gentium* 52 in *The Documents of Vatican II*, ed. Austin Flannery (Collegeville, Minn.: The Liturgical Press, 1975), 413.

5. St. Justin Martyr, *Dialogue with Trypho*, 100, trans. R.P.C. Hanson, *World Christian Books*, vol. 49 (New York: Associated Press, 1964), 60–61 (PG 6.710).

6. Tertullian, *On the Flesh of Christ*, 17, *Ante-Nicene Fathers*, vol. 3 (Grand Rapids, Mich.: Wm. B. Eerdmans, 1963), 536 (CSEL 69–70, p. 233).

7. St. Irenaeus, *Against Heresies*, 3,22,4, *The Ante-Nicene Fathers*, vol. 1 (Grand Rapids, Mich.: Wm. B. Eerdmans, 1987), 455 (PG 7,1.958–59).

8. Ibid., 5, 19, 1, p. 547 (PG 7, 2.1175).

9. St. Cyril of Jerusalem, *Catechesis 12,15, Nicene and Post-Nicene Fathers*, vol. 12, second series (Grand Rapids, Mich.: Wm B. Eerdmans, 1955), 75 (PG 33.742).

10. St. Ephrem Syrus, *Opp. Syr. ii* in John Henry Newman, *Mary—the Second Eve*, ed. Sr. Eileen Breen (Rockford, Ill: Tan Books and Publishers, 1982), 7.

11. St. Epiphanius, *Haer.* 78,18 in *Mary—the Second Eve*, 7 (PG 42.730).

12. *Mary—the Second Eve*, 7. The phrase in Latin: "mors per Evam, vita per Mariam" (St. Jerome, *Ep. 22 ad Eustoch.*, 21, CSEL 54.173).

13. Vladimir Lossky, "Panagia" in *The Mother of God, A Symposium* ed. E.L. Mascall (Westminster: Dacre Press, 1949), 31–32. "The first Eve was taken out of Adam; she was one who, at the moment of her creation by God, took unto herself the nature of Adam, to be complementary to him . . . We find an inverse relationship in the case of the New Eve; through her the Son of God became the Last Adam by taking unto himself human nature. Adam was before Eve; the Last Adam was after the New Eve."

Lossky pulls away from the implication of his above words. He goes on to say that the humanity assumed by Christ was not a complement to the humanity of His mother because it is the humanity of a divine person while Mary is a mere creature. He believes he must deny the complementarity of these two persons in order to preserve the headship of Christ. He will not allow Mary to be a "head" of the New Humanity. Yet, we would argue that while Mary is certainly not the head of the New Humanity she is a source of this New Humanity in relation to her Son because she is the *mother* of God.

14. Feuillet, *Jesus and His Mother*, 110.

15. Lossky, "Panagia," 30.

16. Feuillet, *Jesus and His Mother*, 7.

17. E. L. Mascall, "The Dogmatic Theology of the Mother of God," in *The Mother of God*, 30.

18. St. Augustine, *Serm. Frangipane 4, Miscellanea Agostiniana, Sancti Augustini Sermones*, vol. 1, ed. D. Germani Morin (Rome: Typis Polygottis Vaticanis, 1930), 210.

On Mary and the reversal of the created order Augustine states: "Concepit, et virgo est; parit, et virgo est. *Creatus est enim de illa quam creavit.*"

George Florovsky, "The Ever-Virgin Mother of God" in *The Mother of God*, 58.

Aux jours de la création du monde, lorsque Dieu prononça sa parole vivante et puissante: *Qu'il soit fait*, la parole du Créateur produisit dans le monde les créatures; mais en ce jour sans example dans l' existence du monde, lorsque la divine Marie prononca son modeste et obéissant *Qu'il soit fait*, j'ose à peine exprimer ce qui se passa alors:—la parole de la créature fit descendre dans le monde le Créateur.

John Paul II, *Redemptoris Mater*, 10, 25 March 1987 (Boston: Daughters of St. Paul), 15. The authority of Mary's *fiat* as the cause of God's historical existence is implied in the following statement:

Mary receives life from him to whom she herself, in the order of earthly generation, *gave life* as a mother. The liturgy does not hesitate to call her "mother of her Creator" and to hail her with the words which Dante Alighieri places on the lips of St. Bernard: "daughter of your Son."

19. Donald Keefe, S.J., "Mary as Created Wisdom, the Splendor of the New Creation," *The Thomist* 47 (July 1983): 405.

20. According to the Council of Ephesus, Mary is the *Theotokos*, the Mother of God. This means that Mary, contrary to Nestorius, is the mother not only of the human nature or flesh of Christ but of the person of Christ. When we say Mary has provided the *body*

of Christ, we pose no split between the person of Christ and His historical presence. In the Incarnation they are one and the same. Our anthropological starting point is expressed very well in the Vatican document *Instruction on Respect for Human Life in Its Origin and on the Dignity of Procreation*: "in the body and through the body, one touches the person himself in his concrete reality."

21. John Paul II, *Redemptoris Mater*, 13, 25 March 1987 (Boston: Daughters of St. Paul), 18.

22. Ibid., 19

23. Ibid.

24. Rene Laurentin, *Our Lady and the Mass* (New York: Mac Millan, 1959), 27.

25. Feuillet, *Jesus and His Mother*, 121; Bruce Vawter, "The Gospel According to John," in *The Jerome Biblical Commentary*, ed. Raymond E. Brown, et. al. (Englewood Cliffs, N.J.: Prentice Hall, 1968), 427; F. M. Braun, *Jean le théologian: Sa théologie le mystère de Jésus-Christ* (Paris: Librairie LeCoffre, 1966), 146–47.

26. Feuillet, *Jesus and His Mother*, 14.

27. Ibid., 122.

28. Buby, *Mary, the Faithful Disciple*, 98.

29. *Redemptoris Mater*, 21, p. 31.

30. Ibid.

31. St. Justin Martyr, *Dialogue with Trypho*, 100, p. 61. (PG 6. 710)

32. Ibid, 11, p. 16. John Paul II repeats this teaching—that women are at the center of God's saving action in his Apostolic Letter *Mulieris Dignitatem*, (*On the Dignity and Vocation of Women*, 3, *Origins* 18 (6 October 1988): 264. He states:

> The sending of His Son, one in substance with the Father, as a man "born of woman" constitutes the culminating and definitive point of God's self-revelation to humanity. . . . A woman is to be found at the center of this salvific event.

33. John Paul II, *Mulieris Dignitatem*, 11, pp. 269–70.

34. Ratzinger, *Daughter Zion*, 17.

35. Louis Ligier, *Péché d'Adam et Péché du monde*, *Théologie* 43 (Aubier, 1960), 228. Regarding the meaning of Gen. 4:1 Ligier states:

> Enfanter, c'est participer au pouvoir créateur. La femme est finalement, à ce point de vue, une sorte de déesse-mère, comme le suggèrent certain parallèles puniques de son nom. Mais c'est de Dieu que lui viendra sa descendance: car c'est lui qui bâtit la femme. Il multipliera donc ses grossesses. *Des conceptions miraculeuses rappellront cette loi originale.* (Emphasis added.)

André Feuillet, "Les Adieux du Christ à sa mère (Jn 19 pp. 25–27) et la maternité spirituelle de Marie," *Nouvelle Revue Théologique* 86 (1964): 475–76. Feuillet notes that in John 16:21 Jesus makes a connection between His suffering and the pain of a woman in childbirth who then rejoices because she has brought "a man" into the world. By the use of the specific word "man" as opposed to "child" or "son," we are led back to Gen. 3:16 and 4:1. Here Eve is told she will bring children forth painfully yet this does not hinder her from exclaiming with great joy in 4:1 "I have made a man with the help of the Lord."

This pain and joy of the woman is placed at the center of the Cross as the New Eve definitely fulfills the pain and the joy of the first woman in bringing the Son of God into the world destined to suffer, and by this participation in the Cross the New Eve brings all the living into being as well.

36. Fulton Sheen, *The Life of Christ* (New York: McGraw-Hill, 1958), 14.

...every other person came into this world to live. He came into it to die.... In the person of Christ . . . *it was His death that was first and His life that was last....* It was not so much that His birth cast a shadow on His life and thus led to his death; it was rather that the Cross was first, and cast its shadow back to His birth. His has been the only life in the world that was ever lived backward.

37. Feuillet, *Jesus and His Mother*, 8, 126–27.

38. Ibid., 47.

39. Ibid., 52.

40. Ibid.

41. Ibid. Feuillet states: "[T]his Hour of Jesus and the Hour of his mother, the Hour of the Woman, are presented by John as inseparable."

42. Louis Bouyer, *The Seat of Wisdom* (New York: Pantheon Books, 1960), 162–63.

43. Pope Pius XII, *Munificentissimus Deus*, 1950, in *Papal Documents on Mary*, ed. Wm. J. Doheny and Joseph P. Kelly (Milwaukee, Wisc.: Bruce Publishing, 1954), 237.

44. Raymond Brown, *The Gospel According to John XIII-XXI, Anchor Bible*, vol. 29a (New York: Doubleday, 1970), 926. "Perhaps we may also relate Mary the New Eve to Gen iii 15, a passage that describes a struggle between the offspring of Eve and the offspring of the serpent, for 'the hour' of Jesus is the hour of the fall of the Prince of this world (John xii 23, 31)."

45. F. M. Braun, *La Mère des fidèles* (Casterman-Tournai: Cahiers de L' Actualité Religieuse, 1954), 91.

46. Max Thurian, *Mary—Mother of the Lord, Figure of the Church* (London: The Faith Press, 1963), 150. Thurian provides a compelling list of reasons why Christ's address to Mary from the Cross is not simply a son's filial care for his widowed mother. They are: 1) If Christ is concerned for the material welfare of Mary, why does He wait until the last moment of His life to see that her needs are taken care of? 2) Mary at the Cross is already in the company of her kindred and not alone or isolated. 3) Mary is addressed first, then John. If the import of the text were simply to commit Mary to John's care, it is John who would, more likely, be addressed first. 4) A private meaning of the words do not fit the carefully crafted stages of the crucifixion scene and would be entirely out of place at a time when every act and word of Christ carries the greatest public, official import. 5) If the text has a mere private and domestic meaning then Christ would simply refer to Mary as "mother" and not by title of "Woman."

Thurian states:

It is not a question of putting aside the exegesis which sees in this episode a filial act by Christ towards His mother. The conclusive phrase: ". . . the disciple took her to his home," . . . implies a welcome to Mary by the disciple to his own home. Jesus has indeed committed His mother materially to His beloved disciple; but, as we have seen, the context prevents us from resting with this interpretation alone.

47. Ibid., 145.

48. Brown, *The Gospel According to John*, vol. 29a, 923.

49. Pope Pius X, *Ad deum illum*, 2 February 1904, *Papal Documents*, 139.

50. Cyril Vollert, *A Theology of Mary*, 124–25; Juniper B. Carol, *Fundamentals of Mariology* (Chicago: Benziger Bros., 1956), 52–53.

51. Vollert, *A Theology of Mary*, 137.

52. Feuillet, *Jesus and His Mother*, 128. Feuillet is dependent upon an article by M. de Goedt, "Un schema de revelation dans le Quatrieme Evangile" *New Testament Studies* 8 (1962): 142–50. In Goedt's study as related by Feuillet:

> . . . one of the many revelation formulas of John's work consists in this: a divine envoy (John the Baptist, Jesus) *sees* a person whose name is indicated, and by way of introducing this person, he *says* a word which amounts to an oracle: in other words, he makes a declaration which clearly surpasses the object of the physical sight, for it unveils the mystery of a mission and a destiny: cf. Jn. 1:29ff.; 1:35ff.; 1:47. This is exactly what we have in Jn. 19:25–27: the dying Christ *sees* Mary and the beloved disciple, and he *says* something that no one could see or know: that Mary is mother of the disciple and the disciple is her son. This could only suggest that this episode is not informing us of the creation of some new reality, but is simply revealing a reality that already exists.

The *there is* of the "There is your mother" of John 19:27 is the same type of revelatory statement uttered by John the Baptist concerning the reality of Christ "*There is* the Lamb of God" etc. (John 1:36).

53. Ibid., 124. "She plays here, already, the role of spiritual mother to the disciples in the sense that is through the mediation of her faith that they are led to faith in Jesus."

54. P.M.J. LaGrange, *Évangile selon Saint Jean* (Paris: Librairie LeCoffre, 1948), 494. "Jean prèsentait ici tous les fidèles auxquels Marie a été dès lors donnée comme mère." F. M. Braun, *La Mère des fidèles*, 106.

> "En attestant sa présence au pied de la Croix, sous les traits du Disciple, que Jésus aimait . . . l'évangeliste entendait-il personnifer une classe de personnes? L'emphase de l'expression, reforcée par l'article, semble le signifier. Dan ce cas, la première catégories qui vient à l'esprit serait celle de tous les autres disciples, auxquel le Disciple avait servi de prototype."

Raymond E. Brown, *The Gospel According to John*, vol. 29a, 926.

55. Carol, *Fundamentals of Mariology*, 53.

56. Pope Benedict XV, *Inter Sodalicia*, 22 March 1918, in *Mary in the Documents of the Church*, ed. Paul F. Palmer (Westminster, Md.: The Newman Press, 1952), 97.

57. Leo XIII, *Jucunda Semper*, 8 September 1894, in *Papal Documents on Mary*, 92–93.

58. Pope Pius XI, Radio Broadcast, 29 April 1935, *L'Osservatore Romano*, (29–30 April 1935), 1.

59. Pope Pius XII, *Mystici Corporis*, 10, 29 June 1943 (Boston: St. Paul Editions), 66.

60. Bouyer, *The Seat of Wisdom*, 162–63.

> The part Mary took in the Passion of her Son, by uniting herself to it by faith, went to complete her motherhood, and also belongs to its development; it was not merely a subjective accompaniment to this. Mary, by her presence on Calvary, fulfilled all she implicitly consented to in her "fiat," just as her Son then accomplished all that was included in His first acceptance of the Incarnation and Redemption—"Sacrifice and oblation thou didst not desire. . . . Then said I, Behold I come. In the head of the book it is written of me that I should do thy will" (Ps. 39:7–9, applied to Christ in Hebrews 10: 5–7).

61. Ibid., 162.

62. Thurian, *Mary-Mother of the Lord*, 101.

63. Feuillet, *Jesus and His Mother*, 46.

64. Walter Ong, S.J., *Fighting for Life* (Ithaca and London: Cornell University Press, 1981), 101.

65. *Mystici Corporis*, 110, p. 66.

Tibertius Gallus, S.J. "Mater Dolorosa "principium materiale" Redemptionis objec-tive," in *Marianum*, 12 (1950), 227–49. as Quoted in *Mariology*, ed. Juniper B. Carol (Milwaukee: The Bruce Pub. Co., 1957), 415. Gallus argues that Mary's co-redemption comes from her having sacrificed her maternal rights to protect her son from unjust aggres-sion. By this surrender:

> . . . she removed an impediment to her Son's sacrificial immolation and thus Mary furnished the material principle for the redemptive act. The obedience of Christ to His Father's will has a twofold causality: first by a priority of nature, it elevates and actuates Mary's obedience for the same purpose; second, it becomes, together with Mary's obedience, the efficient cause of the entire redemptive work. Hence, our redemption depends on Christ's renunciation as a formal element, and on Mary's renunciation as a material element. . . . The two elements constitute one single moral cause of the Redemption.

66. St. Thomas Aquinas, *Summa Theologica* III, q. 30, a. 1, *Blackfriars*, vol. 51, trans. Thomas R. Heath (Eyre & Spottiswoode, 1969), 71. In answer to the question: "Was It Necessary to Tell the Blessed Virgin What Was to Be Accomplished in Her?" Aquinas states it was necessary because "it brings out that a kind of spiritual marriage is taking place between the Son of God and human nature. The Virgin's consent, then, which was petitioned in the course of the announcement stood for the consent of all men."

Popes Leo XIII and Pius XII teach that Mary represents all mankind. The former in his encyclical *Octobri Mense* and the latter in *Mystici Corporis*.

67. Thurian, *Mary—Mother of the Lord*, 180.

68. Feuillet, *Jesus and His Mother*, 120. On p. 32 Feuillet also states:

> . . . even before Christ is born, the mysterious Woman crowned with stars whom we have recognized to be the Virgin Mary, shares already by participation, and in a definitive manner, in that great triumph over the powers of evil: the Passion and the Resurrection of Christ. It is the Apocalypse alone which, by applying it to the Mother of the Messiah, gives definitive meaning to the oracle of Gn. 3:15, a crucial prediction, though somewhat obscure, of the retaliation of the Woman against the tempting serpent. It is well known that on this great text, as interpreted by the author of the Apocalypse, that the Catholic Church based her proclamation of the two closely linked dogmas of the Immaculate Conception and the Assumption of Mary.

69. Ibid., 17–18.

70. For a lengthy discussion on whether the child born of the woman in the Apocalypse is Christ the Messiah, see F. M. Braun, *La mère des Fidèles*, 141–46.

Also Bernard J. Le Frois, *Woman Clothed with the Sun: Individual or Collective?* (Rome: Orbis Catholicus, 1954), 204, 218–27, 251. This author makes a valuable exegetical comparison between Gen. 3:15 and Apoc. 12 with special attention given to the parallels between "offspring" (τεκν ον) in both texts (220–22).

71. Feuillet, *Jesus and His Mother*, 119. The parallel between Gen.3:15 and Apoc. 12 is also analyzed and affirmed by Bernard J. Le Frois in "The Mary-Church Relation in Apocalypse" in *Marian Studies*, 9 (1958): 95–99.

72. Feuillet, *Jesus and His Mother*, 23.

73. Bernard, J. LeFrois, "The Mary-Church Relationship in the Apocalypse," in *Marian Studies* 9 (1958): 89. LeFrois provides an extended study of the Fathers of the Church on this question in *Woman Clothed with the Sun: Individual or Collective?*, 48–61.

74. LeFrois, "The Mary-Church Relationship," 94. The following quotation explains well in what way Mary and the Church share the same reality:

The Church is not merely personified and decked out with the features of Mary, but the concrete personality of the Virgin Mother of Christ takes on a collective signification, for if the Church is said to bring forth new life in the baptismal waters and to impart the saving light that makes men the sons of God, it is in reality the Mother of Christ who is instrumental in imparting this life and Light divine to men, by her co-operation in the Redemption on Golgotha where the New Eve suffers the messianic birthpangs that bring salvation. If the Church brings forth Christ amid the sufferings of her temporal vocation, it is in reality Mary *sharing her spiritual Motherhood which brought forth each and every member in the birthpangs of Golgotha.* (Emphasis added.)

Henri de Lubac, *Splendour of the Church* (Glen Rock, N.J.: Paulist Press), 199–200.

The links between Our Lady and the Church are not only numerous and close; they are essential, and woven from within. These two mysteries of the faith are not just solitary; we might say that they are "one single and unique mystery."

75. Edward Schillebeeckx, *Christ the Sacrament of the Encounter with God* (New York: Sheed and Ward, 1963). Schillebeeckx's theology *tends* in the direction of an incarnational monism. For him the Church is the sacrament of Christ which leaves little room for a covenantal understanding of redemption in which the Church is man's (graced) response. Indeed Christ is both the offer of grace and the response to that offer: "In his messianic sacrifice, which the Father accepts, *Christ in his glorified body is himself the eschatological redemptive community of the Church. In his own self the glorified Christ is simultaneously both 'Head and members.'"* (P. 48; Emphasis added.) In another place Schillebeeckx states regarding the Church as the prolongation of Christ: "The man Jesus is the presence of the redeeming God among us, though in the mode of a human presence bodying that presence forth to us. Precisely for this reason the plan of the incarnation requires, from the moment of Christ's ascension, a prolongation of his bodily mediation in time. We know already that this sacramental body of the Lord is the Church" (p. 59).

It is true that the Church is the body of the Lord—and thus is the visible mediator of His presence. However, the Church is the body of Christ through a covenantal unity that exists precisely through the differentiation between head and members. This covenantal unity is the New Covenant, and Christ is present because the New Covenant of head and body exists. We must be careful to avoid collapsing the Church into Christ. Redemption is available in the world via their unity—not by the one simply existing as the sign of the other with no redemptive value other than to exist as a sacrament of Christ's presence. Furthermore, we should be careful about identifying the Church simply as a sacrament of Christ. The Church, because she is the body of her Lord in union with her head, is a visible historical sign of his redemptive presence. However, sacraments are a temporary means of mediating Christ's grace. Thus, the Church is not a sacrament in the sense of the seven formal sacraments of the Church. Rather she *is* the body of Christ, and she does not cease to be even in the eschaton while the parousia of Christ will usher in the end of sacramental mediation. What needs to be emphasized is that the Church has a reality beyond any sacramental function which can be legitimately spoken of as long as the world is in need of a sign to mediate Christ's presence. The Church *is* the New People of God, and this people exists because of the sacraments, primarily the sacrament of the Eucharist.

Karl Rahner also speaks of the Church as a sacrament and an extension of Christ. See *Inquiries* (New York: Herder and Herder, 1964). He states (p. 200):

Christ is the primal sacramental word of God, uttered in the one history of mankind, in which God made known his irrevocable mercy that cannot be annulled by God or man. . . . Now the Church is the continuance, the contemporary presence, of that real, eschatologically triumphant and irrevocably established presence in the world, in Christ, of God's salvific will. . . . By the very fact of being in that way the enduring presence of Christ in the world, the Church is truly the fundamental sacrament, the well-spring of sacraments in the strict sense.

Chapter 5. The Feminine Authority of the Church

1. St. Augustine *Sermo 344* 2 (PL 39.1512).

Ama patrem, sed noli super Dominum: ama genitorem, sed noli super Creatorem . . . Ama matrem tuam, sed noli super Ecclesiam, qua te genuit ad vitam aeternam. Denique ex ipsorum parentum amore perpende quantum diligere debeas Deum et Ecclesiam. Si enim tantum diligendi sunt qui genuerumt mortiurum, quanta charitate diligendi sunt qui genuerunt ad aeternitatem venturum, in aeternitatem mansurum?

2. St. Augustine, *Enarr. on the Book of Psalms*, 89, *Nicene and Post-Nicene Fathers*, vol. 8, ed. Philip Schaff (Grand Rapids, Mich.: Wm. B. Eerdmans, 1956), 440 (CCL 39.1241, Ps. 88).

3. St. Augustine, *Sermon 216*, 8, trans. Sr. Mary Sarah Muldowny, R.S.N., *Fathers of the Church*, vol. 38 (New York: Fathers of the Church, 1959), 157–58 (PL 38.1081). "Your Father is God; the Church is your Mother," etc. in Latin: "Pater Deus est, mater Ecclesia. Longe aliter ab his genera bimini, quam ab illis geniti fueratis."

4. Henri de Lubac, *Motherhood of the Church* (San Francisco: Ignatius Press, 1982), 39.

5. St. Cyprian, *On the Unity of the Church*, 6, trans. Maurice Bevenot, S.J., *Ancient Christian Writers*, vol. 25 (Westminster, Md.: The Newman Press, 1957), 48–49 (CCL 3.253). "Habere iam non potest Deum patrem qui ecclesiam non habet matrem."

6. Origen, *Exp. in Prov.* in Joseph C. Plumpe, *Mater Ecclesia: An Inquiry into the Concept of the Church as Mother in Early Christianity* (Washington, D.C.: The Catholic University of America Press, 1943), 78 (PG 17.201). "The Church too is our Mother," etc. in Latin: "Est mater nostra etiam Ecclesia, quam per Spiritum sanctum Deus Pater sibi sponsan copulauit. Gignit enim sibi per ipsam semper filios filiasque."

7. Tertullian, *On Baptism*, 20, *The Ante-Nicene Fathers*, vol. 3, eds. Alexander Roberts and James Donaldson (Grand Rapids, Mich.: Wm. B. Eerdmans, 1957), 679 (CSEL 20.218).

8. Plumpe, *Mater Ecclesia*, 55.

9. Ibid., 50.

10. St. Optatus *Contra Parmenianum Donatistam* 4.2 in Walter M. Bedard, *The Symbolism of the Baptismal Font in Early Christian Thought* (Wash., D.C.: Catholic University of America Press, 1951), 27 (CSEL 26.103).

. . .quos isdem sacramentorum uisceribus una mater ecclesia genuit, quos eodem modo adoptiuos filios deus pater excepit.

11. Ibid., 26.

12. Didymus of Alexandria, *De Trinitate* 2.13, Bedard, 21 (PG 39.691–92).

13. St. Augustine, *Sermon 56*, 5, Bedard, 29 (PL 38.379). The Latin phrase written by Augustine is quite graphic. He uses the word "utero" (uterus) translated "womb" in the Bedard text. Augustine's phrase reads "utero Ecclesiae in fonte pariendi."

14. St. Augustine, *Sermon 119*, 4, *A Library of the Fathers of the Holy Catholic Church*, vol. 16, (Oxford: John Henry Parker, 1844), 506 (PL 38.674). "Ecce sunt: sed ex Deo nati sunt. Vulva matris, aqua Baptismatis."

15. St. Augustine, *Sermon 216*, 7, FC, vol. 17, p. 156 (PL 38.1080).

16. De Lubac, *Motherhood*, 52. "Ecce uterus Matris Ecclesia, ecce ut te pariat atque in lucem fidei producat, laborat in gemitu suo. . . . Illum Patrum, christiane, agnosce, qui . . . suspepit te ex utero matris tuae. . . . Pater Deus est, Mater Ecclesia" (PL, 38, 1080 and 1081, *Sermo 216*, 7–8).

17. Plumpe, *Mater Ecclesia*, 35.

18. Ibid., 95.

19. St. Clement of Alexandria, *The Stromata*, 4, 25, *The Ante-Nicene Fathers*, vol. 2, eds. Alexander Roberts and James Donaldson (Grand Rapids, Mich.: Wm B. Eerdmans, 1962), 439 (PG 8. 1370).

20. St. Ephrem, *Hymni de virginitate* 7.5, Bedard, 19.

21. St. Methodius, *The Banquet*, 8, 6, trans. Herbert Musurillo, *Ancient Christian Writers*, vol. 27 (Westminster, Md.: The Newman Press, 1958), 111–12 (PG 18.147).

22. St. Zeno of Verona, *Tractatus 2: 33, Invitatio as fontem*, Bedard, p. 31 (PL 9.479).

23. Louis Ligier, "The Biblical Symbolism of Baptism in the Fathers of the Church and the Liturgy," in *Adult Baptism and the Catechumenate, Concilium*, vol. 22 (New York: Paulist Press, 1967), 21.

24. St. Theodore of Mopsuestia, *Baptismal Homily III* in Edward Yarnold, S.J., *The Awe Inspiring Rites of Initiation: Baptismal Homilies of the Fourth Century* (Slough, England: St. Paul Publications, 1971), 194–95.

25. St. Augustine, *Confessions* 4, 12, trans. R. S. Pine-Coffin (New York: Penguin Books, 1961), 81 (CSEL 33.79).

26. George A. Maloney, *Mary: The Womb of God* (Denville, N.J.: Dimensions Books, 1976), 147.

27. St. Theodore of Mopsuestia, *Baptismal Homily*, 14, 10 in Ligier, "The Biblical Symbolism of Baptism," 27.

28. Narsai, "Homilies 50 & 52," in Bedard, 23. The thinking here seems to be under platonic influence. We see that the rational is on the side of what is spiritual while the unformed and "dumb" is on the side of creation, i.e., Mary. We need not accept these conclusions to accept the otherwise insightful covenantal aspects of the Spirit and creation.

29. Bedard, 24.

30. Tertullian, *On Baptism*, 4, ANF, vol. 3, 671 (CSEL 20.204).

31. St. Ambrose, *Expositio evangelii sec. Luc.* 2.7, Bedard, 33 (CSEL 32.45).

32. St. Ambrose, *The Mysteries*, 9, 59, *Fathers of the Church*, vol. 44 (Washington, D.C.: Catholic University of America Press, 1963), 28 (CSEL 73.115–16).

33. De Lubac, *Motherhood*, 58.

34. St. Leo the Great, *Sermon 24*, 2, *Nicene and Post-Nicene Fathers*, vol. 12, eds. Philip Schaff and Henry Wace (Grand Rapids, Mich.: Wm. B. Eerdmans, 1956), 135 (PL 54.206).

35. St. Leo the Great, *Sermon 25*, Bedard, 35 (PL 54.211).

36. Karl Delahaye, *Ecclesia mater chez les péres des trois premiers siécles*, Unam Sanctam, vol. 46 (Paris: Éditions du Cerf, 1964), 90. (St. Hippolytus, *De Anti-Christo* 44, PG 10.763).

37. Ibid.

38. St. Augustine, *Sermon Morin*, 1, 8, *Miscellania Agostiniana*, vol. 1, *Sancti Augustini Sermones*, ed. D. Germani Morin, et. al. (Rome: Typis Polygottis Vaticanis, 1930), 448. The Latin passage from which this quotation is taken reads: "Sic et ecclesia parit, et virgo est, et si consideres, Christum parit: quia membra eius sunt, qui baptizantur. VOS ESTIS, [sic] inquit apostolus, CORPUS CHRISTI ET MEMBRA. [sic] Si ergo membra Christi parit, Mariae simillima est." Han Urs Von Balthasar has translated this last phrase "Mariae simillima est" in French: "elle est absolument semblable á Marie" in *St. Augustine, Le visage de l' église*, Unam Sanctam, vol. 31 (Paris: Éditions du Cerf, 1958), 187.

39. Hugo Rahner, *Marie et L'église: Dix méditations sur la vie spirituelle* (Paris: Éditions du Cerf, 1955), 70.

40. Plumpe, *Mater Ecclesia*, 1.

41. Ibid., 62.

42. This passage refers to Israel in exile, thus the images of desertion and widowhood are applied to her.

43. St. Cyril of Jerusalem, *Catechesis 18*, 26, *Nicene and Post Nicene Fathers*, vol. 7, eds. Philip Schaff and Henry Wace (Grand Rapids, Mich.: Wm. B. Eerdmans, 1955), 140 (PG 33, 1047, 1048).

44. F. J. Dolger, "Dominia Mater Ecclesia und die 'Herrin' im zweiten Johannesbrief," *Antike und Christentum* 5 (1936): 214–17.

45. De Lubac, *Motherhood*, 46 (St. Clement of Alexandria, *Adumbratio* in 2 Jn. 1, PG 9.737–38; Tertullian, *Ad martyres* 1, PL 1.691–93).

46. De Lubac, *Motherhood*, 86.

47. Max Thurian, *Mary, Mother of the Lord, Figure of the Church* (London: The Faith Press, 1963), 168.

48. Elizabeth Schüssler Fiorenza, *In Memory of Her* (New York: Crossroad, 1988), 220.

49. Ibid., 235.

50. Plumpe, *Mater Ecclesia*, 8.

51. St. Hippolytus, *Commentary on the Canticle*, Fragm. slav. 15, Delahaye, 93–94.

52. Delahaye, *Ecclesia Mater*, 94.

53. St. Irenaeus, *Against Heresies*, 3, 24, *Ante-Nicene Fathers*, vol. 1, eds. Alexander Roberts and James Donaldson (Grand Rapids, Mich.: Wm. B. Eerdmans, 1987), 458 (PG 7,1.966–67).

54. Plumpe, *Mater Ecclesia*, 43.

55. St. Clement of Alexandria, *The Instructor* 1,6, 42, *The Ante-Nicene Fathers*, vol. 2, p. 220 (PG 8.299–302).

56. Plumpe, *Mater Ecclesia*, 65.

57. St. Cyprian, *The Unity of the Catholic Church,* 5, p. 48 (CCL 3.253). The phrase "one is the headspring, one the source, one the mother" etc. in Latin: "unum tamen caput est et origo una, et una mater fecunditatis successibus copiosa."

58. Ibid., 48–49.

59. Ibid., Ch. 23, 64–65 (CCL 3.265–66).

60. St. Augustine, *Sermon Mai 92*, MA, 332–33.

61. St. Augustine, *Enarr. on the Book of Psalms*, 99, 8, NPNF, vol. 8, 485 (CCL 39.1385, Ps. 98.9).

62. Pope John Paul II, "At the Root of the Eucharist is the Virginal Heart of Mary," *L'Osservatore Romano* (13 June 1983), 2.

63. St. Augustine. *Enarr. on the Book of Psalms*, 127, 4, NPNF, vol. 8, 607 (PL 37.1672, Ps. 126.7).

64. St. Augustine, *Enarr. on the Book of Psalms*, 41, NPNF, vol 8, 131. (PL 36.461, Ps. 40.10).

65. Tertullian *De Anima* 43 (CSEL 20.372).

66. Plumpe, *Mater Ecclesia*, 57.

67. De Lubac, *Motherhood*, 68–69. (The quotation from St. Irenaeus is from *Against Heresies*, 1, 5, 20, 2.)

68. Ibid., 62.

69. Tertullian, *De praescriptione haereticorum* 42 (CSEL 70, p. 55). The word "motherless" in Latin is "sine matre."

70. St. Hippolytus, *The Anti-Christ*, 61, *Ante-Nicene Fathers*, vol. 9, eds. Alexander Roberts and James Donaldson (Grand Rapids, Mich.: Wm. B. Eerdmans, 1957), 36.

71. Pope John XXIII, *Mater et Magistra*, 1, 15 May 1961 (Washington, D.C.: National Catholic Welfare Conference), 3.

72. Thurian, *Mary, Mother of the Lord*, 171.

73. Paul Claudel as quoted by de Lubac, *Motherhood*, 61.

74. Emmett Cardinal Carter, *Do This in Memory of Me*: Pastoral Letter on the Sacrament of the Priesthood, Dec. 8, 1983 (Toronto: Can.), 19.

75. Pope John Paul II, "At the Root of the Eucharist," 2.

76. Joseph Cardinal Ratzinger, "On the Position of Mariology and Marian Spirituality within the Totality of Faith," in *The Church and Women*, ed. Helmut Moll (San Francisco: Ignatius Press, 1988), 76.

77. Yves Congar, *Christ, Our Lady and the Church* (Westminster, Md.: The Newman Press, 1957), 16.

78. Ibid., 17.

79. Ibid., 18. (Quoting Martin Luther, *Dictata Super Psalterium in Ps. 71*, Weimar III, 468 I, 17–19.)

80. Ibid. (Quoting Martin Luther *Dictata Super Psalterium in Ps. 76*, Weimer III, 545.)

81. Congar, *Christ*, 27.

82. Ibid., 27–28.

83. Ibid.

84. Ibid., 30. Congar, because Luther rejected any positive cooperation of humanity in redemption, accuses Protestantism of a Nestorian tendency. The tendency exists because of the wide distance Luther "marks out between the two natures, and the vacuum set up between the *opus Dei*, the Divinity in action on the one hand, and human nature on the other. But by this very fact, because he attributes everything to the divinity he empties of its value the part played by the human nature of the Word made flesh."

85. Erik Erikson, *Young Man Luther: A Study in Psychoanalysis and History* (New York: W. W. Norton, 1958), 71. "We had better prepare ourselves right here for an almost

exclusively masculine story: Kierkegaard's comment that Luther invented a religion for the adult man states the limitation as well as the true extent of Luther's theological creation. Luther provides new elements for the Western male's identity, and created for him new roles; but he created only one new feminine identity, the parson's wife."

Also for a good discussion of Luther's masculinization of Christianity, see Amaury de Riencourt, *Sex and Power in History* (New York: Dell Publishing Co., 1974), 256–63. As an example of this masculinization the author cites the Protestant tendency to interpret Scripture literally versus the symbolic or allegorical interpretation of Scripture that had dominated Catholicism for centuries.

86. *The Constitution on the Sacred Liturgy (Sacrosantum Concilium)* 1, 7, in *The Documents of Vatican II*, ed. Austin Flannery, O.P (Collegeville, Minn.: The Liturgical Press, 1975), 5. On the differentiated relation between Christ and the Church in Eucharistic worship art. 7 states:

> Christ, indeed, always associates the Church with himself in this great work in which God is perfectly glorified and men are sanctified. The Church is his beloved Bride who calls to her Lord, and through him offers worship to the eternal Father.
>
> The liturgy, then, is rightly seen as an exercise of the priestly office of Jesus Christ. It involves the presentation of man's sanctification under the guise of signs perceptible by the senses and its accomplishment in ways appropriate to each of these signs. In it full public worship is performed by the Mystical Body of Jesus Christ, that is, by the Head and His members.
>
> From this it follows that every liturgical celebration, because it is an action of Christ the Priest and of his Body, which is the Church, is a sacred action surpassing all others.

The Vatican II document *Eucharisticum Mysterium*, 12 (*Instruction on the Worship of the Eucharistic Mystery*), Flannery, 111, states clearly that the Eucharist is *offered* by the faithful in union with Christ:

> It is indeed the priest alone, who, acting in the person of Christ, consecrates the bread and wine, but the role of the faithful in the Eucharist is to recall the passion, resurrection and glorification of the Lord, to give thanks to God, *and to offer the immaculate victim* not only through the hands of the priest, but also together with him. (Emphasis added.)

87. Congar, *Christ*, 18.

88. Ratzinger, "On the Position," 72.

89. Ibid., 72–73.

90. Maloney, *Mary, the Womb of God*, 150.

91. *Dogmatic Constitution on the Church (Lumen Gentium)*, 2,10, Flannery, 361.

92. Desmond Connell, "Women Priests: Why Not?," *The Church and Women*, 210.

93. *Mulieris*, 25, p. 278. John Paul II also taught that men take on bridal aspects in relation to Christ:

> Christ has entered this history and remains in it as the bridegroom who "has given himself." *To give* means "to become a sincere gift" in the most complete and radical way: "Greater love has no man than this" (Jn. 15:13). According to this conception, all human beings—both women and men—are called through the church to be the "bride" of Christ, the redeemer of the world. In this way "being the bride," and thus the feminine element, becomes a symbol of all that is "human," according to the words of Paul: "There is neither male or female; for you are all one in Christ Jesus" (Gal. 3:28).

94. C. S. Lewis, "Priestesses in the Church?," in *Women in the Church* (Appendix), (San Francisco: Ignatius Press, 1979), 131.

95. Ratzinger, "On the Position," 77.

96. *Lumen Gentium*, 2,11, Flannery, 362.

97. Connell, "Women Priests: Why Not?," 215.

98. Ibid., 221.

99. Ibid., 223–24.

100. De Lubac, *Motherhood*, 99–100.

101. St. Augustine, *Enarr. in Psalms*, 44, 32, as quoted by de Lubac, *Motherhood*, 90 (CCL 38.516). I have chosen the de Lubac translation over the *Nicene and Post Nicene Fathers*, vol. 8, 155. De Lubac's choice of words "she who gave birth to them" brings out the maternal aspects of the Church's authority more clearly than do the words of the well-known English series: "the Church itself brought them forth." The Latin reads: "Ipsa ecclesia patres illos appellat, *ipsa illos genuit.*"

102. De Lubac, *Motherhood*, 91.

103. Hans Urs Von Balthasar, "Address to the Cardinals and Prelates of the Roman Curia," (22 December 1987) *L' Osservatore Romano* (23 December 1987).

As quoted by John Paul II in *Mulieris Dignitatem*, *Origins* 18 (6 October 1988), 283.

104. De Lubac, *Motherhood*, 120. Even though priestly authority is derivative, de Lubac explains (p. 121) that it is nonetheless a real authority: "This fatherhood of our pastors is nonetheless real, since it derives precisely from the one divine Fatherhood."

105. Leonardo Boff, *The Maternal Face of God* (San Francisco: Harper and Row, 1987), 61.

106. Ibid.

107. Ibid., 63.

108. Ibid., 53–59, 80, 94.

109. Ibid., 89. "The modern understanding that every human being is at once anima and animus, albeit in different proportions depending on the sex of the individual, means that Jesus is masculine and feminine. He lives the masculine fully, since he is male. However, he integrates the feminine perfectly, too. But everything in Jesus is hypostatically assumed by the eternal Word. Therefore, in Jesus the feminine is God. In Jesus the feminine has been divinized. According to the christological principle of the *perichoresis* or *circumincessio*, this feminine, at any rate, is God."

110. Ibid., 81 (Also, 88–89, 91).

111. Ibid.

112. Ibid., 87. Boff is quoting from Victor White, "The Scandal of the Assumption," *Life of the Spirit* 5 (1950): 211–12.

113. Ibid. Boff's conclusions rest on a revisionist Trinitarian theology (see 88–89). In response we would argue that if God the Father can be God the Mother, in other words, if motherhood expresses the reality of God just as well as fatherhood, then ultimately sexuality has no meaning but is purely symbolic.

114. Ibid., 92.

115. Ibid., 93.

116. Ibid., 95.

117. Ibid., 101.

118. Ibid., 100.

119. Ibid., 102.

120. Ibid., 162.

121. Ibid., 154.

122. Ibid.,158.

123. In this book Boff occasionally affirms that Mary represents creation (for example, see p. 254). Also Boff provides an excellent and theologically sound explanation of the human maternity of Mary and why Mary (contrary to Nestorianism) is truly the Mother of God (pp. 158–60).

124. Ibid., 94. Boff implies that this is the case in heaven:

> If the reign of God and happiness in heaven imply the absolute realization of all the innate possibilities of human nature, then the possibility (obediential potency) of human beings to be united with a divine Person will be realized. Therefore, in eternity, all the just, each in his or her own way and to a degree proper to each, will be hypostatically assumed by God, who will thus become "all in all" (1 Cor. 15:28). Thus, human beings will attain the supreme end for which they have been thought of, loved, and created by God: to be happy and to share in God's divine nature, allowing—because they are different from God—God to share in their human nature. God surrenders to human beings and to the point of producing a unity without confusion and without change, without division but without separation, in a manner similar to what occurs in the incarnation of the eternal Son in Jesus Christ. What took place in Christ in time will take place in all of the just in eternity.

Later (p. 153) Boff states rather boldly: "God wills to be a human being, and wills human beings to become God."

125. Hans Urs Von Balthasar, "The Uninterrupted Tradition of the Church," *L'Osservatore Romano* (24 February 1977): 6–7.

Chapter 6. The Authority of Women

1. John Paul II, *Mulieris Dignitatem, Origins* 18 (6 October 1988): 281.

2. Joseph Cardinal Ratzinger, "On the Position of Mariology and Marian Spirituality Within the Totality of Faith and Theology," in *The Church and Women*, ed. Helmut Moll (San Francisco: Ignatius Press, 1988), 77.

3. Walter Kasper, "The Position of Woman as a Problem of Theological Anthropology," *The Church and Women*, 60–61.

4. Jutta Burggraf, "Women's Dignity and Function in Church and Society," *The Church and Women*, 105.

5. E. Danniel and B. Olivier, *Woman Is the Glory of Man* (Westminster, Md.: Newman Press, 1966), 30.

6. Ashley Montagu, *The Natural Superiority of Women* (New York: Macmillan, 1974), 6.

7. Ibid., 85. Montagu cites data from India indicating that under poor nutritional requirements "the greater the lethality of the males; even fetal females are stronger than fetal males. The records uniformly show that from fertilization on, the mortality rates before birth are higher for the male than for the female fetus and that males after birth continue to have a higher mortality rate than females for every year of age."

8. Ibid., 85–86. Montagu argues that the longer life expectancy of women is due to their stronger physical constitution and is not linked to male working conditions as a factor in earlier male deaths. He says: "I am under the impression that most housewives work at

least as hard as their husbands, and under at least as great a strain." In any case the greater instance of male fetal death and male infant mortality, etc., cannot be linked to a work factor (p. 86).

9. Ibid., 93.

10. Ibid., 94.

11. Ibid., 50. Otto Weininger's original statement reads in English, translated from the German: "[M]an possesses sexual organs; her sexual organs possess women" in his book *Sex and Character* (London: William Heineman; New York: G. P. Putman's Sons, 1975), 92.

Actually, Weininger's statement as it is found in this English edition of his book supports rather than denies Montagu's thesis. Weininger's work however is steeped in a negative view of female sexualtiy which he blames as the primary barrier between women and their emancipation. For Weininger, only when womem are free from their biology can they experience social and moral liberation.

12. George F. Gilder, *Sexual Suicide* (New York: Quadrangle/The New York Times Book Co., 1973), 14–15.

Stephen B. Clark, relying heavily on Judith Bardwick and F. J. J. Buytendijk comes to the same conclusion:

> Most of the descriptive authors connect woman's heightened awareness of her body to the fact that her sexuality is more temporally and spacially diffuse, whereas a man's sexuality is more temporally and spatially specific. Women's sexual experience is extended over time in a series of different phases—menstruation, intercourse, conception, pregnancy, childbirth, and lactation. By contrast, a man's sexual experience is simpler and more psychologically delimited—intercourse and pre-intercourse. In similar fashion, woman's sexuality is more extended in space—vagina, clitoris, breasts, and a generally more sensitive body. A man's sexuality is simpler and more localized in space—the phallic region, along with hands and lips. The sexual body thus comes to a woman's consciousness in many forms and at many times, whereas the man's sexual body protrudes into his consciousness in a more consistent form and only at certain times. (*Man and Woman in Christ* [Ann Arbor, Mich.: Servant Books, 1980], 387.)

Also in support of Gilder one may look to Margaret Mead:

> The relationship in the male between his innate sexual impulses and reproduction seems to be a learned response to which the presence of this great variety of conflicting cultural solutions testifies. Male sexuality seems originally focussed to no goal beyond immediate discharge; it is society that provides the male with a desire for children, for patterned interpersonal relationships that order, control, and elaborate his original impulses.
>
> In the female, however, we are confronted by something very different. The male sex act is immediately self-resolving and self-satisfying, but the female analogue is not the single copulatory experience, however self-resolving that may appear to be, but the whole cycle of pregnancy, birth, lactation. (*Male and Female* [Westport, Conn.: Greenwood Press, 1949], 229.)

13. Ibid., 17.

14. Ibid., 18.

15. Ibid., 23.

16. Ibid., 25.

17. Ibid., 35.

18. George Gilder, "The Sexual Revolution at Home," *National Review* (10 October 1986): 34.

19. Pope Pius XI, *Casti Connubii*, 31 December 1930 (Boston: St. Paul Editions), 15.

20. Emmett Cardinal Carter, *Do This in Memory of Me: A Pastoral Letter Upon the Sacrament of Priestly Orders*, Dec. 8, 1983 (Toronto, Can.), 45.

21. Leo Scheffczyk, "Mary as Model of Catholic Faith," in *The Church and Women*, 95. "In Mary the total openness and devotion of the creature corresponds to the absolute sovereignty of God. Something fundamental from the structure of the working of grace is reflected here."

22. Gertrud von le Fort, *The Eternal Woman* (Milwaukee: The Bruce Publishing Co., 1954), from the preface by Max Jordan, vii–viii.

23. Ibid., 9.

24. Ibid., 8–9.

25. Karl Stern, *The Flight from Woman* (New York: Paragon House, 1965), 9.

26. Barbara Albrecht, "Is There an Objective Type 'Woman'?," in *The Church and Women*, 44. Albrecht is quoting N. Bischof, "Is Biology Destiny? Concerning the Natural History of Gender Role Differentiation," in *Emancipation of Woman, between Biology and Ideology*, ed. E. Weinzierl (Publications of the Catholic Academy in Bavaria, no. 90, Dusseldorf, 1980), 33f.

27. Paul Quay, *The Christian Meaning of Human Sexuality* (San Francisco: Ignatius Press, 1985), 31. See also Manfred Hauke, *Women in the Priesthood* (San Francisco: Ignatius Press, 1988), 86. Hauke is quoting Philipp Lersch, *Vom Wesen der Geschlechter* [On the Nature of the Sexes], 4th ed. (Munich and Basel, 1968), 25.

> In the act of coitus, the female naturally has the role of receiving and assimilating, which corresponds to the male role of effecting and imparting. "If what occurs regarding the female is a *centripetal* process, directed from the outside inward toward the center of life, what occurs regarding the male is a *centrifugal* one, directed from the center of life outward."

28. Judith Bardwick, *Psychology of Women* (New York: Harper and Row Publishers, 1971), 123.

29. Ibid., 125.

30. Ibid., 123. Bardwick notes passivity can be assigned these meanings as well.

31. Quay, *Christian Meaning*, 27.

32. Pope John Paul II, *Original Unity of Man and Woman: Catechesis on the Book of Genesis* (Boston: St. Paul Editions, 1981), 71.

> In this way the meaning of man's original unity, through masculinity and femininity, expressed as an overcoming of the frontier of solitude, and at the same time as an affirmation—with regard to both human beings—of everything that constitutes "man" in solitude. In the Bible narrative, solitude is the way that leads to that unity which, following Vatican II, we can define as *communio personarum*.

33. Ibid., 72.

> [I]n this solitude [man] opens up to a being akin to himself, defined in Genesis (2:18 and 20) as "a helper fit for him." This opening is no less decisive for the person of man; in fact, it is perhaps even more decisive than the "distinction" itself. Man's solitude, in the Yahwist narrative, is presented to us not only as the first discovery of the characteristic transcendence peculiar to the person, but also as the discovery of an adequate relationship "to" the person, and therefore as an opening and expectation of a "communion of persons."

The "distinction" John Paul II refers to above is man's distinction from the animals.

34. Samuel Terrien, *Till the Heart Sings* (Philadelphia: Fortress Press, 1985), 9.

35. Ibid., 10–11.

36. Ibid.

37. Ibid., 17.

38. This is the basic thesis of the Vatican document *Instruction on Respect for Human Life in Its Origin and on the Dignity of Procreation*, Congregation for the Doctrine of the Faith, 22 February 1987 (Boston: St. Paul Editions). The condemnation of artificial forms of human reproduction arises out of the meaning of human relatedness upon which the very dignity of human persons depends, including the dignity of embryos and fetuses. Regarding, for example, *in vitro* fertilization the document states *"These procedures are contrary to the human dignity proper to the embryo, and at the same time they are contrary to the right of every person to be conceived and to be born within marriage and from marriage"* (p. 19).

Further on the document more explicitly connects the necessity of personal embodied love of spouses, the communication of personal spousal love (which by definition cannot be separated from the body) and the creation of a new person—whose dignity finds its support in being personally related and brought into existence by his parents through this type of communication for which there is no substitute.

> The origin of the human being thus follows from a procreation that is "linked to the union, not only biological but also spiritual, of the parents made one by the bond of marriage." Fertilization achieved outside of the bodies of the couple remains by this very fact deprived of the meanings and the values which are expressed in the language of the body and in the union of human persons. (p. 28)

39. Montagu, *Natural Superiority*, 199–200.

> Every living thing comes into being originally in this fundamentally interdependent manner. It is in the process of origin of one living thing from another, in the biologic relation of interdependency which the reproductive process constitutes, that the fundamental meaning of social relationships, of social life, is to be sought and understood. . . .
>
> The social state is the process of interaction between organisms during which they confer survival benefits upon one another. In other words, social relationships are an extension and amplification of the physiologic relations obtaining between maternal organism and offspring.

40. Helene Deutsch, *The Psychology of Women* (New York: Grune and Stratton, 1945), 131. Thus it is not surprising that according, to Deutsch women who choose elective abortion feel they have destroyed not simply a child, but part of themselves (pp. 183–84).

See also *The Psychological Aspects of Abortion*, eds. David Mall and Walter F. Watts (Washington, D.C.: University Publications of America, 1979) for further elaboration on the effect of abortion upon mother-child bonding, in particular Philip G. Ney's contribution to this volume "Infant Abortion and Child Abuse: Cause and Effect," 25–38.

41. Deutsch, *The Psychology of Women*, 126.

42. Edith Stein, "Spirituality of Christian Women," in *The Collected Works of Edith Stein*, vol. 2, eds. Dr. L. Gelber and Romaeus Leuven (Washington, D.C.: ICS Publications, 1987), 95.

43. Von le Fort, *The Eternal Woman*, 78.

44. Stein, "The Ethos of Women's Professions," in *The Collected Works of Edith Stein*, vol. 2, 43.

45. Bardwick, *Psychology of Women*, 100

> Regarding learning differences between boys and girls, Bardwick (p. 110) states
>
> I suspect that there is a general and consistent selectivity in cognitive skills where boys have some tendencies toward the objective and "thing-related" and girls toward the intuitive, verbal, and "people related." The cognitive skills that are developed become congruent not only with the current role expectations but with the personality characteristics of the sexes. It is not surprising,

therefore, that most professional women who have doctorates are in education, certain aspects of medicine, and psychology—professions in which interpersonal sensitivity is an advantage.

For a good discussion of the differences in intellectual qualities between men and women see Clark, *Man and Woman in Christ*, 383–86.

46. Clark, *Man and Woman in Christ*, 384.

47. Hauke, *Women in the Priesthood?*, 94.

48. Bardwick, *Psychology of Women*, 164. One can locate the Church's own catholicity, that is, her own universality—to incorporate all men within her—within the maternal unifying nature of women.

49. Ibid., 158. Bardwick's basic conclusion affirms the importance of the maternal aspect of women:

> It is probably clear by now that I believe the female's need to establish herself in a loving, intimate relationship, to love and be loved is dominant. I also believe that the gratification of maternal needs are necessary for feelings of well-being. And I think that for most women in our society gratification of those needs, at home or at work (e.g. nursing, teaching), are dominant motives. (pp. 158–59)

Bardwick, however, concludes that for the college-educated, middle-class woman, her sense of identity and self-esteem will be inadequately met solely through devotion to husband and family (p. 159).

50. Clark, *Man and Woman in Christ*, 389.

51. Bardwick, *Psychology of Women*, 54. At the time of Bardwick's writing of the book this study included 150 women.

52. Ibid., 55.

53. Montagu, *Natural Superiority*, 171.

54. Bardwick, *Psychology of Women*, 160.

55. Stein, "The Ethos of Women's Professions," 48.

56. Bardwick, *Psychology of Women*, 204.

57. Montagu, *Natural Superiority*, 176.

58. St. Augustine, *Sermo 192*. 2 (PL 38.1012–1013).

59. St. Augustine, *Sermon Mai 92*, *Miscellanea Agostiniana*, *Sancti Augustini Sermones*, vol. 1, ed. D. Germani Morin (Rome: Typis Polygottis Vaticanis, 1930), 332.

> "Fratres quia una nos genuit ecclesia mater."

60. Pierre Batiffol, *Le Catholicisme de St. Augustine* (Paris: Librairie LeCoffre, 1929), 274.

61. St. Clement of Alexandria, *The Instructor*, 1, 5, 20, *Ante-Nicene Fathers*, vol. 2, eds. Alexander Roberts and James Donaldson (Grand Rapids, Mich.: Wm. B. Eerdmans, 1956), 214 (PG 8.275, 276).

62. Ibid., 1, 6, 42, p. 220 (PG 8.301, 302).

63. St. Cyprian, *Epistle 16*, 3 in Joseph C. Plumpe, *Mater Ecclesia: An Inquiry into the Concept of the Church as Mother in Early Christianity* (Washington, D.C.: The Catholic University of America Press, 1943), 84 (CSEL 3, 2.515).

64. St. Cyprian, *The Unity of the Catholic Church*, 5, trans. Maurice Bevenot, *Ancient Christian Writers*, vol. 25 (Westminster, Md.: The Newman Press, 1957), 48 (CCL 3.253).

65. Ibid., 23, pp. 64–65 (CCL 3.265–66).

66. Ibid., 23, p. 65 (CCL 3.266).

67. Henri de Lubac, *The Motherhood of the Church* (San Francisco: Ignatius Press, 1982), 70. (Here de Lubac is quoting St. Cyprian *De Unitate* 23, CCL 3.266.) De Lubac translates the term "parent-stock" used in the *Ancient Christian Writers* series (referred to in footnote 64) as "womb of the mother." The phrase in Latin reads: "quicquid a matrice discesserit."

68. Plumpe, *Mater Ecclesia*, 91. Earlier in this book Plumpe comments upon the letter of the confessors of Lyons and Vienne:

> . . .[W]hen some of their fellow Christians momentarily became weak and disavowed Christ, the παρθένος Μήτηρ was said to have suffered a miscarriage; when they repented and rejoined their brethren doomed to die in the arena, they were conceived again in the womb of their Mother. Her parturition of them was completed only when they had died in loyalty to her Spouse. (pp. 77–78)

69. De Lubac, *Motherhood of the Church*, 69.

70. Ibid., 71.

71. Tertullian, *The Prescription Against Heretics*, 42 in Plumpe, *Mater Ecclesia*, 55–56 (CCL 70.55). I have chosen the Plumpe translation of this passage over that of the *Ante-Nicene Fathers*, vol. 3, p. 264 because Plumpe's choice of words beautifully emphasizes the isolation and rootlessness of those without Mother Church. Tertullian's phrase in Latin: "sine matre, sine sede, orbi fide, extorres quasi veritate vagantur."

72. This truth is poignantly captured in the words of an old Negro slave song *Motherless Child*:

> Sometimes I feel like a motherless child,
> sometimes I feel like a motherless child.
> So far from home.
> So far from home.

It is significant that the song originated among Negro slaves in America. It was the slave's frequent experience to have familial ties torn asunder in which the loss of the mother bond was the experience of homelessness.

73. De Lubac, *Motherhood of the Church*, 156.

74. Here we see how feminine authority as the preserver of personal identity is the exact antithesis of what Rosemary Radford Ruether proposed concerning the existence of the *self*. According to Ruether the person with their own individual identity is unimportant, in fact, after death it is annihilated. The person dissolves back into the "cosmic matrix of matter/energy." The only thing that continues is the "great collective personhood" she calls the "Holy Being" of which the person now has become a part, but the individual self as such does not exist (see *Sexism and God-Talk*, 257–58).

75. De Lubac, *Motherhood*, 156–57.

76. Maggie Gallagher, *The Enemies of Eros: How the Sexual Revolution Is Killing Family, Marriage and Sex and What We Can Do About It* (Chicago: Bonus Books, 1989). Gallagher provides a good analysis of the philosophy that human beings are first isolated individuals without inherit ties to one another in light of surrogate motherhood and the infamous "Baby M" case. Here lies the clear instance of the state ignoring all familial ties, in particular the tie between a mother and her child. If human beings stand outside of familial bonds which determines identity and responsibility, then these bonds are created by the sheer fiat of legal contact. On contract versus the family Gallagher states:

In the pursuit of the widest field for liberty, extended family obligations have been shucked off one-by-one, leaving the reproductive core: father, mother and 1.8 children. In the last two decades, we have gone post-nuclear and deeply weakened men's sense of obligation to their offspring, encouraging the formation of a yet more liberated family: the single parent household. And with the new institutions like surrogate motherhood, we are prepared to go one step further: The mother-child dyad itself will be broken down. Women will be further liberated from the burden of knowing that the child in our womb is our responsibility. All these various developments are, at the deepest level, one and the same phenomenon.

The back door way to destroy the family is through contract. Re-imagining bonds of kinship as bonds of contract leaves women and children dangerously vulnerable. But making contract the basis of kinship is more than dangerous, it is false. The contract model does not explain how families are formed or sustained; in fact it makes families inexplicable. (p. 162)...

The lure of the contract model of the family is that it breaks the bonds of flesh. Contract is clean, contract is disembodied, contract gives us the illusion of control. (p. 187)

The modern quest for women's liberation is a "freedom" for women achieved by the denial of these "bonds of the flesh" of which the woman is the source and center. Liberation means one has the right and the power to actually make or *deny* bonds of human relatedness. Notice, this is why legalized abortion on demand has become, along with contraception, the chief means of assuring female autonomy—abortion assures the woman that she is not controlled by the "bonds of flesh" but she can control, at her own whim, to whom she will be related and at what depth of commitment, if any.

77. In 1987 two nuns, Srs. Barbara Ferraro and Patricia Hussey, traveled about the United States delivering speeches in favor of legalized abortion until they finally left their religious order, the Sisters of Notre Dame de Namur. In response to the nuns' philosophy that women are "autonomous moral decision makers," this author responded:

What is the crux of the battle Ferraro and Hussey are waging? They and others who share their views want to be loosened from the Catholic Church's teachings on sex so that they may gain absolute power over human life and human relationships. This power is to be used to sever ourselves from each other. In this severing we will be free from human responsibility, free from suffering, free from the cross of Christ.

Against the dogma of power manifested in abortion stands the Catholic teaching that human beings are bound to each other. To be human and to be fulfilled humanly is to be bound. Men and women are bound and they are bound to their children and their children are bound to them. And before all this, men and women are bound to their sexuality and what human sexuality created by God means for the world. The nuns' support for abortion would do away with all this intrinsic love and commitment. Ferraro and Hussey's dogma of power begins with an escape from the feminine service to life and ends in a disintegrated world. ("Pro-abortion Nuns at Marquette: The Will to Power," *Crisis* 6 [March 1988]: 15)

78. Albrecht, 39. Quoting Pater Kentenich: "We understand that the devil when he wishes to wield power over an entire civilization and over all humanity, first persecutes women."

79. The human isolation radical feminism advocates as a principle tenet is expressed in the feminists' own rhetoric on abortion. For example, such phrases as "I have a right to control my own body" is meant to speak that the woman has power to separate herself from all others in the world whereby the decision whether another lives or dies is rendered in alienation. Indeed, the unborn can only be put to death by such alienation that only a woman, because of the authority of her sex, is in a position to create.

80. Wherein then would equality lie? Two male homosexuals who appeared on the "Oprah Winfrey" television program supplied the answer. The two homosexuals looked upon their relationship as a marriage—on equal terms with any heterosexual marriage. They can marry *in the same way* a man and woman marry because in their words marriage "takes place in the heart." In other words, the human body, male and female, is irrelevant to the marriage commitment and what it stands for morally and culturally. If we absent the body, all inequalities are dissolved. The true person is present only on the level of the spirit or by what "takes place in the heart." Indeed, there really can be no such thing as marriage as a historical, embodied, objective reality. And if not, then we would have to conclude that there is no *good creation*. The world itself would be absent of any inherent moral order. It would possess only the moral order the human heart could give to it (see John Lofton, "Fear and Loathing on the Oprah Show," *Fidelity* 9 [July-August 1990]: 20–23).

81. Von le Fort, *The Eternal Woman*, 10–11.

82. De Lubac, *Motherhood*, 159.

83. Hans Küng, *On Being a Christian* (Garden City, N.Y.: Doubleday & Co., 1976), 523. Küng states:

> And now, when the authority, unity, credibility of this Church have been shaken in a variety of ways as a result of the evident failure of its leaders, when it is increasingly seen to be weak, erring, searching for directions, there are not a few who will say what they never said in former times of triumph: "We love this Church, as it is now and as it could be." They love it, not as "mother," but as the family of faith, for the sake of which the institutions, constitutions, authorities exist at all and sometimes simply have to be endured.

Not surprisingly Küng rejects loving the Church as a "mother" in the section of his book explaining why, though he disagrees with much Catholic teaching and the institutional Church, he nevertheless opts to remain a Christian within it.

84. Leo Scheffczyk, "Mary as Model of Catholic Faith," in *The Church and Women*, 89.

85. Ibid., 100.

86. Von Balthasar as quoted by Leo Scheffczyk, "Mary as Model of the Church," in *The Church and Women*, 100.

87. De Lubac, *Motherhood*, 164.

88. Ibid., 166. Also pp. 267–68 are helpful:

> Too elaborate an organization of these regional groups of bishops risks doing harm to the personal initiative of each of them, absorbing him in specialized tasks which take him away from his diocesan laity and priests, paralyzing him sometimes in his essential ministry, perhaps even dulling his consciousness of his personal obligations as much as with regard to a universal catholicity as in the government of his own church. What would tend to prevail in this case would be an impersonal, anonymous leadership developing into a bureaucracy; it would by that very fact be a theoretical, abstract teaching of neutral tone, without human warmth, in which the faithful would no longer recognize the voice of their pastor.

89. Ibid., 167.

90. This "tearing of the body" experience may not be so acute in the case of a lapsed Protestant. The Protestant falls away from a set of beliefs and practices shared by a particular community, but the Church is not the source of spiritual life for the Protestant in the same organic kind of way it is for a Catholic. The lapsed Protestant may decide to join another congregation. From the perspective of the Catholic Church as mother, the force of whose maternal tie is profoundly bound to the piety of Catholics, the devout Catholic feels the painful loss, scandal, and anxiety that the exit of a member signifies to the whole maternal

body. For the Catholic it is never enough that the lapsed one maintain his faith in terms of certain fundamental beliefs but that he be personally *related* to the Church as she is true mother and bride of Christ.

91. Stern, *The Flight from Woman*, 296.

92. Von le Fort, *The Eternal Woman*, 97.

93. Stein, "The Separate Vocations of Men and Women According to Nature and Grace," 77–78.

Hauke discusses reasons why women are generally more religious than men in *Women and the Priesthood?*, 93–94.

It should also be noted that in the growing home-schooling movement in the United States the chief educator of children is the woman, both in academics and religion. This movement gives women influence over their children unheard of perhaps in centuries.

94. Gilder, *Sexual Suicide*, 57.

> The essential pattern is clear. Women manipulate male sexual desire in order to teach them the long-term cycles of female sexuality and biology on which civilization is based. When men learn, their view of the woman as an object of their own sexuality succumbs to an image of her as the bearer of a richer and more extended eroticism and as the keepers of the portals of societal immortality. She becomes a way to lend elaborate continuity and meaning to the limited erotic compulsions of the male.

95. Montagu, *Natural Superiority*, 98–99.

96. Ibid., 184. I reject any notion of women turning men *into women* as a means of making things "just" in the world. The kind of love and cooperation Montagu speaks of must be understood within a covenantal aspect of male-female sexuality in which man and woman cannot be reduced to each other. Love and cooperation can simply be understood as the male fulfilling himself within the human relatedness of the familial project which is mediated to him by the woman. Concerning the importance of the family and the woman within it Gilder states:

> But it is foolish to imagine that the complex roles and relationships sustained by the housewife can be abolished or assumed by outside agencies. *Her role is nothing less than the central activity of the human community.* All other work—the business and politics and entertainment and service performed in the society—finds its ultimate test in the quality of the home. The home is where we finally and privately live, where we express our individuality, where we make and enjoy love, and where we cultivate our children as individuals. All very pedestrian, perhaps, but there is not very much more in civilized life.
>
> The central position of the woman in the home parallels her central position in all civilized society. Both derive from her necessary role in procreation and from the most primary and inviolable of all ties, the one between mother and child. In those extraordinary circumstances when this tie is broken—as with some disintegrating tribes—broken as well is the human identity of the group. Most of the characteristics we define as humane and individual originate in the mother's love for her children. (*Sexual Suicide*, 245)

97. Ibid., 193.

98. Gilder provides a good discussion of the effect of the welfare state in rendering the male occupational role irrelevant and obsolete, thus taking men out of long-term familial ties to women and to the children they father (see pp. 167–68).

99. *Mulieris*, 274.

100. Walter Ong, *Fighting for Life* (London: Cornell University Press, 1981), 74.

101. Gilder, *Sexual Suicide*, 93.

102. Ibid., 94.

103. Stein, "Spirituality of Christian Women," 111.

104. St. Augustine, *Sermon Mai 92, Miscellanea Agostiniana, Sancti Augustini Sermones*, vol. 1, ed. D. Germani Morin (Rome: Typis Polygottis Vaticanis, 1930), 332.

105. Stein, "The Separate Vocations of Man and Woman According to Nature and Grace," 69.

106. Henri de Lubac, *The Eternal Feminine* (New York: Harper and Row Publishers, 1971), 104.

107. St. Hippolytus, *Benedic. de Jacob* 7, in Karl Delahaye, *Ecclesia Mater, Unam Sanctam*, vol. 46 (Paris: Éditions du Cerf, 1964), 90.

108. Tertullian, *De Baptismo* 20, (CSEL 20.218).

109. Plumpe, *Mater Ecclesia*, 109.

110. St. Clement of Alexandria, *Paedagogus* 3.12.99 (PG 8. 677,678).

111. St Irenaeus, *Against Heresies*, 4 pref., as quoted by de Lubac in *Motherhood of the Church*, 118 (PG 7,1.975). De Lubac's quotation is based on the following phrase of St. Irenaeus: "Dei formatus est, et per manus ejus plasmatus est, hoc est per Filium et Spiritum."

112. De Lubac, *Motherhood*, 118.

113. *Mulieris*, 273.

114. Luke 24:10b-11 states that the Apostles refused to believe the women but their incredulity is not based on a discrimination against the female sex of the message bearers. It is the message itself that is disbelieved: "the story seemed like nonsense" (v. 11).

Let us note, that while Mary Magdelene is disbelieved so also are the two men "on their way to the country" to whom Jesus appeared as recorded in Mark 16:13. The Apostles put no more faith in the testimony of men than of women regarding the resurrection. To his credit, Luke 24:12 reports that Peter, lone among the Apostles, properly responded to the witness of the women. John 20:3 states that both Peter and John listened to the words of the Magdelene.

Chapter 7. Women, the Covenant Partners of Christ

1. St. Ambrose, *Liber De Viduis* 7.38 (PL 16.259).

2. Ibid., 3.14 (PL 16.252).

3. Ibid., 3.15.

4. Ibid., 3.16 (PL 16.252–53).

5. St. Ambrose, *Concerning Widows*, 7,38, trans. H. De Romestin, *Nicene and Post-Nicene Fathers*, vol. 10, ed. Philip Schaff (Grand Rapids, Mich.: Wm. B. Eerdmans, 1955), 398 (PL 16.259).

6. St. Ambrose, *Liber De Viduis* 7.40 (PL 16.260).

7. St. Ambrose, *Concerning Widows*, 7,41, NPNF, vol. 10, p. 398 (PL 16.260).

8. Ibid., 8,44, p. 399 (PL 16.261).

9. Ibid. "Non ergo natura rea est culpae, nec infirmitati obnoxia: strenuos no sexus, sed virtus facit."

As with nearly all the Church Fathers, Ambrose reveals inconsistencies in his thought. Earlier in the same treatise he expressed the commonly held view of the time that women are the weaker sex in terms of bravery and the ability to lead (*Concerning Widows*, 7,37, p. 397, PL 16.259).

10. Ibid., 8, 45,46, p. 399 (PL 16.261–62).

11. Ibid., 8, 46 (PL 16.262).

12. Ibid., 8, 47.

13. Ibid., 8, 48.

14. Ibid., 8, 50 (PL 16.263).

15. St. Hippolytus, *Fragmenta in Danielem, in Susannam* 15 (PG 10.691,692).

16. Ibid., 22 (PG 10.693,694).

17. St. Hippolytus, *Fragments From Commentaries, On Susannah*, 24, *Ante-Nicene Fathers*, vol. 5, eds. Alexander Roberts and James Donaldson (Grand Rapids, Mich.: Wm. B. Eerdmans, 1957), 193 (PG 10, 695, 696).

18. *The Passion of SS. Perpetua and Felicity*, I,1 in *The Living Testament: The Essential Writings of Christianity Since the Bible*, ed. M Basil Pennington, et al. (San Francisco: Harper and Row, 1985), 30 (PL 3.14–62).

19. Ibid., I, 2.

20. Ibid.

21. Ibid., II, 1. p. 31.

22. Ibid., II, 2.

23. Ibid., V, 2, p. 33.

24. Ibid., VI, 1, p. 34.

25. Ibid., VI, 3.

26. Ibid., III, 2, p. 32.

27. Ibid., VI, 3, p. 34.

28. Ibid., VI, 4, p. 35.

29. Ibid., VI, 3.

30. Eusebius's chief source is the *Epistle of the Church of Vienne and Lyons* which contains the acts of the martyrs persecuted in this region. *The Fathers of the Church* series, vol. 19, p. 273 has a detailed footnote regarding this letter which states that the letter "bears all the marks of authenticity and its genuineness has never been questioned."

31. Eusebius *Historia ecclesiastica* 5.1 (PG 20.415, 416).

32. Eusebius, *Ecclesiastical History*, 5, 1, trans. Roy J. Deferrari, *The Fathers of the Church*, vol. 19 (New York: Fathers of the Church, Inc., 1953), 282 (PG 20.425,426).

33. Ibid., 285 (PG 20.431,432).

34. Ibid.

35. Ibid., 283 (PG 20.427,428).

Quippe mortua jam Ecclesiae membra, viventium ope atque auxilio ad vitam revocata sunt: et martyres gratificati sunt iis qui fidem negaverant: ingentique gaudio mater eademque virgo Ecclesia cumulata est, cum eos quos tanquam exstinctos abortu ejecerat, vivos jam ac spirantes recuperaret. Etenim per illos sanctissimos martyres, hi qui fidem negaverant, rursus in utero delineabantur, rurus concipiebantur , et vitali calore reparato rurus fidem confiteri discebant. Cumque jam ad vitam revocati roboratique essent, Deo qui non vult mortem peccatoris, sed pro sua benigniate ad poenitentiam potius invitat.

36. Ibid., 5, 2, p. 289 (PG 20.435,436). "Cumque pacem dilexissent, pacem nobis commendassent, ipsi cum pace migraverunt ad Deum: non dolorem matri."

37. Joseph C. Plumpe, *Mater Ecclesia: An Inquiry into the Concept of the Church as Mother in Early Christianity* (Washington, D.C.: The Catholic University of America Press, 1943), 37.

38. Ibid., 38.

39. Ibid., 39.

40. St. Augustine, *Confessions*, 5,7,13, trans. R. S. Pine-Coffin (New York: Penguin Books, 1961), 99 (CSEL 33.99–100).

41. Ibid., 5,8,15, p. 101 (CSEL 33.101).

42. Peter Brown, *Augustine of Hippo* (Berkeley: University of California Press, 1967), 30. This quotation is taken from Brown's translation of *Conf.* 5, 9, 16. It is preferred to the Pine-Coffin translation as it brings out more clearly the character of Monica's spiritual motherhood. The original Latin reads: "Non enim satis eloquor, quid erga me habebat animi et quanto maiore sollicitudine me parturiebat spiritu, quam carne pepererat" (CSEL 33.103).

43. *Augustine of Hippo*, 53.

44. Henri de Lubac, *The Motherhood of the Church* (San Francisco: Ignatius Press, 1982), 159.

45. *Confessions* 3,11, p. 68 (CSEL 33.61).

46. Ibid., 68 (CSEL 33.60).

47. Ibid., 9,9, p. 194 (CSEL 33.213).

48. St. Augustine *Confessionum*, 9,9 (CSEL 33.213).

49. *Confessions*, 9,9, p. 196 (CSEL 33.215).

50. Ibid. (CSEL 33.214).

51. Ibid. (CSEL 33.215).

52. Ibid., 9,11, p. 200 (CSEL 3.219).

53. *Confessionum* 9.13 (CSEL 33.224–25).

54. St. Augustine, *Enarr. on the Book of Psalms*, 45,29 *Nicene and Post Nicene Fathers*, vol. 8, ed. Philip Schaff (Grand Rapids, Mich.: Wm. B. Eerdmans, 1956), 155 (CCL 38.516, Ps. 44.33).

55. Igino Giordini, *Catherine of Siena: Fire and Blood* (Milwaukee, Wisc.: Bruce Publishing, 1959), 137. For a first hand look at the authority of St. Catherine of Siena in her struggle with bishops, cardinals, and popes, the reader is directed to the letters of St. Catherine of Siena, which have been translated into English and edited by Suzanne Noffke, O.P. in *The Letters of St. Catherine of Siena, Medieval and Renaissance Texts and Studies*, vol. 52 (Binghamton, N.Y.: 1988).

56. Ibid., 179.

57. Ibid., 182.

58. Ibid., 218.

59. Katherine M. Longley, *St. Margaret Clitherow* (Wheathampsted, Hertfordshire, England: Anthony Clarke, 1986), 63.

60. Ibid., 99.

61. Ibid.

62. Ibid.

63. Ibid., 90.

64. We have already seen how Mother Church is in anguish when certain Christians of Vienne and Lyons denied the faith (see *Eccl. Hist.* 5.1). Origen also expressed the travail of the Mother Church over unrepentant sinners:

> And such as are reared in knowledge and wisdom are the joy of both God the Father and of Mother Church; but she is smitten with bitter pain and grief over their stupidity—when we refuse to repent, remaining attached to our depravity. (*Exp. in Prov.*, 17,25 as quoted in Plumpe, p. 78, PG 17.201)

65. Longley, *St. Margaret Clitherow*, 99.

66. Evelyn Waugh, *Edmund Campion* (Boston: Little, Brown, 1948), 172–75. Mrs. Yate had responsibility for hosting Campion's visit to her house and for hiding him and the other priests. Her husband was gone from the premises, already imprisoned for practicing the Catholic faith (p. 165).

67. Longley, *St. Margaret Clitherow*, 87.

68. Ibid., 103.

69. Ibid., 151–52.

70. Ibid.

71. Ibid., 154–55.

72. Ibid., 156.

73. Ibid., 49.

74. Ibid., 50.

75. Ibid.

76. Ibid., 61, 71.

77. Ibid., 73.

78. Ibid., 72–73.

79. De Lubac, *Motherhood*, 56.

80. *The Dogmatic Constitution on the Church* (*Lumen Gentium*), 63, in *The Documents of Vatican II*, ed. Austin Flannery (Collegeville, Minn.: Liturgical Press, 1975), 419–20.

81. Ibid., 64, p. 420.

82. Pope Pius XII, *On Holy Virginity*, 25 March 1954 (Derby, N.Y.: The Daughters of St. Paul), 14.

83. Ibid., 3.

84. Ibid., 8.

85. Ibid., 13.

86. Ibid., 6.

87. Leo Scheffczyk, "Mary as Model of Catholic Faith," in *The Church and Women*, ed. Herbert Moll (San Francisco: Ignatius Press, 1988), 96.

88. Ibid.

89. Ibid.

90. Ibid., 97.

91. Ibid., 98. Scheffczyk is quoting from St. Augustine's *Sermon 132*.

92. St. Jerome, *Letter 22 to Eustochium*, 38, trans. Hon. W. H. Fremantle, *Nicene and Post Nicene Fathers*, vol. 6, second series, ed. Philip Schaff and Henry Wace (Grand Rapids, Mich.: Wm. B. Eerdmans), 39 (CSEL 54.204).

93. *On Holy Virginity*, 21.

94. Ibid., 19.

95. Richard Cowden-Guido, *You Reject Them, You Reject Me: The Prison Letters of Joan Andrews* (Manassas, Va.: Trinity Communications, 1988), 16.

96. Ibid., 17.

97. Ibid., 172. Joan explains her call to noncooperation in prison in a letter she wrote to Joseph Foreman who himself was sentenced in August 1990 to a one-year jail term in an Atlanta, Georgia prison for his attempt to block the door to an abortion clinic in that city.

98. Ibid., 21.

99. Ibid., 219.

100. Ibid., 177.

101. Karl Stern, *The Flight from Woman* (New York: Paragon House, 1965), 286.

102. According to Stern it is a masculine tendency to appreciate the human being on the level of what is practical. He gives a critique of the character Raskolnikov from Dostoievsky's novel *Crime and Punishment*. The character murders a man for whom he sees no value. Stern calls this "Life seen in terms of logistics—this is sheer *maleness*, unfettered and crazed" (p. 268). See also p. 278 for a good discussion of "power versus love."

103. Bishop Austin Vaughn's speech is recorded in an unpublished manuscript by Richard Cowden-Guido, *The History of Operation Rescue*.

104. Stern, *The Flight from Woman*, 285. Extrinsic organization is a masculine tendency. Stern comments:

Now from what we have seen, that which we call here the "sense of organism" is the feminine, and the "sense of organization" masculine. Those who are wary of the trap of cliches should study the sources of the empirical observation in psychoanalysis and phenomology which we have quoted. Woman as real or potential mother possesses the sense of creativeness by which one lets something grow, nurtures it, allows it to follow its own mysterious law of becoming. Man's sense of creativeness is that of making things work. Hence the strange "maleness" of that entire universe of the organizational. It has been pointed out that Kafka's haunting world of the "Trial" and the "Castle" is run by men, and the women who do occur are either themselves eminently phallic or masochistically submit to, and "go along with," the apparatus. (285-86)

105. Ibid., 154–55.

106. Ibid., 270.

107. Ibid., 146–47.

Bibliography

Albrecht, Barbara. "Is There an Objective Type 'Woman'?" In *The Church and Women*, edited by Helmut Moll, 35–49. San Francisco: Ignatius Press, 1988.

Allen, Christine Garside. "Plato on Women." *Feminist Studies* 2 (1975): 131–37.

Allen, Prudence. *The Concept of Woman: The Aristotelian Revolution*. Montreal: Eden Press, 1985.

Ambrose, Saint. *Concerning Virgins*. Translated by H. De Romestin. The Nicene and Post-Nicene Fathers. Vol. 10. Edited by Philip Schaff. Grand Rapids, Mich.: Wm. B. Eerdmans, 1955.

———. *Concerning Widows*. Translated by H. De Romestin. The Nicene and Post-Nicene Fathers, Vol. 10. Edited by Philip Schaff. Grand Rapids, Mich.: Wm. B. Eerdmans, 1955.

———. *The Mysteries*. Vol. 44. Translated by Fathers of the Church. Washington, D.C.: Catholic University of America Press, 1963.

———. *Paradise*. Translated by John Savage. Fathers of the Church. Vol. 42. New York: Fathers of the Church, 1961.

Andriessen, Paulus. "The New Eve, Body of the New Adam." In *The Birth of the Church*, 111–39. Staten Island, N.Y.: Alba House, 1968.

Augustine, Saint. *City of God*. Translated by Marcus Dods. *The Works of Aurelius Augustine, Bishop of Hippo*. Vol. 2. Edinburgh: T & T Clark and Co., 1878.

———. *Confessions*. Translated by R. S. Pine-Coffin. New York: Penguin Books, 1961.

———. *Enarr. on the Book of Psalms*. Nicene and Post-Nicene Fathers. Vol. 8. Grand Rapids, Mich.: Wm. B. Eerdmans, 1956.

———. *Faith and the Creed*. Translated by John H. S. Burleigh. *Augustine: Earlier Writings*. Library of Christian Classics, Vol. 6. Philadelphia: The Westminster Press, 1953.

———. *The Good of Marriage*. Translated by T. Wilcox. Fathers of the Church, Vol. 27. New York: Fathers of the Church, 1955.

———. *Letter 127*. Translated by Sr. Wilfred Parsons. Fathers of the Church, Vol. 18. New York: Fathers of the Church, 1953.

———. *The Literal Meaning of Genesis*. Translated by John Hammond Taylor, S.J. Ancient Christian Writers. Vol. 42. New York: The Newman Press, 1982.

———. *On the Trinity*. Translated by Authur West Haddan. *The Works of Augustine of Hippo*. Vol. 7. Edited by Rev. Marcus Dods. Edinburgh: T & T Clark, 1873.

———. *Sermon on the Mount*. Translated by Denis J. Kavanagh. Fathers of the Church, Vol. 11. New York: Fathers of the Church, Inc., 1951.

————. *Sermon 119*. A Library of the Fathers of the Holy Catholic Church, Vol. 16. Oxford: John Henry Parker, 1844.

————. *Sermon 216*. Translated by Sr. Mary Sarah Muldowny, R.S.N. Fathers of the Church, Vol. 17. New York: Fathers of the Church, 1959.

Baer, Richard A. *Philo's Use of the Categories Male and Female*. Leiden: E. J. Brill, 1970.

Bardwick, Judith. *Psychology of Women*. New York: Harper and Row, 1971.

Barret, C. K. *A Commentary on the First Epistle to the Corinthians*. New York: Harper and Row, 1968.

————. *From First Adam to Last*. New York: Charles Scribner's Sons, 1962.

————. *The Gospel According to John*. Philadelphia: Westminster Press, 1978.

Barth, Karl. *Christ and Adam*. New York: Octagon Books, 1956.

Batiffol, Pierre. *Le Catholicism de St Augustine*. Paris: Librairie LeCoffre, 1929.

Bedale, Stephen. "The Meaning of κεφαλή in the Pauline Epistles." *Journal of Theological Studies* 5–6 (1954–55): 211–15.

Bedard, Walter M. *The Symbolism of the Baptismal Font in Early Christian Thought*. Washington, D.C.: Catholic University of America Press, 1951.

Benedict XV, Pope. *Inter Sodalicia*. (22 March 1918) In *Mary in the Documents of the Church*, edited by Paul F. Palmer. Westminster, Md. The Newman Press, 1952.

Benoit, Pierre. "Corps, tête et plérôma dans les épîtres de la captivité." *Revue Bibl.* 63 (1956): 107–53.

————. "The Accounts of the Institution and What They Imply." In *The Eucharist in the New Testament*, 71–101. Baltimore and Dublin: Helicon Press, 1965.

Best, Ernest. *One Body in Christ*. London: SPCK, 1955.

Boff, Leonardo. *The Maternal Face of God*. San Francisco: Harper and Row, 1987.

Bouyer, Louis. *The Seat of Wisdom*. New York: Pantheon Books, 1960.

Braun, F. M. *Jean le Théologian: Sa théologie le mystère de Jésus-Christ*. Paris: Librairie LeCoffre, 1966.

————. *La Mère des fidèles*. Casterman-Tournai: Cahiers de L' Actualite Religieuse, 1954.

Brown, Marie P. "The Fallacy of the Fempriest." *Homiletic and Pastoral Review* (October 1981): 18–25.

Brown, Peter. *Augustine of Hippo*. Berkeley: University of California Press, 1967.

Brown, Raymond E. *The Gospel According to John: I–XII*. The Anchor Bible, Vol. 29. Garden City, N.Y.: Doubleday and Co., 1966.

Burggraf, Jutta. "Women's Dignity and Function in Church and Society." In *The Church and Women*, edited by Helmut Moll, 103–14. San Francisco: Ignatius Press, 1988:

Carter, Emmett Cardinal. *Do This in Memory of Me: Pastoral Letter on the Sacrament of the Priesthood*. Archdiocese of Toronto, Can.: 8 December 1983.

Cerfaux, Lucien. *Christ in the Theology of St Paul*. New York: Herder and Herder, 1959.

————. *The Church in the Theology of St Paul*. New York: Herder and Herder, 1959.

Christus Dominus. (*Decree on the Pastoral Office of Bishops in the Church*.) In *Documents of Vatican II*, edited by Austin Flannery, O.P. Collegeville, Minn. The Liturgical Press, 1975.

Chrysostom, Saint John. *Homily 9*. Translated by Philip Schaff. "Homilies on Timothy." Nicene and Post-Nicene Fathers. Vol. 13. Wm. B. Eerdmans, 1956.

————. *Homily 61*. Translated by Sr. Thomas Aquinas Goggin. Fathers of the Church. Vol. 41. New York: Fathers of the Church, Inc. 1960.

————. *On the Priesthood*. Edited by Rev. W. R. W. Stephens. Nicene and Post-Nicene Fathers of the Christian Church. Vol. 9. Grand Rapids, Mich.: Wm. B. Eerdmans Pub. Co., 1956.

Church, F. Forrester. "Sex and Salvation in Tertullian." *Harvard Theological Review* 68 (1975): 83–101.

Clark, Stephen B. *Man and Woman in Christ*. Ann Arbor, Mich.: Servant Press, 1980.

Clement of Alexandria, Saint. *The Instructor*. Ante-Nicene Fathers. Vol. 2. Grand Rapids, Mich.: Wm. B. Eerdmans, 1962.

————. *The Stromata*. Ante-Nicene Fathers. Vol. 2. Grand Rapids, Mich.: Wm. B. Eerdmans, 1956.

Congar, Yves. *Christ, Our Lady and the Church*. Westminster, Md.: The Newman Press, 1957.

————. "Marie et l'église dans la pensee patristique." *Revue des Sciences Philosophiques et Theologiques* 38 (1954): 3–38.

Connell, Desmond. "Women Priests: Why Not?." In *The Church and Women*, edited by Helmut Moll, 207–27. San Francisco: Ignatius Press, 1988.

Cornford, F. M. *From Religion to Philosophy: A Study in the Origins of Western Speculation*. New York: Harper and Brothers, 1957.

Cowden-Guido, Richard. *You Reject Them, You Reject Me: The Prison Letters of Joan Andrews*. Manassas, Va.: Trinity Communications, 1988.

Coyle, Kevin J. "The Fathers on Women and Women's Ordination." *Église et Théologie* 9 (1978): 51–101.

Cranfield, C. E. B. *The Epistle to the Romans*. Vol. 1. Edinburgh: T & T Clark, 1975.

Cyprian, Saint. *On the Dress of Virgins*. Translated by Roy J. Deferrari. The Fathers of the Church. Vol. 36. New York: Fathers of the Church, 1958.

————. *On the Unity of the Church*. Translated by Maurice Bevenot, S.J. Ancient Christian Writers, Vol. 25. Westminster, Md.: The Newman Press, 1957.

Cyril of Jerusalem, Saint. *Catechesis 18*. Nicene and Post Nicene Fathers, Vol. 7. Edited by Philip Schaff and Henry Wace. Grand Rapids, Mich.: Wm. B. Eerdmans, 1955.

Daly, Mary. *Beyond God the Father*. Boston: Beacon Press, 1973

————. *Gyn/Ecology*. Boston: Beacon Press, 1978.

————. "The Qualitative Leap Beyond Patriarchal Religion." *Quest*, 1 (1975).

Danniel, E., and B. Olivier. *Woman Is the Glory of Man*. Westminster, Md.: The Newman Press, 1966.

Delahaye, Karl. *Ecclesia Mater chez les péres des trois premiers siécles*. Unam Sanctam, 46. Paris: Éditions du Cerf, 1964.

Delorme, J. "The Last Supper and the Pasch in the New Testament." In *The Eucharist in the New Testament*: 21–67.

De Lubac, Henri. *The Eternal Feminine*. New York: Harper and Row Publishers, 1971.

————. *Motherhood of the Church*. San Francisco: Ignatius Press, 1982.

————. *The Splendour of the Church*. Glen Rock, N.J.: Paulist Press, 1956.

Deutsch, Helene. *The Psychology of Women*. New York: Grune and Stratton, 1945.

Dölger, F. J. "Dominia Mater Ecclesia und die 'Herrin' im zweiten Johannesbrief." *Antike und Christentum* 5 (1936): 211–17.

Eusebius. *Ecclesiastical History*. Translated by Roy J. Deferrari. The Fathers of the Church, Vol. 19. New York: Fathers of the Church, 1953.

Feuillet, André. "Les Adieux du Christ à sa mère Jn 19, 25–27 et la maternité spirituelle de Marie." *Nouvelle Revue Theologique* 86 (1964): 469–89.

———. "La Digniteé et le rôle de la femme d'apres quelques textes Pauliniens: Comparaison avec L'Ancien Testament." *New Testament Studies* 21 (1975): 157–91.

———. *Jesus and His Mother.* Still River, Mass.: St. Bede's Publications, 1984.

Florovsky, George. "The Ever-Virgin Mother of God." In *The Mother of God*, 51–63. London: Dacre Press, 1949.

Gallagher, Maggie. *The Enemies of Eros: How the Sexual Revolution Is Killing Family, Marriage and Sex and What We Can Do About It.* Chicago: Bonus Books, 1989.

Galot, Jean. *Theology of the Priesthood.* San Francisco: Ignatius Press, 1984.

Gilder, George F. *Sexual Suicide.* New York: Quadrangle/The New York Times Book Co., 1973.

Giordini, Igino. *Catherine of Siena: Fire and Blood.* Milwaukee, Wisc.: Bruce Publishing, 1959.

Goldenberg, Naomi. *Changing of the Gods: Feminism and the End of Traditional Religions.* Boston:Beacon Press, 1979.

Hauke, Manfred. *Woman and Priesthood?.* San Francisco: Ignatius Press, 1988.

Hennessy, Thomas E. D. "The Fatherhood of the Priest." *The Thomist* 10 (July 1947): 271–306.

Hippolytus, Saint. *The Anti-Christ.* The Ante-Nicene Fathers. Vol. 9. Edited by Alexander Roberts and James Donaldson. Grand Rapids, Mich., 1869.

Hitchcock, George S. *The Epistle to the Ephesians.* London: Burns and Oates and Chicago: Benziger Bros., 1913.

Huby, Joseph. *St Paul: Les Épistres de la Captivité.* Paris Beauchesne et ses fils, 1935.

Irenaeus, Saint. *Against Heresies.* Ante-Nicene Fathers. Vol. 1. Grand Rapids, Mich.: Wm. B. Eerdmans, 1967.

Inter Insigniores. (*Declaration on the Admission of Women to the Ministerial Priesthood.*) In *Vatican Council II: More Postconciliar Documents.* Vol. 2. Edited by Austin Flannery O.P. Collegeville, Minn.: The Liturgical Press, 1982.

Jeremias, Joachim. *The Eucharistic Words of Christ.* Oxford: Basil Blackwell, 1955.

Jerome, Saint. *Letter 22 to Eustochium.* Translated by W. H. Fremantle. Nicene and Post-Nicene Fathers. Vol. 6. Grand Rapids, Mich.: Wm. B. Eerdmans.

John XXIII, Pope. *Mater et Magistra* (15 May 1961) Washington, D.C.: National Catholic Welfare Conference.

John Paul II, Pope. "At the Root of the Eucharist Is the Virginal Heart of Mary." *L'Osservatore Romano* (13 June 1983): 1.

———. *Mulieris Dignitatem.* (On the Dignity and Vocation of Women). *Origins* 18 (6 October 1988): 1, 263–83.

———. *The Original Unity of Man and Woman.* Boston: St. Paul Editions, 1981.

———. *Redemptoris Mater.* (25 March 1987) Boston: Daughters of St. Paul, 1987.

Justin Martyr, Saint. *Dialogue With Trypho.* Translated by R. P. C. Hanson. World Christian Books, Vol. 49. New York: Associated Press, 1964.

Kasper, Walter. "The Position of Woman as a Problem of Theological Anthropology." In *The Church and Women*, edited by Helmut Moll, 51-64. San Francisco: Ignatius Press, 1988.

Keefe, Donald J. "Authority in the Church: An Essay in the Theology of History." *Communio* 7 (Winter 1980): 343–63.

———. "Gender, History, and Liturgy in the Catholic Church." *Review for Religious* 46 (November–December 1987): 866–81.

———. "Mary As Created Wisdom, the Splendor of the New Creation." *The Thomist* 47 (July 1983): 395–420.

————. "Sacramental Sexuality and the Ordination of Women." *Communio* 5 (Fall 1978): 228–51.

Kiefer, Ralph. "Christ in Liturgical Prayer." In *Women and Priesthood*. Edited by Carroll Stuhlmueller, C.P. Collegeville, Minn.: The Liturgical Press, 1978: 103–10.

Kilmartin, S, Edward, "Apostolic Office: Sacrament of Christ." *Theological Studies* 36 (1975): 243–64.

LaGrange, P.M.J. *Évangile Selon Saint Jean*. Paris: Librairie LeCoffre, 1948.

Laurentin, Rene. *Our Lady and the Mass*. New York: MacMillan Co., 1959.

LeFrois, Bernard. *Woman Clothed With the Sun: Individual or Collective?*. Roma: Orbis Catholicus, 1954.

————. "The Mary-Church Relationship in the Apocalypse." In *Marian Studies* 9. Paterson, N.J., 1958: 79–106.

Leo the Great, Saint. *Sermon 24*. Nicene and Post-Nicene Fathers, Vol. 12. Edited by Philip Schaff and Henry Wace. Grand Rapids, Mich.: Wm. B. Eerdmans, 1956.

Leo XIII, Pope. *Jucunda Semper*. (8 September 1894) In *Papal Documents on Mary*, edited by Wm. J. Doheny and Joseph P. Kelly. Milwaukee, Wisc.: Bruce Publishing, 1954.

Lewis, C. S. "Priestesses in the Church?." In *Women in the Church*, appendix, 123–32. San Francisco: Ignatius Press, 1979.

Lightfoot, R. H. *St John's Gospel*. London: Oxford University Press, 1957.

Ligier, Louis. "The Biblical Symbolism of Baptism in the Fathers of the Church and the Liturgy." In *Adult Baptism and the Catechumenate*. 16–30. Concilium, Vol. 22. New York: Paulist Press, 1967.

————. *Péche d'Adam et Péche du monde*. Théologie 43. Aubier, 1960.

Little, Joyce A. "Sexual Equality in the Church: A Theologicaal Resolution to the Anthropological Dilemma." *Heythrop Journal* 28 (1987): 165–78.

Long, Steven A. "The Metaphysics of Gender and Sacramental Priesthood." *Faith and Reason* 10 (Fall 1984): 207–21.

Longley, Katherine M. *St Margaret Clitherow*. Wheathampsted, Hertfordshire, England: Anthony Clarke, 1986.

Lumen Gentium. (*Dogmatic Constitution on the Church*). In *Vatican Council II: The Conciliar and Post-Conciliar Documents*, edited by Austin Flannery, O.P. Collegeville, Minn.: The Liturgical Press, 1975.

Maloney, George A. *Mary: The Womb of God*. Denville, N.J.: Dimensions Books, 1976.

Mascall, E. L. *Christ, the Christian and the Church: A Study of the Incarnation and Its Consequences*. London: Longmans, Green 1946.

————. "The Dogmatic Theology of the Mother of God." In *The Mother of God*, edited by E. L. Mascall, 37–50. London: Dacre Press, 1949.

McNamara, Jo Ann. "Equality in the Cult of Virginity in Early Christianity." *Feminist Studies* 4 (1976): 145–58.

Mead, Margaret. *Male and Female*. New York: Dell, 1949.

Methodius, Saint. *The Banquet*. Translated by Herbert Musurillo. Ancient Christian Writers, Vol. 27. Westminster, Md.: The Newman Press, 1958.

Miletic, Stephen F. *"One Flesh": Eph. 5.22–24, 5.31 Marriage and the New Creation*. Analecta Biblica, 115. Roma: Editrice Pontificio Istituto Biblico, 1988.

Miller, John W. "Depatriarchalizing God in Biblical Interpretation: A Critique." *Catholic Biblical Quarterly* 48 (October 1986): 609–16.

Montagu, Ashley. *The Natural Superiority of Women*. New York: Macmillan, 1974.

Morin, Germani, D., et al., eds. *Sancti Augustini Sermones. Miscellania Agostiniana*. Rome: Typis Polygottis Vaticanis, 1930.

Muller, Earl. *Trinity and Marriage in Paul: The Establishment of a Communitarian Analogy of the Trinity Grounded in the Theological Shape of Pauline Thought*. New York: Peter Lang, 1990.

Neely, James C, M.D. *Gender: The Myth of Equality*. New York: Simon and Schuster, 1981.

Newman, John Henry. *Mary—the Second Eve*. Edited by Sr. Eileen Breen. Rockford, Ill.: Tan Books, 1982.

Ong, Walter, S.J. *Fighting for Life*. London: Cornell University Press, 1981.

Origen. *Hom. in Jos.*, and *Hom. in Ezech*. Translated by Henri Crouzel. *Virginité et Mariage Selon Origène*. Paris: Desclee de Brouwer, 1963.

Osiek, Carolyn. "The Ministry and the Ordination of Women According to the Early Church Fathers." In *Women and Priesthood: Future Directions*, edited by Carroll Stuhlmueller, 59–68. Collegeville, Minn.: The Liturgical Press, 1978.

Parry, R. St John. *The First Epistle of Paul the Apostle to the Corinthians*. London: Cambridge University Press, 1937.

The Passion of SS. Perpetua and Felicity. In *The Living Testament: The Essential Writings of Christianity Since the Bible*, edited by M Basil Pennington, et. al., 29–35. San Francisco: Harper and Row, 1985.

Paul VI, Pope. *Mysterium Fidei*. (September 1965) St. Paul Editions: Boston, 1965.

Paulinus of Nola, Saint. *Letter 23*. Translated by P. G. Walsh. *Letters of St. Paulinus of Nola*. Westminster, Md.: The Newman Press, 1967.

Pius X, Pope. *Ad deum illum*. (2 February 1904) In *Papal Documents*, edited by Wm. J. Doheny and Joseph P. Kelly. Milwaukee, Wisc.: Bruce Publishing, 1954.

Pius XI, Pope. *Casti Connubii*. (31 December 1930) Boston: St. Paul Editions.

Pius XII, Pope. *Munificentissimus Deus*. (1950). In *Papal Documents on Mary*, edited by Wm. J. Doheny and Joseph P. Kelly. Milwaukee, Wisc.: Bruce Publishing, 1954.

———. *Mystici Corporis*. (29 June 1943) Boston: St. Paul Editions.

———. *On Holy Virginity*. (25 March 1954) Derby, N.Y.: The Daughters of St. Paul, 1954.

Plumpe, Joseph C. *Mater Ecclesia: An Inquiry Into the Concept of the Church as Mother in Early Christianity*. Washington, D.C.: The Catholic University of America Press, 1943.

Prat, Ferdnand. *The Theology of St Paul*. Vol. 2. Translated by John L. Stoddard. Westminster, Md.: The Newman Bookshop, 1927.

Prysbyterium Ordinis. (*Decree on the Ministry and Life of Priests*.) In *Documents of Vatican II*. Edited by Austin Flannery, O.P. Collegeville, Minn.: The Liturgical Press, 1975.

Quay, Paul. *The Christian Meaning of Human Sexuality*. San Francisco: Ignatius Press, 1985.

Quinn, James. "Priesthood and Maleness." *Homiletic and Pastoral Review* (November 1984): 23–29.

Rahner, Hugo. *Marie et l' église: Dix méditations sur la vie spirituelle*. Paris: Éditions du Cerf, 1955.

Raming, Ida. *The Exclusion of Women from the Priesthood: Divine Law or Sex Discrimination?*. Metuchen, N.J.: The Scarecrow Press, 1976.

Ramsay, William. *The Cities of St Paul: Their Influence on His Life and Thought*. Grand Rapids, Mich.: Baker, 1949.

Ratzinger, Joseph Cardinal. *Daughter Zion*. San Francisco: Ignatius Press, 1983.

———. *Introduction to Christianity*. New York: Herder and Herder, 1969.

———. "On the Position of Mariology and Marian Spirituality within the Totality of Faith." In *The Church and Women*, edited by Helmut Moll, 67–79. San Francisco: Ignatius Press, 1988.

Robinson, J. Armitage. *St Paul's Letter to the Ephesians*. London: James Clarke and Co. Ltd., 1922.

Ruether, Rosemary Radford. *Sexism and God-Talk: Toward a Feminist Theology*. Boston: Beacon Press, 1983.

———. "Misogynism and Virginal Feminism in the Fathers of the Church." *In Religion and Sexism*, edited by Rosemary Radford Ruether, 150-83. New York: Simon and Schuster, 1974.

Sacrosanctum Concilium. (*The Constitution on the Sacred Liturgy*.) In *The Documents of Vatican II*, edited by Austin Flannery. Collegeville, Minn.: The Liturgical Press, 1975.

Sampley, J. P. *And the Two Shall Become One Flesh*. New York: Cambridge University Press, 1971.

———. "The Letter to the Ephesians." In *Proclamation Commentaries*, edited by Gerhard Krodel, 9–39. Philadelphia: Fortress Press, 1978.

Scheffczyk, Leo. "Mary as Model of Catholic Faith." In *The Church and Women*, edited by Helmut Moll, 81–102. San Francisco: Ignatius Press, 1988.

Schroeder, H. J. *Canons and Decrees of the Council of Trent*. St. Louis, Mo.: Herder, 1941.

Scroggs, Robin. *The Last Adam: A Study in Pauline Anthropology*. Philadelphia: Fortress Press, 1966.

Schüssler Fiorenza, Elizabeth. "Breaking the Silence—Becoming Visible." In *Women Invisible in Church and Theology*, edited by Elizabeth Schüssler Fiorenza and Mary Collins, 3–16. Concilium, 182. Edinburgh: T & T Clark Ltd., 1985.

———. *In Memory of Her*. New York: Crossroad, 1983.

Stafford, Archbishop J. Francis. *The Mystery of the Priestly Vocation*. *Origens* 18 (10 November 1988): 1, 351–60.

Stein, Edith. *The Collected Works of Edith Stein*, Vol. 2: *Essays on Woman*. Edited by Dr. L. Gebler and Romaeus Leuven. Washington, D.C.: ICS Publications, 1987.

Stern, Karl. *The Flight from Woman*. New York: Paragon House, 1965.

Terrien, Samuel. *Till the Heart Sings*. Philadelphia: Fortress Press, 1985.

Tertullian. *A Treatise on the Soul*. The Ante-Nicene Fathers. Vol. 3. Edited by Alexander Roberts and James Donaldson. Grand Rapids, Mich.: Wm. B. Eerdmans, 1957.

———. *On the Apparel of Women*. Translated by Rev. S. Thelwall. The Ante-Nicene Fathers. Vol. 4. Grand Rapids, Mich.: Wm. B. Eerdmans, 1956.

———. *On Baptism*. The Ante-Nicene Fathers, Vol. 3. Edited by Alexander Roberts and James Donaldson. Grand Rapids, Mich.: Wm. B. Eerdmans, 1957.

———. *The Prescription Against Heretics*. The Ante-Nicene Fathers. Vol. 3. Edited by Alexander Roberts and James Donaldson. Grand Rapids, MI: Wm. B. Eerdmans, 1957.

Theodore of Mopsuestia, Saint. *Baptismal Homily III*. In Edward Yarnold, S.J., *The Awe Inspiring Rites of Initiation: Baptismal Homilies of the Fourth Century*. Slough, England: St. Paul Publications, 1971.

Thomas Aquinas, Saint. *Summa Theologica* I. Translated by Edmund Hill. Blackfriars, Vols. 6, 13. New York: McGraw-Hill; London: Eyre and Spottiswoode, 1964.

———. *Summa Theologica* III. Translated by Thomas R. Heath. Blackfriars. Vol. 51. New York: McGraw-Hill; London: Eyre and Spottswoode, 1964.

Thornton, L. S. *The Common Life in the Body of Christ*. London: Dacre Press, 1942.

Thurian, Max. *Mary—Mother of the Lord, Figure of the Church*. London: The Faith Press, 1963.

Tixeront, J. *Holy Orders and Ordination.* St. Louis, Mo.: Herder, 1928.

Trible, Phyllis. *God and the Rhetoric of Sexuality.* Philadelphia: Fortress Press, 1978.

Van der Meer, S.J., Haye. *Women Priests in the Catholic Church?: A Theological-Historical Investigation.* Philadelphia: Temple University Press, 1973.

Vawter, Bruce. "The Gospel According to John." In *The Jerome Biblical Commentary,* edited by Raymond E. Brown, et al., 414–66. Englewood Cliffs, N.J.: Prentice-Hall, 1968.

Von Balthasar, Hans Urs. "The Uninterrupted Tradition of the Church." *L'Osservatore Romano* (24 February 1977): 6–7.

———. *St. Augustine, Le Visage de L'Église.* Unam Sanctam. Vol. 31. Éditions du Cerf, 1958.

Von le Fort, Gertrud. *The Eternal Woman: The Woman in the Timeless Woman.* Milwaukee, Wisc.: Bruce Publishing, 1954.

Von Rad, Gerard. *Genesis: A Commentary.* Philadelphia: Westminster Press, 1961.

Weaver, Mary Jo. *New Catholic Women: A Contemporary Challenge to Traditional Religious Authority.* San Fransisco: Harper and Row, 1985.

Zimmerman, Marie. "Neither Clergy or Laity: Women in the Church." In *Women Invisible in Church and Theology,* edited by Elizabeth Schüssler Fiorenza and Mary Collins, 29–37. Concilium, 182. Edinburgh: T & T Clark, 1985.

Zimmern, Alice. *The Home Life of the Ancient Greeks.* New York: Cooper Square Publishers, 1906.

Index

Abraham, 80, 81, 147

Adam, 28, 34, 35, 36, 37, 43, 44, 54, 59, 60–62, 64, 56, 68, 69, 71, 81, 94, 116, 118, 119, 123, 124, 125, 132, 133, 141, 156, 161, 167, 169, 178, 235 n.46

Allen, Prudence, 35, 36

Ambrose, St., 40, 44, 197, 198, 199, 270–71 n.9; on Church's motherhood, 38, 145; on Mary, 145; on virginity, 38, 215

Andrews, Joan, 217–20

Andriessen, Paulus, 59, 164

Androcentrism, 5–6, 9. *See also* Patriarchy

Apostolic succession, 92–93, 102, 164

Aquinas, St. Thomas, 65, 86–88, 100, 110, 111

Aristotle, 5, 22, 107, 110, 111

Athanasius, St., 113

Augustine, St., 28, 36, 44, 115, 205, 206, 207; on the Church, 33–34, 156, 164, 182; on the Church as mother, 34, 138–40, 141, 142, 147, 153, 154, 192, 205 on the Church as virgin, 147; on the Eucharist, 154; on goodness of female body, 31, 32, 36, 37, 38, 97, 229 n.129; on the image of God, 29–30; on marital equality, 41–42; on Mary, 32, 127, 144, 147; on resurrection of body, 97; on virginity, 37, 38, 39, 40, 214

Authority, ix, 44–47; of apostles, 47, 88–92, 94, 96–97, 101–6, 114, 136, 194; of bishops, 92–93, 102, 103, 106, 114, 188, 226 n.53; of the Church, 147, 158, 163; of Christ, xii, 52, 57, 74, 89, 92 (*see also* Christ); covenantal, x, xi, xiii, 44–46, 49, 76, 77, 194, 220–21; of females, ix, xi, xii, xiii, 3, 42, 43, 45, 48, 66–69, 72, 73, 75, 76, 78, 95, 98, 99, 107, 109, 111, 112, 114, 121, 123, 131, 134, 136, 137–38, 143, 155, 159, 161, 165, 168, 170, 171–74, 175, 176, 179–80, 182, 186, 190, 191, 212, 227; females' eucharistic authority, 95; females as source of life, 68, 69, 125, 164; of husbands, 65, 69, 71, 74; of males, 46, 63, 64, 65, 68, 72, 73, 74, 75, 76, 78, 95, 99, 102, 190, 191–92, 231; marital aspects of, 60, 69, 72, 73, 88, 89, 90, 114, 139, 175; of Mary, xii, 47, 119, 121–22, 123, 125, 126, 129, 130, 133, 135, 168, 195, 218, 221 (*see also* Mary); one flesh union of, 6, 59, 68, 73, 74, 136, 194; of priests, 4, 45, 47, 48, 75, 91, 92–95, 96, 101–6, 109, 114, 162; as responsibility for life, xi, x, 46, 48, 57, 79, 83, 93, 131, 137, 153, 170, 171, 174, 175, 176, 179–80, 184, 186, 190, 195; of wives, 41–43, 44, 74, 209, 216, 230 n.149, 231 n.155

Baptism, 99, 104, 105, 140–47, 156, 163, 182, 183, 193, 205

Bardwick, Judith, 177, 180, 181

Barrett, C. K., 64, 67

Barth, Karl, 61, 160

Barth, Marcus, 55

Bedale, S., 53

Benedict XV, 131

Beniot, Pierre, 59

Bernard of Clairvaux, St., 162

Blandina, 202–4

Boff, Leonardo, 165–68

Braun, F. M., 128

Brown, Raymond, 82, 105, 129
Buytendijk, F. J. J., 108

Caesarius of Arles, St., 42
Campion, St. Edmund, 208, 209, 211, 212
Carol, Juniper B., 131
Carter, Emmett Cardinal, 73
Catherine of Siena, St., 207–8
Christ, Jesus, 31, 32, 36 authority of,
    54–56; as bridegroom, 50, 68, 72, 74,
    89, 93, 95, 105; and the Church, 36, 72,
    73, 74, 75, 95, 100, 113, 134, 163, 196;
    fatherhood of, 103–6; feminist view of,
    10–12, 14; headship of, 49, 50, 51–57,
    62, 63, 64, 69–70, 71, 73–74, 75, 77,
    88, 92, 93, 94, 97, 104, 114, 121, 129,
    137, 159, 208, 230, 237 n.74; masculin-
    ity of, 75, 80, 85, 88, 89, 97–98, 100,
    112, 113, 159, 166; as New Adam, 34,
    54, 60–62, 73, 90, 92, 115, 116, 118,
    119, 128, 132, 134, 151, 152, 153, 154,
    156, 163, 169; sacrifice of, 51, 56–57,
    60, 61, 62, 73, 74, 76, 77, 82, 88, 89,
    90, 92, 93, 105, 112, 121, 129, 134,
    154, 159; as shepherd, 78–79, 82, 83,
    88, 89, 90, 93, 102, 104; as source, 58,
    60, 62, 68, 71, 72, 74, 75, 77, 92, 94,
    106, 115, 129, 157, 159; virginity of,
    33
Chrysostom, St. John: authority of wives,
    42–44, 70, 101, 123
Church, 20, 96, 98, 188; as body of Christ,
    52, 57–58, 59, 69–70, 71, 73–74, 97,
    134, 153, 159, 161, 232 n.4; feminist
    view of, 17–21, 73; as fullness of
    Christ, 70–71, 75, 238 nn. 77 and 78;
    motherhood of, 38, 48, 136, 137–44,
    145, 146, 147, 148, 149, 151–57, 163,
    164, 165, 170, 177, 182–85, 187,
    188–89, 203, 204, 205, 209, 218, 219;
    as New Eve, 33, 54, 60, 61, 71, 73,
    134, 150, 151, 152, 153, 154, 155, 169;
    as source, 163, 164; source of unity,
    182–89; as teacher, 157–59; virginity
    of, 37, 38, 147, 151, 214. See also
    Authority: of the Church
Claudel, Paul, 159
Clement of Alexandria, St., 28–29, 40, 93,
    142, 149, 153, 183, 193
Clitherow, St. Margaret, 208–12

Congar, Yves, 160
Consecrated virginity, 37, 38, 39, 40,
    212–15. See also Fathers of the Church
Cornford, F. M., 23, 27
Council of Trent, 92
Cyprian, St., 44, 140, 142, 153, 157, 183,
    188, 213, 214
Cyril of Jerusalem, St., 117, 149

Daly, Mary, x, 24–25, 38
Deborah, 198–200
De Lubac, Henri, xiii, 149, 192; on the
    Eucharist, 93; on motherhood of Church,
    139, 141, 188, 193, 205; on priesthood,
    102, 164; on virginity of Church, 212
Deutsch, Helene, 179
Didymus, St., 141
Dolger, F. J., 149

Ephrem, St. Syrus, 117, 142
Epiphanius, St., 118
Eucharist, xii, 17, 45, 47, 77, 82, 89, 90,
    91–92, 93, 96, 103, 111, 136, 145, 151,
    154, 160, 162, 163, 207, 209; feminist
    view of, 10, 16, 45, 113, 163;
    institution of, 242–43 n.37; marital
    meaning of, 49, 50, 89, 93, 94, 95, 97,
    159, 161, 168; and Mary, 155
Eusebius, 44
Eve, 28, 34, 35, 36, 37, 43, 44, 54, 57, 68,
    69, 81, 94, 115, 116–18, 123, 124,
    125–26, 127, 133, 141, 150–51, 156,
    157, 161, 167, 169, 170, 176, 178

Fatherhood, of apostles, 101–6; of
    bishops, 102–3, 158; of Christ, 103–6;
    of God, xii, 64, 65, 77, 79–80, 80–83,
    85–88, 89, 100, 101, 104, 109, 110,
    133, 137–40, 142, 144, 149, 153, 154,
    185, 193, 240 n.4; of men, 101, 111,
    138–39, 178, 190, 191–92, 214; of
    priests, xii, 103, 104, 106, 158, 164,
    165, 207, 260 n.104; as source, 101
Fathers of the Church, 138; on Church
    authority, 44–45; on feminine virtue,
    44; on Mary, 116, 118, 127, 130; on
    motherhood of Church, 142, 151, 157;
    Neo-platonism of, 28, 29, 31, 39, 98,
    99, 224; on women and marriage,
    39–40, 41, 42; on virginity, 37, 39, 214

Feminist theology, xi, 3–4, 7, 15, 17, 63, 162, 186, 224n.9, 226n.56; on Christ, 112, 113 (*see also* Ruether, Rosemary Radford); on fatherhood of God, 77; gnostic aspects of, 22, 73, 266n.74; on motherhood of God, 83

Feuillet, Andre, 66, 122, 127, 132, 135

Fiorenza, Elizabeth Schüssler, x, 4–6; biblical theology of, 8–9; Christology of, 14; on the Church, 17–18; on fatherhood of God, 240n.4; on patriarchy, 5–6, 151

Fisher, St. John, 211

Gilder, George, 172, 173, 174, 181, 190

Gnosticism, 22–28, 98

Goldenberg, Naomi, xi, 8

Gregory the Great, St., 215

Hennessy, Thomas, 104, 105

Hippolytus, St., 146, 152, 193, 200

Hitchcock, George S., 70

Holy Spirit, 143, 144, 145, 146, 152, 155, 156, 157, 158, 163, 166, 167

Huby, Joseph, 55, 58, 70

Inter Insigniores, 49–50, 89, 95

Irenaeus, St.: on Church as mother, 157, 193; on Mary as New Eve, 34–35, 117, 151, 152, 153

Isaac, 80–81, 148

Jeremias, J., 55

Jerome, St., 21, 32–33, 70, 98; on Mary, 118; on priesthood, 106; on virginity, 33, 37, 38, 39, 40, 44, 214

John XXIII, 158

John Paul II, 72, 95, 120, 155, 156, 159, 170, 191

Judith, 196–98, 199

Kasper, Walter, 170

Keefe, Donald, S.J., xiii

Kiefer, Ralph, 98

Kilmartin, Edward J., S.J., 96, 97, 98, 103

Küng, Hans, 187, 268n.83

Laurentin, Rene, 121

LeFrois, Bernard J., 136

Leo the Great, St., 146

Lewis, C. S., 162

Ligier, Louis, 143

Luther, Martin, 160, 258–59n.84

Maloney, George, 144

Martyr, St. Justin, 35, 117, 124

Mascall, E. L., 119

Mater et Magistra, 158

Methodius, St., 142, 215

Miletic, Stephen F., 62, 72, 74

Monica, St., 204–7

Montagu, Ashley, 171, 172, 181, 182, 190, 191

Montanism, 19, 21

Motherhood: of Church, xiii, 38, 48, 138–47, 163, 164, 165, 182, 203 (*see also* Church); of Eve, 94, 126, 127; of God, 83–85, 166–68, 241n.17; of Israel, 83–84; of Mary, 116, 121, 122, 166–68 (*see also* Mary); of virgins, 37; of women, xiii, 98, 110, 127, 138–39, 167, 170, 174, 177, 178–79, 185, 191, 218

Mulieris Dignitatem, 125, 170, 191

Muller, Earl, S.J., 67, 68

Mysterium Fidei, 91

Mystici Corporis, 131, 134

Nathanson, Adele, 215–17

Neely, James C., 107

Nicodemus, 144, 145

Ong, Walter, S.J., 107, 108, 133, 182

Optatus, St., 141

Origen, 32, 70, 140

Patriarchy, 4–5, 7, 19, 227n.84, 231n.164

Paul VI, 91

Paul, St., 49, 50–51, 53, 54, 56, 57, 58, 59, 61, 63, 64, 66, 67, 68, 74, 98, 99, 101, 106, 116, 118, 147, 149, 150, 151, 153, 161, 221, 234n.29, 236n.63

Paulinus of Nola, St.: authority of wives, 44; on Mary, 127

Perpetua and Felicity, SS., 200–202

Philo, 23, 24, 25, 27

Pius X, 130

Pius XI, 131, 174

Pius XII, 131, 134, 213, 215

Plato, 5, 22, 23, 27

Platonism, 28, 29, 30, 32, 38–39, 98, 99, 224n.9

Plumbe, Joseph, 140, 148, 151, 156, 204
Presbyterorum Ordinis, 104
Priesthood, 50, 106, 121, 152, 164,
    244 n.51; authority of, 57, 75, 91,
    92–95, 101, 154; of faithful, 161–63;
    feminist view of, 16; masculine essence
    of, 49, 50, 75, 77–78, 89, 92, 100–101,
    102, 108, 111, 114, 144, 161–62. *See
    also* Women's ordination
Protogospel, 124–26, 128, 129, 134, 136

Rahner, Karl, 188, 254–55 n.75
Raming, Ida, xi
Ratzinger, Cardinal Joseph, 85, 125
Redemptoris Mater, 120, 125
Robinson, J. Armitage, 55
Ruether, Rosemary Radford, x, 7–8; bibli-
    cal theology of, 9; Christology of,
    10–12, 15–16, 113; Ecclesiology of,
    18–19; gnostic theology of, 25–27; on
    Mary, 13

Sarah, 80, 148
Scheeben, Mathias, 139
Schillebeeckx, Edward, 244–45 n.64,
    254 n.75
Stafford, Bishop Francis, 103
Stein, Edith, 3, 139, 179, 180, 182, 185,
    190, 192, 224 n.2
Stern, Karl, 189, 219, 220, 221
Subordination, 74–75, 101, 174–77,
    239 n.88
Susannah, 200–202

Teilhard de Chardin, Pierre, 187, 192
Tertullian, 117, 140, 145, 149, 156, 158,
    184, 193
Theodore, St., 143, 144
Thurian, Max, 150, 158
Trinity, 73, 86, 88, 141, 166

Van der Meer, Haye, 98, 99, 100, 103
Vaughn, Bishop Austin, 219–20
Vollert, Cyril, 30
Von Balthasar, Han Urs, xiii, 108, 109,
    164, 168, 173
Von le Fort, Gertrude, 75, 175, 179, 186,
    189
Von Rad, Gerhard, 80

Weininger, Otto, 172
Widows, 196, 197, 198
Women: authority of, 132, 177, 178,
    194–95, 237 n.66 *(see also* Authority
    of females); and the Eucharist, 162;
    psychology of, 108; as savior, 178;
    sign of the Church, 143, 148, 149–50,
    159, 161, 162, 163, 165, 168, 189, 194,
    199, 200, 203, 204, 208, 210, 211, 212,
    213, 219; source of life, 115, 184, 185,
    186; source of relatedness, 177–82;
    source of unity, 182–89; as teacher,
    189–92
Women's ordination, 75, 76–77, 78,
    95–101, 113, 163, 220

Zimmerman, Marie, 14